CONSTITUTIONALISM
Philosophical Foundations

This is the second volume in a subseries of commissioned collaborative volumes on key topics at the heart of contemporary philosophy of law that will appear regularly in *Cambridge Studies in Philosophy and Law.*

A distinguished group of legal theorists examines the issue of constitutionalism and poses such foundational questions as Why have a constitution? How do we know what the constitution of a country really is? How should a constitution be interpreted? Why should one generation feel bound by the constitution of an earlier one?

The volume will be of particular importance to those in philosophy, law, political science, and international relations who are interested in whether and what kinds of constitutions should be adopted in countries without them and who are involved in debates about constitutional interpretation.

Cambridge Studies in Philosophy and Law

GENERAL EDITOR: GERALD POSTEMA
(UNIVERSITY OF NORTH CAROLINA, CHAPEL HILL)

ADVISORY BOARD
Jules Coleman (Yale Law School)
Antony Duff (University of Stirling)
David Lyons (Boston University)
Neil MacCormick (University of Edinburgh)
Stephen R. Munzer (UCLA Law School)
Philip Pettit (The Australian National University)
Joseph Raz (University of Oxford)
Jeremy Waldron (Columbia University)

Other books in the series:
Jeffrie G. Murphy and Jean Hampton: *Forgiveness and Mercy*
Stephen R. Munzer: *A Theory of Property*
R. G. Frey and Christopher W. Morris (eds.): *Liability and Responsibility: Essays in Law and Morals*
Robert F. Schopp: *Automatism, Insanity, and the Psychology of Criminal Responsibility*
Steven J. Burton: *Judging in Good Faith*
Jules Coleman: *Risks and Wrongs*
Suzanne Uniacke: *Permissible Killing: The Self-Defense Justification of Homicide*
Jules Coleman and Allen Buchanan (eds.): *In Harm's Way: Essays in Honor of Joel Feinberg*
Warren F. Schwartz (ed.): *Justice in Immigration*
John Fischer and Mark Ravizza: *Responsibility and Control*
R. A. Duff (ed.): *Philosophy and the Criminal Law*

CONSTITUTIONALISM

Philosophical Foundations

Edited by

LARRY ALEXANDER

CAMBRIDGE
UNIVERSITY PRESS

PUBLISHED BY THE PRESS SYNDICATE OF THE UNIVERSITY OF CAMBRIDGE
The Pitt Building, Trumpington Street, Cambridge, United Kingdom

CAMBRIDGE UNIVERSITY PRESS
The Edinburgh Building, Cambridge CB2 2RU, UK
40 West 20th Street, New York, NY 10011-4211, USA
10 Stamford Road, Oakleigh, Melbourne 3166, Australia
Ruiz de Alarcón 13, 28014 Madrid, Spain
Dock House, The Waterfront, Cape Town 8001, South Africa

http://www.cambridge.org

© Cambridge University Press 1998

This book is in copyright. Subject to statutory exception
and to the provisions of relevant collective licensing agreements,
no reproduction of any part may take place without
the written permission of Cambridge University Press.

First published 1998
First paperback edition 2001
Reprinted 1999

Typeset in Times Roman 10/12 pt, in QuarkXPress™ [AG]

A catalog record for this book is available from the British Library

Library of Congress Cataloging in Publication data is available

ISBN 0 521 48293 3 hardback
ISBN 0 521 79999 6 paperback

Transferred to digital printing 2005

Contents

Contributors

LARRY ALEXANDER   University of San Diego, School of Law

RICHARD S. KAY   University of Connecticut, School of Law

FRANK I. MICHELMAN   Harvard University Law School

MICHAEL J. PERRY   Wake Forest University, School of Law

JOSEPH RAZ   Columbia University Law School

JED RUBENFELD   Yale University Law School

LAWRENCE SAGER   New York University, School of Law

JEREMY WALDRON   Columbia University Law School

Introduction

LARRY ALEXANDER

Constitutionalism is a rich vein for philosophical inquiry. For example, what, if anything, makes a constitution legitimate? Is there any difference between a constitution and a Hartian rule of recognition,[1] or between a constitution and other laws? Relatedly, of what if any importance is "writtenness"?[2] And how do the questions of legitimacy, of hierarchical status, and of writtenness bear on such questions as how constitutions should be interpreted (e.g., by reference to original intentions, to common understandings, or to moral rights) and by what institutions (e.g., by courts or by popular bodies)?

Of particular philosophical significance is the relationship among a constitution's authority, its identity, and possible methodologies of interpretation. Thus, if authority stems from acceptance by the governed – whatever that means – then that might suggest that the identity of a constitution can vary from moment to moment because it is dependent on what is accepted as supremely authoritative. And the identity of a constitution might also seem inseparable from the question of what interpretive methodology is correct and even whose interpretation should be authoritative. These possible connections among legitimate authority, identity, and interpretation suggest that debate over constitutional interpretation and judicial review should focus on what we (who?) do accept and what we (who?) should accept as supremely authoritative. On the other hand, if authority stems not from acceptance but from content, how does that change the answers to questions of constitutional identity and interpretation?

Consider the following account of constitutionalism and the various philosophical problems that it entails. At step 1, I begin with my own current views about principles of justice and other aspects of political morality, about principles of wise governance, and about the institutional arrangements best suited to realizing these various principles. If I could impose these principles and institutions by myself, I would do so (unless they included principles, such as democratic side constraints, that prohibited their unilateral imposition). Because I do not have such power, however, I need the assistance of others, others who will not share all of my views about political morality, wise governance, and institutional arrangements.

At step 2, then, I seek wide agreement on rules of governmental behavior and rules defining governmental institutions that realize my own personal principles and views to a greater extent than any alternative set of such rules on which I can obtain wide agreement. In other words, under my own principles, it is preferable that they not be fully realized than that anarchy prevail (because of lack of wide agreement), but that they be realized as fully as possible consistent with wide agreement. Others who hold different principles and views will reason similarly, which will result in agreement on rules of governmental behavior and rules defining institutions that no one believes are optimal but that most believe are good enough – that is, superior to anarchy.[3] (Obviously, not just any set of rules will be superior to anarchy according to everyone's principles of political morality and wise governance; the rules must be the best that can be widely agreed upon and above everyone's anarchy threshold of acceptability.)

The rules widely accepted at step 2 may be entrenched to various degrees. That is, it may be widely accepted that these rules may not be altered ever, may not be altered for a certain length of time, and/or may not be altered except by extraordinary procedures. We may believe that we have the best rules we can ever have, and that there is far more danger of loss of political wisdom and morality or of political akrasia than there is danger that wide agreement on better rules will be thwarted.

At the moment of agreement on the entrenched rules at step 2, the rules mean what we who have agreed to them mean by them. In other words, we have not merely agreed to certain symbols or sounds, but to particular meanings of those symbols and sounds. Our agreement can be memorialized only in symbolic form, however, which means that the symbols we have agreed upon and what we meant by them can come apart. Therefore, at step 2 we might agree not only on the rules of governmental behavior and institutions, but also on rules about who is to decide at later times what we meant by those rules.

It might be useful, then, to distinguish a constitution as a collection of agreed-upon symbols from a metaconstitution (or preconstitutional rules),[4] with the latter consisting of agreed-upon norms – metarules – about which particular set of symbols is the constitution, who is to interpret those symbols, and whose semantic intentions shall count as the authoritative meaning of the symbols. The constitution and the metaconstitution are inseparable at the moment of agreement in step 2, but they can come apart at any time thereafter. Thus, although we may at some later time lack the earlier substantive agreement regarding the content of the rules that we had at step 2 – for example, we might now disagree about what freedom of speech should cover or about whether separation of powers is a good idea – we can still have wide agreement on the metaconstitution. And that agreement might still be sufficient under our principles of political morality to favor the constitution over anarchy.

This discussion of the metaconstitution and its relation to the symbolic constitution illustrates various ways that a constitution might change at step 3. First, the symbolic constitution might change without a change in the metaconstitution. Constitutional amendment in pursuance of the (original meaning of the) rules laid down in the symbolic constitution changes the original constitution organically.

Second, a constitutional revolution might occur in which agreement on the first metaconstitution is replaced by agreement on another metaconstitution that in turn picks out a different symbolic constitution. We may draft a brand new constitution, widely agree on what it means and that it is more desirable than the current constitution, and also agree that it, and not the current constitution, shall now be authoritative for us. (Arguably, the United States Constitution itself was the product of such a constitutional revolution.)[5]

Third, the symbolic constitution might remain the same, but the metaconstitution might change. Thus, the original metaconstitutional agreement might be supplanted at step 3 by a new metaconstitutional agreement, one that deems some parts of the symbolic constitution to be nonauthoritative, that substitutes a new understanding of the symbols for their original meaning, or that "ratifies" otherwise improper interpretations of the symbolic constitution.[6]

Just as it is understandable how people of differing moral and political views could nonetheless agree to entrench a set of constitutional rules and metaconstitutional rules, so it is understandable how they might come to agree on new rules and metarules and hence effect a constitutional revolution. Because it is only the agreement that these rules and metarules shall be supremely authoritative that makes them so, any subsequent agreement can supplant the original agreement to this effect. Of course, some who might have gone along with the original agreement and its constitution may not go along with the later one. For them, the new constitution will not be authoritative even if it is obliging. At least, it will not be so if their political-moral beliefs favor anarchy or resistance to the new constitution. But that will be the case for any dissenters from a constitutional agreement as long as their acceptance of the constitution is not necessary to achieve the degree of effectiveness required to sustain the others' acceptance of the constitution.

Why should anyone at step 4 accept as authoritative a constitution or constitutional provision – whether in the original constitution of step 2 or a supplanting constitution of step 3 – if she does not view the constitution or the relevant provision thereof to be morally and prudentially ideal? The reason is the same one we had at steps 1 and 2: an effective set of relatively good en-

trenched rules, even if nonideal, may be ranked by our own ideal political
morality as better than either anarchy or any other set of entrenched rules that
has a chance of gaining wide agreement.[7]

Finally, there is the question of why we should ever accept any rule or
metarule as authoritative – that is, as providing us with a content-independent
reason for action. What I have argued thus far is that we can have content-
dependent reasons – reasons derived from our political morality – to establish
and entrench rules that others recognize as authoritative. But why should *we*
recognize those rules as authoritative? Why should we not depart from them
whenever our political morality marks disobedience as the preferable course?
Of course, if our political morality supports these rules as the best we can get
agreement upon, then our political morality will never dictate disobedience if
that would undermine agreement. But it might well dictate secret disobedience.[8]

This is the central dilemma of rule-following. Following a rule because it is
a rule is what is meant by attributing practical authority to the rule. But if
practical authority is impossible, claims of practical authority will be false,
and hence rules *qua* rules will be undermined, which by hypothesis is morally
nonoptimal. So it appears, paradoxically, that it is morally optimal to make
claims on behalf of rules that one knows to be false.[9] And what goes for rules
generally applies equally to the entrenched rules of constitutional law.[10]

The foregoing is a sketch of my own answers to the philosophical questions about constitutionalism that I have posed. Let me turn now to the answers proffered by the authors in this collection.

Richard Kay's treatment of constitutionalism's philosophical issues is perhaps the closest to the one I have just outlined. For Kay, the purpose of a constitution is to lay down fixed rules that can affect human conduct and thereby
keep government in good order. Constitutionalism implements the rule of
law: It brings about predictability and security in the relations of individuals
to the government by defining in advance the powers and limits of that government.

The price of constitutionalism's securing the rule of law – binding the government by rules laid down in advance of its actions – is rigidity or, put differently, suboptimal response to change. Kay disagrees with Joseph Raz, who
argues that judges may from time to time improve law. Constitutionalism,
Kay says, sides with risking rigidity rather than risking security. And in response to those like Jeremy Waldron who extol democratic decision-making
and the right of majorities to implement their own judgments about individual
rights and liberties, Kay argues not only that democracy is not a preemptive
value, but that it also may trample rights and, through destabilization, undermine liberty. Constitutionalism prefers the constancy of a single privileged

judgment about powers, rights, and liberties to the inconstancy of shifting democratic decisions.

Kay next takes on those who are skeptical of the capacity of written rules to convey fixed meanings. That skepticism, Kay says, is belied by our everyday experience of successful communication. The idea that we cannot in fact successfully communicate is, according to Kay, "operationally self-defeating."

A constitution's rules are to be interpreted according to the intent of their authors. In the case of the United States Constitution, Kay argues that we *now* accept the lawmaking authority of the framers *then* (in 1789). That is, we now accept a meta- or preconstitutional norm that locates authority in the framers, which in turn means that the Constitution's rules *qua* supreme law mean what the framers meant by them. (I would argue, and I believe Kay would agree, that the actual metaconstitutional norm we accept is more complex and gives a role to Supreme Court precedents that conflict with original intent; indeed, there may be no metaconstitutional norm that commands widespread acceptance except one that leaves all of these matters to the Supreme Court to resolve by a majority vote of the justices.)[11]

Why would we accept the authority of those who acted more than two hundred years ago? Kay contends that for our acceptance of this metaconstitutional norm to be rational, all we need to believe is that the framers did a pretty good job – and, I would add, as good a job as any alternative on which we could possibly achieve widespread agreement. If, on the other hand, we make our acceptance of the Constitution's authority dependent on its squaring perfectly with our present political and moral views, the Constitution's stability – its raison d'être – will be undermined. That is why "reading" the Constitution as containing broad delegations to judges to apply contemporary political and moral views – versus delegations to legislatures to act within the constraints set by fixed rules – is itself antithetical to constitutionalism, the purpose of which is to limit government by rules.

Finally, Kay takes up the problem of how rules can ever be authoritative and make good their claim to allegiance in any case where they produce suboptimal results. His discussion of this and the related problem of how final authoritative decision-makers can be expected to conform to rules with which they do not fully agree merits close attention.

Frank I. Michelman's central concern with constitutionalism is what he calls the authority–authorship syndrome: "We ought to do it because they said so." Constitutions are legislated by human authors. Their norms are intentional creations. Yet, Michelman says, one cannot posit what ought to be; what ought to be is independent of our positing it. Therefore, he asks, how can we accept a rule of recognition that directs us to do what the constitutional authors said because "they said so"?

Basically, the problem Michelman wrestles with is the general problem of rule-following. How can a datable act of human will preempt as a matter of practical rationality one's own current judgment about what ought to be done? The answer, as I have indicated, is paradoxical: We have good moral reasons to posit fixed rules that claim preemptive authority over our moral reasoning. If such authority is impossible, then perhaps we have moral reasons to deceive ourselves, at least in our everyday affairs, so that we come to believe that the impossible is true. Not just the moral advantages of constitutions, but the moral advantages of *all* rules, are at stake.

Michelman has surely identified the deepest problem of constitutionalism, but only because it is the deepest problem of law generally. Even democratic decision-making, which is frequently contrasted with constitutionalism, cannot escape the authority–authorship syndrome. If rules are entrenched for some period of time – and a rule must be so to function as a rule – then even unanimously approved rules are subject to the authority–authorship syndrome. For why should I act against my better judgment *now* just because *I* said so then?

Michael J. Perry's take on constitutionalism is in many respects very similar to Kay's and mine. Like us, he rejects the notion that the Constitution *qua* supreme law is just the configuration of marks on the parchment in the National Archives. Rather, the Constitution is composed of the norms those marks were intended by their authors to symbolize. Like us, he answers the question of why norms should ever be entrenched against majority repeal by reference to distrust of our future politics. Again like us, he argues that present acceptance of constitutional norms posited in the (distant) past is justified by the need for a widely agreed upon constitutional arrangement and the difficulty of recoordinating an alternative superior one. Finally, like us, he notes that because the Constitution of 1789 is authoritative because we now accept a metaconstitutional rule to that effect, a change in the metaconstitutional rule can effect a change in the Constitution *qua* norms even if it does not change the Constitution *qua* symbols. Thus, norms that were not intended by the framers of 1789 (or 1791 or 1868, etc.) – such as the practice of judicial review and finality, or the application of equal protection principles to the federal government – are now part of the Constitution due to a change in our metaconstitutional rule of recognition.

Perry devotes a lot of attention to issues of interpretation. He distinguishes between the norms the framers intended and the specification of those norms. The framers' intentions are authoritative with respect to the identity of constitutional norms but not with respect to their specification, which is the process of deciding what the norm requires in a particular context.

Perry presupposes an ontology of norms such that it is possible for the "norm" but not its applications to be dependent upon the framers' intent. In places Perry refers to specifying "indeterminate" norms, suggesting that he is distinguishing within the universe of intended norms between rules and standards. Standards would be intentional delegations of norm-elaborating authority to other decision-makers, whereas the extension of rules would be totally dependent upon the intentions of their authors.

In other places, however, Perry appears to make a more global claim about norms in general and to assume that the norm can be authorial-intention-dependent while its applications are not. This means that the norm and its applications have different ontological statuses, the former belonging to the realm of fact, the latter to the realm of evaluation.

It would seem, however, that this ontological bifurcation of norms would be difficult to sustain and that it would spill over into all norm-governed activities. Thus, is it possible that when I use the word "dog," its semantic meaning *is* dependent on a psychological fact – did I have in mind canines? – but any particular application (e.g., to wolves or jackals) is purely evaluative and can be at odds with what I had in mind?[12] Perry – quite rightly, I believe[13] – rejects the notion that intentions themselves are purely evaluative, for he attributes facticity to the question of what norms the framers intended. On the other hand, he rejects the position held by Kay and by me that makes the meaning of an intended norm and how it applies inseverable inquiries.[14]

The final part of Perry's contribution focuses on institutional relations in specifying norms. In particular, he is interested in the extent to which the courts should be the primary constitutional norm-specifiers and to what extent they should defer to the norm-specifications of other branches of government.

Joseph Raz's principal focus is the question of a constitution's authority and its source. Raz is, of course, well known for his work on practical authority in general and legal authority in particular.[15] In this respect, Raz's views on constitutional authority are entailed by his general jurisprudential approach.

According to Raz, a constitution has authority if one does better morally by following its dictates than by following one's own moral views. Therefore, a constitution has authority if its authors have sufficient moral expertise and if the moral benefits of its symbolism and the coordination it provides are sufficiently great that society does morally better by following its dictates than by not doing so. What gives constitutional law the basis for its claim of authority is its facticity – its consisting of posited concrete determinations about what morally ought to be done, determinations that can be unpacked without recourse to the less determinate moral considerations the determinations are meant to resolve. For the facticity of constitutional determinations – together with a sufficient degree of moral expertise in the authors – is what renders a constitution capable of providing enough moral guidance and coordination to make good the claim that we will do better morally by treating it as authoritative.

Raz's account of constitutional authority is thus at bottom the same kind of account that Kay and I give. Raz departs somewhat from us, however, in his account of constitutional interpretation. Raz argues that the three bases for constitutional authority – moral expertise, coordination, and symbolism – cannot support timeless authority. At some point, the claim that we will do better morally by following a particular constitution will become false. So Raz argues that in constitutional interpretation by judges, reasons for remaining faithful to the original meaning of the constitution compete with and can be outweighed by reasons for innovative interpretations.

Now I would claim that "innovative interpretations" is an oxymoron. What Raz is really dealing with is not constitutional interpretation but constitutional change or constitutional revolution. Constitutional change and revolution may be morally desirable in many circumstances, but they are not and cannot be interpretations of the constitution that exists up to that time. Of course, the constitution or metaconstitution may authorize judicial amendments to the constitution, in which case innovative "interpretations" effect change but not revolution. When the understanding, however, is that judges will be faithful to the original meaning, and amendment, if any, is left to other processes, then a forthrightly innovative decision – if it is accepted – will signal a constitutional revolution. Although at the end of his essay, Raz takes up this rejoinder and disputes it, it seems difficult to deny that in many cases of innovative decisions, a new constitution will have supplanted the old one.

The four contributions discussed thus far, despite their differences, display relatively similar views of the philosophical terrain of constitutionalism and indeed take relatively similar positions on the principal philosophical issues. The remaining three contributors, however, depart from this orthodoxy.

Jed Rubenfeld is preoccupied with the same problem of time that Michelman struggles with: Why ought the majority *now* to feel bound by what a majority – even a supermajority – said *then*. Rubenfeld rejects the answer that at least Kay, Perry, Raz, and I offer, namely, that a sufficient number of us (for effectiveness) accept *now* that we are so bound because we believe that the moral advantages so achieved make the old constitution a better moral bet than the vicissitudes of democratic politics. Rubenfeld believes, by contrast, that invoking contemporary consent to be bound, instead of resolving the problem of time, repudiates constitutionalism altogether.

Rubenfeld therefore tries a different tack to solve the problem of how a constitution authored then can legitimately bind now. The solution to the problem will entail a theory of constitutional interpretation that will give a proper place to each half of law's double nature, namely, datable acts of will (*then*) and right reason (*now*). The methodology of interpreting according to the intent of the constitutional authors subordinates right reason to past will, whereas the methodology of interpreting according to one's views of political morality subordinates past will to right reason.

Rubenfeld argues that true freedom requires commitment over time, for the uncommitted person is not truly free. A constitution represents the commitments of *a* people, commitments that are perforce temporally extended. We are bound *now* to constitutional commitments then because we are the same "people," even if we are not the same individuals, who authored the Constitution. Rubenfeld refers to this central feature of the Constitution as its "writtenness."

At this stage of his argument it would seem that Rubenfeld has solved the problem of time by deeming individuals past and present to be one "people" and by deeming the Constitution to embody the commitments of that "people," but that in doing so he has opted for originalism and thus subordinated right reason to past will. For how do we ascertain "our" commitments except by reference to the intentions of our past selves?

But Rubenfeld denies this consequence of his theory. Commitment, he says, is not the same thing as choice or consent. The latter occur at a particular point in time, whereas commitments are temporally extended.

If not original intentions, then what establishes and defines our commitments? Rubenfeld argues that the proper interpretive methodology for the Constitution as the commitments of a people is what he calls the paradigm-case method of interpretation, which picks out the historical evils to which various constitutional provisions were responses and which employs right reason within the bounds of fidelity to the paradigm cases. In this way, law's dual aspect is given its due, and the problem of time is solved.

Lawrence Sager contrasts historicist and justice-seeking accounts of the United States Constitution. He argues that historicist accounts – those that take the meaning of the Constitution to be dependent on the intentions of the authors – cannot properly answer the question of why the past should govern the present. Sager sides with justice-seeking accounts, according to which the Constitution stands for broad principles of justice that both the popular and judicial institutions of government are obligated to implement.

Sager focuses most of his contribution on two distinctions. The first is the distinction between the part of justice that is constitutionally committed to judicial enforcement and the part of justice that is constitutionally committed solely to legislative protection. The second is the distinction between the part of justice that has been constitutionalized and the part that has not been. The second

distinction seems problematic given the first: If not all of justice is constitutionally committed to the judiciary for enforcement, why should it matter whether
the part remaining entirely in the hands of the legislature is deemed "constitutional" or "nonconstitutional"? After all, the courts will not overturn the legislative judgments in either case. And presumably the legislature is as morally obligated to pursue justice outside the constitutional realm as within it.

It might seem that for Sager the justice-seeking, nonhistoricist Constitution
could be reduced to those portions establishing the institutions of government
plus the single injunction "Do justice." But Sager denies this. At one point he
indicates that the judicial quest for constitutional justice will be "guided . . .
by the text of the Constitution," albeit "only broadly." At another, he writes of
particular rights that are "insufficiently connected to the dictates of text and
history." These sound like points that would be made by a historicist, not by
one who endorses justice-seeking constitutionalism.

Perhaps, however, Sager distinguishes between the text of the Constitution,
which does constrain the Constitution's pursuit of justice, and the intentions
of the text's authors, which do not. The difficulty with this position is that it
does make us bound "because they said it." We are bound by the framers' intended text. If that text constrains our pursuit of justice as we see it, then
Sager has not answered the question he puts to the historicist of why the past
so binds us.

Moreover, Sager needs to tell us why the framers' textual intentions bind us
but their semantic intentions do not. Or, going in the opposite direction, why
are we not bound only by the marks they intended rather than their text, marks
that we could turn into a language and text of our choosing and whose meanings would be more conducive to justice-seeking? If authored intentions bind
us not only to marks but also to an English text, why do they not bind us all
the way down to specific intended meanings? And if they do not bind us all
the way down, why do they bind us at all, even at the level of marks?

Near the end of his contribution, Sager hints that, for the United States
Constitution at least, the historicist/justice-seeking dilemma may not exist.
For he says that "the framing constitutional generations [were] . . . speaking
at a high level of moral generality or abstraction in the liberty-bearing provisions of the Constitution." In other words, their *intention* was so general as to
be translatable as "Do justice as you see it." We can be both faithful to history
and unconstrainedly justice-seeking in constitutional interpretation. We need
not choose between the past and the present.

Jeremy Waldron's central concern is the conflict between constitutionalism
and democratic decision-making. Waldron quite correctly argues that constitutionalism is not democratic even if it is established democratically. Likewise, a democratic delegation to the courts of the power to invalidate legisla-

tion in the name of rights does not make such judicial invalidations democratic. Moreover, the fact that we accept the legitimacy of these systems, even when they thwart our democratic judgments, does not make such systems democratic in Waldron's eyes.

Now I do not read Waldron as arguing that democratic decision-making about matters of justice is itself a principle of justice that is lexically superior to all other principles of justice. Such an argument would, of course, undermine constitutionalism, but it is surely not self-evident. Would two thugs have a right to take my property – and would I have no right to resist – merely because they were two and I am but one?

In any event, Waldron does not explicitly make the argument that democratic decision-making always trumps all other principles of justice. What, then, *is* the source of his democratic complaint against constitutionalism?

Waldron does not distinguish among the following ways that constitutionalism might thwart current majorities:

(1) We might have, as Sager suggests we do have in part, a constitution that directs the judiciary to determine our moral rights and to impose those rights despite their legislative rejection. That version of constitutionalism would be a judicial aristocracy. We might accept such a system, even as it thwarted our democratic judgments, perhaps because we trusted judges more than legislatures on the ground that the judicial process is more conducive to arguments of principle and hence to ascertaining where justice lies, or on the ground that judges are less subject to political akrasia (succumbing to pressures to depart from justice).

(2) We might have our rights determined by past majorities and entrenched against present majorities, a system that we might now accept even if the rights so entrenched are not ideal under anyone's political morality. We might accept those rights over present democratic outcomes if they are good enough and if present democratic bodies are subject to political akrasia or to the problems of social choice associated with Kenneth Arrow.[16] That is, we might prefer the menu of rights the framers left us to the menu that shifting majorities would produce.

Under the system of rights entrenched by past generations, we need to distinguish four variants for handling cases where it is not clear what rights were established by the constitutional framers:

(2a) We could have a system in which the legislature, by majority vote, determined the historical question of what the framers intended. The decision would be democratically made, but it would not be a decision about the present majority's views of rights.

(2b) We could have a system that left the historical meaning of unclear rights to the courts.

(2c) We could have a system in which, when the framers were unclear about rights, the legislature resolved the lack of clarity by reference to its own judgments about rights, and not by reference to historical evidence of what the framers intended.

(2d) We could have a system in which, when the framers were unclear about rights, the judiciary resolved the lack of clarity by reference to its own judgment about rights, and not by reference to historical evidence.

Both system (1) and system (2) are undemocratic in Waldron's terms. Under system (2), only variant (2c) satisfies Waldron's conception of democracy, and it operates within the undemocratic bounds set by the clear rights established by the constitutional framers.

The system that is generally understood to be authoritative in the United States is that described by (2b). One could accept (2) for reasons previously given and still reject (2b) in favor of (2c), the most democratic version. That is, we might agree that the clear rights bequeathed us by the constitutional framers are superior to those that would most likely arise through pure democratic decision-making and yet not accept those other rights bequeathed us that we do not presently understand.

On the other hand, if the rights bequeathed us are for the most part clear – and if we believe that the marginal applications that are unclear will not be seriously misguided, perhaps based on the evidence provided by the clear applications – then we may still prefer the historical inquiry to current judgments as the method for clarifying the rights. And given the nature of courts and legislatures, we could surely prefer that courts undertake the historical inquiry, (2b), rather than that legislatures do so, (2a).

Parts of Waldron's argument against constitutionalism appear to be directed at judicial supremacy on questions of what rights we have (as opposed to what rights the constitutional framers entrenched as a historical matter). In other words, these parts of the argument respond to systems (1) and (2d) but not to the other possibilities.

Still other parts of Waldron's argument subtly shift from one system to another. Thus, he describes a shift in views about rights from the constitutional founding at time$_1$ to the decision of a legislative majority at time$_2$ to the decision of a judicial majority at time$_3$. His critique of judicial supremacy works much better, however, if the judicial decision at time$_3$ is on the same issue as that raised in the legislature at time$_2$ and by the founders at time$_1$. That would be true if the system were (2d), for example. That would *not* be true, however, if the system were (2b), for in that system, the judicial decision, unlike the founders' and the legislature's, is a historical one, not one involving the court's own views of political morality.

At other points, Waldron's comments about precommitment, although correct as far as they go, misdescribe the situation in constitutionalism. For if we *now* accept the metaconstitutional norm that makes what we judged *then* to trump what we judge *now,* then *we,* not some third party, are holding ourselves to our earlier commitment. Why should we do so? For the usual reasons about political akrasia, Arrow's problem, and so forth discussed earlier.

Finally, even democratic decision-making requires some entrenchment against the democratic will. For example, democratic parliaments would find it highly desirable to have a rule – an entrenched one – saying that those who lose a legislative battle over the enactment of a law may not reintroduce the issue immediately. Indeed, it might be desirable to have an entrenched rule against reintroducing the issue during the same legislative term, perhaps with an exception when reintroduction is favored by a supermajority. Those rules, however, differ in degree but not in kind from the constitutionally entrenched rules that Waldron attacks.

Notes

1 See H. L. A. Hart, *The Concept of Law* (Clarendon Press, 1961), 92.
2 Rubenfeld, Chapter 5, this volume.
3 See Larry Alexander, *The Constitution as Law,* 6 Constitutional Commentary 103, 106–9 (1989). See also David A. Strauss, *Common Law Constitutional Interpretation,* 63 University of Chicago Law Review 877, 910–11 (1996); Michael J. White, *Guide for Perplexed Liberals: Second Installment,* 15 Law & Philosophy 417, 429–30 (1996).
4 See Richard S. Kay, *Preconstitutional Rules,* 42 Ohio State Law Journal 187 (1981).
5 See Kay, Chapter 1, n. 108, this volume; Richard S. Kay, *Comparative Constitutional Fundamentals,* 6 Connecticut Journal of International Law 445 (1991); Richard S. Kay, Book Review, 7 Constitutional Commentary 434 (1990).
6 See Kay, Chapter 1, n. 108, this volume; Frederick Schauer, *Amending the Presuppositions of the Constitution,* in *Responding to Imperfection: The Theory and Practice of Constitutional Amendment* (S. Levinson, ed., Princeton Univ. Press, 1995), 145–61.
7 See Alexander, supra note 3, at 106–9.
8 See Larry Alexander and Emily Sherwin, *The Deceptive Nature of Rules,* 142 University of Pennsylvania Law Review 1191 (1994); Larry Alexander, *Pursuing the Good – Indirectly,* 95 Ethics 315, 325–9 (1985).
9 See Alexander and Sherwin, supra note 8; Larry Alexander, *Law and Exclusionary Reasons,* 18 Philosophical Topics 5, 9–11 (1990).
10 See Larry Alexander, *Originalism, or Who Is Fred?* 19 Harvard Journal of Law & Public Policy 321, 325–6 (1996).
11 See id. at 324–6:

... Originalism in constitutional law is Fred determining the rules for our club. If there is
some fact of the matter based upon Fred's psychological states about what he determined
those rules should be, and he intended that the document he gives us communicate those determinations, then our rules *are* the determinations Fred recorded in that document. In all theories of constitutional interpretation, the model remains the same. As our preconstitutional
norms change, only Fred's identity changes. And although our preconstitutional norms can
change the identity of Fred – say, from the Constitutional Convention to the state ratifiers to
a hypothetical average user of English in 1787 (or in 1995) – and can limit Fred's authority in
various ways – say, by treating the authoritative Constitution as that document in the National Archives minus the Second Amendment – we cannot eliminate Fred – some Fred – altogether.

So once we have determined who Fred is in our constitutional scheme – whose determinations are supremely authoritative – it follows tautologically that Fred's determinations are
supremely authoritative. It is redundant to speak of that Fred's *original* determinations.

Now, the Framers might be Fred. Or the Ratifiers might be Fred. Or an average speaker of
English in 1787 might be Fred, except when a 1787 dictionary and grammar do not produce
single answers or produce absurd ones, in which case the Framers or the Ratifiers might be
Fred. So it all boils down to, "Who is Fred?"

In the footnote to the last sentence just quoted I wrote:

Here is a thumbnail account of constitutionalism that provides a context for the "Who is
Fred?" problem:

1. We have a state of moral uncertainty. Either we disagree about certain moral norms, or
   we agree about them at a certain level of generality but disagree about what they demand
   at a more concrete level.
2. We need to resolve this moral uncertainty by accepting as authoritative certain methods
   for resolving the uncertainty.
3. A particular set of norms of authority – norms that prescribe the authoritative practice referred to in 2., that is, preconstitutional norms, presuppositions, rules of recognition,
   groundnorms – becomes accepted, because we all agree that it is the morally best such
   ... [set of norms] upon which we can agree in our state of moral uncertainty.
4. [Those norms] ... of authority describe "Fred." For purposes of resolving our moral uncertainty, Fred might be the actual determinations of what ought to be done by the
   Framers, or by the ratifiers, or by the public (what the words in their context would have
   meant to an average person at the time of ratification), and so on.
5. Because 4. might be uncertain, our norms of authority might designate an authoritative
   interpreter – for example, the Supreme Court. The norms of authority would also resolve
   the question when and over whom the authoritative interpreter is authoritative (for example, does the President have to follow the Court in cases on all fours with the case the
   Court has decided?).
6. Because an interpretation of 4. per 5. might differ from a later understanding of 4., we
   also need norms of authority for resolving the conflict between precedent and Fred – for
   example, Fred trumps precedent, precedent trumps Fred, or Fred trumps precedent, but
   only under certain circumstances. (If precedent can trump Fred, then we really have two
   Freds – Fred the interpreted and Fred the interpreter – and our norms of authority dictate
   how these Fred versus Fred conflicts should be resolved.)
7. Our norms of authority could limit Fred's and the interpreter's authority on substantive
   grounds – for example, the Constitution or constitutional precedents are authoritative unless they are too unjust. In this way *justice can enter as a limit on authoritative practices.*
8. But, *justice cannot be weighed in the balance alongside authoritative practices because
   justice and authoritative practices are norms of different ontological types.* Justice belongs to the realm of *morality.* Authoritative practices are posited, and the contents of
   their prescriptions are *matters of fact.*
9. One *can* ask whether one should follow Fred or follow justice. But if one does so one
   confronts the paradox of authority: Fred's authority was a morally required response to

moral uncertainty. That is, we all agreed, whatever our moral views, that it was morally better to have Fred and Fred's authority to deal with moral uncertainty than to have no moral authority. If we now ask whether we morally ought to follow Fred or follow morality, the latter will be what we morally ought to do, but morality also dictated that there be Fred.

10. We have a constitutional crisis if we cease to agree over our norms of authority, that is, over who Fred is. That seems to be our current situation. We do not agree about whose Constitution is authoritative, or about the authority of precedent, the role of substantive morality, and so forth.

11. *But,* we may have a second order norm of authority that we all do agree upon that resolves first order disagreement about norms of authority. That rule might be, "Whatever the Supreme Court decides about who Fred is is authoritative." In this case, the real Fred for the rest of us is the Supreme Court, though for the Supreme Court, Fred is someone else.

Id. at 326 n. 17.

12 See Larry Alexander, *All or Nothing at All? The Intentions of Authorities and the Authority of Intentions,* in *Law and Interpretation* (Andrei Marmor, ed., Clarendon Press, 1995), 356–404, 375–9.

13 See id. at 375–9, 394–5.

14 See id. at 368–79; Richard S. Kay. *Adherence to the Original Intentions in Constitutional Adjudication: Three Objections and Responses,* 82 Northwestern University Law Review 226 (1988).

15 See Joseph Raz, *The Authority of Law* (Clarendon Press, 1979), 233–49; Joseph Raz, *Authority, Law and Morality,* 68 The Monist 295 (1985).

16 See Kenneth J. Arrow, *Social Choice and Individual Values* (Wiley, 2d ed., 1963), 2–8.

1

American Constitutionalism

RICHARD S. KAY

As the twentieth century comes to a close, the triumph of constitutionalism appears almost complete. Just about every state in the world has a written constitution. The great majority of these declare the constitution to be law controlling the organs of the state. And, in at least many states, that constitution is, in fact, successfully invoked by courts holding acts of the state invalid because inconsistent with the constitution.[1] This development is generally thought to be a tribute to an especially American idea.[2] Although there is considerable variation in the substantive contents and structural machinery of constitutionalism in various countries,[3] the central idea, forged in the American founding, of public power controlled by enforcement of a superior law is present everywhere constitutional government is proclaimed.

In this essay I hope to elaborate what I take to be the essential premises of that idea. I do not mean that these premises are always reflected in the actual practice of constitutionalism in the United States or elsewhere. But I believe they continue to provide the indispensable ideological supports on which every exercise of authority in the name of the constitution rests, even when such an exercise of authority is, in fact, inconsistent with them.

I find these premises neatly summarized in the sentence with which Walton H. Hamilton opened his article entitled "Constitutionalism" in the 1930 *Encyclopedia of Social Sciences:* "Constitutionalism is the name given to the trust which men repose in the power of words engrossed on parchment to keep a government in order."[4] Hamilton, as the balance of his article makes clear, regarded that trust with an amused contempt. An economist at Yale Law School who had no formal legal education, he was one of that group of skeptical academics who were creating the jurisprudence of American Legal Realism.[5] Hamilton applied to constitutionalism the same "cynical acid"[6] that the realists applied to the idea of constraining rules generally. He mocked, as inevitably futile, any effort to translate fixed constitutional principles into genuine restrictions on government action, referring to constitutional rules as "abracadabra" and to constitutional interpretation as an "ordeal at law."[7]

Hamilton's own doubts to the side, his opening description remains one of the most succinct and telling summaries of the core elements of constitutionalism. It also catalogs those features of constitutionalism that have been the focus of most critiques of it as a plausible political device. I propose to examine constitutionalism by considering each of three components of Hamilton's definition. And because, as he presented them, they are decreasingly problematic, I will take them in reverse order. First, constitutionalism entails an attempt "to keep a government in order." This requires consideration of what it means for a government to be "out of order," the risks of state power that stir people to create constitutional limits. This, in turn, demands some attention to the ways in which human beings conceive of a good life and, given such conceptions, to what kind of political "order" they would aspire. Second, the means to such a result are "the power of words engrossed on parchment." This element of constitutionalism reflects a conclusion, given our prior judgments about the proper shape of state power, that effective constitutional limits require the promulgation of fixed rules. This raises such questions as the source of the rules, the manner in which they should be interpreted, and the costs of fixedness in terms of other social values. Finally, once we have resolved the proper kinds of limits and the ways in which they should be interpreted, we will still have to face the last, and most difficult, problem – how we can translate such abstract rules into human conduct. That capacity depends, at the end, on "the trust men repose" in the ability of human beings to change their behavior in response to law.

I. To Keep a Government in Order

A. *Constitutional Order and the Liberal State*

The theoretical justification for the creation of an independent American nation included, at its center, an assumption that there existed some proper relationship between government and the subjects of government. The Declaration of Independence of 1776 stated the proper ends of government. It then asserted that a state was illegitimate when it became "destructive to these ends": Certain actions are beyond the proper realm of public power. The Declaration was mainly a catalog of such actions insofar as they had been attempted by the British government of North America.

In declaring a right and wrong of government behavior, and in asserting that wrongful behavior deprived the government of a claim to obedience, the American revolutionaries were the conscious heirs to a political theory that had been expounded in the preceding century to justify the English Revolution of 1688–9. That event had been defended on a number of grounds, but the version (a radical version) that most influenced the Americans posited that the state was limited in purpose to the protection of the natural rights of individuals, the rights they had sought to secure when they left the state of nature to enter a governed society. This is the political theory most prominently associated with John Locke, and it is hard to read the *Two Treatises* and the Declaration without becoming convinced of the powerful and direct influence of the former upon the latter.[8]

The idea that the state is in need of limitation followed naturally on the expansion of the relative role of public power in human life. As powerful and centralized nation-states took form in the sixteenth and seventeenth centuries, political theory emerged to explain them. Filmer and Hobbes, although arguing from different premises, found the authority of the sovereign to be more or less plenary.[9] In eighteenth-century Britain, this development took the form of a king-in-parliament that was held to be vested with sovereign – that is, unlimited – power.[10] By 1776 Blackstone was able to write that what Parliament does "no authority upon earth can undo."[11] It was partly in response to the positing of a leviathan-state that the idea of a government of limited purpose, and therefore of limited power, was reformulated and explicated.[12]

Like their English predecessors, the American revolutionaries saw the principal vindication of these limits in the proper distribution of political authority. The seventeenth-century constitutional settlement was, essentially, a change in the relative powers of Crown and Parliament;[13] the Americans transferred authority from distant to local government. But the logic of the underlying notion of a properly limited sphere of public power would necessarily transcend mere structural solutions. If the ultimate desideratum was the restriction of public power to a defined realm and the consequent deference to private persons in the exercise of their natural rights, it made little difference if the transgressing government acted through one kind of machinery or another.[14] The early emergence of American bills of rights that listed kinds of protected private conduct and did not (like the English Bill of Rights of 1688–9) merely specify some allocation of government power confirmed this core conviction.[15]

English history also confirmed a second aspect of the American elaboration of the idea of a properly defined domain for state activity. This was the assumption that the form that restraint of government would take would be that of law. Expressions to the effect that the state was a creature of the law and, by implication, controlled by the law were regular features of English political history, as illustrated by Bracton's remark that the king does not make the law, but the law makes the king.[16] Indeed, the great constitutional controversies of the seventeenth century were, overwhelmingly, argued in legal terms. In 1642, in the midst of his struggle with Parliament, Charles I had posited (in his Answer to the Nineteen Propositions) a distribution of power that was offered as a statement of existing governing law.[17] Those legal disputes were rehearsed in the Restoration, and in 1688–9 the Revolution was justified as necessary for the maintenance of the legal constitution.[18] The capstone of that revolution was not a promulgation, but a *declaration,* of rights. James II had lost his crown by acting "contrary to the known laws and statutes and freedom of this realm," and the revolutionaries, in the declaration, sought to vindicate "their ancient rights and liberties."[19]

While the Declaration of Independence does not, in terms, refer to positive law, an appeal to an English law that presumably limited the acts of government was a substantial ingredient of the political arguments of the American revolutionaries.[20] There was no tension between the claim that British policy impinged on the colonists' natural rights and their claim that they were being denied the legal rights of British subjects. Positive law was the vehicle by which originally natural rights were protected.[21] When the actions of the state failed to vindicate that central purpose, but on the contrary "evince[d] a design to reduce them under absolute despotism," the foundation of state authority evaporated and further submission to it was no longer justified.

The new independent states put this principle into practice by the early adoption of state constitutions. The precise nature of the incapacity of governments to act in ways inconsistent with their limited purposes was spelled out and enacted as positive law. The widespread adoption of bills of rights, already noted, made clear the American conviction that the law could be employed not merely to define the structure of political institutions, but also to fence out certain subjects from potential public regulation.[22]

These two elements – first, that there is a proper and improper use of state authority and, second, that the means of confining its exercise to proper uses are the promulgation and enforcement of positive law – remain the defining features of American constitutionalism. The constitutionalist instinct is that the use of the collective power of society is a special source of danger. Constitutionalism is, therefore, an expression of that view which came to be known as liberalism – the idea that the relevant moral unit in political discourse is the individual or, perhaps more accurately, that the *polis* itself has no moral standing independent of that of its members. A basic premise of this outlook is that the highest human satisfaction can arise only in a life freely chosen.[23] According to Gerald Dworkin, "What makes an individual the particular person he is is his life-plan, his projects. In pursuing autonomy, one shapes one's life, one constructs its meaning. The autonomous person gives meaning to his life."[24] If one accepts this view of the minimum conditions for a successful life, it follows that the coercive power of the state is justified principally as far as it is a means of preserving the capacity of human beings to define their own existences.[25] Public authority exists to facilitate that process:

[I]n the usual sense of purpose, namely the anticipation of a particular foreseeable event, the law does not serve any purpose but countless different purposes of different individuals. . . . [O]f all multipurpose instruments it is probably the one after language which assists the greatest variety of human purposes.[26]

Personal autonomy is prior to, indeed defines, any purpose of the state: Or, as Thomas Paine said, government "has of itself no rights; they are altogether duties."[27]

One may contrast this understanding of the state with another that has also had a powerful presence in Western political thought. That is the idea that the state exists to pursue substantive objectives which are held exclusively by society in its incorporated form, apart from those held by individuals and private groups. Michael Oakeshott called this kind of association *universitas* and contrasted it with *societas,* in which the association is merely instrumental to the achievement of the particular ends of its members.[28] The latter form of association is essential to his idea of a "rule of law" state, one involving "recognition of the authority of known, noninstrumental rules."[29] The alternative state, premised on some collective purposes, is, on the other hand, "a rationally regulated cooperative engagement," which Oakeshott identified with a *Politzeistaat.*[30] This term, which Continental writers on the rule of law have employed,[31] is to be distinguished from the modern English use of "police state," which refers to the repressive character of a totalitarian regime. Oakeshott calls it a "benign conception of the state."[32] It is related to the broader use of "police" in terms like "police power." Both usages, however, share a reference to the state as something with purposes of its own, and the darker version tells us something about the dangers such an idea holds for the advocates of liberal constitutionalism.

This distinction may be put in sharper relief by considering recent attempts to view constitutions and constitutional law mainly as instruments for facilitating a mode of political discourse in which the good is sought in collective decision-making and political association.[33] Contemporary exponents of this "republican" outlook do not, to be sure, suggest that the interests of individuals are to be submerged in the interests of the state. Indeed, they embrace a picture of constitutional restraint not unlike that inferable from liberal premises. But they understand such restraint on state behavior not as a prerequisite to personal self-determination, but as necessary for authentic public deliberation and decision.[34] The differences between this derivation and the more conventional understanding are significant. It may make a difference in the operation of a constitutional regime whether private rights are a means to effective political association or whether political institutions are a means of realizing private rights.

This theme of republican virtue was a substantial one in the political thought of the founding period.[35] Still, it is hard to maintain that what the early American constitution-makers *did* was meant principally to optimize the manner and effectiveness of political decision-making. They rather explicitly intended their specification of governmental institutions to be not merely a way of enhancing public deliberation and of expediting collective action but, in significant part, a technique for thwarting them. The founders attempted to check political overreaching by creating a division of powers. They employed what they understood to be the psychology of power. Ambition, in Madison's well-known phrase, must be made to counteract ambition.[36] The enactors understood these structural features of constitutionalism to be complementary to the more direct limitations of power represented by bills and declarations of rights.[37] This understanding was explicit with respect to the United States Constitution of 1787–9. The principal response to the critics of that document who based their opposition on its failure to express a bill of individual rights was that the same purpose was served, as well or better, by the enumeration of exclusive powers. "The Constitution" itself, said Hamilton, is "to all intents and purposes a bill of rights."[38] This design tracked almost perfectly what has become a central feature of liberal constitutionalism, the assumption that private action is, "*in principle,* unlimited" and that all impingements on it "are to be regarded as exceptions."[39]

This is not to say that the only object of protection of constitutions was the individual human being. De Tocqueville recognized early in the history of the United States the importance of groups and associations of every kind.[40] The freedom to associate and act collectively is itself a natural and important consequence of constitutional limitations. The unique subject of constitutional restraint is the state, which is unlike every other human institution. As a practical matter, of course, the state is, save in extraordinary situations, the holder of formidable powers of compulsion. More to the point, the theoretical claims of the post-Hobbesian state include plenary authority over every act within its jurisdiction and the exclusive and ultimate right to employ physical force to accomplish its objectives. Every other actor in the polity is subject to restraints created and enforced by the state. However, the state, as the holder of legislative power, is itself subject to no constraint but that of the constitution.[41] The constitution must, then, be understood as a protection for every potential subject of state authority – individuals, families, groups.[42] (When the 1787–9 Constitution was drafted and ratified, the subjects whose autonomy was to be protected were, mainly, the individual states. For the purposes of that enterprise, the states stood in relation to the new national government as the individual or private association stood to the unitary state.)

To take this perspective it is not necessary to assume, as some writers have argued, that rights of individuals and associations are in some sense "prepolitical."[43] Quite to the contrary, the idea of preserving autonomy through the imposition of rules on the state presupposes that the planning and acting that are to be protected must take place in a social environment. The value

central to this understanding of the relative role of public and private authority is not mere independence but, as Neil MacCormick put it, "independence
in interdependence, independence in community."[44] Therefore, no constitution supposes that public authority is an unqualified evil. Locke's hypothe-
sized state of nature was no desert island but an inhabited community. But in
such an ungoverned society it was impossible for the inhabitants to protect
their natural rights effectively, to rule their own lives – thus "governments are
instituted among men."[45]

B. Constitutional Order and the Rule of Law

Constitutions restrict the reach of the state by a proper specification of what it
may and may not do. They may do this by defining an exclusive grant of public power and/or by removing from its control certain favored private activities. But they achieve their more general aim of reducing the danger from the
state in another way as well – one unrelated to the particular set of powers and
rights set out in them. The existence of *any* a priori statement of the scope of
state power "keep[s] a government in order." Any particular exercise of
power is less threatening if it occurs within preexisting known limits. In fact,
a constitutionally defined government with extensive granted powers is, in
some ways, less dangerous than a weak government whose powers are not defined by prior law.

   The advantages of dealing with predefined power are akin to those more
generally associated with the "rule of law." Joseph Raz has identified a cluster
of propositions generally associated with that idea:

1. All laws should be prospective, open, and clear. . . . 2. Laws should be relatively
stable. . . . 3. The making of particular laws . . . should be guided by open, stable and
clear general rules. . . . 4. The independence of the judiciary must be guaranteed. . . .[46]

While an enacted constitution is not indispensable to the creation of a regime
adhering to these propositions, the presence of such a constitution extends
these features to the lawmaking power itself.[47] The capacity for personal self-
determination is protected if the sources of potential interference with that capacity are known in advance. Personal autonomy consists not merely of freedom of action but also, critically, of the capacity to plan actions over time. A
central danger of state regulation is its power to wipe out the planned results
of personal decision. The ability to predict when such authority will, and,
more important, when it will not, be employed permits the making out of a
space for planning and undertaking actions with some confidence that they
will be allowed and that their results will be permitted to stand.[48]

   We can put the same conclusion another way. One of the most serious injuries the state can inflict on its subjects is to commit them to lives of perpet-

ual uncertainty. Our picture of the totalitarian state is associated with the surprise knock on the door that can come on any day at any hour, by the threat of punishment for the violation of standards of conduct that were different or unknown before enforcement, with official behavior that is uncontrolled by any preexisting patterns or restraints. This kind of existence is like a journey, full of dangerous obstacles and risks, undertaken in total darkness. The political writers of the founding generation quoted Montesquieu: "Political liberty consists in security, or at least, in the opinion we have of security."[49]

The character of these concerns, and the way in which constitutional rules respond to them, may be made clearer by imagining the situation of two people shipwrecked on a desert island. Caliban is powerful. He is also impulsive, violent, and selfish. Prospero is weak and old and terrorized by his companion. He lives his life at Caliban's whim. Where he goes, what he does, what he has are all subject to interruption and destruction at any time. Assume, however, that Caliban has one moral capacity, the ability to keep promises. If Caliban can be prevailed on, in a moment of sympathy, to promise not to enter a certain physical space, or not to injure Prospero at certain times, or to announce his approach when he comes near, or to forgo one or two particularly offensive forms of maltreatment, Prospero's life will be profoundly improved. This will be so even if we concede that in every other way Caliban remains as vicious as ever. Such an improvement will, moreover, be superior to one in which Caliban agrees merely to consider Prospero's interests before acting, even if he does consider those interests and actually refrains, from time to time, from injuring him. Prospero might prefer the former reform even if he knew that, in a given period, Caliban would interfere with him more often that he would under the latter. Only in the first case has Prospero acquired the capacity, however limited, to live according to plan.

The special virtue of constitutionalism, therefore, lies not merely in reducing the power of the state, but in effecting that reduction by the advance imposition of rules. The affinity of the American constitution-makers for limitation by law made this combination natural to them. When Walton Hamilton spoke of the need to keep government "in order," he touched (albeit inadvertently) on this critical feature. The advantage of the use of a priori legal rules to define the sources, procedures, and extent of public power is that it imparts to that power some minimum of orderliness, of regularity, and thus makes it a thing capable of being rationally known. Those rules state attributes of public action that make such action valid or invalid. Individuals may then focus on the presence or absence of such attributes in potential state action that might impinge on their plans.[50] The availability of such defined criteria substantially simplifies the estimation of potential state interference. The subject thereby acquires a greater ability to place every planned action in one of two categories, one subject to undoing by the state, the other immune to such authority. And within that second category, however narrow, a person may construct his or her own life.

C. Constitutional Order, Public Action, and Democracy

The personal liberty and order facilitated by a constitutional regime are not the only values that might be given consideration in designing a government. I have already noted an alternative conception of the state as the means to accomplish corporate goals rather than to facilitate private planning. Even if we give priority to private planning and action, we might think that the conditions of modern life require extensive public intervention to supply the minimal material preconditions of private self-determination or to provide the necessary coordination for such plans to have a chance to succeed.[51] In either case the fixed quality of constitutional rules entails substantial costs because it makes it impossible for the state to respond to such changes in circumstances. This is an aspect of all regulation by rule that, by definition, precludes reference to all of the individual features of any case governed by the rule. To embrace constitutionalism is to concede the costs of suboptimal public responses to change as an acceptable price to pay for the security obtained. Constitutionalism is risk-averse in the sense that it prefers the awkwardness of rigidly bound state action to the possibility that government will overshoot the mark in dealing with new circumstances and thus needlessly restrict private action.[52] That may, in fact, be an especially worrisome hazard in a democratic regime where a government will be especially vulnerable to the appeal of short-term considerations of collective welfare at the expense of the liberties of individuals and minorities.[53]

Therefore, I am unable to agree with the notion of constitutional interpretation suggested by Joseph Raz in Chapter 4, this volume. He posits that both continuity and innovation are moral qualities in the governance of a society. It follows, as a matter of political morality, that judges may be obliged to require or forbid state actions in ways not provided for by the original enactors when "the need to improve the law is greater than the need for continuity on the point, and when there is an interpretation that improves the law."[54] Such a policy commits the ultimate judgment on the propriety of innovation to the judges and, while it contemplates judges sensitive to the value of continuity as well as change, it effectively replaces the "hard" limits of fixed rules with the more malleable restraint of judicial balancing. In some ways it is attractive to substitute a conscious and intelligent human judgment for the dumb and insensate abstractions of preexisting rules, but, for reasons already articulated, the risks of that substitution are exactly what animates constitutionalism in the first place.[55] It is true, as Raz notes, that there is a sense in which the effective constitution in a regime of regular judicial improvements is the "same" constitution as that originally enacted.[56] But, if we are concerned with stable and knowable rules that allow us to distinguish permissible from potentially regulable conduct, which, as I have argued, is the point of constitutionalism, it is quite certainly not the same constitution. Indeed, in such a regime there is no identifiable constitution at all, merely a practice of constitutional interpretation.

Constitutional obstacles to state flexibility may be valuable even in a state premised on the achievement of collective objectives. Long-term social objectives might be better approximated by adherence to more or less permanent rules than by a series of infinitely revisable decisions. To the extent that the state objectives rely on private actions, an unpredictable political environment may chill them. Even the actions of the government itself require some assurance of permanence to have an effect. To make a state constantly vulnerable to total redefinition is to "introduce an element of nervous hysteria into the heart of democratic politics."[57] Just as with private parties, the state requires some stability if it is to carry out any chosen policy.[58]

Similar considerations are relevant to the objection to constitutional rule based on its supposed inconsistency with democratic government. The most familiar example of the operation of constitutional rules is the judicial invalidation of unconstitutional acts of the legislature. It should be stated immediately that the preference for a constitutional regime depends on an implicit or explicit judgment that self-government, immediate or long-term, is not a preemptive value. In its strongest form the argument for democracy supposes that what is democratically chosen should be effected simply because it is democratically chosen. Admittedly, in the prevailing political culture, the approval of elected representatives lends critical legitimacy to public decisions. Yet, at bottom, such democratic legitimacy depends on nothing but its source and is, in that sense, a species of what Weber called charismatic legitimacy. As such, by itself, it is irrational and arbitrary and, therefore, in direct contradiction to the core objectives of constitutional government.[59] The framers of the United States Constitution were no less wary of arbitrary power issuing from a legislature than from any other source.[60] When hedged with formal rules for its exercise, the extreme potentialities of this charismatic democratic authority are tempered, domesticated, by a rational-legal authority.

It is possible to conceive of democratic decision-making not as an independent and supreme source of political legitimacy but merely as a component of the liberal state. We may regard it as a sensible complement to constitutional rules. Confiding the necessary powers of government to a periodically elected legislature provides a further safeguard against public action in that it reduces the likelihood that the state will undertake measures that threaten the liberty of the population.[61] Nevertheless, as the American constitution-makers well understood, legislatures could be foolish, venal, even tyrannical, so that the

restraint of limiting rules was still desirable. Even a sober and virtuous legislature could not be counted on to act within the kind of predictable limits that
could be effected only by the establishment of a fixed constitution.

Even if we accepted the political priority of democratic legitimacy, it
would not be obvious that a regime of constitutional rules conflicts with it.
This follows, even more clearly, from reasons already considered in connection with the more general objection to the rigidity introduced by constitutions. The idea of democratic decision-making involves multiple and, perhaps, contradictory meanings. There is no single specification of whose
assent confers democratic legitimacy on a decision. The American enactors
thought the confirmation of the state ratifying conventions made the Constitution an act of "the people" in a way to which no mere legislation could aspire.[62] More recently Bruce Ackerman has argued that only on occasion can
the people muster the intensity sufficient to express themselves on basic constitutional questions.[63] In addition, it is unclear over what period democratic
decision is to be respected. One function of constitutional rule is to maintain
the conditions and institutions of democracy for the future: "By means of a
constitution generation *a* can help generation *c* protect itself from being sold
into slavery by generation *b*."[64] Finally, genuine democratic deliberation requires some background stability with respect to the basic characteristics of
the state and society in which it operates. What does it mean democratically
to establish a rule in a world where every procedure and institution is subject
to immediate and total change, where the very arena of collective choice is
undefined?[65]

The choice of a constitutional regime thus assumes an ordering of values. It
does not exclude attention to the utility of collective action and the propriety
of democratic decision-making. But it requires the accommodation of those
values to the overriding objective of ensuring that human activity can be undertaken in a political environment that has a minimally acceptable degree of
clarity and stability. This liberal conception of the state seems especially congenial to a society in which a plurality of cultures and ethics must coexist. In
a community with a uniform conception of the good life, private happiness
might be nurtured by public means. In such a situation, as Michel Rosenfeld
has noted, "there would be no palpable need to separate the governors from
the governed."[66] Once that unity disappears, however, some definition of
private and public spheres becomes essential. The determination of the public sphere must take account of the diversity of views in the population. The
responsibilities committed to the state need not be without substantive
aim. (The creation of public institutions that protect private liberty of action
is itself a collective aim.) Still, to the extent that those aims must reflect
what Rawls refers to as an "overlapping consensus" of the various value systems present in society, it is natural to expect that rules and institutions vindi-

cating the formal, rule-of-law values will be the state's outstanding features.[67] Agreement on a limited number of constitutional rules, with restricted substantive content, supported from various, and possibly sharply antagonistic, moral-political viewpoints, improves the prospects for a stable pluralist society.[68]

D. Conclusion

Central to constitutionalism, as I have defined it, is security. Effective liberty requires assurance as to its duration and extent. Put another way, constitutionalism aims to invest at least some aspects of life with a promise of psychological repose.[69] There is a popular misconception about the defects of the legal world depicted in Kafka's *The Trial*. A system thick with rules and regulations is disparaged as "Kafkaesque"[70] and, indeed, a proliferation of difficult and contradictory rules may obscure more than it reveals. Yet the terror of *The Trial* is that intrinsic in a world where rules do not exist or do not count. Joseph K has nothing to rely on.[71] It illustrates the kind of society in which the power of the state is not defined – the kind of society that constitution-makers wish to reform. In a much-quoted passage, Grant Gilmore said that "[t]he better the society, the less law there will be. In Heaven there will be no law, and the lion will lie down with the lamb. . . . In Hell there will be nothing but law, and due process will be meticulously observed."[72] If so, for the reasons discussed, for mortals at least, Heaven may be a fearful place.

II. Words Engrossed on Parchment

A. *Written Rules as Instruments of Restraint*

To say that constitutionalism necessarily entails the creation of prior rules to define and limit the power of the state is to invoke some fixed verbal formulation of those rules. A legal rule that cannot be stated is no rule. The medium by which the formulation is preserved and communicated is not crucial. It could be oral or electronic, but for the founders of the United States Constitution, of course, it was written. They referred incessantly to the desirability of written instruments of government. One wrote in 1776 that "all Constitutions should be contained in some written Charter."[73] In *Marbury v. Madison*, Chief Justice Marshall referred to "what we have deemed to be the greatest improvement on political institutions, a written constitution."[74] Ten years earlier a Virginia judge had written that "with us the Constitution is not an ideal thing, it has a real existence; it can be produced in a visible form."[75]

For that founding generation, writtenness was attractive because it *fixed* the rules. Such ideas as "fundamental principles of government" and natural rights were subject to endless disputation. A written rule narrowed, if it did not eliminate, differences as to its meaning. In his well-known judgment in *Calder v. Bull,* Justice Iredell disparaged the idea of referring challenged acts to the criteria of "natural justice which are regulated by no fixed standard." The point of the Constitution was "to define with precision the objects of the legislative power, and to restrain its exercise within marked and settled boundaries."[76] In another expression, Iredell linked the precision of constitutional rules with their tangible written quality: The Constitution was not "a mere imaginary thing about which ten thousand opinions may be formed."[77] In *Marbury,* Marshall made the same association: "The powers of the legislature are defined and limited; and that those limits are not mistaken, or forgotten, the constitution is written."[78] In the same year Jefferson wrote that "[o]ur peculiar security is possession of a written constitution. Let us not make it a blank paper by construction."[79]

Considering this history, it is ironic that some modern commentators have seized on the written nature of the Constitution as the basis for arguing that it is incapable of yielding rules sufficiently determinate to effect real limits on the state. Drawing upon relatively recent writing in the philosophy of language and literary criticism, these authors deny that language use is capable of communicating a determinate meaning. Every text is strewn with inherently ambiguous, indeed self-contradictory, tropes. It is, moreover, impossible for a reader to puzzle out the text's one "correct" interpretation. There is no such thing as an independent text, author, or reader. All are linked in a single and inevitably self-referential social practice. The destructive power of this outlook is total:

It calls into question and explodes our faith in the author (someone who is in command of language and creates the text); in the text itself (a stable entity that yields stable meanings); in interpretation (an activity that aims to extract univocal meanings from texts); and in literary, cultural, and other [we might add legal] kinds of history (a story or narrative that "progresses" from one period to the next).[80]

Applying this idea to law, one not atypical exponent says, "Each attempt to fix meaning is belied by the dependence of meaning on language."[81]

Whatever the merits of this way of perceiving linguistic expression for literary critics, its implausibility as a description of the practice of reading and writing texts in general and legal texts in particular is plain.[82] It is at odds with the everyday successful verbal communication we all experience. With respect to the efficacy of legal communication, parties contract and then (usually) behave in the ways sought to be prescribed in the contract; legislatures reduce speed limits and motorists (generally) slow down; judges hand down sentences and defendants (almost always) go to prison. Scholars propound theories of interpretation and others agree with them or denounce them. In-

deed, this claim may be one of those "operationally self-refuting propositions" described by John Finnis as "inevitably falsified by any assertion of
them."[83] If it were valid, any discussion of the character of constitutionalism (not to mention any discussion at all) would be futile. A limitation imposed by unknowable rules is indistinguishable from the total absence of
rules. This would, to use Marshall's words again, "reduce[ ] to nothing what
we have deemed the greatest improvement on political institutions, a written
constitution."[84]

B. *Meaning, Text, and Intent*

One need not, however, embrace this extreme view of the impossibility of linguistic communication to share Walton Hamilton's skeptical view of the capacity of words to limit public power. Even if every use of language cannot
mean everything, words, taken by themselves, may denote more than one
thing. This idea – that there is a range of meanings of which constitutional
words are capable – seems to present the possibility of an attractive compromise between the benefits of flexible state authority and the security of hard
and fast restrictions on its exercise. A court interpreting constitutional rules
may adapt the powers of government to the changing needs of the polity, but
only within the play allowed by the possible meanings attached to the words
of the rules by the (changing) conventions of the language.[85] The United
States Constitution, on this reading, provides an especially fertile source for
varying constitutional meaning. Phrases like "necessary and proper," "faith-
fully execute," "freedom of speech," "due process," and "equal protection"
provide a clear opportunity for, if not an invitation to, such a judicial response. Thus, Justice Jackson described one task of the Supreme Court as
"translating the majestic generalities of the Bill of Rights, conceived as part
of the pattern of liberal government in the eighteenth century, into concrete
restraints on officials dealing with the problems of the twentieth century."[86]

There is, however, a serious objection to this understanding of the limits
imposed by constitutional rules. It assumes that the limits on the state are
somehow associated with the words of the text considered apart from the history of their adoption. But the capacity of words engrossed on parchment to
keep government in order depends on more than the physical location of the
relevant words in a document calling itself the Constitution. The choice of political actors to change their behavior in response to constitutional words is
(as will be further explored in the next section) a political phenomenon. What
is it in the fact of constitutions that induces the desired conduct? It must be
something about the historical fact of constitution-making that commends its
product to those whom it is supposed to influence. In Chapter 2, this volume,
Frank Michelman rightly emphasizes the widely shared assumption that the

Constitution gets its authority because it is a "designed creation[ ] by responsible human authors . . . law[ ] that lawmakers legislate. . . ." No one, to paraphrase Walter Benn Michaels, would pay attention to a constitution "if everyone thought it had been put together by a tribe of monkeys with quills."[87]

We can describe the quality that makes a constitution (or any law) seem worthy of being obeyed as "legitimacy." For most law, in an established legal system, legitimacy is conferred by another rule of law, one granting lawmaking power to the legislator. A constitution, on the other hand, usually is legitimized not by promulgation according to preexisting law[88] but by a widely shared political consensus as to the nature of the constituent authority in a polity.[89] The constituent authority in the United States in the constitution-making period, as far as its exact features are concerned, was, and no doubt still is, a highly controvertible matter. Nevertheless, its broad character has been shown fairly clearly. The Constitution took its authority as the act of the "people." By the time the United States Constitution was being written and ratified, the idea of some abstract model of properly arranged and balanced state powers had given way to the view that the people had sweeping authority to specify the forms and limits of government power.[90] This understanding is reflected in the declarations of rights of the earliest state constitutions.[91] Throughout *The Federalist* are frequent appeals to the consent of the people as the foundation of government. In No. 22 Hamilton called that consent "the pure original fountain of all legitimate authority," and in No. 46 Madison reminded the opponents of the Constitution that "ultimate authority, wherever the derivative may be found, resides in the people alone."[92] James Wilson's description of the relationship between constitutions and the people sums up this view:

From [the people's] authority the constitution originates; for their safety and felicity it is established: in their hands it is as clay in the hands of the potter: they have the right to mould, to preserve, to improve, to refine, and to finish it as they please.[93]

By the time of Marshall's opinion in *Marbury,* he could refer confidently to the people's "supreme and original will," which organizes the government and sets limits to its power.[94]

Of course, the way "the people" expressed themselves in 1787–9 seems insufficient today. Ratification was committed to separate conventions called for the purpose in the original thirteen states. Although qualifications for electors choosing the delegates to these conventions varied from state to state, the most liberal excluded major components of "the people" conceived of in modern terms. Even putting these limitations aside, the elections of these assemblies were tainted by improprieties.[95] Still, whatever the reality of their representative capacity, the conventions were, at the time, understood to be a proper way, perhaps the only way, that "the people" could express their constituent power. (The word "convention" had by the late eighteenth century acquired a special connotation as a legally irregular, but politically authentic medium of popular will.)[96] Any deficiencies were quickly forgotten, and the identification of "the people" as the true authors of the Constitution, as assumed in *Marbury v. Madison,* was firmly established. This attribution of the legitimacy of the Constitution to the authority of the "people" as exercised in the eighteenth-century founding appears to have continued to the present day.[97] To be sure, it is possible that this is the kind of case referred to by Joseph Raz as one in which although "respect for the authors of the constitution is very much a living political force" such respect has ceased to be a ground "for the legitimate authority of [the] constitution[ ]."[98] This kind of question is fairly impervious to conclusive empirical inquiry. Those familiar with the ubiquitous appeals to the American founders in every kind of invocation of constitutional authority, however, are likely to doubt that we have really severed the link between their action and the continuing potency of the Constitution.

If the Constitution does derive its legitimacy, its power to restrain, from assumptions about this historical-political act that created it, the idea that it is to be understood in any of the various senses that might be supported by its words as a matter of contemporary usage becomes insupportable. What commands obedience is not a mere set of words, but the expression of an intentional historical-political act. Any attempt to apply the Constitution's terms in a sense not intended by the human beings participating in that historical-political act, therefore, fails to invoke the only phenomenon that marks the Constitution off as worthy of obedience. Treating the Constitution as composed of meanings unrelated to its history makes it a different text, one no more legitimate for the purpose of limiting government than the constitution of another state or the rules of major league baseball.[99]

It follows that the implementation of a regime of constitutional restraints entails the interpretation and application of the fixed rules (rules committed to writing) created by the constitution-makers and in the sense understood by those constitution-makers. It calls, that is, for adherence to the "original intent" of the constitutional enactors. Academic lawyers and political scientists have hashed and rehashed the appropriateness and practicality of such a practice since the founding, and particularly intensively over the past twenty years.[100] I will consider briefly the standard objections. First, however, it is important to be clear about the role that original intentions should play in constitutional interpretation if it is to be consistent with the considerations surveyed in this essay. Since the principal feature of constitutionalism is its employment of fixed, a priori rules, constitutional interpretation cannot be a direction to decide individual controversies over the use of public power in whatever way is thought would be most congenial to the constitutional enactors. Such disputes are to be resolved, rather, by reference to the constitutional *rules*. Recourse to the original intentions is proper in determining the content of those rules. Once the intended scope of the rules is decided, however, the relevance of the original intentions is exhausted.

This reasoning is consistent with the premises of constitutionalism canvassed in the preceding section. I stated at the outset that constitutionalism depends on some a priori assumption as to the proper definition of public power. Why then, one might ask, should a society adopt constitutional rules solely because they express the will of the sovereign people as represented by the constitutional founders? It is possible to relieve, if not resolve, this tension by supposing that the "people," expressing themselves after their most careful and solemn deliberation, are especially qualified to define a government most appropriate to the core objectives of constitutionalism. If the principal justification of state power is related to its capacity to supply the preconditions necessary for the effective self-governance of private individuals and groups, the specification of the exact form of governmental structures and limitations employed might sensibly be committed to a political process representing the broadest consensus – to the representatives of the people.[101]

Several contributors to this volume have raised the possibility that constitutional rules may acquire legitimacy not by association with an intentional historical act but by their mere acceptance in society at a given time. As elaborated in the next section, I agree that the legal effectiveness of a constitution depends critically on the continuing acknowledgment of its legal authority. It is also true that there are species of law – customary law, common law, constitutional conventions – that attract such acceptance even in the absence of any recognized moment of lawmaking. We should not, however, expect a similar phenomenon with respect to law associated with a specific written text – enacted law. That kind of acceptance cannot be a "brute fact" of the physical world. It must issue from some explicit or tacit human judgments about political and moral right and prudential response.[102] As Frank Michelman notes in Chapter 2, there is nothing inconsistent in the assertions that law depends on social agreement and that such agreement is itself premised on a shared regard for the relevant enactors.

Constitutional rules so created will then be regarded as legitimate, as worthy of obedience. We may assume that such rules, being genuinely agreed on by such a constituent process, will represent a fair approximation of what is understood at that time and place to be proper functions of government. That those rules do not represent the optimum arrangements that might be imagined for the underlying purpose is an expected consequence of proceeding by fixed rule. And, for reasons considered in the preceding section, reliance on fixed rules is itself an indispensable element of constitutional limitation.

C. *Constitutional Legitimacy over Time*

If rules, so created, are effectively to serve the aims of constitutionalism, it is essential that they be relatively long lived. This is, in large measure, a matter of practicality. "[M]ankind are more disposed to suffer, while evils are sufferable, than to right themselves by abolishing the forms to which they are accustomed,"[103] and the exercise of the constituent power "is a very great exertion" that cannot "be frequently repeated."[104] But it is also inherent in the meaning of constitutionalism itself. The utility of constitutional rules depends on the limits they put on inconstant, and thus unknowable, state conduct. That value diminishes as the constitutional rules themselves are subject to constant rewriting.

This is not to say that constitutional rules need be, or may be, immutable. Those rules are effective only as long as they continue to be regarded in the polity as legitimate. I have already mentioned that this legitimacy depends on the historical-political process from which they issue. This factor might be called historical legitimacy. But it does not follow that any rules produced by a process that has such legitimacy will maintain their effectiveness indefinitely. Sometimes (this may be the case in the United States) the passage of time will make the founding generation appear wiser and its constitution-making legitimacy will be enhanced.[105] But there is also a risk that time will eviscerate the claim of the constitution-makers to speak for "the people."[106] Nevertheless, the inertia to which I have already referred may suffice to maintain the authority of a given set of rules as long as they retain a second characteristic – substantive legitimacy. That is, the content of the rules – the structures, procedures, and limitations they create – must retain a minimum political acceptability in the society. A particular specification of the powers of the state will lose such substantive legitimacy if, because of changed circumstances, it becomes so unsuitable that the corresponding rules cannot, as a political matter, maintain that regard which is necessary if they are to continue to control government conduct. This may be either because the original specification deprives the state of a power that is now essential for adequately protecting private decisions or because it grants government powers that have become intolerable.

One response to this possibility is to provide a procedure for constitutional amendment that can both refresh the historical legitimacy of the constitutional rules and permit their substantive realignment with the political realities. But the availability of such a procedure cannot be proof against the loss of substantive legitimacy. If constitutional rules are to limit legislative power, they must, of necessity, be entrenched beyond any alteration that could be effected by the ordinary expression of political will. Article V of the United States Constitution is frequently cited as an example of such an especially difficult process.[107] It is possible to conceive of circumstances in which the political need for constitutional change is so great as to subvert the substantive legitimacy of the Constitution, but in which the particular pattern of political forces favoring that change is unable to express itself in a form that can satisfy the amending formula. In such a situation the positive constitutional rules will, sooner or later, have to give way to the more generally held specification of the proper definition of state authority.

This phenomenon calls for some elaboration because it is a critical, though often ignored, aspect of constitutionalism. As noted, constitutionalism assumes a right and wrong of state power that is prior to government itself. This model is effected by the creation of a set of entrenched legal rules that effect a political specification of that model of public authority. Still, the legal-constitutional rules are, necessarily, merely means for accomplishing the proper limitation. If the underlying political judgments that inform the constitutional definition change, the constitutional instrument no longer serves a sensible purpose. And the result is the same when those judgments remain constant but other changes in society make the constitutional instrument obsolete as a means of achieving them. In such cases, if the positive constitutional rules do not contain an adequate legal mechanism for restoring a viable relationship between the constitution and the prior social ideas about public power, some alegal change is inevitable. Thus, constitutionalism always presupposes a reserved right of revolution.[108]

It is at least equally important, however, to remember that such events must be the rare exception. If constitutions are to provide the genuine limitations that justify their existence, they must remain fairly stable. Thus, necessarily, there cannot be a perfect correspondence between the constitutional rules and the ideal definition of political authority held in a society at any given time. It must be emphasized that to say that the legitimacy of a constitution is based, in part, on respect for the popular character of its creation is not the same thing as to say that a constitutional regime is justified only by some theory of democracy, by some notion of explicit or tacit consent. The priority of such considerations in justifying constitutional constraint has already been considered and rejected as subordinate to the value of stable and knowable rules for the conduct of the state. Moreover, that principal objective makes long-term rules indispensable and, necessarily, those rules will, over time, present an increasingly poor fit with the most appropriate substantive values to govern public action. That is, at any given moment, the constitutional rules in place will not be those that would be chosen by an equally representative and reflective constituent process. Rather, the popular origins of the rules provide a necessary ingredient in their achieving constitutional status and in maintaining that status while their substantive content retains some minimal level of social acceptance. Only when those rules depart substantially from important, widely shared, and intensely held political values can the substantive utility of constitutional redefinition justify its costs to social peace and personal security.

D. *The Interpretation and Application of Constitutional Rules*

It follows that the demands of constitutionalism in normal times require adherence to the rules fixed in the written constitution in the senses intended by the legitimate constitution-makers. It is sometimes argued, however, that the determination of the originally intended meaning is not possible in most cases. In its most extreme form this argument adopts the radical critique on the possibility of determinate language meaning already discussed. More moderate versions do not attack the very idea of linguistic meaning, but claim merely that the determination of the original meaning of a constitutional rule, drafted in the distant past, cannot be accomplished with an acceptable degree of certainty.

One aspect of this criticism centers on the fact that the rules in question are the creations not of one person, but of groups. In the case of the United States Constitution, the problem is multiplied because the enacting authority, as noted, was not a single assembly but a combination of conventions in the various states. The idea of a group intention may initially appear to be a peculiar one.[109] It is easy, however, to conceive of more than one person sharing an identical intention. When both Susan and John sign a letter inviting Tom to visit them, it is no solecism to say *they* share an intention as to the meaning of the words used. When we speak of the intention of a group, therefore, we mean an identical intention shared by some number of its members authorized to act as the group on various occasions. We deal with such intentions all the time. Legislatures, faculties, committees, and families make decisions according to their own rules or practices and express those decisions with words. In political bodies (and this was the case with the eighteenth-century state conventions) it is usually assumed that a majority can act for the group. This explanation is particularly appealing in light of the prior discussion concerning historical legitimacy. What creates that legitimacy in a regime founded on the consent of "the people" is the agreement of a sufficient number of people whose representative capacity makes their joint will an acceptable surrogate for "the people" itself.

It is possible, of course, that different members of a majority attach different meanings to the same agreed-on language.[110] Yet it will be a truly unusual case where there is not a core of common meaning shared by every member of a constitution-making majority. Differences will more normally appear with respect to fringe applications of the language chosen. All of the constitution-makers who agreed to protect "freedom of speech" surely intended by the use of the word "speech" to indicate nondefamatory spoken and written opinions about political matters. Whether a sufficient number intended those words to extend to sexually explicit works of fiction is more doubtful. The investigation of intended meaning in this context is an inquiry into the broadest meaning of the language chosen that is believed to have been shared by a number of people sufficient to act for the legitimate constitution-making group.

This statement of the manner in which the meaning of constitutional rules should be inferred may seem to confirm the positions of those who suggest it is a task too difficult and imprecise to provide a confident basis from which to restrain the actions of the state. But, as a practical matter, it is hardly necessary to investigate, one by one, the mental states of each of the human beings involved in the constitution-making process. A good idea of the meanings entertained by the relevant majority will generally be apparent from the language chosen, the context in which it was adopted, and the character of the debate surrounding the particular provision at issue, both inside and outside the body that adopted it.

There will certainly be cases of doubt, and that doubt will be intensified as the historical distance between the moment of enacting and the moment of interpretation becomes greater.[111] Still, the archival evidence available will, in the usual case, be rich enough that an honest inquiry will make one meaning more plausible than its competitors. This is especially true given the most likely forum in which questions of constitutional meaning will arise, namely in a judicial contest. It is in the nature of such events that the question presented will be whether a particular proffered interpretation is or is not correct. That is, the question presented will not be "What is a bill of attainder?" but "Is this a bill of attainder?" The second question can be answered only yes or no, and one of these answers will almost always appear better than the other. It is true that in difficult cases there will be disagreement and, to that extent, the efficacy of constitutional rules as fixed and reliable limits on government conduct will be reduced. But if there is a historical fact of the matter about intended meaning,[112] it is reasonable to think that diligent and good-faith investigation will, over time, narrow the differences as to intended meaning.

Before leaving this subject, it is necessary to consider one possibility that would make largely irrelevant the conclusion that constitutionalism requires reference to the meaning of constitutional rules fixed by the constitution-makers at their creation. That is the case in which the constitution-makers' intention is that the rules they write down should not decide, or should not decide completely, the validity or invalidity of allegedly unconstitutional actions. There is a sense in which this is necessarily true. Constitutional rules cannot map out and permit or forbid, in terms, every possible state action into the indefinite future. Of necessity, the constitution-makers dealt with categories of actions. The Eighth Amendment of the United States Constitution does not speak, in terms, to the punitive use of electric cattle prods on convicted criminals, but it almost surely prohibits such use – by proscribing a category of conduct that includes it.

If this is all that is meant, we can still speak comfortably of limitations effected solely by the preexisting rules. The subsequent interpreters, in the manner discussed, weigh the historical evidence and decide whether the scope of the rule does or does not cover the challenged instance. But it is sometimes suggested that, at least sometimes, constitution-makers intended the constitutional rules to be "indeterminate" so that, in applying them, opposite results might be equally correct. Take, again as an example, the constitutional rule prohibiting the infliction of "cruel" punishment. The view of constitutional interpretation sketched earlier supposes that the underlying intentions of the rule-makers define a category of action. A particular action – say, the imposition of solitary confinement – is or is not within that category. Two judges, each honestly attempting to apply the intended meaning, may disagree on that question, but each will suppose that only one of them can be right. The position under consideration, on the other hand, might hold that the constitution-makers intended that the question of whether the rule did or did not apply in a given case should not be decided until the question actually arose and that, when it did arise, it should be determined (within certain constraints) by the judges at the time, on the basis of factors not identified by the Constitution. In that case, neither of the two disagreeing judges would be right or wrong *with respect to the correct application of the rule as intended by its enactors.* In that sense, at least, there is no such thing as a "correct" application.[113]

To the extent that this is an accurate description of constitutional rules, it is subversive of the goals of constitutionalism spelled out earlier. The limits of governmental power in this situation are necessarily defined on the occasion, not imposed by preexisting rules. State decision-making in this kind of regime will not, it is true, be just the same as it would be were the political departments subject to no constitutional constraint. But neither will it exhibit the special values of the rule of law discussed in the preceding section. Now, it would not be impossible for the enactors of constitutional rules to contemplate, as Lawrence Sager puts it in Chapter 6, this volume, a "transtemporal partnership between founding generations and judges" more or less to delegate to judges or some other officials the determination, from time to time, of some of the permissible limits of public power. But how can we know whether a constitutional provision was really intended to be of this kind? The fact that an inspection of the text does not suggest an immediately recognizable meaning is no proof of this type of indeterminacy. The very point of the inquiry into the original intentions of the enactors is to determine a meaning for texts that are the subject of dispute. Nor should this conclusion be drawn merely because the historical evidence of intended meaning is itself subject to differing interpretations. As already argued, the mere fact of disagreement is not conclusive evidence that no fact of the matter exists.[114]

To construe a constitutional text as incomplete in this way requires historical evidence of an affirmative intention of the constitution-makers to create rules that let some possible applications be decided by constitutional interpreters at a later time. The presence or absence of such intentions is a question of historical interpretation like any other. But, given the tension with the aims of constitutionalism this situation would create, why would makers of a constitution regard their rules as having this "partial" quality? One reason suggested by Michael Perry, citing H. L. A. Hart, is the known incapacity of rule-makers, as mere human beings, to anticipate, with sufficient certainty, all the circumstances in which their rule might be applied.[115] That is, constitution-makers, aware of the inevitably changing character of social life, would be disinclined to define the role of government within the rigid limits of outdated rules. But the drafting of "indeterminate" rules is not the only way to respond to this question. In the case of the United States Constitution, Philip Hamburger has demonstrated that the enactors were well aware of this reality, but dealt with it by narrowing the degree to which government was constitutionalized. For most public decision-making, flexibility was ensured by leaving the political departments to deal with change, unconstrained by prior constitutional rule. In those areas where constitutional limits were imposed, they were content to take the risk of obsolete rules to achieve the security of legal limits.[116]

It is often thought that the constitution-makers' intention to leave questions undecided is proved by their use of broad and unspecific language.[117] But the use of such language is not dispositive. Inquiry may reveal that what appears broad to later readers was intended by the enactors as a term of art. That is, at least, a reasonable conclusion with respect to the Fourteenth Amendment of the United States Constitution.[118] More generally, the use of broad language may reveal nothing more than an attempt to deal with large categories of state conduct. The interpretive problem of locating a particular action within or without that category may, indeed, be more difficult than would be the case if more precise language had been used, but, as already noted, there is nothing in such a practice that prevents the honest interpreter from acting entirely on the basis of a directive perceived *in* the constitutional rules. That is a more plausible explanation if we take the enactors to have been animated by the values of constitutionalism. For the American constitution-makers, it is confirmed by what we know of their general view of constitutions. As noted, they were nearly uniformly attached to the idea of a *fixed* constitution. They were, moreover, entirely aware that a special source of danger for the efficacy of legal limits was the power of judges to alter the law in the course of construing it.[119]

E. Conclusion

If it were necessary that a judicial conclusion as to the originally intended meaning of a constitutional rule be provable beyond reasonable doubt, it is true that such interpretation, in this sense, would be impossible. Experience tells us that such freedom from doubt is simply not available. There is some tendency in modern commentary to conclude that because, in many cases, no conscientious judge can always defend the meaning he or she thinks most likely as certain, or even nearly certain, the entire enterprise of searching for intended meaning is futile.[120] John Locke summarized the fallacy in this argument:

He that, in the ordinary affairs of life, would admit of nothing but direct plain demonstration would be sure of nothing in this world but of perishing quickly. The wholesomeness of his meat or drink would not give him reason to venture on it, and I fain know what it is he could do upon such grounds as were capable of no doubt, no objection.[121]

There is, therefore, a sense in which "words engrossed on parchment" can "keep a government in order." It supposes that rules formulated at one time have a fixed content that can be sufficiently appreciated to be acted upon at a subsequent time. For people familiar with the operation of legal rules this does not seem a particularly audacious claim. But in constitutional law, as in every kind of law, there is a critical gap between the creation of rules and their consequences. The existence of that gap is the most serious problem for constitutional government. And, as Walton Hamilton recognized, it is a gap that can be bridged only by trust.

III. Trust

A. Rules and Conduct

No verbal rule is self-executing. Walton Hamilton illustrated that obvious truth in the absurd figure of an inscribed parchment controlling the behavior of government officials. In the first chapter of Genesis, God says, "Let there be light," and there is light. In that case saying is literally doing.[122] It is common to talk about the law prohibiting or requiring some action, but human legislation "being but words and breath, [has] no force to oblige, contain, constrain or protect any man."[123] Its effect on action is, necessarily, indirect.

Still, the idea that legal rules, especially written legal rules, have independent potency is well entrenched in our culture. It is illustrated by the probably apocryphal story of the Charter Oak. In 1687 Sir Edmund Andros, the royal governor of the new "New England province," demanded the return of the Connecticut Charter of 1662 that had granted the colony a large measure of self-government. In a dramatic meeting with Connecticut freemen, the Charter was snatched from under Andros's nose and hidden in the hollow of a large oak tree for two years, until the old government was restored in the wake of the Revolution of 1688–9. The (historically entirely false) inference to be taken from this story seems to be that the physical preservation of the Charter preserved the liberty of the colonists.[124] In some ways, we still act as if there were an independent power in the written document. The original of the United States Constitution is preserved in the National Archives with a security that cannot be explained by its merely antiquarian value.

Simply memorializing a proposition in a formal writing seems to change the way it is regarded. At some point in Western history, written expression acquired a special claim to human attention.[125] The American constitution-makers were, it has already been noted, convinced of the unique effectiveness of written law.[126] Thus, they commonly associated the written constitution with images of physical force. A dictum of Jefferson's best expresses this attitude: "In questions of power, then, let no more be heard of confidence in man, but bind him down from mischief by the chains of the Constitution."[127] Even when acknowledging the inevitable need for some human intermediary between the rules and the actions dictated by the rules, advocates of government under law have described a passive, mechanical role for the interpreter and applier of rules. Montesquieu, whose influence with the American founders was great, said the judges were "no more than the mouth that pronounces the words of the law, mere passive beings, incapable of moderating either its force or its rigor," and consequently the judicial power was "in some measure, next to nothing."[128]

As simplistic as such figures are, they express what experience shows to be a common perception – that, although written words can exert no direct restraint on human beings, the formal promulgation of rules by legitimate authorities results in texts that exert a normative force on the persons to whom the rules are addressed. To understand constitutionalism is to understand the operation of that force. This phenomenon is not peculiar to constitutions. It is basic to the effectiveness of law generally. Every act, formulating a legal rule – the establishment of a constitutional right, the articulation of the standard of care in a common law tort case, or the specification of procurement procedures in an agency regulation – presupposes that human beings will read the rule, will understand from it that some behavior is called for, and then will choose to behave in that way, at least in part, because of the existence of the rule.[129]

The actual effect of legal rules is, necessarily, a complex matter, one not reducible to a uniform description. Notwithstanding our metaphors, we know that the correspondence between rules and actions is far from perfect. Comprehension of and reaction to law may be partial, mistaken, or even perverse. Conduct and practice influence law as well as the other way around. The nature of the relationship will, moreover, differ for different categories and instances of law.[130] It is equally unrealistic, however, to suppose that law and conduct are unrelated. Much conduct is explained by the phenomenon of rule-following. That experience provides a basis for believing that constitutional rules may be effective as well. If we consider the common explanations for compliance with legal rules, we can expect to see the same factors, perhaps in modified form, present when we examine the effects of constitutions.

B. Sanctions and Courts

The most prominent explanation for law-following is the presence of sanctions for noncompliance. The existence of such sanctions presupposes the existence of institutions and procedures for detecting violations and for imposing penalties on delinquents. There is no reason this might not hold true for public agencies with respect to their adherence to governing rules of public law. The constitutional system of separated powers and checks and balances is designed to do just that. Agency A monitors the legality of the behavior of Agency B. B watches C, and C watches A. Each agency depends on one or more of the others to accomplish anything.[131] Thus, a system of mutual regulation is created. But the successful operation of this scheme is far from certain. It supposes, first, that the state agencies will not sometimes find it in their interest to cooperate to effect an illegal action. One may imagine a system of trade-offs allowing a regular circumvention of legal limits by all of the institutions involved. Beyond this, the system of mutual regulation assumes that certain other legal rules will not be transgressed – namely those rules that define the relative competences of the various departments. Checks and balances assume the agencies will observe those definitional rules that deprive them of the powers for lack of which they must depend on the other agencies. The executive's power to exact property from the population is to be checked by the need for legislative authorization for any taxing scheme. But if the executive ignores its own constitutional disability and promulgates and proceeds to collect a new tax without such authorization, the restraining capacity of the legislature comes to nothing.

The primary constitutionalist solution to such risks involves the presence of one agency with no incentive to make deals to enhance its own authority and, indeed, with no political interests of its own. That agency could be entrusted with the task of supervising the restriction of the more political departments within their constitutionally defined powers and enforcing the substantive constitutional limits on the exercise of those powers. This is the special constitutional role of courts. To the extent that its business is the resolution of disputes and the award of compensation for injuries suffered as a result of illegal action, the judiciary is merely another functioning agency of government. But the American courts were, from the outset, recognized as having an additional and unique responsibility. That was to declare, elaborate, and enforce the legal limits on public action. In his defense of the federal courts in *The Federalist,* No. 78, Alexander Hamilton called them the "bulwarks of a limited Constitution." Judges, who were expected to cleave to the legal restraints of the Constitution in opposition to the political actors who might transgress them, would require "an uncommon fortitude." The constitution-makers invested them with permanent tenure to shield them from the political give and take to which other agencies were necessarily subject. This arrangement was meant to discourage them from "consult[ing] popularity [and] justify a reliance that nothing would be consulted but the Constitution and the laws."[132]

The introduction of the judiciary as an independent agency, the sole interest of which was faithful application of the Constitution, appeared to reduce the risks associated with self-application of the constitutional rules by the other agencies of the state. But, as is well known, it simultaneously created a different problem. The independence from political control, which enables the judges to deal dispassionately with the legal transgressions of other parts of the government, raises the possibility of incorrigibility when the courts themselves depart from the law.[133] *Within* the judiciary, to be sure, a hierarchical system of appeal and review may restrain the inferior courts. But, in any such system, there must necessarily be a last, and therefore unreviewable, judgment. Hobbes thought that the inevitability of a final decision-maker in any state refuted the idea that final authority could rest in law.[134] It is no accident that American students of constitutional theory are preoccupied with the behavior of the United States Supreme Court. The essential question in any constitutional system must be: Qui custodet ipsos custodes? The dangers to constitutionalism of a final but lawless constitutional court are multiple. Not only are such a court's actions illegal themselves but, by distorting the meaning of the constitutional rules, they subvert the effectiveness of constitutional limitations throughout the government.[135]

The plausibility of the enterprise of constitutional government, therefore, depends in large measure on the plausibility of the assumption that the constitutional court of last resort will refrain from abusing its unique position or, put positively, that it will adhere to the rules of the constitution. It is sometimes assumed that the power to upset governmental decisions, combined with the absence of effective review, creates a temptation so great as to make unrealistic any prospect that the Supreme Court will confine itself to the application of the preexisting rules of the Constitution.[136] But this presumption of noncompliance is at odds with our experience as to law-following generally. We know that people often conform to legal rules without either supervision or compulsion. It is reasonable to suppose that the same general factors that induce that behavior affect justices of the Supreme Court as well.

In some measure, judges, like everyone else, conform to the law as a matter of personal prudence. The law subjects even life-tenured judges to some external constraint. They may not, that is, regularly disregard with impunity the governing legal rules. There are ways of disciplining renegade judges. Impeachment and removal from office are available as a last resort. Of course, the imprecision of law application, already referred to, means that the departure from law would have to be egregious for these sanctions to be invoked. Still, they provide some outer limit to judicial independence from the law. The less formal censure of public and professional criticism is probably also effective in limiting the extent of judicial adventuring.[137]

C. Compliance without Sanctions

Such explanations, however, are far from complete. In more prosaic circumstances we usually assume that people obey the law for reasons other than the fear of personal sanction. People do stop at stop signs when no other people, including police officers, are anywhere to be seen.[138] We must seek the reasons for this behavior outside the law itself. It explains nothing to say that the law imposes a duty that legal rules be observed. The phenomenon of law-following has been the subject of description and analysis from many different viewpoints – moral, psychological, sociological.[139] There is no need to rehearse that literature here. But it is worth noting some of the factors thought to explain that behavior and, in light of the particular doubts about the restraining capacity of constitutional rules, considering the extent to which they apply to this one special case of submission to preexisting legal rules – that of the constitutional judge purporting to apply the constitution.

As with the case of other forms of compliance with law, to say that a judge adheres to the rules of the constitution is to say that he or she decides a case in a certain way because he or she understands that result to be the one dictated by the rule. Mere coincidence of a result reached by a judge and a result indicated by the rule does not demonstrate a case of rule compliance if the judge reaches that result for reasons other than the force of the rule as a rule of the

legal system. So a judge may, for reasons of personal taste or political principle, believe the state ought never to confiscate private property without compensation. When such a judge declares an uncompensated taking invalid, we
cannot be sure that the constitutional rule is the effective cause of that decision. This quality of genuine law-following has been summed up by describing the obligation of the judge to apply the law as *content-independent*.[140] The
practical test of action pursuant to such a commitment is the decision made
by a judge who would, but for this obligation, decide a given case the opposite way.

What is it that would cause a judge to regard the mere fact of a valid rule, independent of its substantive content, to be a reason for decision? Again, this is
but a particular instance of the more general question as to why individuals regard legal rules as binding.[141] With respect to the constitutional judge, the
short answer is that, at some level of consciousness, he or she accepts the force
of at least some of the arguments for a constitutional state that I have summarized in this essay. Much of what follows is a rehearsal of those reasons as they
might be understood by the judge facing a constitutional decision.

The judge may be convinced that the constitution-makers were simply better qualified to determine the proper limits of public action than he or she is
likely to be. While on particular occasions, the underlying objectives of the
constitutional state might, indeed, be better served by their direct application
to a particular controversy, the consistent application of the rules will result in
more correct applications, or correct applications in more important cases,
than will the case-by-case evaluation of the judge.[142] In the case of the application of constitutional rules, we have seen that there are some entirely sensible reasons why a judge might come to such a conclusion. A judge might assume that the special process by which the constitution was created was likely
to yield especially sound rules for governing the exercise of public power.[143]
Constitutions are usually drafted in circumstances that impress upon the participants the importance of their actions. They understand that the rules being
created will have serious effects on a large number of people and that they
will probably endure for a fairly long time. This is likely to impart a seriousness and intensity to the constituent decisions that cannot be reproduced
every time a constitutional dispute arises. Moreover, the constitution-makers
will be writing rules for a large number of cases, the specific aspects of which
will be unknown to them. They are, therefore, less likely to be swayed by personal interests and sympathies than may be the case when flesh-and-blood individuals in specific circumstances are involved.[144] None of these generalizations will always hold and each is subject to reasonable counterargument. But
they are plausible enough that we can understand that they might influence a
judge to submit his or her individual judgment to a different one found in the
constitutional rules.

It is possible, moreover, that a judge might have reasons to apply constitutional rules that are independent of any conclusion that fidelity to such rules is likely to achieve results superior to the unfettered application of the judge's own evaluation of the merits of one decision or another. That may be because the judge accepts, as a matter of political morality, that it is better for the constitution-makers to decide some aspects of state power in advance by fixed rule. That is, the same factors already mentioned that, as a matter of social acceptance, confer legitimacy on a constitution may provide reasons for a judge to adhere to its rules. The judge may regard the process by which the constitution was created as possessing a political license for making constitutional rules that he or she lacks. I have noted that some combination of esteem for the constitution-making sources and an at least minimal acceptance of the substantive suitability of the rules that the process generated allows a constitution to continue to be generally regarded as fundamental law. The same factors may convince a judge that it is his or her duty to be faithful to that law in the process of adjudication.[145]

Perhaps, more plausibly, the judge may be convinced of the special value of limiting governmental power by clear and stable rules discussed in the first section. As a matter of current political morality, a judge may decide that social well-being is better served by the thorough and consistent application of one set of constitutional rules than by the enforcement of shifting standards of public conduct, formulated case by case according to the best lights of the current occupants of the final constitutional court.[146]

This recognition of a political-moral duty to subordinate the judge's own view of the merits of constitutional controversies to what appear to him or her to be the inferior solutions derived from the original constitutional rules may be a particular instance of a more general explanation of why people treat any law as a content-independent reason for action. Some writers have described the obligation to obey the law as a moral duty of individuals living in and benefiting from a free society. Such individuals recognize (or ought to recognize) that it is essential to the functioning of such a society that there exist general rules and that they be generally observed. A practice of deference to those rules is part of the essential cooperation that members of society owe each other.[147] These considerations obviously hold for public officials as well as for private persons. Indeed, the assumption of special public responsibilities may give particular force to the duty of cooperation in maintaining the effective functioning of society. One might suppose, moreover, that this obligation would be felt unusually poignantly by judges whose duty requires them to pronounce on the effective limits of state authority. For the reasons already canvassed, the potential injury from the disregard of those rules might be thought especially severe and the delinquency of the judge who indulged in such disregard particularly worthy of censure.

Since, as noted, judges in courts of last resort are, for the most part, free of the risk that they will suffer personal adverse consequences if they fail to be guided by legal rules, these non-sanction-based reasons for law-following may not be as effective as they are when combined with a fear of penalty. But there is one sense in which the force these considerations carry for the judge will be greater than their force in influencing individuals to conform to law in their primary conduct. The reasons for following the law that I have summarized are not preemptive in the sense that they preclude reference to any other relevant reasons for acting or not acting in the way the legal rules indicate. It is enough for the effectiveness of law to say that the existence of a legal rule provides *a* content-independent reason for action. If so, it follows that sometimes the fact of a controlling rule alters the balance of reasons and, therefore, the outcome contemplated by the rule results.[148] On this view, the force of a rule of law depends on the strength of the reasons for following it and also on the strength of independent, nonlegal reasons for not following it. Besides non-law-based reasons of political morality, private individuals may have reasons for not following a rule of law related solely to their personal welfare. If we posit an honest judge, acting exclusively in his or her capacity as an official devoted to the public good, the political-moral reasons for following the law must compete only with the political-moral reasons for acting contrary to the law on the particular occasion. Those public reasons for departing from the law may be compelling from time to time.[149] But the relative weight of the rule-of-law values will more often be greater than when private considerations are also part of the decision-making mix.

The discussion to this point has cataloged explicitly the kinds of reasons that might move a judge (even a judge usually beyond the reach of formal sanctions) to comply with constitutional rules in their originally intended sense. In doing so it has necessarily distorted the actual explanation of the way in which most judges choose to be guided by preexisting law. It is surely not the case that, on every occasion for adjudication, a judge reconsiders and recalculates the reasons for and against following the rules. Rule-following, rather, becomes the normal, "natural" habit of the judge. Judges in this respect are like individuals who learn unselfconsciously to follow applicable rules – of the family, the workplace, or the state.[150] A motorist approaching a stop sign does not mull over the state of traffic, the importance of his or her schedule, the competence of the traffic engineer, and the moral authority of the state.

In some respects this tendency to follow rules may be an essential part of our makeup. Human beings are "rule-following animal[s] as much as purpose-seeking one[s]."[151] The number of factors that might logically bear on any decision is so great that only choice according to some predetermined and relatively abstract rules, which exclude consideration of most of these factors, prevents paralysis. The capacity to act according to rule has sometimes (and especially with respect to judicial behavior) been disparaged as requiring an unrealistic "compartmentalization" of reasons for action. But such compartmentalization is a common and necessary feature of human existence. We simply do not, could not, consider every consequence, immediate and remote, of every alternative action open to us.[152] Some form of "selective attention" is an inescapable aspect of judicial decision.[153] In normal times, the exclusive authority of legal rules on such decisions will usually be taken for granted.

The widespread existence of such an attitude is an expectable consequence of the way judges are chosen and the social context in which they work. Judges everywhere, and certainly in the United States, have a marked similarity of training and background. It is a truism to say that law school education and legal practice are mainly about the creation, interpretation, and application of legal rules. Such an experience will naturally inculcate a feeling of the importance of rules in deciding controversies:

Through their training, then, lawyers and judges acquire habits of thought that limit the range of arguments that they will find acceptable for the kinds of decisions that they will be willing to advocate and reach. They learn substantive norms that tell them what kinds of principles are legitimate and illegitimate. They learn "procedural" norms that tell them what kinds of evidence and procedures are permissible. They learn ethical norms that deter them from exercising their discretion in self-serving ways.[154]

The day-to-day context in which lawyers and judges operate reinforces this tendency. Judges live and work with colleagues, clerks, and lawyers who share this general orientation toward rule-based adjudication and who may criticize (not to say reverse) decisions on these grounds. It is reasonable to expect, moreover, that judges will respond to these attitudes not simply out of a calculated concern for their reputation, but because they have, in fact, adopted those ideas of proper conduct for themselves.[155] Judges, like anyone else engaged in a lifelong pattern of conduct, develop for themselves certain "role expectations." They incorporate those expectations into their definition of what it means to be a judge.[156] In our culture that definition includes a duty of fidelity to prior law, even when it is in opposition to the judge's extralegal conception of right policy.[157] It is through this pervasive process of unreflective socialization that the more substantive considerations discussed take hold.

To summarize, it follows that, while words on parchment can do nothing themselves, it is not altogether outlandish to think that the directives intended by the human beings who put those words to parchment might be discovered and followed by judges whose decisions are then largely respected by the officials whose conduct is at issue. Such a practice is technically, logically possible. There are good reasons why judges and public officials might follow it, and there is even some evidence that they see their jobs in those terms. Consequently, the "trust" derided by Walton Hamilton might not be misplaced after all.

There is, however, strong evidence for the contrary view – that constitutions in the hands of judges are not, cannot be, translated into fixed restraints on government action. The influences of training and professional and social relations do not all point toward rule-following. "Great" judges are often thought to be daring or creative judges. The opportunity to shape as well as follow the law and the opportunity to do good at the same time surely presents a temptation.[158] More powerful still is the recognition that, to a significant degree, the large corpus of constitutional law formulated by the United States Supreme Court in almost two hundred years of decision-making cannot be squared with the rules of the Constitution in the senses that they were intended by the constitution-makers to carry. The fact that many of the most famous constitutional judgments of the Court meet this description can hardly be denied. Neither the extended authority of the federal Congress nor the insistence on respect for many individual rights by the states can be justified as required by the rules intended by the relevant constitutional enactors. Considering this experience, one may ask whether American constitutionalism is not more accurately characterized by a description of this history of judicial invention in the name of the Constitution than by the abstract picture of limited government under preexisting rules.

One need not deny that constitutional history in the United States has been associated with important cases of non-rule-based adjudication to believe that, on the whole, the enterprise of constitutionalism has had an important and salutary effect on the exercise of public power and that this effect has been, to a significant degree, in the direction of realizing the rule of law. The impact of the Constitution is not restricted to the adjudication of the Supreme Court. Certain aspects of the text are so plain that not even the most imaginative public official would require a judicial pronouncement to understand the limitations they create. No Congress has attempted to extend the terms of its members beyond those specified in Article I. The prohibitions on ex post facto laws and bills of attainder have required judicial interpretation, but the core ideas are sufficiently plain that few legislatures will have the temerity to legislate the criminal punishment of an individual for a completed act that was legal when undertaken. Like all law, the Constitution requires litigation to make it effective only in the pathological case. The Constitution did settle, to a very great extent, the shape and reach of governmental power. It did this so effectively and so obviously that those limitations are taken for granted.[159]

This is not to say that the well-known judicial deviations from the constitutional rules are inconsequential, nor to deny that they represent a disproportionately important aspect of the history of constitutional government in the United States. But, put in perspective, these instances are still deviations. The norm of constitutional government is rough compliance with the fixed rules of the Constitution. The social science evidence on the attitudes and behavior of judges is not easy to evaluate. But it appears that, despite their deliberate insulation from sanctions and other forms of external pressure, judges do feel an obligation to act on the basis of norms that are independent of their own views of the intrinsic justice of the causes before them.[160] The decision-making of the Supreme Court has been found to show far less correlation with perceived measures of public opinion than is the case for the other, "political" branches of government.[161] We can agree that even the most responsible judges cannot free themselves of their own deeply held, perhaps subconscious, extralegal convictions and that legal interpretation is sufficiently imprecise that the opportunities for such influences to be felt cannot be avoided. But this tendency can be greater or lesser. It is a meaningful position to urge the adoption of a serious commitment to reach the decisions called for by legal rules. Such a commitment can change the results of adjudication and that change would, consistent with the purpose of constitutionalism, tend toward a more stable jurisprudence.[162]

It is worth considering, finally, that the success of the United States government has been substantially established on a wide and deep popular attachment to the Constitution and to the idea of constitutional government in general.[163] Part of that attachment is associated with a belief that the Constitution does limit governmental action and that the courts will, when called on to do so, apply those limitations. The Supreme Court has maintained a high degree of public confidence. That regard is premised not on the substantive results that the court has reached, but on a perception that the Court acts on a legal assessment of the merits of the claims before it and not on the basis of "political pressure and personal opinion."[164] This public conviction is also a matter of trust. It cannot be verified and, on many occasions, it may well be mistaken. But the actions of the government, as a whole, are not so far removed from the general understanding of constitutional restraint that that critical trust has yet disappeared.

In the end constitutionalism, law generally, and most of what we value in a civilized society are artifice. We construct rules, institutions, relationships, values and then live in them. The character and success of our lives are genuinely determined by those creatures of our own intelligence and imagination. "Final belief," Wallace Stevens wrote, "[m]ust be in a fiction."[165] Those fictions can work only if we generally ignore their artificial character.[166] But in evaluating the utility of our institutions, there is some value in reminding ourselves, from time to time, of the fictions that support them and our stake in behavior that conforms to those fictions. With respect to law, Neil

MacCormick has explained the nature of such an evaluation, noting that law is a "thought object" in the sense that it "exist[s] by being believed in, rather than being believed in by virtue of [its] existence."

We have to ask: *should* it be believed in, and thus brought into existence by our beliefs? This is nothing other than the question whether it makes a difference to practical or political life if we postulate and sustain the ideal of rules and rights. . . . Such beliefs have been differentially sustained at different times and places, and in my judgment the effects of the beliefs have on the whole been preferable to the effects of their rejection.[167]

With respect to constitutionalism it may be that our very capacity to live in safety depends on the a priori creation of abstract limits, on an honest effort by our public actors to stay within those limits, and on an ordinarily uncritical trust by the rest of us that they will – more or less – succeed.

Notes

Carol Weisbrod made useful suggestions on a prior draft.

1 What exactly counts as a governing constitution is not always agreed on. Two states, Israel and New Zealand, are often cited as being without written constitutions. Israel, however, has a series of Basic Laws that purport to be entrenched beyond ordinary legislative modification. Expressions in a recent decision of the Israeli Supreme Court strongly indicate that state action may be held invalid because in conflict with a Basic Law. United Mizrachi Bank v. Migdal, C.A. 6821/93 (1995), summarized in Asher Landau, *Justices: Courts Have Right to Review Statutes,* Jerusalem Post, January 1, 1996, Features Section, 7. New Zealand has long been governed under a United Kingdom statute that created its basic public institutions and procedures. In 1990 Parliament enacted a statutory bill of rights that explicitly forbade judicial invalidation of statutes, but that encouraged courts to construe legislation so as to be consistent with the rights listed. The New Zealand judiciary has been moderately active in utilizing this power. See Michael Principe, *The Demise of Parliamentary Supremacy? Canadian and American Influences upon the New Zealand Judiciary's Interpretation of the Bill of Rights Act of 1990,* 16 Loy. L. A. Int'l and Comp. L. J. 167 (1993). The only state unambiguously without a written constitution today appears to be the United Kingdom, and even it is subject to the constitution-like restraints of the European Convention on Human Rights enforceable by the European Court of Human Rights in Strasbourg. See Mark Janis, Richard Kay, and Anthony Bradley, *European Human Rights Law: Texts and Materials* 450–65 (1995).

2 See, e.g., F. A. Hayek, *The Constitution of Liberty* 176–92 (1960); Louis Favoreu, *Constitutional Review in Europe,* in *Constitutionalism and Rights: The Influence of the United States Constitution Abroad* 38 (L. Henkin & A. J. Rosenthal, eds., 1990).

3 See Louis Favoreu, *American and European Models of Constitutional Justice,* in *Comparative and Private Law: Essays in Honor of John Henry Merryman on His Seventieth Birthday* 105 (David S. Clark, ed., 1990).

4 Walton H. Hamilton, *Constitutionalism,* 4 Encyc. Soc. Sci. 255 (Edwin R. A. Seligman & Alvin Johnson, eds., 1931).

5 Fred Rodell, *A Sprig of Rosemary for Hammy,* in *Rodell Revisited: Selected Writings of Fred Rodell* 44 (L. Ghiglione, J. Rodell, & M. Rodell, eds., 1994). After retiring from Yale, Hamilton was admitted to the Georgia bar by special act of the legislature. John Henry Schlegel, *American Legal Realism and Empirical Social Science* 265 (1995). A more extended, but kindred realist criticism of conventional constitutionalism is Karl Llewellyn, *The Constitution as an Institution,* 34 Colum. L. Rev. 1 (1934).

6 Oliver Wendell Holmes, *The Path of the Law,* 10 Harv. L. Rev. 457 (1897).

7 Hamilton, supra note 4 at 257–8.

8 Modern scholarship has rightly stressed that the revolutionaries' position was formed under the inspiration of various underlying political philosophies, both European and homegrown. But the texts, as well as extrinsic evidence, show that no single source exerted an influence more important than that of Locke. Rogers M. Smith, Liberalism and American Constitutional Law 43–4 (1985). See also Bernard Bailyn, *The Ideological Origins of the American Revolution* 30 (1967) ("[E]xcept for Locke [European Enlightenment figures'] influence . . . was neither clearly dominant nor wholly determinative"). Cf. John Locke, *Treatise of Civil Government and a Letter Concerning Toleration* Paras. 223, 225, 230 at 149–54 (Charles L. Sherman, ed., 1937) with Declaration of Independence Para. 4 (U.S. 1776). But see Garry Wills, *Inventing America: Jefferson's Declaration of Independence* 171–5 (1978).

9 See Robert Filmer, *"Patriarcha" and Other Political Works* 93–6, 102–6 (P. Laslett, ed., 1949); Thomas Hobbes, *Leviathan* 237–50 (M. Oakeshott, ed., 1962). On the late emergence of this understanding of public power see Pasquale Pasquino, *Political Theory, Order and Threat,* in *Political Order* (Nomos 38), 19, 21 (Ian Shapiro & Russell Hardin, eds., 1996).

10 Bailyn, supra, note 8 at 180, 222; G. Wood, *The Creation of the American Republic, 1776–1787* 264–5 (1969). John Phillip Reid argues that, at the time of the prerevolutionary struggle, the idea of an unlimitable sovereign power was still in contest with the older notion of inherent legal limits on all state power. The latter position, in his view, while viable in both Britain and the colonies, was especially vital in America and provided the underpinning for colonial arguments against the authority of Parliament to legislate for America. John Phillip Reid, *Constitutional History of the American Revolution: The Authority to Legislate* 60–4, 127 (1991).

11 1 *Blackstone's Commentaries* 156 (1983).

12 "Thus the *Rechtstaat,* as the controlling arrangement of law, presupposes the existence of the *Machtstaat,* the political power apparatus to be controlled." Rune Slagstad, *Liberal Constitutionalism and Its Critics: Carl Schmitt and Max Weber,* in *Constitutionalism and Democracy* 108 (Jon Elster & Rune Slagstad, eds., 1988). See id. at 110.

13 Richard S. Kay, *Substance and Structure as Constitutional Protections: Centennial Comparisons,* Pub. L. 428, 428–9, 433 (1989).

14 See Bailyn, supra, note 8 at 46–7. The Declaration states plainly, if not expressly, that Parliament, as well as the king, had transgressed the proper boundaries of state power. Para. 18 ("He has combined with others . . .").

15 See Thomas Paine, *The Rights of Man,* in *The Life and Major Writings of Thomas Paine* 343, 383 (P. Foner, ed., 1974); Wood, supra, note 10 at 271–3.

16 See Henry deBracton, 2 *The Laws and Customs of England* 33 (Samuel Thorne, trans., 1968).

17 See generally Corinne C. Weston and Janelle R. Greenberg, *Subjects and Sovereigns: The Grand Controversy over Legal Sovereignty in Stuart England (1981).*

18 See generally, Howard Nenner, *By Colour of Law: Legal Culture and Constitutional Politics in England,* 1660–1689(1977).

19 On the Declaration of Rights see generally Lois G. Schwoerer, *The Declaration of Rights* 1689 (1981). The Declaration and the quoted passages are reproduced in id. at 295, 296.

20 See Bailyn, supra, note 8 at 30.

21 Philip A. Hamburger, *Natural Rights, Natural Law, and American Constitutions,* 102 Yale L. J. 907, 930 (1993). See Reid, supra, note 10 at 5.

22 Walter Fairleigh Dodd, *The Revision and Amendment of State Constitutions* 1–3 (1910). For the texts of early state constitutions and original charters see generally *The Federal and State Constitutions, Colonial Charters and Other Organic Laws of the States, Territories and Colonies Now or Heretofore Forming the United States of America* (Francis Newton Thorpe, ed., 1909).

23 Joseph Raz, *Ethics in the Public Domain: Essays in the Morality of Law and Politics* 105 (1994). See generally id. at 104–5; John Finnis, *Natural Law and Natural Rights* 103–5, 129–30 (1980); Bhikhu Parekh, *Oakeshott's Theory of Civil Association,* 106 Ethics 158, 159, 170 (1995).

24 Gerald Dworkin, *The Theory and Practice of Autonomy* 31 (1988). See also Stephen Gardbaum, *Liberalism, Autonomy and Moral Conflict,* 48 Stan. L. Rev. 385, 394–7 (1996).

25 Western political philosophy has produced many versions of this "liberal" outlook. It is implicit in much of the work of John Locke, whose views on the legitimacy of government were so important to the American founders. See Smith, supra, note 8 at 28–30. Its relationship to the power of the state was crystallized in the work of John Stuart Mill. See John Stuart Mill, *On Liberty,* in *J. S. Mill on Liberty in Focus* 72–80 (John Gray & G. W. Smith, eds., 1991). The relation between Mill's political liberalism and his understanding of the privileged character of autonomous decision-making is explored in Isaiah Berlin, *John Stuart Mill and the Ends of Life,* in id. at 131, 135–6, 146–8, and John Gray, *Mill's Conception of Happiness and the Theory of Individuality,* in id. at 190, 190–3, 202–7. See also John Rawls, *A Theory of Justice* 408–14, 548–67 (1971).

This perception of the roles of state and subject depends on an assumption that subjects have sufficient capacity to evaluate and choose among options. With respect to persons (most notably children) lacking such capacity, the extent to which decision-making authority should be in the state, or in some intermediate institution such as the family (however defined), becomes a much more difficult issue. See John H. Garvey, *What Are Freedoms For?* 81–122 (1996); Carol Weisbrod, *Family Governance: A Reading of Kafka's Letter to His Father,* 24 U. Toledo L. Rev. 689, 696 (1993). That is an issue not considered in this essay.

26 Friederich A. Hayek, *Law Legislation and Liberty* (Volume 1: *Rules and Order*) 113 (1973).

27 Paine, supra, note 15 at 379.

28 Michael Oakeshott, *On Human Conduct* 201 (1975). For a useful discussion see Parekh, supra, note 23 at 174–80.

29 Michael Oakeshott, *The Rule of Law,* in *On History and Other Essays* 118, 136 (1983).

30 Id. at 153.

31 See Gottfried Dietze, *Two Concepts of the Rule of Law* 21 (1973).

32 Oakeshott, supra, note 29 at 153.

33 See, e.g., Frank Michelman, *Law's Republic,* 97 Yale L. J. 1493 (1988); Cass Sunstein, *Beyond the Republican Revival,* 97 Yale L. J. 1539 (1988).

34 See, e.g., Sunstein, supra, note 33 at 1551.

35 See, e.g., Richard Fallon, Jr., *What Is Republicanism and Is It Worth Reviving?* 102 Harv. L. Rev. 1695, 1696 (1989).

36 *The Federalist,* No. 51 at 321–2 (J. Madison) (C. Rossiter, ed., 1961).

37 See generally Kay, supra, note 13. For this reason, I am unable to disagree with Jeremy Waldron that there is a fairly clear distinction "between constitutional constraints and the constitutive rules of political institutions." See Waldron, Chapter 7, this volume.

38 *The Federalist,* No. 84 (A. Hamilton), supra, note 36 at 513–14.

39 Slagstad, supra, note 12 at 105.

40 Alexis De Tocqueville, 1 *Democracy in America* ch. 12 (Henry Reeve, trans., 1966).

41 See Richard S. Kay, *The State Action Doctrine, the Public Private Distinction and the Independence of Constitutional Law,* 10 Const. Comm. 329, 342 (1993).

42 See generally Kathleen Sullivan, *Rainbow Republicanism,* 97 Yale L. J. 1713 (1988).

43 See, e.g., Michelman, supra, note 33 at 1503.

44 Neil MacCormick, *The Ethics of Legalism,* 2 Ratio Juris 184, 188 (1989). See also Gardbaum, supra, note 24 at 394.

45 Declaration of Independence, Para. 2 (U.S. 1776); Locke, supra, note 8 at 90–4 (Paras. 136–8).

46 Joseph Raz, *The Rule of Law and Its Virtues,* in *The Authority of Law: Essays on Law and Morality* 210, 214–15 (1979).

47 Some of the benefits of a regime committed to the rule of law have little to do with the risks of government overreaching – the need "to keep a government in order." For example, insofar as the rule of law involves the periodic creation of entrenched standards of government behavior, it may be understood as a way to get the government to *work better,* better in the sense of better approximating some shared, public objectives. It may be that any state, a *Rechtstaat* or a *Polizeistaat,* will be more effective if it employs well-thought-out, long-term rules than if it freshly

54   RICHARD S. KAY

applies underlying social desiderata to each successive decision. See Larry
Alexander and Emily Sherwin, *The Deceptive Nature of Rules,* 142 U. Pa. L. Rev.
1191, 1194–7, 1214–15 (1994). Constitutionalism involves, in part, a conscious
abnegation of the critical evaluation of particular social decisions in terms of the
overriding goals of the polity, for the very purpose of securing those goals – thus
the common analogies of Ulysses bound to the mast and the appeal of the people
drunk to the people sober.
48 See, e.g., F. A. Hayek, supra, note 6 at 158, 178 (1960); Rawls, supra, note 25 at
   239; Frederick Schauer, *Playing by the Rules: A Philosophical Examination of
   Rule-Based Decision-Making in Law and in Life* 95, 140–2 (1991); Jules L. Coleman and Brian Leiter, *Determinacy, Objectivity and Authority,* 142 U. Pa. L. Rev.
   549, 582–3 (1993); Stephen Macedo, *The Rule of Law, Justice and the Politics of
   Moderation,* in *The Rule of Law* (Nomos 36) 148, 154–5 (I. Shapiro, ed., 1994);
   Raz, supra, note 46 at 220.
49 Quoted in Michael Kammen, *Sovereignty and Liberty: Constitutional Discourse in
   American Culture* 51 (1988). This notion, therefore, cannot coexist with the version of constitutionalism described by Jed Rubenfeld in Chapter 5, this volume,
   which encompasses the accretion to the state of the power to impose burdens on
   individuals that are "both onerous and unexpected."
50 See Schauer, supra, note 48 at 140–2.
51 See Gardbaum, supra, note 24 at 401–3.
52 See Schauer, supra, note 48 at 154.
53 See Jon Elster, Introduction to *Constitutionalism and Democracy* 1, 5–6 (Jon
   Elster & Rune Slagstad, eds., 1988).
54 Raz, Chapter 4, this volume.
55 See Waldron, Chapter 7, this volume.
56 Raz, Chapter 4, this volume; see also Rubenfeld, Chapter 5, this volume.
57 Stephen Holmes, *Precommitment and the Paradox of Democracy,* in *Constitutionalism and Democracy* 195, 221 (Jon Elster & Rune Slagstad, eds., 1988).
58 "Current power is self-destructive — 'instant power is objectless.' Some sort of
   negative power is necessary not only to check, but paradoxically also to protect
   positive power." Francis Sejersted, *Democracy and the Rule of Law: Some Historical Experiences of Contradictions in Striving for Good Government,* in *Constitutionalism and Democracy* 131, 145 (Jon Elster & Rune Slagstad, eds., 1988) (citing Jon Elster, *Logic and Society: Contradictions and Possible Worlds* 128
   [1978]).
59 See Slagstad, supra, note 12 at 127. Before the Revolution, one American pam-
   phlet denounced "absolute power" and continued that "it matters not whether it be
   an absolute royal power or an absolute legislative power, as the consequences will
   be the same to the people." Quoted in Reid, supra, note 10 at 146. On the risks of
   exclusive reliance on popular sanction see J. L. Talmon, *The Origins of Totalitarian Democracy* 1–13 (1960).
60 See *The Federalist,* No. 6 (A. Hamilton), supra, note 36 at 56–7.
61 See *The Federalist,* No. 51, supra, note 36 at 323 (A "dependence upon the people
   is, no doubt, the primary control on the government"); Sejersted, supra, note 58 at

135 ("Democratic elements were introduced to check and not to legitimize state power").

62 See *The Federalist,* No. 39 (J. Madison), supra, note 36 at 243. Hamilton's justification of judicial constitutional review is founded on the same idea: "If there should happen to be an irreconcilable variance between [a legislative act and the Constitution], that which has the superior obligation and validity ought, of course, to be preferred; or, in other words, the Constitution ought to be preferred to the statute, the intention of the people to the intention of their agents." *The Federalist,* No. 78 (A. Hamilton), supra, note 36 at 467.

63 See generally Bruce Ackerman, *We the People* (1991). A similar argument is considered and rejected by Waldron, Chapter 7, this volume.

64 Holmes, supra, note 57 at 226.

65 See Sejersted, supra, note 58 at 145–8.

66 See Michel Rosenfeld, Book Review, 11 Const. Comm. 32 (1994).

67 See John Rawls, *The Priority of Right and Ideas of the Good,* 17 Phil. & Pub. Affairs 251, 269–70 (1988).

68 See Michelman, Chapter 2, this volume.

69 While no life can be lived in a state of total uncertainty, the relative attractions of stability and spontaneity differ from person to person. One's affinity for constitutionalism, therefore, may be a function of personal temperament. See Schauer, supra, note 48 at 140.

70 See, e.g., Nancy Rutter, *Michele Corash: Fast Action Hero,* Forbes, February 28, 1994, at 88 ("In the Kafkaesque world of Superfund . . ."); George F. Will, *Events and Arguments,* Newsweek, October 16, 1995, at 38 ("Kafkaesque regulation").

71 Franz Kafka, *The Trial* (1937). One deletion from *The Trial* suggests that Kafka may at one point have understood the state to be a necessary source of stability and hence to provide a possible escape from the (presumably nonstate) unfathomable agencies with whom Joseph K had to deal. In a deleted passage, K was to whisper to one man, "What if I transferred the trial into the domain where the writ of the state law runs?" Weisbrod, supra, note 25 at 716. By finally leaving open the possibility that it was the state that commanded or participated in K's persecution, the terror of the experience is intensified.

72 G. Gilmore, *The Ages of American Law* 111 (1977).

73 *Four Letters on Interesting Subjects* 15 (1776), quoted in Wood, supra, note 10 at 268. See id. at 266–8, 293–5.

74 5 U.S. (1 Cranch.) 137, 178 (1803).

75 Kamper v. Hawkins (Va. 1793) quoted in Henry P. Monaghan, *Stare Decisis and Constitutional Adjudication,* 88 Colum. L. Rev. 723, 769 (1988).

76 3 U.S. (3 Dall.) 386, 399 (1796).

77 Quoted in Thomas Grey, *The Constitution as Scripture,* 37 Stan. L. Rev. 1, 15 (1984).

78 5 U.S. (1 Cranch) at 176.

79 Letter to Wilson Cary Nicholas, September 7, 1803, quoted in Raoul Berger, *Government by Judiciary: The Transformation of the Fourteenth Amendment* 336 (1977).

80 William E. Cain, *The Crisis in Criticism: Theory, Literature and Reform in English Studies* 31–2 (1984).

81 Gary Peller, *The Metaphysics of American Law,* 73 Calif. L. Rev. 1151, 1170 (1985).

82 The serious exponents of this school do not suppose otherwise. See Richard S. Kay, *Adherence to Original Intentions in Constitutional Adjudication: Three Objections and Responses,* 82 NW. U. L. Rev. 226, 236–43 (1988). The most thorough critic of various forms of this position in the context of literary analysis is E. D. Hirsch. See his *Validity in Interpretation* (1967). See also Coleman and Leiter, supra, note 48 at 570–1.

83 Finnis, supra, note 23 at 74.

84 5 U.S. (1 Cranch) at 178.

85 See, e.g., John J. Gibbons, *Intentionalism, History and Legitimacy,* 140 U. Pa. L. Rev. 613, 614 (1991) (quoting Judge Anthony M. Kennedy); Frederick Schauer, *Precedent and the Necessary Externality of Constitutional Norms,* 17 Harv. J. L. & Pub. Pol'y 45, 53 (1994).

86 West Virginia Board of Education v. Barnette, 319 U.S. 634, 639 (1943). It is sometimes not noticed that Justice Jackson immediately described that task as "one to disturb self-confidence." Id.

87 Walter Benn Michaels, *The Fate of the Constitution,* 61 Tex. L. Rev. 765, 774 (1982).

88 This is usually (although not inevitably) so even if a constitution is promulgated according to the forms of preexisting law. Such regularity of form may be counted on only to provide a "relationship of validating purport." See H. L. A. Hart, *Kelsen's Doctrine of the Unity of Law,* in *Essays in Jurisprudence and Philosophy* 309, 318 (1983). But such regularity of form need not mirror the actual political explanation for the acceptance of a constitution as law. See Richard S. Kay, *Comparative Constitutional Fundamentals,* 6 Conn J. Int'l L. 445 (1991).

89 See generally, Richard S. Kay, *Pre-constitutional Rules,* 42 Ohio St. L. J. 187 (1981). Joseph Raz makes a similar point in Chapter 4, this volume.

90 See Bailyn, supra, note 8 at 175–6; Wood, supra, note 10 at 289–93, 600–5.

91 See generally, Thorpe, supra, note 22.

92 *The Federalist,* No. 46 (J. Madison), supra, note 36 at 294; No. 22 (A. Hamilton), supra, note 36 at 152.

93 James Wilson, *Lectures on Law,* in *The Works of James Wilson* 304 (Robert Green McCloskey, ed., 1967).

94 5 U.S. (1 Cranch) at 176. See also M'Culloch v. Maryland, 17 U.S. (4 Wheat.) 316, 403 (1819) ("The government proceeds directly from the people" and is " 'ordained and established' in the name of the people"). The idea that a constitution derives its binding force from the consent of "the people" is, at the present time, a standard explanation of its legitimacy. A 1978 survey of 142 world constitutions showed that 76, or 53.6%, referred explicitly to the sovereignty of the people. See Hence van Maarseveen and Ger van der Tang, *Written Constitutions: A Computerized Comparative Study* 93 (1978).

95 See generally, Jackson T. Main, *The Anti-Federalists: Critics of the Constitution, 1781–88* 187–248 (1961).

96 See Richard S. Kay, Book Review, 7 Const. Comm. 434, 437–8 (1990).

97 See, e.g., Michael Kammen, *The Machine That Would Go of Itself* 13 (1986). A 1986 public opinion poll indicated that 82% of participants believed the phrase "of the people, by the people and for the people" was in the Constitution. *Knowledge of the Constitution* (Hearst Corp., 1986), question No. 6 (Lexis News Library; RPOLL file).

98 See Raz, Chapter 4, this volume.

99 See Richard S. Kay, *Original Intentions, Standard Meanings and the Legal Character of the Constitution,* 6 Const. Comm. 39 (1989). See also Larry Alexander, *All or Nothing at All? The Intentions of Authorities and the Authority of Intentions,* in *Law and Interpretation: Essays in Legal Philosophy* 358, 360–6 (Andrei Marmor, ed., 1995); Paul Campos, *Three Mistakes about Interpretation,* 92 Mich. L. Rev. 388, 389–90 (1993).

100 See Daniel Farber, *The Originalism Debate: A Guide for the Perplexed,* 49 Ohio L. J. 1085 (1988).

101 See Hamburger, supra, note 21 at 930–44. The role of popular assent in legitimizing constitutional rules, therefore, does not depend, as Jed Rubenfeld suggests, in Chapter 5, this volume, on an inference of continuous assent. Rather the understanding of the constitutional rules as issuing from a "people" who acted, and are represented as acting, with unusual care and wisdom makes it more plausible to expect that those rules will be deemed acceptable over a longer period of time. Of course, as explained in the next subsection, that acceptance can never be permanent.

102 See Raz, Chapter 4, this volume.

103 Declaration of Independence, Para. 2 (U.S. 1776).

104 Marbury v. Madison, 5 U.S. (1 Cranch) 137, 176 (1803). On the intensity of the political exercise of constitution-making see generally Ackerman, supra, note 63.

105 Eighty percent of Americans polled in 1987 said they believed the views of the founders were a "very reliable" or "somewhat reliable" guide to solving modern problems. William S. Smith, *The People's Court: Do Americans Understand the Constitution the Way the Supreme Court Does?* Pol'y Rev. 56 (Winter 1987).

106 See Gibbons, supra, note 85 at 621 ("The sanction behind constitutional law is not derived from the long deceased founders, whose only present power is to intercede for us in heaven"). See also the similar views expressed by Jed Rubenfeld, Chapter 5, and Lawrence Sager, Chapter 6, both in this volume.

In Chapter 3, this volume, Michael Perry suggests that the passage of time may also generate *new* constitutional norms, perhaps from mistaken holdings of constitutional courts. Such mistakes attain constitutional status if they "become such a fixed and widely affirmed and relied-upon (by us the people of the United States now living) feature of the life of our political community that the premise (or the practice) is, for us, bedrock." I agree that such a phenomenon is possible. But its occurrence may be regarded as anticonstitutionalist in the sense that the obscurity of the criteria for "quasi-constitutional" status diminishes the clarity of the constitutional rules and such clarity is at the center of constitutionalist values.

107 See, e.g., John R. Vile, *Constitutional Amending Process,* in *The Oxford Companion to the Supreme Court of the United States* 179, 181 (Kermit L. Hall, ed., 1992).

108 See generally, Kay, supra, note 96 at 445. In Chapter 4, this volume, Joseph Raz correctly points out that a single constitutional text may, over time, come to be supported by different sources of authority. If, as a consequence of such a change, the meanings of the constitutional rules are also understood in a different sense, I think it is still proper to say that a revolution has taken place, albeit one that is unannounced and nonobvious. A state of affairs in which the formal artifacts of a constitutional regime remain in place but in which the political underpinnings of those artifacts are in contest may last for a substantial time. Sooner or later, however, a case will arise in which a matter of great substantive importance will turn on constitutional interpretation and constitutional interpretation will turn on settling the authority on which the constitution rests. At such moments of constitutional crisis it will be necessary for one or another version of the authority of the constitution to prevail and to be articulated. See Kay, supra, note 88.

109 Paul Brest, *The Misconceived Quest for the Original Understanding,* 60 B.U. L. Rev. 204, 214–15 (1980).

110 See Alexander, supra, note 99 at 387–80.

111 See Mark Tushnet, *Following the Rules Laid Down: A Critique of Interpretivism and Neutral Principles,* 96 Harv. L. Rev. 781, 783–804 (1983).

112 This too, of course, is a contested matter. See Kay, supra, note 82 at 251–2. For many of the same reasons discussed in connection with the argument on radical linguistic indeterminacy, I assume that, when we are talking about particular facts (including mental states), and not characterizations or evaluations, there is such a thing as historical truth and that it may be approximated by reliance on reason and evidence. Id. at 252–3.

113 In describing decision-making under the aegis of "deliberately indeterminate" legal directives, Michael Perry (Chapter 3, this volume) quotes Richard Posner in referring to "a creative decision, involving discretion, the weighing of consequences, and, in short, a kind of legislative judgment."

114 Thus, it seems unwarranted to take, as Michael Perry does in Chapter 3, this volume, the test of indeterminacy to be whether people "*can* reasonably disagree with one another about how, given [a constitutional directive], the conflict should be resolved."

115 Perry, Chapter 3, this volume; see also Michael J. Perry, *The Constitution in the Courts* 76–8 (1994).

116 Philip Hamburger, *The Constitution's Accommodation of Social Change,* 88 Mich. L. Rev. 239 (1989). It is this view of the Constitution as allowing flexibility by political response that underlies the routinely miscited (although not by Michael Perry) dictum of Chief Justice Marshall in M'Culloch v. Maryland, 17 U.S. (4 Wheat.) 316, 407 (1819), that "we must never forget, that it is *a Constitution* we are *expounding.*"

117 See, e.g., Ronald Dworkin, *The Forum of Principle,* 56 N.Y.U. L. Rev. 469, 494 (1981); cf. Henry P. Monaghan, *Our Perfect Constitution,* 56 N.Y.U. L. Rev. 353, 361–7 (1981). A similar conclusion about the U.S. Constitution has been advanced on the basis of historical claims about the general views of law and interpretation held in the constitution-making period. See H. Jefferson Powell, *The*

Original Understanding of Original Intent, 98 Harv. L. Rev. 885 (1985). I have responded to the latter argument in Kay, supra, note 82 at 263–73.

118 See Berger, supra, note 79 at 110–21.

119 On the fixed constitution see Hayek, supra, note 6 at 470 n. 9. On attitudes toward the judges see Berger, supra, note 79 at 300–11.

120 See, e.g., Brest, supra, note 109 at 222. ("The defense that 'We're doing the best we can' is no less available to constitutional interpreters than to anyone else. But the best is not always good enough. . . . It seems peculiar, to say the least, that the legitimacy of a current doctrine should turn on the historian's judgment that it seems 'more likely than not' or even 'rather likely' that the adopters intended it some one or two centuries ago.")

121 John Locke, *An Essay Concerning Human Understanding* 372 (John W. Yolton, ed., 1993).

122 There is a sense in which human saying is also doing. By convention, we can determine in advance that certain utterances will change relationships in a certain way and the legal system is especially rich with such instances. See generally J. L. Austin, *How to Do Things with Words* (1962). The problem referred to by Walton Hamilton, and the subject of the discussion in text, is the capacity to establish such conventions with respect to the promulgation of constitutions.

123 Hobbes, supra, note 9 at 135.

124 See Albert van Dusen, *Connecticut* 87–90 (1961).

125 See Bernard J. Hibbitts, *"Coming to Our Senses": Communication and Legal Expression in Performance Cultures,* 41 Emory L. J. 873, 873–88 (1992). J. G. A. Pocock recounts a parallel development in his description of the historiographical transition of the seventeenth century whereby sources of authority could no longer be justified by the citation of immemorial custom but had to be located in the act of a historical sovereign. J. G. A. Pocock, *The Ancient Constitution and Feudal Law* (1987). Thus, for Coke, who represents the earlier attitude, Magna Carta was not the source of legal liberties but a solemn confirmation of preexisting law. Id. at 45.

126 See also Robert N. Clinton, *Original Understanding, Legal Realism and the Interpretation of "This Constitution,"* 72 Iowa L. Rev. 1177, 1187–90 (1987) (recounting the founders' "love affair with the written word and its power to control human destiny and limit government abuse"). Id. at 1188.

127 Quoted in Berger, supra, note 79 at 252. See also *The Federalist,* No. 41 (J. Madison), supra, note 36 at 257 ("If a federal Constitution could chain the ambition or set bounds to the exertions of all other nations, then indeed might it prudently chain the discretion of its own government, and set bounds to the exertions for its own safety"); id. No. 44 (J. Madison), supra, note 36 at 282 (concerning the prohibition of bills of attainders by states: "Our own experience has taught us, nevertheless, that additional fences against these dangers ought not to be omitted. Very properly, therefore, have the convention added this constitutional bulwark in favor of personal security and private rights"); id. No. 78 (A. Hamilton), supra, note 36 at 469 (Courts are to be "bulwarks of a limited constitution against legislative encroachments").

128 Baron de Montesquieu, *The Spirit of the Laws* 156, 159 (Thomas Nugent, trans., 1949). See also Oakeshott, supra, note 29 at 147.

129 See Steven J. Burton, *Particularism, Discretion and the Rule of Law,* in *The Rule of Law* (Nomos 36) (I. Shapiro, ed., 1994).

130 To a large degree this is a problem of the extent to which people are aware of law and are able to identify its directives. See Carol Weisbrod, *On the Expressive Functions of Family Law,* 22 U. Cal. Davis L. Rev. 991, 995–1004 (1989). This factor may be less important when we confine our consideration to the impact of the law on the constitutional judge. See Sejersted, supra, note 58 at 148; Richard A. Posner, *The Jurisprudence of Skepticism,* 86 Mich. L. Rev. 827, 832 (1988) ("The vast majority of legal questions can be and are resolved syllogistically . . .").

131 The classic formulation is in *The Federalist,* Nos. 47–51 (J. Madison), supra, note 36 at 300–25.

132 *The Federalist,* No. 78 (A. Hamilton), supra, note 36 at 469–71. It is true, as Michael Perry points out in Chapter 3, this volume, that the text of the U.S. Constitution "does not state that the Supreme Court of the United States is to be the arbiter of . . . disagreements" among the branches of the national government. But I think the creators of the Constitution did empower the courts to exercise constitutional judicial review when they granted them a "judicial power" over cases "arising under the Constitution." See Raoul Berger, *Congress vs. the Supreme Court* 50–116 (1969). The expressions quoted indicate to me that the courts, having no interest but the law, were understood as essential institutions in making the Constitution effective. As noted in text, the courts also have an ordinary subconstitutional public purpose. The extent to which that function should be emphasized relative to that of constitutional exposition may be a matter of reasonable disagreement. See Alexander M. Bickel, *The Least Dangerous Branch: The Supreme Court at the Bar of Politics* 173 (1962).

133 See William B. Fisch and Richard S. Kay, *The Legitimacy of the Constitutional Judge and Theories of Interpretation in the United States,* 42 Am. J. Comp. Law (Supplement) 517, 527–30 (1994).

134 See Hobbes, supra, note 9 at 240.

135 There is another critical prerequisite to effective constitutional government that I will not discuss in this essay. Assuming that courts, more or less, restrict themselves to the application of preexisting law, it will be necessary that the other agencies of government comply with the constitutional decisions of the courts. As the courts have no means of coercion, this might well seem the more substantial problem. I think that the reasons I suggest in the balance of the essay as to why we can expect courts generally to adhere to the preexisting rules apply as well to the other government departments adhering to the judgments of the courts. The assumption that they will so comply is fairly well borne out by U.S. history. Submission even to very unpopular decisions of the Supreme Court, while not invariable, has been pretty much the rule.

136 See, e.g., Lino A. Graglia, *Do Judges Have a Policy-Making Role in the American System of Government?* 17 Harv. J. L. & Pub. Pol'y 119, 122–3 (1994).

137 See Schauer, supra, note 48 at 123–4.

138 See Tom R. Tyler, *Why People Obey the Law* 3 (1990). In a 1995 public opinion survey 81% of respondents said it was very important for good citizens to "obey

all laws"; 97% said it was very important or somewhat important. Newsweek Poll, June 28, 1995 (Lexis News Library, RPOLL file). In a 1985 poll, while 53% of respondents said that there were "exceptional occasions" when people might follow their own consciences, 40% said people should obey the law "without exception." National Opinion Research Center Poll, 1985 (Lexis News Library. RPOLL file).

139 See generally Tyler, supra, note 138; Joseph Raz, *The Morality of Freedom* 28–100 (1986).

140 Raz, supra, note 139 at 40. See id. at 35, 40–8. See also Schauer, supra, note 48 at 51–2; Heidi Hurd, *Challenging Authority,* 100 Yale L. J. 161, 1631–2 (1991); MacCormick, supra, note 44 at 186.

141 Scc Schauer, supra, note 48 at 125.

142 See Raz, supra, note 139 at 68; Schauer, supra, note 48 at 124–5.

143 The judges, that is, might feel swayed by the "theoretical authority" of the constitution-makers. See H. L. A. Hart, *Essays on Bentham* 263 (1982); see also Alexander and Sherwin, supra, note 47 at 1214–15.

144 On the impartiality engendered by general lawmaking see Richard Flathman, *Liberalism and the Suspect Enterprise of Political Institutionalization: The Case of the Rule of Law,* in *The Rule of Law* (Nomos 36), 297, 306–7 (I. Shapiro, ed., 1994). Flathman argues that the necessary ignorance of the specific consequences of general rules is in tension with the liberal constitutionalist goal of predictability. It is true that the more general the rule the more difficult it will be for individuals to predict its effect on their planned actions. But for reasons already given, this is a problem only at the margin of meaning. It is also true that the necessary ignorance of consequences that accompany the creation of general rules means that the lawmakers or constitution-makers will not be able to know with any assurance how their rules will play out over time. But with respect to the particular constitutionalist values discussed, there is no particular reason why *lawmakers* ought to be able to predict the cumulative outcomes of their legislation. It is sufficient if subjects can predict whether their conduct on a given occasion will or will not be proscribed, or in the case of constitutions, be proscribable. The cost of this technique for social policy is the necessary price for subordinating the interests of the state to the interests of the subjects.

145 See Alexander and Sherwin, supra, note 47 at 1219–20.

146 See John Dickinson, *Legal Rules: Their Function in the Process of Decision,* 79 U. Pa. L. Rev. 833, 845 (1931).

147 See J. L. Mackie, *Obligations to Obey the Law,* 67 Va. L. Rev. 143, 151–3 (1981); Joseph Raz, *The Authority of Law* 250–9 (1979); Raz, supra, note 139 at 97–8; Tony Honore, *Making Law Bind: Essays Legal and Philosophical* 117–19 (1987).

148 See Burton, supra, note 129 at 190–1.

149 See, e.g., R. Cover, *Justice Accused* (1975).

150 Max Weber, *Law in Economy and Society* 12 (Max Rheinstein, ed., 1966) (Rule-following is, in large part, "a result of unreflective habituation to a regularity of life that has engraved itself as a custom").

151 Friederich A. Hayek, supra, note 26 at 11.

152 See Gerald F. Gaus, *Public Reason and the Rule of Law,* in *The Rule of Law* (Nomos 36) 328, 333 (I. Shapiro, ed., 1994).

62   RICHARD S. KAY

153 See Larry Alexander, *The Gap,* 14 Harv. J. L. & Pub. Pol'y 695, 701 (1991). See generally Meir Dan-Cohen, *Decision Rules and Conduct Rules: Acoustic Separation in Criminal Law,* 97 Harv. L. Rev. 625 (1984).

154 Carl E. Schneider, *Discretion and Rules: A Lawyer's View,* in *The Uses of Discretion* 47, 81 (Keith Hawkins, ed., 1992). See also Martha S. Feldman, *Social Limits to Discretion: An Organizational Perspective,* in id. at 163, 176–7.

155 See Feldman, supra, note 154 at 182–3; see also Scott Altman, *Beyond Candor,* 89 Mich. L. Rev. 296, 309 (1990).

156 See H. L. A. Hart, supra, note 143 at 158–9, 265; James L. Gibson, *Judges' Role Orientations, Attitudes and Decisions: An Interactive Model,* 72 Am. Pol. Sci. Rev. 911, 917–21 (1978).

157 The force of role definition for lawyers and judges is illustrated by an anecdote told in connection with James II's attempt to pack the benches of the royal courts with men who would support his power to suspend acts of Parliament. When the king dismissed Thomas Jones from the Court of Common Pleas for failing to give the proper assurances he is reputed to have answered, "Your majesty may find twelve men of your mind, but hardly twelve lawyers." T. B. Macaulay, 1 *History of England to the Death of William III* 585 (Heron Books, ed., 1967).

158 The philosophy of one federal judge illustrates this, not uncommon, theme: "The expansive view of our Constitution, the one I espouse, involves a rather optimistic view of life and human nature. The philosophy sees our nature and our world as evolving in a progressive manner, recognizing new human rights as our consciousness grows and develops. This view takes a document that has phrases such as "equal protection" and "due process," and seeks to discover what the phrases mean by re-examining them from time to time in light of what we have learned — as we increase our understanding of human nature, the nature of society and the universe." Stephen Reinhardt, *The Supreme Court as a Partially Political Institution,* 17 Harv. J. L. & Pub. Pol'y 149 (1993).

159 See Frederick Schauer, *Easy Cases,* 58 So. Cal. L. Rev. 399 (1985).

160 See Gibson, supra, note 156 at 919–21; Schneider, supra, note 154 at 69–70.

161 See James Stimson, Michael B. Mackuen, and Robert B. Erickson, *Dynamic Representation,* 89 Am. Pol. Sci. Rev. 543, 555–6 (1995).

162 Cf. Altman, supra, note 155 at 289–310.

163 See Sanford Levinson, Constitutional Faith 14–15 (1988); Kammen, supra, note 97 at 331 (1986).

164 See Tom R. Tyler and Gregory Mitchell, *Legitimacy and the Empowerment of Discretionary Legal Authority: The United States Supreme Court and Abortion Rights,* 43 Duke L. J. 703, 713, 728, 754 771, 786–7, 798 (1994). See generally Dean Jaros and Robert Roper, *The U.S. Supreme Court: Myth, Diffuse Support, Specific Support, and Legitimacy,* 8 Am. Politics Q. 85 (1980). In a 1990 poll, 44% of respondents said they believed the Supreme Court decided cases primarily on the basis of the law and facts. Twenty-eight percent thought "political pressures" were the primary determinant, and 19% thought the influence of personal beliefs was foremost. Marcia Coyle, *How Americans View the High Court,* National Law Journal, February 26, 1990, 1.

165 Wallace Steven, *Asides on the Oboe,* in *The Palm at the End of the Mind: Selected Poems and a Play* 187 (1971).
166 See Alexander and Sherwin, supra, note 47 at 1198, 1202–10.
167 MacCormick, supra, note 44 at 191.

2

Constitutional Authorship

FRANK I. MICHELMAN

We, the people of the United States, . . . do ordain and establish this Constitution for the United States of America.[1]

The ratification of the Conventions of nine States shall be sufficient for the establishment of this Constitution between the States so ratifying the same.[2]

This Constitution and the laws which shall be made in pursuance thereof . . . shall be the supreme law of the land. . . .[3]

The Congress, whenever two thirds of both Houses shall deem it necessary, shall propose amendments to this Constitution, or . . . shall call a convention for proposing amendments, which . . . shall be valid . . . as part of this Constitution, when ratified by the Legislatures of three-fourths of the several States, or by conventions in three-fourths thereof. . . .[4]

I. Constitution as Legislation

The Constitution of the United States is an enacted law, a piece of legislation, the intentional production of a political will. So at any rate it styles itself and so we are pleased to regard it. To be sure, such an authorial view of constitutional origins is the sheerest banality, a view as simplistic as it is inevitable, a commonplace vernacular notion that cannot withstand critical examination. It is nevertheless with us for the duration, because perception of the Constitution's enactedness figures crucially in the country's acceptance of it as supreme law. We examine in this chapter the impossible, unrelinquishable idea of the intentional constitution, of constitution as legislation – or, as it has sometimes been put, as "writing."[5]

If someone says, "The United States has a strong constitution," we hear metaphor. The speaker, we gather, is evoking the idea of the country's hardihood in its environment by likening U.S. society, government, economy, culture – the country's endowment of organs and metabolisms, so to speak – to a thriving animal's physical makeup. By contrast, "The United States has an old constitution" undoubtedly refers, quite literally,[6] to the country's express political charter; or if not exactly to that, then to the country's somehow otherwise established set of governing norms for "constitutional essentials" meaning (a) the plan of political government – offices, branches, levels, procedures, power distributions, and competency ranges – and (b) the list of personal rights and liberties, if any, that the constituted government is "bound to respect."[7] In what follows, we speak of constitutions in this political-regime or charter sense of the term.

Lacking special contextual cues to the contrary, "The United States has a good constitution" doubtless praises our regime- or charter-sense constitution, not any other features of U.S. society's so to speak congenital profile of as it were organs and metabolisms. Does the statement, however, carry praise of any agent for making our constitution a good one? A central claim of this chapter is that it does, because we incorrigibly think of good constitutional charters or regimes not as blessings that luckily befall us as strength and health befall an animal, but as designed creations by responsible human authors: as laws that lawmakers *legislate* and as laws, moreover, whose expressly legislated character is a part, at least, of what gives them their claim on our allegiance and support.

I just mentioned a "we" who think in this legislative way of constitutions and their bindingness. I use the term to refer to whoever reading this will admit to thinking, sometimes, in the ways I am here beginning to map, my use of it thus representing my bet that you, Reader, are one of the party, some if not all of the time. For us (for you), I am saying, a political-institutional constitution has always – I do not mean constantly, but forever recurrently – the character of a law expressly and designedly laid down by politically circumstanced human agents, which gains its bindingness on us at least in part by force of its reputed intentionality as a product of their express political exertion.[8]

As distinguished from a product of what? There are two major alternative possibilities to consider, which we may denominate the existential and the rational. *The existential possibility:* A constitution is binding as a product of a sociocultural fact of acceptance of it as the country's constitution. Or rather, to speak more precisely, a social fact of this kind (and nothing directive or evaluative or argumentative or otherwise rife with intention) is all that a constitution's bindingness consists in. *The rational possibility:* A constitution is binding (insofar as it is) as a product – a dictate – of right reason (insofar as it is). This gives us, then, a triptych of possibilities: constitutional bindingness-as-law is (a) "existential," a matter of how things are (what I see that we in this country just happen to find ourselves doing);[9] or (b) "rational," a matter of the right (what I see that reason requires that we do); or (c) "decisional," a matter of sovereignty (what I see that some agent whose entitlement to rule I recognize has, as it happens, decided we are to do). Let us be clear that no one can hold strictly to all three possibilities at once (although, of course, anyone can, and most of us do, switch around among them all the time with the speed of light). When and insomuch as I am feeling bound by some prescription for the reason that I perceive it to have been laid down as law at some past time by such and such persons having a title to do so, I cannot also just then be feeling bound for the reason that (as I see or judge for myself) the prescription is right or is currently accepted as law in the territory where I am.

The case, let us suppose, is that I am right now considering myself bound by something having the look of a law – say, "The Constitution of the United States." If I am consciously doing so in virtue of the thing's being right in my judgment, then, at the cost of my fealty to the right, it cannot matter to me who laid it down. If I am consciously doing so in virtue of the entitlement to rule of whoever laid it down, then, at the cost of my fealty to their sovereignty, it cannot matter to me whether I judge it to be right. If I am consciously doing so for either of those reasons, then, at the cost of my fealty either to the right or to sovereign entitlement, it cannot matter to me who else feels bound. And if, on the other hand, I am just being swept along by a tide of general social acceptance of the thing as law, then it is not just then mattering to me how or by whom the thing got laid down or whether it is right in my judgment.

You might object that the following is possible: I see that what my country's people just happen to find themselves doing is ascribing constitutional bindingness to the intentional acts of certain agents under certain conditions, it being their belief (and this belief of theirs being a part of my description of what they are doing) both that these agents own a title to decide constitutional matters and that their acts under these conditions reveal or define what reason requires.[10] Accordingly, I follow suit. You might say this is a case in which all three of our possible bases of constitutional bindingness are simultaneously in play. If it seems so, though, that is only because the ultimate motivation of my conduct is insufficiently specified. At the very instant of feeling bound by the contingency of intentional action ("in that they said so"), I cannot also feel bound by rational necessitation ("in that it is right regardless of what anyone may have said about it") or by intentionless accidents of history ("in that such-and-such complex legal-recognitional norm[11] just happens to prevail in the territory where I am"). And so on around the circle: contingency clashing with necessity, accident with design.

The focus of my explorations here is the moment in thought in which, by the internal act of basing allegiance to the Constitution on its having been authored by whom it was, we set aside, if only momentarily, whatever concerns we may also have with either the bare facticity or the rational necessity of society's acceptance of it as the basic law of the country. The object of investigation is not, please note, the bare fact of our regarding the textual or documentary Constitution as a historical product of episodes of authorship. The obvious reason for *that* is that it is, and very interestingly. The issue here is the connection we draw between perceived historical facts of the textual "Constitution's" authorship and the current normative authority for us, as law, of a body of practical political principles that we take this text to express or represent. By the "normative authority" of a political directive I mean its serious impingement on our feelings and judgments about what is required and permitted in the conduct of the political affairs. The connection we draw between normative authority and perceived historical facts of authorship ("we ought to, because they said so") I sometimes refer to below as the authority–authorship syndrome. I do not mean by "syndrome" to call the connection pathological, which I do not consider it to be. I do mean that something strong must be motivating the connection – the syndrome – because, as we shall soon start to notice, linkage of the Constitution's authority to its authorship is a sitting duck for critique.

Explanation for the syndrome does not obviously lie, as you may think it does, in the idea of an expoundable or interpretable constitution. Perhaps it seems that the very possibility of the Constitution's force as law – the possibility of "applying" the Constitution to the run of cases supposed to be under its legal control – depends on attribution of it specifically to someone's authorship. Lacking such attribution, you might think, one would lack all basis for referring questions of the Constitution's meaning-in-application to the motive, vision, purpose, aim, or understanding, at any level of generality or abstraction, at any moment past or present, of anyone in particular – any "framer" or all of them, any "ratifier" or all of them, any past or contemporary court or member thereof, any past or contemporary electorate or citizenry or "generation."[12] And wouldn't a so-called text cut off from all such reference be strictly meaningless? (How, in that case, could one even have a basis for construing those marks as tokens of the English language?)[13]

The answers are that it needn't be (and one could). Interpretability of a thing that has the look of being a text in English need not presuppose the interpreter's belief in its having been intentionally created by anyone. The thing, let us say, is found on the beach.[14] It might just be a pattern made by waves in the sand; no one is certain. Legibility does not depend on the answer. As long as it looks like English words and sentences, you can "read" it if you know English. (It appears to say, "Everyone has the right of freedom of speech.") Furthermore, as long as the words and sentences that it looks like come somewhere within shouting distance of making sense in your culture, you can interpret it, imbue it with meaning, even if the apparent meaning is quite unexpected. (It appears to say: "Everyone has the right to dishwater.")

Now consider the following: In any country at any time, a legal culture may sustain some distinct notion (by which I do not necessarily mean an uncontested notion) of the legal category "constitution" and its office in the ordering of social life. Suppose there comes within our field of vision an object that has the look of being a text in a language we know, and the text that the object looks like has the look of being part of a constitution according to our culturally embedded notion of that category. The object, by appearance, roughly fits or calls to mind our constitutional notion. Even if it also contains variations and anomalies, that object, in our culture, will be interpretable as a constitution-part.

Of course, "application" to particular cases of a legal text that is couched in generalities does require ascriptions of point or purpose. The question, say, is how or whether the free-speech guarantee applies to governmental restrictions on expenditures in political campaigns. Given a known, historical author, we could have committed ourselves to answering by doing our best to seek out the author's relevant intention or expectation. But in the case I am posing, we know of no author whose purpose we might seek out. Structural relations among the focal clause and other parts of the constitutional text (assuming we have the rest available) may doubtless help to frame the inquiry, but any further inputs of purpose or value will have to be supplied by the constitutional notion itself, the working theories of personality and society, and of government by or under law, that lead us to see the thing as a piece of a legal constitution in the first place.[15] Instead of debating over what the "framers" meant or contemplated, a group of judges – more or less sharing a specific, if always contestable, political-cultural inheritance – would have to debate the content of the constitutional notion. From it they would have to draw their claims about whether a true or proper constitution, granting rights of "freedom of speech," would or would not better have meant those terms to cover political campaign expenditures.

The point is that all this can be done by interpreters while making no supposition whatever about the actual authorship of the constitution. I therefore conclude that the demands of interpretability cannot explain our predilection to premise the bindingness of a constitution on attributions of its authorship.

II. Constitution as Proposition of Fact: Legal Nonvolitionism

A norm for an agent is a directive the agent does not feel rightly free to ignore. It is something saying efficaciously to the agent that not everything is rightly permitted, that within some range of action choices otherwise open to her, at least one ought to be done or not done. The authority–authorship syndrome is the connection we draw between two poles of our everyday knowledge of the Constitution, one of which is our experience of it as a norm or container of norms. If the Constitution somehow came to figure for us as not a norm at all (a directive or ought-statement that we don't feel rightly free to ignore) but rather only as a fact (a happening of history), then one of the syndrome's poles would be missing. It would seem, then, that you could deconstruct the syndrome by teaching people to see the Constitution as fact-not-norm. That might seem a tall order, at least when "norm" is defined broadly enough to include the possibility of agents gathering directives from what they perfectly well know to be intentionlessly grown facts of social practice.[16] It could nevertheless be understood (or rather misunderstood) as the project of a certain branch of legal positivism.

In contemporary jurisprudential debates, use of the term "legal positivism" is notoriously vagrant.[17] The term has been used to name the view that the status of a norm as part of a country's law depends on facts of social acceptance, either of that norm specifically or of the authority of certain officers or institutions in a country to pronounce what norms are and are not law there. Such a broad usage, however, unfortunately makes a legal positivist of anyone who insists on distinguishing the category of "law" or "the legal" from that of "morals" or "the moral" (or "reason" and "the reasonable"), if only for the purpose of raising and pursuing the question of the relations between these categories. Once that categorial distinction is drawn, who can deny that to speak of a *legal* order actually subsisting in a country is always to speak of an ongoing social process in that country of recognition and acceptance of that order as the legal order of that country?[18]

A question that then divides legal positivists from other legal theorists is that of the relation, if any, between the possibility of a norm's being made a valid legal one by social acceptance of it as such and the moral status of that norm whether in the eyes of an external observer of the social order in question or of an internal participant. Legal positivists deny that either the true moral status of a norm in the sight of an observer or its perceived moral status in the sight of participants has any necessary bearing on the possibility of the norm's being made a legal one by social acceptance of it as such.[19] They assert the possibility of a legal system in which there is neither "external" nor "internal" connection between considerations of the transcendent morality of a norm and either social acceptance of it as law or the efficacy of such acceptance to make the norm truly a legal one.[20]

Within legal positivism thus defined, we can detect a smaller camp of what I will call "legal nonvolitionists." What distinguishes them is insistence that the foundations of legal orders are and can only be organically grown facts of social practice, as distinguished from acts or expressions of anyone's will.[21] Straightforwardly, a going legal system is an effectively regulative social practice of reference to an identifiable collection or system of norms. Some of the norms are "primary," immediately regarding what is and is not to be done.

Some are "secondary," regarding the modes and means by which primary norms are determined. Among the secondary norms are "rules of recognition," among which there must logically be an "ultimate" rule of recognition, controlling which purported determinations of primary normative contents, uttered by whom, in what forms and circumstances, are to be respected and given effect.[22] Now, this ultimate rule of legal recognition, legal nonvolitionists point out, cannot itself consist in the command of any sovereign, because it supplies the standard by which the identity of the sovereign is ascertainable. Therefore, the legal nonvolitionist concludes, the normative system's ultimate ground can, in the last analysis, be only a social fact that is not itself a norm.

In a legal nonvolitionist account, the authority-as-law of the United States Constitution (and of legislative and judicial law declarations made in pursuance thereof) flows in the last analysis from facts of social acceptance of *the Constitution* – of the collection of secondary norms in which it consists – as the society's ultimate rule of legal recognition. The point is, social acceptance of *the Constitution* as supreme law is a very different matter from acceptance of *someone's entitlement* to make the Constitution be supreme law by legislating it as such. The latter sort of acceptance still traces legal bindingness to facts about someone's exercise of a legislative will; the former does not.

It is always possible, of course, that some society's prevailing, ultimate legal-recognitional standard would appear to take the form: such-and-such classes or descriptions of persons acting by such-and-such procedures are entitled to legislate whatever they will as this country's "law of laws."[23] That indeed appears to be true for the United States, where the strongly prevailing although not uncontested view (among those who have a view) is that such an entitlement was and is available to be claimed by or on behalf of any collection of actors who did or may in the future successfully carry out the ratification and amendment processes laid out in Articles VII and V of the Constitution.[24] But you do not faze the legal nonvolitionist by posing this sort of case, of an apparently ultimate legal recognitional standard cast in terms of someone's entitlement by act of will to legislate the constitution or law of laws. When you pose the case, she cheerfully rejoins that this recognitional standard itself, then, is to all intents and purposes the country's real law of laws – its small-*c* constitution as I'll sometimes hereafter refer to it, as distinguished from the big-*C* Constitution whose recognition-as-law the small-*c* constitution underwrites – and that this standard is not itself conceived of as a product of anyone's willful act.[25] If you object that, to the contrary, Articles VII and V gain *their* authority as (secondary, recognitional) law from a social perception of them as having been enacted through certain procedures by certain descriptions of persons ("framers," "ratifiers," the confederation Congress), she just pushes her argument up a notch (or down, your choice): It is *that* procedure, then, that is really the country's law of laws and the status-as-law of *that* procedure, she says, is that of a social fact making no reference to anyone's exercise of will. You and she can replay your respective moves an indefinite number of times moving up (or down) an indefinite number of notches, but it seems that she must eventually prevail because you must sooner or later run out of historically plausible enactment claims. Her point – the legal nonvolitionist's point – is that references to entitled authorship of laws are in the last analysis inessential to the phenomenon of legality.

Here, then, is where we have come: Everyone who conceptually distinguishes "law" from "morals" (or "reason") agrees that to speak of legal ordering in a country – to speak of the country's being in a legally ordered condition – is to speak of social convergence on some ultimate rule of legal recognition. Legal positivists properly so called maintain that such a convergence is sufficient for legality regardless of anyone's view (or of the truth) about the moral status of the recognition rule or of any other norm in the system. Legal nonvolitionists insist further on the point that such an ultimately grounding so-called rule or norm is more accurately classed as a *fact*. It consists in a socially shared understanding of who, selected by what means and marks and acting by what forms and in what combinations, has final authority to say what is or will be valid law, and to say further what this law concretely requires of inhabitants and officials in various circumstances. True, this must be in a quite strong sense an intersubjectively shared understanding, because a crucial part of what inhabitants (or maybe it is only "officials") must share is awareness of each other sharing this awareness of a shared understanding.[26] Still, it remains in the end that the recognition "rule" is neither an intentional production nor a rational necessitation but just a matter of reflexive social practice being what it is. The "rule" consists in a pattern of interconnected responses on the part of a critical mass of a country's people (or officials) to certain classes of social events that they have culturally learned to construe as "Parliament" enacting a "statute," as the "decree" of a "court," as a "police car's" beacon, or what have you. In sum, according to the legal nonvolitionist view, a country's constitution – its really operative constitution – is not itself finally graspable as a prescriptive law or any other kind of norm but only as "a matter of social fact" to be discovered not by analysis of propositions but by "empirical investigation."[27]

You feel drawn to object. You want to say, by way of counterexample, that – obviously – the Constitution of the United States both (a) gathers its effective legal force from public accreditation of it as an intentional act of legislation and (b) is or provides the ultimate rule of legal recognition in U.S. territory. The legal nonvolitionist then poses her challenge: You say the Constitution binds legally as the product of someone's act of legislating a law meant to contain the country's ultimate rule of legal recognition. But if so, then the said someone – the framers, the ratifiers – must have been legally entitled to lay down basic law to the country in this way. And what rule of recognition, then, confirms this constitutional legislator's entitlement? Your best rejoinder, I think, would be: a recognition rule that was historically co-original and congruent with certain acts of constitutional lawmaking that it authorized. Why not? There seems to be no reason why a single transformative passage of national history cannot contain both and simultaneously (and even reciprocally) (a) a series of legislatively intended public actions and events that succeeds, in fact, in laying down law to the country and (b) the emergence in society – the coming-into-practice – of the precise "rule of recognition" that the legislative efficacy of this particular series of events implies. For illustration, it seems we need look no further back than the recent history of South Africa[28] and no further abroad than the American constitutional founding, the course of events from the run up to the Philadelphia convention of 1787 through the convention itself and its ratificational aftermath.[29]

It's a nice thought, this idea of historical coincidence between the occurrence of a legislative endeavor conforming to a certain (broadly speaking) procedural specification and the coming-into-being of a social practice of attributing legislative efficacy to endeavors falling under that same procedural specification. But still this idea misses the point of the legal nonvolitionist's challenge to your attempt finally to ground the Constitution's *current* legal force in a *current* perception of it as a product of someone's *past* exercise of an entitlement to legislate. The legal nonvolitionist is making a charge of incoherence against all claims of this sort. She is saying that no one can base the Constitution's authority on its legislative character without, in the very thought, positing some preconstitutional ground of the authority-to-make-something-be-law-by-legislating-it of whoever is supposed to have made the Constitution be law by legislating *it*.[30] The point, in other words, is that a law that we right now see as legally forceful by virtue of its having been duly legislated cannot itself right now also be or contain our legal order's ultimate rule of recognition. So it cannot be, in that sense, what we also think a constitution is.[31]

It remains only to point out that if whatever-it-is – the real or meta or small-c constitution – that is supposed to drape the mantle of legislative authority on whoever is supposed to have legislated "the Constitution" is, in its turn, conceived of as a legislated law, then the same argument recurses on it. The recursion recurs for as long as the successive mantles of authority are said to consist in legislated laws; we tumble in the void of infinite regress. Hans Kelsen saw this problem long ago.[32] From it he deduced what he called "the transcendental-logical condition" of any possible "grounding" of the validity of a legal order.

"Only a norm," offered Kelsen, can ground "the validity of another norm."[33] Therefore, when we regard a legal order as grounded we must – logically must – be positing a "historically first constitution," together with a socially prevailing "basic norm" conferring on that first constitution's promulgators the authority to make it be the law, and thereby to obligate the country's posterity (assuming the basic norm remains operative for them) to grant the force of law to everything that has issued from or pursuant to a chain of amending clauses depending from that first constitution.[34]

Just as the "first constitution" and its promulgators are pure abstractions – "transcendental-logical" categories necessitated by the prior determination of a thinker to regard his legal order as "grounded" – so then is the basic norm. Perhaps that is why contemporary legal nonvolitionism has turned away from Kelsen's dictum that "only a norm" can ground "the validity of another norm," offering instead to block the regress by shifting attention from the space of norms to the space of facts, and specifically to the convenient fact that a critical mass of the country's inhabitants (or officials) does, as it happens, intersubjectively concede a regulative force to an actually operative practice of government that these inhabitants for some reason or other tend to identify with (or hypostatize as) a textoid that they call "the Constitution."[35] What those reasons may be are a part of what we are after here. We should be clear, though, that the legal nonvolitionist argument, cogent as it is, in no way impugns this chapter's thesis that Americans do in fact recurrently *think of* the Constitution as containing the ultimate legal grounding, the law of laws, of the American legal order and, furthermore, as doing so by virtue of its legislated character.

What the nonvolitionist argument shows is that a social practice of legal validation must ultimately ground itself in something that is not itself a validated law in terms of the system's own ultimate standards of legal validation – something that rather, then, must be "merely" a social practice of referring questions of legal validity to those particular standards. But full knowledge of a social practice includes knowledge of how participants in the practice experience it, "from the inside" so to speak, and the legal nonvolitionist argument neither says nor decides anything about the internal-experiential dimension of any given society's legal-recognitional practice.[36] More precisely, the argument does not preclude the practice's being one that has this as one of its features: that participants refer all questions about legal authority and validity to sets of standards to which, whenever they make such referrals, they attribute the character of having been intentionally legislated.

The legal nonvolitionist argument accordingly does not preclude but rather sharpens this chapter's thesis that we trace the Constitution's bindingness on us at least partly to its reputation-as-legislated. In the face of an apparently cogent refutation of any essential tie between the legal force of a country's constitution and attributions of its authorship, we persist in tying our constitution's authority for us – small-c and large-C – to attributions of its authorship. The question is why.

III. The People's Title to Rule: Sovereignty, Democracy, and "Political Identity"

In any search for what might be motivating a population's habit of tracing a constitution's normative bindingness to perceived facts of its authorship, a glaringly obvious hypothesis is the influence on that population of a theory of sovereignty. Normative bindingness sometimes flows from legal bindingness, insomuch as that which I perceive to bind me legally also, in some substantial measure, binds me normatively. Now, to say that someone is sovereign in a country is to ascribe to that person a legal title to rule the country in whatever way she decides to do, and an acknowledged sovereign, therefore, is within her legal entitlement to legislate for the country whatever constitution she may wish. What makes for her constitution's legal (hence normative) bindingness on me as an inhabitant, then, is all and only my recognition of her legal title to rule. My own judgments of the rightness of what she rules are then beside the point, as are my observations regarding anyone else's acceptance of her rule. As long as I acknowledge her title of rulership, I am bound to follow her constitutional directives, to the best of my ability to find out what those directives are and what she meant for them to have me do in one or another specific set of circumstances. An acknowledgment of sovereignty would thus supply a perfect explanation for the authority–authorship syndrome.

But of course the explanation is only as good as its underlying supposition of our attachment to an idea of sovereignty. And there we run into a complication. For it seems safe to say that we as we actually are do not recognize the title of anyone save the people of a country to rule it. Democratic sovereignty is the only sovereignty we accredit. And the idea of democratic sovereignty, I am now going to argue, is special in the very respect that it cannot maintain a separation between judgments of the pretending sovereign's title to rule (or judgments of the pretender's actual identity as the entitled sovereign) and judgments of the rightness of the pretender's constitutional-legislative acts.

If you attribute sovereignty to another, then the authority–authorship syndrome holds for you with respect to the bindingness on you of the other's legislative acts. But suppose, instead, that you attribute sovereignty to yourself. In that case, it seems, the syndrome must break. If you feel bound at all by what you ruled before, it won't normally be because it was ruled, or was ruled by you. If you feel bound at all, it must be by rightness as you judge it now: what you ruled before still striking you, on current reconsideration, as the right thing to rule. If it does not, why should not you, being sovereign, feel free to amend? Why should you feel bound to stand by your own former judgment?

There are complications, of course. Rightness considerations – of legal "integrity," perhaps – might constrain your freedom to alter some laws that you now judge not quite right.[37] Of more immediate interest: Here you are, considering yourself absolute owner of the country, entitled as such to make laws *ad libitum* for the country and you in it, quite irrespective of getting them "right," whatever that might mean. (That is what it means to be sovereign.) Your only aim in this matter is for the country, and you in it, to be ruled *by you*. If you are tired and not of a mind to rule right now, that aim could make you feel bound by what you ruled before, and for the reason that it was you who ruled it, until such time as you might bestir yourself to rule again. The syndrome would hold. This assumes, of course, either that "you" are ascertainably still the same person as the one who ruled before or else that what matters is not really self-rule – being ruled by yourself – but only being ruled by a pod with your name on it. But suppose neither of those conditions holds. Suppose that self-rule is what matters, and also that "you" are not still ascertainably the same person as the one who ruled before. In that case, the syndrome breaks. Insistence on this point breaks down the radical separation of will from reason that the proposition of democratic sovereignty is often taken to involve – the idea, that is, that a sovereign people is free to legislate to itself whatever law it pleases, just because that is what "sovereign" means.

A. *Two Views of Constitutional Democracy*

Constitutionally speaking, "democracy" in our times certainly signifies something beyond the rule of the many or the crowd as opposed to the few, the best, or "the one." The term names a standard by which a country is not a free one, its inhabitants not free men and women, unless political arrangements are such as to place inhabitants under their own political agency, their own "rule." No doubt the prevailing constitutional-democratic ideal does accept a large amount of rule pro tanto by legislative, administrative, and judicial officers, operating within schemes of representative government. What the ideal tests, in the end, are the constitutive or fundamental laws of a country; the laws, that is, that fix the country's constitutional essentials.[38] There is, however, an ambiguity in the test: Are we talking about the legislation of a country's fundamental laws by its inhabitants collectively, as one agent ("the people"), or by them severally, as individuals? The idea that a country's inhabitants *severally* are morally entitled to be the makers of the fundamental laws of their country I call "liberal constitutional democracy." The contrasting idea that this entitlement belongs to a collective or supraindividual entity, "the people," I call "constitutional populism."[39]

B. Constitutional Populism and the "Generation" Problem

Constitutional populists begin with the proposition that among requirements of rightness in political arrangements the most basic is the entitlement of the people of a country, somehow conceived of as a single situs of political agency or energy, to decide the country's fundamental laws (saving, no doubt, the "law" of the people's title to make the law).[40] It may seem directly clear, then, why for constitutional populists constitutional-legal authority depends on constitutional-legal authorship. That perception, however, is incomplete. For constitutional populists, as I now undertake to show, the deeper basis of constitutional-legal obligation must be rightness, not authorship; authorship either stands in the way of obligation or serves as a figure of thought for the supposition of rightness on which obligation depends.

Explanation begins with the opacity of the normative notion of the will of "the people" or of a decision "by the people." Few who consider the matter with much seriousness believe that this can plausibly be equated with a simple tally of votes taken under any conditions whatever, the vote of the majority then standing for the decision of the people.

Among contemporary American constitutional theorists of populist inclination, Bruce Ackerman is the one who has grappled most seriously with the question of what counts as an expression of the legislative will of the people. Ackerman quite convincingly maintains that, on any plausible conception of a people's constitutional will that is morally deserving of respect, that will (or that "people") can never be corporately or instantaneously present but can only be represented by time-extended courses of political events. Sometimes, Ackerman says, a course of events can disclose the existence of a "mobilized majority" in favor of major constitutional change – by which he means a clear, strong, sustained, and committed majority that arises, consolidates, and persists over a time during which the fundamental, constitutional matters in questions are publicly controverted at a high level of energy and concern. Ackerman believes (and in this respect his view is noncontroversial) that such episodes of constitutionally decisive and transformative popular mobilization have been relatively infrequent in U.S. history.[41]

At a recent conference titled "Fidelity in Constitutional Theory," announcing in effect what he finds in constitution-space that might be worthy of his faith, Ackerman pronounced "the generation" to be the "basic unit" in American constitutional theory: not "the clause" (for which read: some existentially self-warranting, autonomously speaking text) and not "the theory" (for which read: some rightness apple of the beholder's eye) but "the generation" (for which read: the historically acting creator of constitutional law – the creator, that is, on a full and true view of who that is). To those who already agree with him that proper use of the Constitution today requires reference to past historical acts of constitutional creation, Ackerman urges the need to reckon with a certain true fact about historical acts of creation of our constitution, to wit: They were done by a succession of somewhat spiritually separated generations. The constitution we have is a product of a chronologically ordered but nonlinear ("discontinuous") series of creative political events, each one of which rejected some but not all of its predecessors' basic normative premises. As such, then, must the Constitution be construed.[42]

Yes. But when Ackerman posits *the generation* – *not* the clause, *not* the theory – as the basic object of fidelity, he certainly intends a further message: that proper use of the Constitution today does indeed require reference to past historical acts and events. Constitutional law he declares to be constituted by a "conversation between generations."[43] Each generation of Americans is "obligated to honor" the creativities of every predecessor generation (saving certain barren ones).[44] Thus, *our* task today is to say what "*their* sound and and fury" means.[45] The message seemingly could not be clearer: The most compelling what-there-is-to-be-faithful-to, constitutionally speaking, is human political action, the political works and acts of generations. Fidelity does not run to an impersonal prescriptive text that just happens, heaven only knows how, to be shining there before us *in loco constitutionis*. Whatever merits our acceptance – our "reception"[46] – as constitutional law does so precisely by virtue of being the works and acts of the generations whose works and acts it is.

Why so? Why not by virtue of being right (if it is) or by virtue of being there? Because, Ackerman says, of our commitment as Americans to being governed by ourselves as a people. That commitment leaves us with the problem of telling when we as a people have spoken law; it gives us need for a rule of recognition of the people legislating. But the root commitment that raises the need also points to the form of the only admissible answer to it, which is to draw the rule of recognition from the actual historical practice of the country. The country came to treat the semilawlessly enacted Constitution of the 1780s as highest law, as it did the semilawlessly enacted Reconstruction amendments and as it now does (so Ackerman contends and many adamantly deny) an undocumented constitutional-legal quasi-enactment of the New Deal era.[47] The country thus shows to itself what it counts as a mobilized-majoritarian apparition of the legislating people. On this matter as on others, our task is nothing more or less than to listen to ourselves. What could be more in the spirit of democracy as popular self-rule?

The difficulty is as it has ever been (call it "counter-majoritarian,"[48] call it "intertemporal"[49]). They – the generations of the Founding, Reconstruction, and the New Deal – are not in any obvious or self-proving way in unity or unison with us the living. But given that they are not, for us to submit in any degree to governance by their say-so – including not least their say-so regarding rules of recognition – is for us in that same degree to be not governing ourselves. What some prior generation did as distinguished from what we *might* do is extraneous, it would seem, to our self-government, as long as it remains agreed that they (then) are not us (now).

C. Intergenerational Heuristics

Ackerman has a response: Granted, predecessor generations are not us. Neither, on good authority, is Congress us, nor is any other contemporary organ of representative government.[50] If what we mean by democracy is the rule of the people, we must also understand that this people appears in action only sporadically, in moments of exceptional political mobilization that it may not be granted to every generation to know. So in this world of generational finitude and change, to ask for perfect democracy is to ask for too much. The best that any oncoming generation can do, if it means to be ruled by the people, is to receive as its law the most recent word from an adequately mobilized U.S. citizenry, pending that oncoming generation's own arousal (if ever) of the people slumbering within it.

With that in mind, suppose someone, an American, says that his sole objective in life is to live in compliance with a constitution that truly corresponds to the contemporary will of the contemporary American people. I emphasize *contemporary*. This person sees no moral or other value in being ruled from the grave by dead people. What morally moves him is the idea that the living should in concert rule their own lives in their own country. But he finds himself in a state of puzzlement about how he can possibly know what *is* the constitutional will of the contemporary American people, which it is his sole object in life to abide by. So he takes a leaf from Bruce Ackerman's book. He allows himself to be persuaded by Ackerman that the best evidence he can hope to have of the will of the contemporary American people is the facts about where matters constitutional were last left (in the year 1937, by Ackerman's reckoning) by the series of constitutionally decisive, popular mobilizations that have previously occurred in U.S. history.

Here you have a genuine case of the authority–authorship syndrome. Our hero is minded to abide by the Constitution "because they said so," no further questions asked. Given his objective – to live under laws corresponding to the (contemporary) people's will – his heuristic attribution to past historical acts of dependable direction toward that objective not only relieves him but rationally bars him from any further direct inquiry of his own. In this matter, he does truly equate what he ought to do with whatever they said.[51] The authority–authorship syndrome holds for him. Of course, it does so only in a special way, by virtue of a special feature in *his* syndrome that we might call its normative-heuristic structure. Submission to authority may not always be morally motivated, but in our speaker's case it is. His attitude is certainly not one of moral detachment or indifference to the right. As a constitutional populist, he thinks it right to submit himself to the fundamental-legal will of the people. He submits to the authority of past political events because and only because he aims to do what is right, having himself assumed responsibility for the judgment that what is right in these matters is submission to the contemporary people's will. But that, as we are about to see, is not the only or, perhaps, the most telling sense in which a rightness judgment undergirds his regarding what "they" said as normatively authoritative for him.

D. *"Political Identity" and Rightness*

Our hero hazards a probability estimate that the constitutional doings of prior generations of Americans – dead Americans – point with acceptable accuracy toward the will of the contemporary people respecting matters constitutional. On what basis, however, can he count this estimate a rational one? The estimate depends on the supposition that each politically mobilized generation in the American series is an episode or representation of one and the same political family, so to speak, periodically exercising one and the same family-owned title to collective self-rule. But this succession of mobilizational episodes might also, after all, be construed as a temporal series of *different* collective agencies, strangers to each other, each possessed of its own discrete entitlement to rule over its own affairs.

The point is: To think of a people living under a fundamental-legal regime that they themselves make or adopt is already by the thought to confer upon "the people" an identity that is in some respect continuous across events of constitutional mobilization and change. The people need not be unchanging across the higher legislative divide: Agents can change through their acts without loss of identity; Montaigne is made by the book that he makes. But we do need to fix on *something* about this people – presumably it would pertain to their political sensibilities and motivations – that might warrant our calling them the same people after as they were before the event. Unable to affirm a relevant sameness between those who decide upon constitutional innovation and those who must live with the decision, we could not seriously speak of a people living under its own rule.

Popular sovereignty no doubt conceives of constitutional lawmaking events as deliberate acts of a capital-*P* People legislating. What is tricky is that this People legislate not only to the official agents – congresses, presidents, courts – whom they charter or "constitute" by their higher lawmaking acts, but to themselves as the self-same (self-governing) People as those who legislate. They do so at least insomuch as every constitution (worthy of the name) is a law containing a binding rule about how itself (including this rule of which we just now speak) may thenceforth be revised. In the Constitution of the United States, this rule (most observers think) is Article V.[52] It looks like there is a dimension of political freedom that we both attribute to the chartering People (represented as the authors and ratifiers of Article V) and deny to the People as thus chartered, that is, the freedom to decide the terms and conditions of higher lawmaking. The charterers ("We the People of the United States") seem to stand, then, on a different plane of rulership from the chartered ("our posterity"), as creators to creatures. How is it possible to construe such an event as one of the people's self-government?

There are possibility conditions for this, but they are stringent. For a People to be self-governing means for them to legislate to themselves as the self-same (if also the ever-changing) People as those who legislate. This means that the lawmaking act emanates from a People whose collective character or "political identity" (to use Bruce Ackerman's nice term)[53] not only continues through the process of enactment undissolved but also, by the same token, was already established when the process began. We need to say, then, what it is that we think confers political identities on empirical human aggregates, identities of a sort that allows us to check for the sameness of the People who lay down constitutional law and the People to whom it is laid down. What do we think this people-constituting, identity-fixing factor could possibly be? Must it not finally come down to an attitude of expectation or commitment shared by constituent members of the putative capital-P People? An attitude of expectation of the presence among them of some substantially contentful normative like-mindedness, or at the very least of commitment to searching out the possibility of this? An expectation of, or commitment to, some cultural or dispositional or experiential commonality from which they can together try to distill some substantially contentful idea of political reason or right? Something – could it be – along the lines of that constitutional-cultural "notion" to which I have previously made reference?[54]

Think, now, about how matters look from the standpoint of the People on the receiving side of a constitutionally decisive mobilization. As a supposedly self-governing people, they cannot accept constitutional lawmaking from anyone save themselves. But it seems they can know themselves as themselves – can know themselves as, so to speak, a collective political self – only by knowing themselves as a group of sharers, joint participants in some already present, contentful idea, or proto-idea, of constitutional reason or right. This means they can know their lawgivers as legitimate, as the same People as they are, only through *the lawgivers'* perceived or supposed participation in the same set of regulative ideas that they right now hold about what constitutions are for and are supposed to do. What we are saying here, in effect, is that a population's conception of itself as self-governing, as legislating law *to itself,* depends on its sense of its members as, in their constitutional lawmaking acts, commonly and constantly inspired by and aspiring to some distinct regulative idea of constitutional justice, fitness, and right.

What it comes down to is this: For anyone committed to the pursuit of popular sovereignty for the sake of the value of political self-government – the value of a population's being under its own political rule (and why else be committed to the pursuit of popular sovereignty?) – acts of legitimate constitutional lawmaking can never within history be conceived of as writing on a clean slate. Rather, such acts must always be conceived of as outcomes of political interactions that were already framed, when they occurred, by some already present idea of constitutional reason, some constitutional-cultural notion. As devotees of self-rule by the people, we do not and cannot grant binding force to any predecessor constitutional lawgivers' say-so just because it was theirs, without an identity check to make sure that they and we are relevantly the same people, and there appears to be no such relevant check apart from our current judgment as to whether what they did was in accord, or at least tending toward accord, with constitutional reason as it may be given to us the living to know it. In other words, constitutional framers can be *our* framers – their history can be our history, their word can command observance from us now on popular-sovereignty grounds – only because and insofar as they, in our eyes now, were already on what we judge to be the track of true constitutional reason.

We see a hermeneutical circle closing. I have been arguing that, in the production of present-day legal authority, constitutional framers have to be figures of rightness for us before they can be figures of history. But if so, then present-day constitutional interpreters, dedicated to the support of the contemporary normative authority of the Constitution, have no choice but to read the words of the framers with the interpretative charity of the living. In that respect, my argument here is incidentally intended to cause trouble for those who assert that a broadly originalist mode of constitutional interpretation follows directly from the premise that "the Constitution . . . derives its power to restrain from assumptions about [a] historical act that created it."[55]

But to return to our main inquiry: If it is true that, in the production of present-day legal authority, the framers must be figures of rightness before they can be figures of history, then why is not history superfluous to the enterprise? Why don't we dispense altogether with the framers and their authority? Might an answer lie in the fact that we are not only constitutional populists but liberal constitutional democrats as well? I think it may, but in order to explain I will first have to rehearse some liberal constitutional democratic doctrine.

IV. Coercion, Justification, and Conscience in Liberal Constitutional Democracy

A. *Liberal Conscience to Liberal Justice*

The question of the rightness of the fundamental laws hounds us both as the constitutional populists we are and as the constitutional liberals we are, but in different ways.

For us as populists, the question of fundamental-legal rightness merges into that of authorship: What is right in this matter, and all that is right, is that the people make the laws for themselves. The question of the substantive rightness of the laws, of the rightness of the laws as opposed to the right of their makers to make them, enters secondarily, at the point where members of a current generation must accept (or not) that those historical actors whom they credit as lawmakers are the right ones, those who are sovereign for them, themselves.

Matters stand quite differently for us as constitutional liberals. In liberal constitutional thought, the question of the rightness of the fundamental-legal regime is primary. That is because the regime is a program for coercion. When we abide by a constitutional regime in place we collaborate in coercion of the ideally and presumptively free and equal individuals who live or come within its jurisdiction. For that collaboration, we liberally feel, some justification is owing. Justification means (what else could it mean?) a showing that the legal order's constitutive or fundamental laws are substantively right, or at least that there is something about them giving reason for confidence in their tendency toward rightness.[56]

To spell it out a little: Liberals are committed to a certain kind of political regard for individuals, as presumptively invested with "higher-order interests" in the direction of their lives in accordance with goals and values they freely posit to themselves.[57] Given the extent to which a country's laws obviously impinge on the lives of the population, fulfillment of individuals' self-government interests apparently would require that a country's inhabitants be each one a maker of the country's laws. But lawmaking in a modern, plural, diverse society is and must in every discrete instance be a nonunanimous, "collective" activity. It simply cannot be that each and every concrete instance of lawmaking will directly register for each affected person as an instance of self-government.

The problem might seem containable, if not exactly soluble, were liberal thought content to relegate individuals' interests in self-government to some bounded realm of "private" affairs. It grows toward the intractable, though, if we insist that each individual's self-government interest extends across the full range of politically or collectively decidable matters. And why would it not? If it is correct at all to say that I have a basic interest in setting the directions of my life, then how can that interest not extend to the question, for example, of whether there shall or shall not be in force in my country a law against abortion? How, indeed, can it not extend further, to the question of whether there shall or shall not be in force in my country a (higher or constitutional) law against having (ordinary) laws against abortion?

Nevertheless, there may be salvation in the idea of fundamental laws that frame a system for all further lawmaking. If I could see myself as, so to speak, an autonomous author or endorser of the system of lawmaking, then I would also be accepting responsibility for whatever issues from the system. For as long as I consciously endorse the system as a right or fair one, I am bound by that endorsement to accept its specific results even when they revolt me (granting that I might not forever retain confidence in the rightness of a system that I saw issuing in too many revolting laws). The hope of the liberal constitutionalist is that a country's people can severally see themselves in this way as autonomously approving the fundamental laws, and so as autonomously responsible for all further lawmaking that those laws authorize. Whoever could do that would be self-governing with respect to the politically decidable conditions of their lives.[58]

So the liberal constitutional project ideally is that of everyone's actually endorsing the fundamental-legal regime as right, and the first requirement of that ideal project is that everyone reasonably *could* do so. Liberal theorists differ in the details, but that is roughly how liberal reason drives us to define justice in politics. Liberals agree that in order for any regime of political coercion to comport with justice, all those concerned must have true reasons of their own, whether or not consciously held, for agreeing to its basic programmatic terms – reasons that all would discover themselves to have in a wide and general reflective equilibrium,[59] reasons that are objectively consonant with everyone's system of interests (including whatever interests you think everyone has in fair and peaceful social coexistence or cooperation with others) or that are in accord with what all would agree to, according to their understandings of their interests, in the light of a truly democratic debate.[60]

B. Liberal Constitutional Responsibility

If the legal-nonvolitionist argument is correct, the small-*c* constitution, when you get to the bottom of it, is an outcome of "subjectless" social processes."[61] No one in particular made it what it is or, therefore, can be held responsible for its undoubtedly coercive content. It seems, in that way, to be beyond justification. Yet justify and disjustify we incessantly do, even down to pretty deep small-c constitutional levels.[62] The legal-nonvolitionist argument may leave us wondering what we then think we are doing, or why we don't just take our *justificandum* to be what legal-nonvolitionist analysis so compellingly reveals it to be: a subsisting, observable, sociocultural evolutionary fact, assured as such of the only sort of justification – that is, facticity, existence – that a fact can ever have and that all existent facts always have. To that question, liberal conscience provides an answer.

Legal nonvolitionism, let us imagine, somehow insinuates its message into the country's drinking-water supplies, and Americans predominantly come to share a sense of currently accepted legal-recognitional standards as having no author, as having been "subjectlessly" produced. This sensing might, perhaps, occur only in some vestibule of consciousness, so that neither the content of the standards nor the fact of their acceptance ever entered the field of anyone's focused, critical contemplation. But surely it wouldn't have to work that way. *Pace* Kelsen,[63] it seems we can easily maintain awareness of being under the sway of directives that we consciously hold to be subjectless, and can furthermore make these directives, or norms, focal objects of inquisitive and critical thought. As agents or "persons" we can reflect critically on what we "just happen" to find ourselves doing, and when we do reflect on our subjectlessly grown legal-recognitional practice or small-c constitution, it cannot then be for us a value-neutral fact. If a legal order inevitably coerces, then so, too, does the small-c constitution that grounds it. If we collaborate, we need to justify. A small-c constitution is not after all like the weather, beyond anyone's ability to affect by action. From a sense or perception that no one made the small-c constitution what it is today, nothing follows about the possibility of working to change it by deliberate action now. We can always, therefore demand, of ourselves if of no one else, reasons for leaving the small-c constitution as we find it.

C. Responsibility and the Authority–Authorship Syndrome

Thus, liberal conscience gives us a straightforward response to our question about what could possibly possess anyone to demand justification for, or debate the moral merits of, a constitutional practice that on due reflection he or she has to see as grounded in social facts that no one willed or intended and for which no one is responsible. However this small-c constitution came to be what it is, there is always the question of leaving or not leaving it as we find it. In that sense, a liberal constitutionalist cannot help assuming the role of constitutional author. But there is here no explanation, as yet, for the authority–authorship syndrome, the "drawn connection" between something's authorship and its commandingness as law ("because they said so"). Awareness that you or I could work at changing the received small-c constitutional content does not make us its authors in that sense. A part of what we are trying to explain here is displacement of agency to another ("because they said so") as opposed to acceptance of it on one's own ("because I right now judge that it is [or would be] right regardless of what anyone may ever have said about it"). At stake is exactly the difference between what I earlier distinguished as the rational and the decisional groundings of constitutional bindingness. People's acceptance of responsibility for moral improvement of the constitution from here on out just *is* their embrace of the rational grounding, whereas it is the country's attachment to the decisional grounding that we are engaged here to explain.

D. Authorship in Default of Agency?

A legal order coerces. So then does its small-*c* constitution. When we abide by a constitutional regime in place, we collaborate in coercion. For that collaboration we require justification. Our direct perception of the regime's moral rightness or justice in all important respects would give us what we require, but many or most of us unfortunately do not have that perception. Some believe or suspect the regime to be wrong in some basic way;[64] some just do not know and do not try to judge, or do not trust themselves to do so given limits on the effort they are willing to invest in the question. Even if the regime is in our view badly wrong in some way, we may despair in practice of getting the fault corrected, or we may decline the effort for reasons of prudence (regard for overriding values of legal unity and stability)[65] or of principle (respecting the evident predominant disposition of our mates in political cooperation).[66] For any or all of such reasons, a concurrent endorsement of the justice of the coercive regime may be unavailable to us as our reason for abiding by and thereby helping to sustain it. Authority, then – "because they said so" – could supply the reason we want. And authority here requires – presupposes – an author.

In sum: For liberals, that the constitution is *there* can never suffice as a reason for abiding by it; it also has to be morally supportable as just or at least as "justice-seeking."[67] Somewhere, it seems, liberals have to locate accountability and responsibility for the constitution's conformity to justice or at least for good-faith effort in that direction. Those who stand accountable and responsible for a constitution's justice-seeking character are its agents, its doers, its authors. The idea of constitutional authorship, I am suggesting may serve us as a projection and signifier of moral agency and accountability in the matter of politics.

V. The Lost Democrat?

Some parallels appear between the views we hold as constitutional populists and the views we hold as liberal constitutional democrats. In neither view

does intentionless existence sufficiently ground constitutional-legal normative force or justification, and in neither can the grounding be completed
without reference to rightness. Liberal constitutional democracy grounds justification in rightness itself, in the warrantable justice or justice-seekingness
of basic political arrangements. Constitutional populism grounds normative
force not in rightness but in will – specifically, in the contemporary will of the
people. However (if Ackerman's argument is correct), there is no discovering
what that will is without reference to an historical series of political acts; and
furthermore (if my argument is correct), there is no deciding which acts belong to the series without a view as to which ones fall along what is now
found to be a right track by (a duly deliberated or chastened) contemporary
public opinion.

"Rightness," however, stands differently positioned in the two views. For
constitutional populism, the relation of rightness to contemporary political
expressions of popular intuitions and judgments is one of immanence,
whereas for liberal constitutional democracy, it is one of transcendence. For
populism, the question is one of construing one's own political past, con-
structing one's own political biography, in the process simultaneously engag-
ing and (re)producing one's own notion of the right in politics. For liberals,
the question is one of testing what exists by comparison with an independent
critical standard. To put it another way: In populist thought, rightness does
not seem to fight in principle against democracy; in liberal thought, it does.
How, then, does liberal constitutional democratic thought preserve a place for
democracy at all?

I mean "democracy" in the unrestricted procedural sense of the term. It is
all too easy to say: By constitutional "democracy" liberals mean and can only
mean something substantive, not anything deeply procedural – that is, they
mean only that the country's basic laws, regardless of how those laws came to
be in force, provide for more or less popularly accountable day-to-day government based on a more or less equally distributed franchise; for nondiscriminatory lawmaking and prohibition of caste distinctions; for protection
against arbitrary and oppressive uses of state powers; for strong rights of
moral autonomy, freedom of thought, freedoms of political expression and association; for whatever one's profile for democracy requires. If the provisions
match our profile, we judge the regime democratic, no matter its authorship.
By contrast, on what I mean by the unrestricted procedural sense of "democracy," the regime is not democratic, no matter the democratic nicety of its
fundamental-legal prescriptive content, unless the country's people at all
times retain appropriate joint control over that content, too. The question, to
repeat it, is how it is possible for constitutional liberals also to be constitutional democrats in the full procedural sense of the term.

Many of us do try. Take as a case in point Jürgen Habermas. When it comes
to the matter of constitutional law, he is expressly committed both to bottom-

less procedural democracy and to liberal justice. As a democratic procedural-ist, Habermas complains about the effort of John Rawls to find a ground for liberal constitutionalism in the hypothetical deliberations of parties in a philo-sophically constructed "original position." He writes:

> From the perspective of the [philosophically elaborated] theory of justice, the act of founding the democratic constitution cannot be repeated under the institutional condi-tions of an already constituted just society. . . . It is not possible for the citizens to . . . reignite the radical democratic embers of the original position . . . , for . . . they find the results of the theory already sedimented in the constitution. . . . [T]he citizens can-not conceive of the constitution as a *project*."[68]

That, plainly, is a call for democratic procedure even at the point of deciding the *most* fundamental laws of the regime or, indeed, of formulating principles or norms by which to test the laws. "The democratic procedure for the pro-duction of law," Habermas declares, "forms the only . . . source of legiti-macy" for our "postmetaphysical" age.[69]

Yet Habermas along with Rawls undoubtedly belongs to the family of lib-eral political moralists, those who judge political arrangements by asking whether the arrangements sufficiently honor elementary moral entitlements attributed to individuals. Along our "liberal" – "populist" divide, the thought of Habermas falls decidedly on the liberal side of the line. It deeply shares with the thought of Locke, Kant, Mill, Rawls, and Dworkin a view of human individuals as severally possessed of capacities for rational agency, for taking some substantial degree of conscious charge of their own minds and lives, making and pursuing their own judgments about what is good and what is right.[70] Accordingly, it also deeply shares with theirs a sense of the inelim-inable coerciveness of political government and a concomitant view of what it must mean to defend against complaint the governmental presence in peo-ple's lives – which is to show that all affected persons severally have what are actually, for them as individuals, good reasons for consent at least to the fun-damental laws that constitute the system of government they are under.

A Habermasian version of this line of thought appears in the propositions that he labels "U" and "D":

[U] [F]or a norm to be valid [meaning for the norm to be observable "out of respect for" it], the consequences and side effects that its general obser-vance can be expected to have for the satisfaction of the particular inter-ests of each person affected must be such that all can accept them freely;[71]
[D] [O]nly those norms of action are valid to which all possibly affected per-sons could assent as participants in rational discourses.[72]

D as written is not quite a procedural equivalent or translation of U; rather, the two propositions jointly asserted reflect upon each other's meanings.[73]

But it is clear that the statements together characterize political justification in terms of *hypothetical* universal agreement, by those who stand to be affected and who reason correctly. And hypothetical consent based on correct reasoning is a substantive, not a procedural, test for the justified character of a set of fundamental laws. So if – as the U–D coupling apparently implies – liberal-individualist premises require that sort of test, then Habermas has no argument yet for a requirement of an actual democratic-procedural provenance for a set of fundamental laws. If anything, he has an argument *against* such a requirement. There is, after all, an obvious conceptual gap between a procedure designed to issue in a set of fundamental laws that can be rationally approved by everyone and a procedure designed to afford a full and equal part to everyone in fundamental lawmaking. An elitist institution could turn out to be just the ticket for the first requirement, even as the second would surely disqualify it. Whence, then, from here? How does Habermas get from here to the conclusion that "the democratic procedure for the production of law . . . forms the only post-metaphysical source of legitimacy?"

Does it help if one infers from the Habermasian U–D coupling that there is one and only one basic individual right to be satisfied by constitutional arrangements, namely, a procedural right to participate as an equal in political self-government? It does not. That proposed basic right has a democratic-procedural content, to be sure, but the fact of its being a basic right (if it be one) is not itself contingent on the performance or outcome of any democratic procedure. Liberal constitutional justice may or may not require that there be placed in operation a democratic procedure for the further determination of people's rights (and of other dimensions of the right in political arrangements) but no procedural fact of democratic debate or decision can settle whether or not it does. What settles that question can only be philosophical competence, or, in other words, reason.[74]

At this point, I think, liberal constitutional democrats have to alter slightly the question under consideration. From the question of a given regime's actual consonance with justice, in the liberally defined sense of all individuals' hypothetically having reason for their own to agree whether they know it or not, we move to the question of the moral justifiability of supporting the coercive regime in the face of actual unliquidated disagreement among individuals and population groups about whether the regime really does satisfy justice in that same sense. These two questions are obviously related in some way, but they are not identical, or at any rate liberals had better hope that they are not.

That is because of a fact, as I take it to be, related to what John Rawls calls "the fact of reasonable pluralism." I will call mine "the fact of reasonable interpretative pluralism." Rawls means that there are a plurality of conflicting but all of them reasonable, ethical-philosophical views – "comprehensive doctrines" – that develop and survive under free institutions.[75] Now, surely this fact has replicative consequences on the "lower" level of deciding on a codified set of fundamental laws or constitutional essentials that everyone has reason to agree to in the country's historical circumstances. Surely "burdens of judgment" guarantee unliquidatable reasonable disagreement on this "interpretative" level, too.[76] Consider, for example, a liberal bill of rights. Any such empirical-legal enumeration of rights must always, in the first place, offer an interpretation, for the country in its historical circumstances, of some more abstract conception of human right such as that adumbrated by Habermas through propositions U and D or by Rawls through the original position and the two principles of justice as fairness.[77] Given the burdens of judgment, the interpretations conveyed by the enumeration are bound to be in many respects reasonably contestable. (Consider the glaring differences among liberal constitutional democracies about whether or how to deal with property rights or positive social rights in a constitutional bill of rights.) Reasonable contestation must also attend major judicial interpretations of the enumerated articles – such as interpretation of "the equal protection of the laws" to mean a requirement of color-blind law.

Rawls posits reasonable pluralism as one of those general social facts that bear crucially upon people's reasons for agreeing or not to one or another set of public practical norms, and that thereby affect the very content of justice.[78] But, I want to suggest, the consequences of the burdens of judgment cannot be so confined. This fact about our situation has the further consequence of making nondemonstrable by public reasoning any authoritative truth about what it is that everyone in this country now has reason to agree to in the matter of legal basic-rights codifications and interpretations. I don't mean it makes truth in this matter *philosophically* unavailable, or beyond reasoned argument, or just a matter of opinion or desire or power. I mean it makes it *politically* unavailable among people who, aware of human frailty and burdens of judgment, all sharing "a desire to honor fair terms of cooperation," all sharing a belief that there is a truth of the matter of what those are, can neither all agree on what that is nor dismiss as unreasonable their opponents' positions.[79] The fact of reasonable interpretative pluralism thus opens a gap between the question of justice and the question of legitimacy, of what it would be morally right or justifiable for anyone to do about the matter of political coercion. What is more and what is worse, liberals by affirming reasonable interpretative pluralism (as it seems to me they must) present themselves with the possibility that there is no answer at all to the question of what it would be right for anyone or any society to do about this matter – or, in other words, that nothing that is done about it can be right or morally justifiable, that all there can be is facts of power. This, indeed, is what John Rawls calls "the problem of political liberalism."[80]

For liberals, the grim conclusion must be avoidable; but how do we escape it? If we can, it can only be by our being able to identify some possible attribute in a currently prevailing set of human-rights codifications and interpretations, *other than the reasonably contested attribute of actual congruence with justice,* that could underwrite the moral justifiability of acts in support of a coercive political regime that contains this set of codifications and interpretations. But then what could this other attribute be?

One might liberally think that acts in support of a prevailing set of human rights prescriptions are morally justified, as long as there is something about the set in virtue of which everyone is able to observe and abide by what it contains, not just out of desire to avoid legally administered punishment or loss but also out of consciously held "respect for" the interpretations. Habermas sometimes calls such a property in a legal regime its "validity."[81] But then what can confer validity on a regime of fundamental-legal enumerations and interpretations? What possible fact about the laws – apart from the unavailable one of public and certain knowledge of their conformity to justice – might make it possible for everyone to observe them out of respect for them, without regard to any adverse institutional consequences of nonobservance?

A possible such fact might be that the regime's human rights prescriptions are in some way made continuously accountable to an influential process of truly democratic critical reexamination that is fully receptive to everyone's perceptions of situation and interest and, relatedly, everyone's opinion about justice. Respectable reasons could be supplied why a well-advised, liberal-minded philosopher in search of constitutional justice would submit his efforts to such a critical review: first, a belief that only in the wake of democratic debate can anyone hope to arrive at a reliable approximation to true answers to questions of the justice of proposed constitutional norms, understood as consisting in their universalizability over everyone's interests or their hypothetical unanimous acceptability in a democratic discourse; and, second, that only in that way can anyone hope to gain a sufficient grasp of relevant historical conditions to produce for the country in question, in a legally workable form, an apt interpretation of whatever abstract practical norms can pass the justice tests of universalizability and democratic-discursive acceptability. (The epistemic or truth-seeking character of these reasons bears comparison with the Ackermanian constitutional populist's heuristic search in history for guidance to the will of the people now.) One might, with Habermas, conclude on the basis of such reasons that only the submissibility of the justice question at any time to an actual and influential democratic-discursive forum can sustain a validity-conferring "presumption" that nonunanimously enacted and nonunanimously interpreted constitutional laws are universally rationally acceptable.

I am not here making the claim that a regime's ongoing procedural-democratic accountability can in all truth justify collaboration in the coercive imposition of it on a contentious country. My claim is only that liberal constitutional democrats seem driven to the view that it can. Notice, though, that a response in this form to someone demanding justification for your support of a given constitutional regime can never be complete. A "truly democratic" process is itself inescapably a legally conditioned and constituted process. It is constituted, for example, by laws regarding political representation and elections, civil associations, families, freedom of speech, property, access to media, and so on. Thus, in order to confer legitimacy on a set of laws issuing from an actual set of discursive institutions and practices in a country, those institutions and practices would themselves have to be legally constituted in the right way. The laws regarding elections, representation, associations, families, speech, property, and so on, would have to be such as to constitute a process of more or less "fair" or "undistorted" democratic political communication, not only in the formal arenas of legislation and adjudication but in civil society at large.

The problem is that whether they do or not may itself at any time become a matter of contentious but reasonable disagreement, according to the liberal premise of reasonable interpretative pluralism. Examples abound in our constitutional law. Is the regime properly democratic only in the absence (as some claim) or only in the presence (as others claim) of state-administered corrections of market-based distributions of economic means? Only in the absence (or only in the presence) of affirmative action, or of cumulative voting or proportional representation? Only in the absence (or only in the presence) of federalism, separation of powers, and other checks and balances? In the absence (or in the presence) of gun control, or of regulation of political spending, or of guarantees of procreational autonomy, or of barriers to religious expression in public educational and other spaces? Lacking politically authoritative answers to questions such as those, how can we justify forceful imposition on the country of whatever answers we arrive at?

Only, it would seem, by establishing the validity of those answers, which again we would do by showing the continuous submissibility of them to the critical rigors of an influential, properly formed democratic debate. But then the question of what *is* a properly formed democratic debate still looms, and we are caught in an infinite regress of validity claims. Habermas is thoroughly aware of the problem. A legitimate legal order, he writes, is "one that has become reflexive with regard to the very process of institutionalization." "The idea of the rule of law sets in motion a spiraling self-application of law." "The citizens themselves . . . decide how they must fashion the rights that give the discourse principle legal shape as a principle of democracy. . . . [They] make an originary use of a civic autonomy that thereby constitutes itself in a performatively self-referential manner."[82] But then the question must be: Where in history can this "originary" constitutive moment – this founding act of citizens' authorship – ever be fixed or anchored?

Surely what we have here is pure abstraction, a transcendental-logical deduction necessitated by the prior determination of a thinker to think something. In Hans Kelsen's case it was that the constitution is grounded. In the case of Habermas – and he stands, I believe, for liberal constitutional democratic thought at large – it is that support of the constitution might somehow possibly be morally justified. Either way, we produce an author because we have to.

Notes

1 U.S. Const., Preamble.
2 Id. Art. VII.
3 Id. Art. VI, §2.
4 Id. Art. V.
5 See William F. Harris II, *The Interpretable Constitution* (Baltimore: Johns Hopkins University Press, 1993); Jed Rubenfeld, Chapter 5, this volume.
6 But the political-institutional and the related legal-textual senses of "constitution" are themselves nodes in a complex web of metaphor. Consider " 'Old Ironsides' has a strong constitution." Compare allusions by the American framers – e.g., by Hamilton in *The Federalist,* No. 78–to the "limited Constitution" they had fashioned for the country.
7 John Rawls, *Political Liberalism* (New York: Columbia University Press, 1993) 227.
8 Compare Richard Kay, Chapter 1, this volume. For a strong expression of this view, see Bruce Ackerman and David Golove, "Is NAFTA Constitutional?" *Harvard Law Review* 108 (1995): 799, 907 (raising the question of "why the Constitution deserves our respect in the first place" and beginning the answer with a reference to "constitutional self-consciousness"); id. at 908 (continuing the answer with a reference to "citizens" engaged in "a principled overhaul of constitutional arrangements"); id. at 916 (referring to "America's overriding commitment to popular sovereignty"); id. at 924 (reserving valid constitutional lawmaking for "those rare moments in American history when the mass of Americans get into the act").
9 For discussions of reasons that people might have for preferring not to monkey with an imperfect constitution currently in force – pertaining, for example, to the desirability of resolution and stability in the law – see Michael Perry, Chapter 3, this volume; Joseph Raz, Chapter 4, this volume; Russell Hardin, "Why a Constitution?" In Bernard Grofman and Donald Wittman, eds., *The Federalist Papers and the New Institutionalism* (New York: Agathon Press, 1989) 100. Compare Larry Alexander and Frederick Schauer, "On Extrajudicial Constitutional Interpretation," *Harvard Law Review* 110 (1997): 1359–87 (advancing similar reasons for a practice of "judicial supremacy" in constitutional interpretation).
10 Compare Lawrence G. Sager, "The Birth Logic of a Democratic Constitution," paper presented to the NYU Colloquium on Constitutional Theory, New York, February 1995; David R. Dow, "The Plain Meaning of Article V," in Sanford Levin-

son, ed., *Responding to Imperfection: The Theory and Practice of Constitutional Amendment* (Princeton, N.J.: Princeton University Press, 1995) 117, discussed in Frank I. Michelman, "Thirteen Easy Pieces," *Michigan Law Review* 93 (1995): 1297–1332, at 1315–17. See also Lawrence G. Sager, "The Incorrigible Constitution," *New York University Law Review* 65 (1990): 893–961, at 902 ("The claim of privilege [for popular will] . . . would have to be that popular will enjoyed a powerful advantage in accuracy or reliability [given a metric of what makes a political choice good] over other possible means of choosing among social options.") My express references to various of Professor Sager's writings do not fully convey their effect on my thinking about the matters discussed herein.

11 For an idea of how complex it is likely to be, see Kent Greenawalt, "The Rule of Recognition and the Constitution," *Michigan Law Review* 85 (1987): 621–71.

12 See Bruce Ackerman, "A Generation of Betrayal?" *Fordham Law Review* 65 (March, 1997): 1519–36.

13 See Hilary Putnam, *Reason, Truth, and History* 4–5 (Cambridge University Press, 1981).

14 The example is adapted from id. at 1.

15 For an example of an express theory of constitutional interpretation that exemplifies this model, see Lawrence Sager, Chapter 6, this volume. Interestingly, the model seems to uphold the "textualist sensibility of American constitutional culture," which Michael Perry urges that we try to maintain for the sake of the constraint it provides on the "awesome power of judicial review." See Perry, Chapter 3, this volume.

    A constitutional notion may or may not be considered to encompass such broadly applicable components of "public reason" as "general beliefs and forms of reasoning found in common sense" and widely accepted basic scientific theories and facts and prevailing canons of logical and material (social-causal) inference. See Rawls, *Political Liberalism* 224. If we define the notion strictly so that it does not include these, then the sources of the purpose-inputs required for constitutional-legal interpretations may be said to include not only the (authorless) constitutional notion but also these components of (equally authorless) public reason.

16 Hans Kelsen for some reason defined "norms" more narrowly, as "the [objective] meaning of acts of will that are directed toward the conduct of others." See Kelsen, "The Function of a Constitution," in Richard Tur and William Twining, eds., *Essays on Kelsen* (Oxford: Clarendon Press, 1986) 109–111. If, following Kelsen, you define "norm" to include only such directives as agents see issuing from some other agent's "act of will," then it becomes relatively easy to defeat any claim that the directive contents of regime-fixing constitutions are eo ipso "norms." All you then need do to defeat it is establish the possibility of agents taking direction from what they perfectly well know to be intentionlessly grown facts of social practice.

17 For pertinent analyses of variant usages, see Anthony J. Sebok, "Is the Rule of Recognition a Rule?" *Notre Dame Law Review* 72 (1997): 1539–63; Sebok, "Misunderstanding Positivism," *Michigan Law Review* 93 (1995): 2054–132; Jules L. Coleman, "Negative and Positive Positivism," *Journal of Legal Studies* 11 (1982): 139–64; and Frederick Schauer, "Constitutional Positivism," *Connecticut Law Review* 25 (1993): 797–841.

18 See Coleman, "Negative and Positive Positivism" 139.
19 What H. L. A. Hart calls "soft" positivism (in contradistinction to "plain-fact" positivism) allows for the *possibility* of a legal practice, properly so called, in which people's judgments of justice or morality do in fact figure in the processes of social acceptance that constitute the practice as a legal one. See H. L. A. Hart, "Postscript," in Penelope A. Bulloch and Joseph Raz, eds., *The Concept of Law,* 2d ed. (Oxford: Oxford University Press) 247, 250–1. What unites all legal positivists, on the definition I am offering here, is insistence that it is nevertheless, in the last analysis, only a fact of acceptance, and not anyone's consideration or judgment of the moral justifiability of the acceptance, that can and does essentially constitute certain social practices as legal ones.
20 This is a somewhat more elaborate version of the "separability thesis" in what Jules Coleman terms "negative positivism." See Coleman, "Negative and Positive Positivism" 140–3.
21 For example, this is how I understand Frederick Schauer, "Amending the Presuppositions of a Constitution," in Levinson, ed., *Responding to Imperfection* 145, 148–52 (referring to works of Hans Kelsen and H. L. A. Hart).
22 H. L. A. Hart, *The Concept of Law* (Oxford: Clarendon Press, 1961) 92, 96.
23 Cf. Jed Rubenfeld, Chapter 5, this volume.
24 Cf. Richard S. Kay, Chapter 1, this volume. For the contestation, see generally Levinson, ed., *Responding to Imperfection.* For Articles VII and V, see the epigraphs to this chapter.
25 My usage of "small-*c* constitution," which follows that of Frederick Schauer in "Amending the Presuppositions of a Constitution," should be contrasted with Michael Perry's distinction between "Constitution$_1$" (the words) and "Constitution$_2$" (the norms of supreme law, some but not all of which are gathered from directives recorded in the words). See Perry, Chapter 3, this volume.
26 Cf. Hart, "Postscript" 267 ("[S]urely . . . an American judge's reason for treating the Constitution as a source of law having supremacy over other sources includes the fact that his judicial colleagues concur in this as their predecessors have done"). Hart takes the view that conscious acceptance of the recognitional rule or practice as such need occur only among legal officials, those whose work requires them to determine whether a given norm is or is not part of the law, and not necessarily among the population at large who need only "obey." See Hart, *The Concept of Law* 110–13. The difference does not matter for any argument I make here.
27 Schauer "Amending the Presuppositions of a Constitution" 152.
28 For a respected journalist's account of the origins of the Constitution of South Africa, see Allister Sparks, *Tomorrow Is Another Country: The Inside Story of South Africa's Road to Change* (New York: Hill & Wang, 1995).
29 See, e.g., Bruce Ackerman and Neal Katyal, "Our Unconventional Founding," *University of Chicago Law Review* 62 (1995): 475–573; Akhil Reed Amar, to the contrary, argues vigorously (although not in these words) that the promulgation and ratification of the Constitution were in basic accord with a *preexisting* rule of recognition. See Amar, "The Consent of the Governed: Constitutional Amendment Outside Article V," *Columbia Law Review* 94 (1994): 457–508.
30 Cf. Alexander and Schauer, "Extrajudicial Constitutional Interpretation" 1370 ("[I]t is only the present [and not the past] that can constitute a legal order for a

population, and the question of what [has and should have] the status of law can only be decided non-historically").

31 For a recent vivid example of the view that a country's constitution *has to* contain the country's ultimate rule of recognition, see Laurence H. Tribe, "Taking Text and Structure Seriously: Reflections on Free-Form Method in Constitutional Interpretation," *Harvard Law Review* 108 (1995): 1221, 1246–7 (speaking of constitutional amendment): "[W]e must look to the Constitution to determine how [the institutions that it calls into being] are to operate and when their products are to be regarded as law. . . . We can know that something has the binding force of law only if it complies with the requirements that, as a matter of social fact, we have agreed must be met when a law is to be made. . . . Pending some upheaval [of revolutionary magnitude], the only such requirements for our polity are those that are, for the time being at least, embodied in our Constitution's text."

32 See Kelsen, "Function of a Constitution" 111.

33 Id. at 115.

34 Id. at 114–16. On the reduction, for these purposes, of small-*c* constitutions to their amending clauses, see id.; Peter Suber, *The Paradox of Self-Amendment: A Study of Law, Omnipotence, and Change* (New York: Peter Lang, 1990).

35 "Textoid," not "text" or "instrument," to make allowance both for textually nonreduced or noncodified (but still institutionally recognizable) constitutions like the British and for lawyers' knowledge that the political-legal-institutional Constitution of the United States is not confined to the instrument thus captioned but consists also of interpretative and other practices containing and surrounding the instrument.

36 Compare H. L. A. Hart, "Postscript" 242 ("[T]here is . . . nothing in the project of a descriptive jurisprudence . . . to preclude a non-participant external observer from describing the ways in which participants view the law from . . . an internal point of view").

37 See Ronald Dworkin, *Law's Empire* (Cambridge, Mass.: Harvard University Press, 1986) 176–224.

38 On "constitutional essentials," see Section 1 and note 7.

39 Cf. the distinction drawn by J. M. Balkin, "Populism and Progressivism as Constitutional Categories," *Yale Law Journal* 104 (1995): 1935–90.

40 See Richard D. Parker, *"Here the People Rule:" A Constitutional Populist Manifesto* (Cambridge, Mass.: Harvard University Press, 1994).

41 See Bruce Ackerman, *We the People: Foundations* (Cambridge, Mass.: Harvard University Press, 1991) 236, 260–2, 274–5, 285–8.

42 Ackerman, "Generation of Betrayal" 1519–20.

43 Id. at 1524.

44 Id. at 1522.

45 Id. at 1523 (emphasis added).

46 Id. at 1524.

47 See Bruce Ackerman, *We the People: Transformations* (Cambridge, Mass.: Harvard University Press, forthcoming).

48 Alexander M. Bickel, *The Least Dangerous Branch: The Supreme Court at the Bar of Politics* (Indianapolis: Bobbs-Merrill, 1962) 16–23.

49 Bruce Ackerman, "The Storrs Lectures: Discovering the Constitution," *Yale Law Journal* 93 (1984): 1013.

50 See Frank I. Michelman, "Foreword: Traces of Self-Government," *Harvard Law Review* 100 (1986): 4, 75 ("The Air Force is not us. Congress is not us. The President is not us. 'We' are not 'in' those bodies. Their determinations are not our self-government. Judges overriding those determinations do not, therefore, necessarily subtract anything from our freedom, although the judges also, obviously, are not us").

51 For a definitive discussion of the kind of heuristic or epistemic authority I am pointing at here, see Joseph Raz, *The Morality of Freedom* (Oxford: Clarendon Press, 1986) 21–105.

52 We noticed in Section II and note 24 that a minority of theorists hold to the view that Article V is not correctly construed as setting forth the exclusive procedural avenue to valid amendments of the Constitution. The minority theorists do not, however, all suggest that the Constitution, correctly construed, contains no binding amendment rule at all. In "The Consent of the Governed," Akhil Amar says the Constitution's rule is a deliberative majority vote.

53 See Ackerman, *Foundations* 204. Ackerman writes, it seems to me paradoxically, of "an entire People . . . break[ing] with its past and construct[ing] a new political identity for itself." See Michelman, "Thirteen Easy Pieces" 1325.

54 At the end of Section I.

55 Richard Kay, Chapter 1, this volume.

56 John Rawls is representative. From the coerciveness of politics, he writes, flows a moral duty of "civility" – "to be able to explain to one another," when "fundamental questions are at stake," how the "principles and policies we advocate can be supported" in the lights of "principles and ideals acceptable to [all] as reasonable and rational." Rawls, *Political Liberalism* 226. Cf. Christine Korsgaard, "Commentary on Cohen and Sen," in Martha Nussbaum and Amartya Sen, eds., *The Quality of Life* (Oxford: Clarendon Press, 1993) 54–61, at 55 ("Only the pursuit of certain kinds of aims, in special circumstances, can justify the use of coercion; only these, therefore, can be legitimate political objectives"); Bernard Manin, "On Legitimacy and Deliberation, *Political Theory* 15 (1987): 338–68, at 338 ("The most radical form of liberalism maintains that protection against arbitrary coercion is the sole common aim of human beings living in society").

57 See Rawls, *Political Liberalism* 73–4.

58 Cf. John Rawls on "full autonomy" in id. at 77–8. By honoring what they themselves have judged to be basic principles of justice in politics, Rawls says, citizens "show themselves autonomous, politically speaking." See Frank I. Michelman, "The Subject of Liberalism," *Stanford Law Review* 46 (1994): 1807–43, at 1826–30.

59 See Rawls, *Political Liberalism* 8 and n. 8.

60 See Jürgen Habermas, *Between Facts and Norms: Contributions to a Discourse Theory of Law and Democracy* (Cambridge, Mass.: MIT Press, 1996) 107, 447–8, 459, 566 n. 15.

61 I take the term "subjectless" from id. 486.

62 A vivid example is the Supreme Court's authority to decide, finally and independently, disagreements over the meaning of the Constitution, at least insofar as such disagreements bear on the actual or anticipated disposition of cases at law. This

obviously "bedrock" (see Michael Perry, Chapter 3, this volume) and also obviously "preconstitutional" (see Alexander and Schauer, "Extrajudicial Constitutional Interpretation" 1377) norm or feature of American constitutional practice is a constant topic of justificational discourse.

63 See Section II, note 16.

64 As, for example, Bruce Ackerman finds wrong our small-*c* constitution's commitment to "dualist democracy" as opposed to "rights-foundationalism" (see Bruce Ackerman, "Rooted Cosmopolitanism," *Ethics* 104 (1994): 516, 535) and both Ackerman and David Abraham find wrong its cast against positive rights against the state (see Abraham, "Liberty without Equality: The Property-Rights Connection in a 'Negative Citizenship' Regime," *Law and Social Inquiry* 21 [1996]: 1–65).

65 See Alexander and Schauer, "On Extrajudicial Constitutional Interpretation."

66 See Amy Gutmann and Dennis Thompson, *Democracy and Disagreement* (Cambridge, Mass.: Harvard University Press, 1996): 2–3; Michelman, "Thirteen Easy Pieces" 1325–6.

67 See Lawrence G. Sager, Chapter 6, this volume; Sotirios Barber, "Justice-Seeking Constitutionalism and Its Critics," paper presented at the Colloquium on Constitutional Theory, New York University, April 20, 1995; Anthony J. Sebok, "Justice-Seeking Constitutional Theory and the Problem of Fit," paper presented at the Colloquium on Constitutional Theory.

68 Jürgen Habermas, "Reconciliation Through the Public Use of Reason: Remarks on John Rawls's Political Liberalism," *Journal of Philosophy* 92 (1995): 109–31, at 128.

69 Habermas, *Between Facts and Norms* 448.

70 It by no means follows that Habermas is an anthropological "atomist," which of course he is not. Liberal thought as I am now rendering it easily accommodates, as exemplified by the thought of Habermas, a "relational" view of human severalty, one that fully recognizes the importance of groups and relationships in the lives of individuals, the existence of co-dependencies not only among individuals' interests but among their consciousnesses of self – the "symmetrical relations of recognition," and their consequences, that are "built into communicatively structured forms of life in general." Id. at 109.

71 Id. at 447–8, 566 n. 15.

72 Id. at 107, 459.

73 Suggesting, for example, such possibilities as that "rational" discourses in D are the set of procedures that issue in unanimous assent to a norm if and only if that norm satisfies U, or that "free" acceptance in U is acceptance that would issue from a D-type rational discourse.

74 It is worth pointing out that the conflict here is between reason and procedural-sense democracy, not between philosophical competence and individual self-government. My self-government depends on my having, on due reflection, approved the fundamental laws of my country as true laws of justice, and that condition can be satisfied by the very sort of Rawlsian grounding for constitutional principles – everyone arrives separately at a reflective considered judgment that some or other philosopher has gotten them right – that Habermas has said he finds democratically wanting.

75 See Rawls, *Political Liberalism* 36–7, 60.

76 "Burdens of judgment" are the causes of unliquidatable disagreement about contestable questions among persons who, as reasonable, all observe and report honestly, argue cogently, and share "a desire to honor fair terms of cooperation." Among the causes Rawls posits is the following: "To some extent (how great we cannot tell) the way we assess evidence and weigh moral and political values is shaped by our total [life] experience, . . . and our total experiences must always differ. Thus, in a modern society with its numerous offices and positions, its various divisions of labor, its many social groups and their ethnic variety, citizens' total experiences are disparate enough for their judgments to diverge, at least to some degree, on many if not most cases of any significant complexity." Id. at 55–7.

77 See John Rawls, *A Theory of Justice* (Cambridge, Mass.: Harvard University Press, 1971) 291.

78 See id. at 36. The fact of reasonable pluralism, for example, gives people reasons for accepting entrenched norms of toleration that they might not otherwise have.

79 See id. at 55.

80 See id. at xviii.

81 See Habermas, *Between Facts and Norms* 448.

82 Habermas, *Between Facts and Norms* 39, 74, 128.

3

What Is "the Constitution"?
(and Other Fundamental Questions)

MICHAEL J. PERRY

Several of the most divisive *moral* conflicts that have beset us Americans in the period since the end of World War II have been transmuted into *constitutional* conflicts – conflicts about what the Constitution of the United States forbids – and resolved as such. The most prominent instances include the conflicts over racial segregation, affirmative action, sex-based discrimination, homosexuality, abortion, and physician-assisted suicide, each of which has been resolved – at least in part, and at least for a time – on the basis of a claim about what the Fourteenth Amendment forbids. Which of the conflicts, if any, understood as constitutional conflicts, have been resolved as they should have been resolved – that is, which have been resolved on the basis of *the Constitution* as they should have been resolved? If one wants, as I do, to pursue that inquiry, one must first answer three questions: What is "the Constitution"? What does it mean to interpret the Constitution? Is the Supreme Court supreme in interpreting the Constitution? Although this chapter is, then, preparatory, the questions I address here – connected questions – are fundamental.

I. What Is "the Constitution"?

A. Herein of the Constitution$_1$ and the Constitution$_2$

The referent of the phrase "the Constitution of the United States" is sometimes the document – the text – called the Constitution of the United States. But the referent is sometimes – indeed, often – the norms that constitute "the supreme Law of the Land." (Article VI of the Constitution declares, "This Constitution . . . shall be the supreme Law of the Land. . . .") That there is no disagreement about what sentences the Constitution in the first sense (the Constitution$_1$) contains[1] does not mean that there is no disagreement about what norms the Constitution in the second sense (the Constitution$_2$) consists of. The Constitution$_1$ (the document called the Constitution) is not identical to the Constitution$_2$ (the norms that constitute "the supreme Law").

What is the Constitution$_2$ – what norms does it consist of? The Preamble to the Constitution (the Constitution$_1$) declares, "We the people of the United States ... do ordain and establish this Constitution for the United States of America."[2] In American constitutional culture, few if any persons – even, remarkably, few if any constitutional theorists – disagree that the norms the Constitution$_2$ consists of include at least some directives issued by – that is, some norms "ordained and established" by – "We the people." More to the point, few disagree that the Constitution$_2$ consists of some such norms partly because the norms were "ordained and established" by "We the people."[3] It is now a convention – an axiom – of American constitutional culture that "We the people of the United States" not only "do ordain and establish this Constitution for the United States of America" but *may* ordain and establish it. This is not to say that *only* "We the people" may establish norms as constitutional. I will say more about that later.[4]

What directives have "We the people" issued, what norms have they established? When "We the people," through their representatives, put words into the Constitution$_1$, they do so for the purpose of issuing – and, in that sense, establishing – one or more constitutional directives. The Constitution$_1$, in each and all of its various parts, is the yield of political acts of a certain sort: acts intended to establish not merely particular configurations of words but, ultimately, particular norms, namely, the norms that "We the people" understood – or would have understood, had they been engaged, had they been paying attention – the particular configurations of words to communicate. Does anyone really believe that were *we* to amend the Constitution$_1$ in our day, it might be a political act of a different sort: an act intended to establish not, ultimately, a particular norm but merely a particular configuration of words? If not, why would anyone believe that when *they* amended the Constitution$_1$ in their day, they acted to establish merely a particular configuration of words? Establishing, in a political or legal document, a norm to govern the future – unlike establishing, in such a document, merely a particular configuration of words – is a recognizably human act. "[I]t is hard to think of any recommendation for a regime of law created by the 'interpretation' of disembodied words that have been methodically severed from the acts of mind that produced them."[5] Therefore, the norm (or norms) that "We the people" established, in putting a particular configuration of words into the Constitution$_1$, is the norm they understood (or would have understood) their words to communicate. They did not establish a norm they would not have understood their words to communicate. In what sense would "We the people of the United States ... ordain and establish this Constitution for the United States of America" if the norm they are deemed to have established is one they would not have understood their words to communicate?[6]

B. Why Bow to Old Constitutional Directives? And Why Issue New Ones?

I said that few if any persons disagree that the norms the Constitution (the Constitution$_2$) consists of include some directives issued by "We the people of the United States." (From here on, I will use the subscript only occasionally, for emphasis. It should be clear from the context whether I am referring to the Constitution as law, as a set of legal norms [the Constitution$_2$], or simply as a text, a statement [the Constitution$_1$].) The "people of the United States" who did "ordain and establish" the Constitution in 1787–9 – and the Bill of Rights in 1789–91 – are long dead. So, too, are the people who amended the Constitution in the aftermath of the Civil War. (They amended the Constitution$_1$ so as to amend the Constitution$_2$.) Why, then, should *we,* the people of the United States *now living,* accept constitutional directives issued by persons long dead as our "supreme Law of the Land"?[7] Some of the directives of which the Constitution consists, including some of the oldest ones, are directives that we, the people of the United States now living, should want to be a part of our constitution if they were not a part of it already. In the view of some of us, however, not every directive that is a part of our constitution should be a part of it.[8] Why should those of us who believe that a directive should not be a part of our constitution bow to the directive – that is, bow to it unless and until we succeed in disestablishing the directive in a constitutionally ordained way? Put another way, why should we follow the convention established by the directive? Why shouldn't we follow a different, competing convention – one not established by the Constitution but, nonetheless, more to our liking?

We might try to change the existing convention by amending the Constitution in a constitutionally ordained way – for example, in the way ordained by Article V.[9] But to pursue that strategy is to follow a convention established by the Constitution. The question at hand, however, is whether we should follow a convention not established by the Constitution that competes with a constitutionally established convention. Why should we do *that?* Why should those of us who believe that a directive should not be a part of our constitution bow to the directive unless/until it is disestablished in a constitutionally ordained way? Why shouldn't we (or our representatives) try to disestablish the directive in a way that is not constitutionally ordained? (In what way that is not constitutionally ordained?) Indeed, why shouldn't we try to establish a new constitutional directive in a way that is not constitutionally ordained?

The most basic reason for bowing to a constitutional directive, unless/until it is disestablished in a constitutionally ordained way, is practical.

Contracts are generally backed by external sanctions; constitutions are more nearly backed by default, by the difficulty of recoordinating on an alternative arrangement. . . . [O]nce we have settled on a constitutional arrangement, it is not likely to be in the interest of some of us then to try to renege on the arrangement. And this is generally true not because we will be coerced to abide if we choose not to but because we generally cannot do better than to abide. To do better, we would have to carry enough others with use to set up an alternative, and that will typically be too costly to be worth the effort.[10]

Trying to disestablish a constitutional directive or to establish a new one in a way that is not constitutionally ordained would be an exemplary instance of "try[ing] to renege on the arrangement." Because to succeed in that effort "we would have to carry enough others with us to set up an alternative, and that will typically be too costly to be worth the effort," it is not surprising that there is no significant support – nor, without a severe constitutional crisis, is there ever likely to be such support – for disestablishing or establishing a constitutional directive in an other than constitutionally ordained way. Those of us who believe that an existing directive should not be a part of our constitution usually have no option but to bow to the directive (unless/until it is disestablished in a constitutionally ordained way), because "we generally cannot do better than to [do so[." Similarly, those of us who believe that a directive should be a part of our constitution usually have no option but to bow to the fact that the directive is not a part of our constitution (unless/until it is established in a constitutionally ordained way) because "we generally cannot do better than to [do so]."[11] This is not to deny, however, that in truly extraordinary circumstances (e.g., a revolution, a civil war, or a great depression) some of us could disestablish a directive, or could establish one, in an other than constitutionally ordained way.[12] For example, Bruce Ackerman has argued – persuasively, in my view – that the Fourteenth Amendment was neither proposed by Congress nor ratified by the states in full accord with the requirements of Article V.[13] (Ackerman's project is not to challenge the constitutional status of the Fourteenth Amendment, but to demonstrate that the ways in which "We the people of the United States . . . do ordain and establish this Constitution for the United States of America" are sometimes different from, and more complex than, those authorized by Article V.) Moreover, it is almost certainly the case that in at least a few instances Supreme Court justices have disestablished a directive, or have established one, or have done both. I will say more about this state of affairs in Subsection C of this section.

We can disestablish a constitutional directive, in a constitutionally ordained way, without establishing (issuing) a new directive in its place. However, some day we might want to establish a constitutional directive (whether or not in place of an existing one). What reasons might we have for wanting to establish the directive as a *constitutional* directive – for wanting to establish it, that is, not, or not merely, by means of an ordinary statute, but by means of a constitutional amendment?

Whereas a statute typically may be revised or repealed by a legislative majority, national constitutions typically require much more than a legislative majority to amend the constitution. According to Article V of the Constitution, for example, "The Congress, whenever two thirds of both Houses shall deem it necessary, shall propose Amendments to this Constitution, or, on the Application of the Legislatures of two thirds of the several States, shall call a Convention for proposing Amendments, which, in either Case, shall be valid to all Intents and Purposes, as Part of this Constitution, when ratified by the Legislatures of three fourths of the several states, or by Conventions in three fourths thereof, as the one or the other Mode of Ratification may be proposed by the Congress. . . ."[14] For us to establish a directive by means of a constitutional amendment, then, is for us to try to make it especially difficult, both for ourselves at a later time and for our political descendants at a much later time, to disestablish the directive. Opting for the constitutional strategy rather than for, or merely for, the statutory one is to decree that the directive may be disestablished, not by a legislative majority acting through the ordinary politics of legislative revision, but only by a supermajority acting through the extraordinary politics of constitutional amendment.[15]

What reasons might we have for wanting to make it so difficult to disestablish a directive? We might be skeptical about the capacity of our ordinary, majoritarian politics to safeguard the directive adequately, especially during politically stressful times when the directive might be most severely challenged. We might fear that, at some time in the future, we who are so enthusiastic about the directive – for example, a directive expressly limiting the power of government – might lose our political dominance and that those who take our place might be hostile to the directive. We might fear too that even if we hold on to our political dominance, our political representatives, over whom we exert imperfect control, might fail to safeguard the directive adequately. In short, we might distrust – we might lack faith in – our (future) politics.

Not that there aren't other reasons for pursuing the constitutional strategy. For example, a political community might need to establish, or to reestablish, its basic institutions, institutional arrangements, and practices, so that its day-to-day politics might then begin, or begin again, to operate. Or it might want to remove certain issues from the agenda of its ordinary politics because it fears, not that its politics cannot be trusted to resolve the issues, but that a contest about how they should be resolved might tear or even destroy the bonds of community.[16] Even when a political community has already established its basic institutions, institutional arrangements, and practices, however, and even when it has no reason to fear that a contest about how a certain issue should be resolved might tear, much less destroy, the bonds of community, the community might be skeptical about the capacity of its ordinary, majoritarian politics, especially during stressful times, to safeguard adequately a directive the community deems important. In a federal political community, like our own, such skepticism might focus, at one time, less on the capacity of the politics of the states to safeguard a directive than on the capacity of the politics of the national government to do so. At another time, it might focus more on the capacity of the politics of the states, or of some of them.

C. *What Norms Does the Constitution₂ Consist of?*

Again, few if any persons disagree that the norms the Constitution consists of include some directives established by "We the people" (and that it includes some such norms partly because they were "ordained and established" by "We the people"). However, that the Constitution consists of some such norms does not entail that it consists *only* of such norms. As I now explain, few constitutional scholars disagree that the Constitution consists of at least some fundamental norms that were probably never established by "We the people." (Although few scholars disagree that the Constitution consists of at least some such norms, whether one or another norm was established by "We the people" is often a matter of controversy – as is the question whether one or another norm not so established is nonetheless a part of the Constitution.)

Under what circumstances, if any, is it legitimate for the Supreme Court to strike down as unconstitutional a law or other governmental action on the basis of a norm that, in the Court's view, is not part of the Constitution that was "ordained" and "established" by "We the people of the United States" through their political representatives – that is, a norm that no generation of "We the people" understood, or would have understood, themselves to be establishing in putting particular words into the text of the Constitution? In our constitutional culture, it would be extremely difficult to justify such an action. It is widely accepted among us that "We the people of the United States" – not "We the justices of the Supreme Court" – should "ordain and establish" the Constitution of the United States.[17] By what right, then, would the Court impose on a branch of the national government – or even on state government – a norm that in its view no generation of "We the people" had ever established?[18]

The issue, however, is rarely so simple. Assume that, a generation or even longer ago, the Supreme Court struck down as unconstitutional a law or other governmental action on the basis of a norm that, in the view of the Court today, is no part of the Constitution ordained and established by "We the people." It doesn't matter, to the inquiry I want to pursue here, whether the past Court based its decision on an honest but mistaken view about what norm the text of a constitutional provision was understood to establish, or on pretense – a lie – about what norm the provision was understood to establish, or on an unreasonable specification of an indeterminate constitutional norm,[19] or even on a theory of constitutional adjudication according to which the Court may enforce, in the name of the Constitution, norms that no one, past or present, could fairly understand any language in the Constitution to establish. Under what circumstances, if any, should the Court today acquiesce in that old ruling rather than overrule it? Few constitutional scholars insist that the Court should never acquiesce in old constitutional rulings it now believes to have been wrong; the disputed question is when – under what conditions – the Court should do so.[20]

I don't mean to provide an exhaustive answer here, but I do want to float one suggestion: If, over time, the practice or the premise decreed by the old, wrong (at the time) ruling has become such a fixed and widely affirmed and relied-upon (by us the people of the United States now living)[21] feature of the life of our political community that the premise (or the practice) is, for us, bedrock, then the premise has achieved a virtual constitutional status;[22] it has become a part of our fundamental law – the law that is constitutive of ourselves as a political community of a certain sort.[23] Such a premise ought not now to be overturned by the Court. Even Robert Bork has argued that some mistaken constitutional precedents "have become so embedded in the life of the nation, so accepted by the society, so fundamental to the private and public expectations of individuals and institutions, that the result should not be changed now."[24] (Because Article V's processes of constitutional amendment are supermajoritarian, for the Court to overturn such a premise would be for it to empower a minority to impede the reestablishment of the premise as a part of our constitutional law. Perhaps ultimately the minority would fail, but given the reality of so much of our politics – logrolling, sound bites, demogoguery, and so on – one couldn't be sure.) Moreover, after declining to overturn such a premise, the Court should not treat the premise as a sport and refuse to go further.[25] By hypothesis, we are talking about a premise that has achieved a virtual constitutional status, that has become a part of our fundamental law. It would be anomalous, therefore, for the Court to refuse to weave the premise into the fabric of the constitutional law that, in its "common law" mode, the Court develops over time.

What premises would satisfy the condition articulated in the preceding paragraph? What premises are constitutional bedrock for us the people of the United States now living – and would remain so even if all of us who pay attention to such things came to be persuaded that no constitutional norm established by "We the people" warranted the premises?

- Consider, for example, the premise that the privileges and immunities – the rights and freedoms – protected against the national government by the Bill of Rights are protected against state government by the Fourteenth Amendment. It has been controversial whether that or any similar premise was, as the Supreme Court's "incorporation" jurisprudence holds, established by the Fourteenth Amendment. I believe that the premise was established by the Fourteenth Amendment,[26] but even if we were to discover tomorrow that it was not – that the generation of "We the people" that made the Fourteenth Amendment a part of the Constitution did not understand the amendment to communicate any such premise – the premise is now constitutional bedrock; no Court would (or should) overturn it.[27]

• Consider in particular the premise that not only the national government, but state government too, may not establish religion or prohibit the free exercise thereof or abridge the freedom of speech or the freedom of the press. It is at least somewhat controversial whether, even if the Fourteenth Amendment made (i.e., was meant to make) applicable to the states the norms, or some of the norms, made applicable to the national government by the Second through Eighth Amendments of the Bill of Rights, the Fourteenth Amendment made the norms of the First Amendment applicable to the states.[28] But even if we were to discover tomorrow that, contrary to what the historical record seems to show[29] and to what the Court's rulings have long affirmed, the Fourteenth Amendment did not "incorporate" the First Amendment, thereby making its norms applicable to the states, the premise that First Amendment norms are applicable to the states – that no state may establish religion or prohibit the free exercise thereof or abridge the freedoms of speech and of the press – is constitutional bedrock for us the people of the United States now living; no Court would (or should) overturn it.

• Finally, consider the premise that whatever antidiscrimination norm is applicable to state government under the Fourteenth Amendment is applicable to the national government as well. The Supreme Court has hung this premise on the due-process provision of the Fifth Amendment, which states that "[n]o person shall be . . . deprived of life, liberty, or property, without due process of law. . . ."[30] However, it is implausible that the due process provision of the Fifth Amendment – which, unlike the Fourteenth, applies to the national government – was understood by the generation of "We the people" that made the Fifth Amendment a part of the Constitution (the founding generation) to communicate any antidiscrimination norm, much less the same antidiscrimination norm established by a later generation of "We the people" when they made the Fourteenth Amendment a part of the Constitution.[31] I argue elsewhere that a historically accurate reading of the Ninth Amendment, mediated by a modest judicial strategy for determining what unenumerated rights against the national government are "retained by the people," warrants subjecting the national government to the same antidiscrimination norm to which state government is subject under the Fourteenth Amendment.[32] But even if we were to discover tomorrow that no constitutional norm established by "We the people" warrants doing so, the premise that the same antidiscrimination norm that applies to state government also applies to the national government is now constitutional bedrock and no Court would (or should) overturn it.

Whatever other premises satisfy the condition I have sketched here,[33] the three fundamental premises just listed surely do satisfy it.

I mean the condition articulated here to be a sufficient condition for the Court's acquiescing in mistaken constitutional precedent, not a necessary condition. I am presently agnostic about whether it should also be a necessary condition.[34] It does seem to me that the condition is appropriately stringent. Nonetheless, there would doubtless be self-serving and implausible, even frivolous, claims to the effect that a premise is, for us the people of the United States now living, constitutional bedrock and ought not to be overturned by the Court.[35] But that even most such claims would be implausible does not entail that no such claim would be compelling. One might doubt that the premises to which I referred in the preceding paragraph are "mistaken" constitutional precedents. But whether or not they are – and, so, even if they are – mistaken, the premises are, for us the people of the United States now living, constitutional bedrock.

Although, as I have said, the Constitution consists of norms established by "We the people" (and not subsequently disestablished by them) in a constitutionally ordained way, it does not consist only of such norms. Both as a description of our practice and as a prescription for the continuance of the practice, the Constitution also consists of premises that, whether or not any generation of "We the people" meant to establish them in the Constitution, and, so, even if no generation of "We the people" meant to establish them, have become such fixed and widely affirmed and relied-upon (by us the people of the United States now living) features of the life of our political community that they are, for us, constitutional bedrock – premises that have, in that sense, achieved a virtual constitutional status, that have become a part of our fundamental law, the law constitutive of ourselves as a political community of a certain sort. If such a premise is inconsistent with a norm established in the past by "We the people," the premise has, in our practice, lexical priority.[36]

II. What Does It Mean to Interpret the Constitution?

A. *Interpreting the Constitution$_1$*

If one wants to argue that a governmental action – for example, a state law – violates the Constitution$_2$, the least controversial basis on which to do so, in American constitutional culture, is a norm established as a part of the Constitution$_2$ by "We the people." Certainly the least problematic basis on which the Supreme Court can rely in invalidating a governmental action is such a norm. (As I mentioned earlier, it is widely accepted among us that "We the people of the United States" – not "We the justices of the Supreme Court" – should "ordain and establish" the Constitution of the United States.) "We the people," through their representatives, sometimes put words into the Constitution$_1$ that, even after more than two hundred years, succeed in communicating, without much interpretive inquiry by readers of the words, the norm that "We the people" understood the words to communicate and, through their representatives, meant to establish. Two such provisions are the part of Article I, Section 3, that states that "[t]he Senate of the United States shall be composed of two Senators from each State" and the part of Article II, Section 1, that states that "neither shall any person be eligible to that Office [of President] who shall not have attained to the Age of thirty-five Years." Thus, we may say that the sentence "The Senate of the United States shall be composed of two Senators from each State" is a part of the Constitution$_1$ and the norm that the Senate of the United States shall be composed of two senators from each state is a part of the Constitution$_2$. To say (as I did in Section I.A) that the Constitution$_1$ is not identical to the Constitution$_2$ is not to say that every provision of the Constitution$_1$ must undergo a significant interpretive inquiry – that every provision must be decoded or translated – if we are to discern what norm the provision was understood to communicate.

Sometimes, however, constitutional language does not communicate, without significant interpretive inquiry, the norm that "We the people" understood (or would have understood) it to communicate; sometimes a constitutional provision is, if not opaque, at least vague or, especially, ambiguous and so must be clarified. (The unintelligibility of a text is not necessarily either–or; it can be, and often is, a matter of degree.) Concomitantly, sometimes we readers of a constitutional provision can reasonably disagree, even after significant interpretive exertions, about what norm "We the people" understood a provision to communicate. Consider, for example, that part of the First Amendment that forbids government to "prohibit[ ] the free exercise [of religion]."[37] It is safe to assume that the free-exercise language was not understood to communicate a norm forbidding government to prohibit each and every imaginable religious practice. (One need not concoct frightening hypotheticals about human sacrifice to dramatize the point. One need only point, for example, to the refusal of Christian Science parents to seek readily available lifesaving medical care for their gravely ill child.)[38] What norm, then, was the free-exercise language understood to communicate? The language is ambiguous about what directive "We the people" meant to issue, what norm they meant to establish. Was it a norm forbidding government to engage in prohibitory action that discriminates against religious practice – that is, that disfavors religious practice *as such:* as religious practice, practice embedded in and expressive of one or more religious beliefs?[39] Or was it a broader norm, one that forbids, in addition to prohibitory action that discriminates against religious practice, at least some prohibitory action that, although nondiscriminatory, nonetheless impedes religious practice?[40] The position of five justices of the Supreme Court, in 1990, was that the free-exercise language represents a norm that forbids only discriminatory action. The position of the remaining four justices – and of the Congress that, in 1993, passed the Religious Freedom Restoration Act and of the president who signed it into law – was that the free-exercise norm also forbids some nondiscriminatory action that impedes religious practice.[41]

Consider next Section 1 of the Fourteenth Amendment, which states, among other things, that "[a]ll persons born or naturalized in the United States, and subject to the jurisdiction thereof, are citizens of the United States and of the State wherein they reside" and that "[n]o State shall make or enforce any law which shall abridge the privileges or immunities of citizens of the United States." We the people of the United States now living cannot discern what norm "We the people" then living understood the privileges-or-immunities language to communicate without strenuous interpretive inquiry, because we cannot know, without such inquiry, what the particular generation of "We the people" who put the language into the Constitution – the generation that had just lived through the Civil War and the abolition of slavery – understood the phrase "the privileges or immunities of citizens of the United States" to mean. We need to pursue a clarification of the language, which, by itself, is ambiguous about what norm they, through their representatives, meant to establish. Does the privileges-or-immunities norm they established protect only the privileges and immunities that persons who are citizens of the United States are due under the law, including the Constitution, of the United States?[42] Or does it protect not only those privileges and immunities, but also all the privileges and immunities that persons who are citizens of the United States are due under the law of the state "wherein they reside"? Or does it protect, if not all the privileges and immunities citizens are due under the law of their state, at least some of them – and, if so, which ones?[43]

And whatever privileges and immunities are protected by the privileges-or-immunities norm that "We the people" established, what kind or kinds of state legislation does the privileges-or-immunities norm established by "We the people" protect the protected privileges and immunities from or against: laws that discriminate on a racist basis? laws that discriminate on the basis of race, whether or not the discrimination is "racist"? some other kinds of discriminatory laws, too? (what kinds?) even some kinds of nondiscriminatory laws? (what kinds?)[44] And who – what class of persons – does the norm protect: just citizens of the United States (all of whom are also citizens of the state wherein they reside) or all persons? (The very same sentence that contains the privileges-or-immunities language also contains this language: "[N]or shall any State deprive *any person* of life, liberty, or property, without due process of law; nor deny to *any person* within its jurisdiction the equal protection of the laws" [emphasis added].) The language of the privileges-or-immunities provision is undeniably limited to the privileges and immunities *of* such citizens (whatever those privileges and immunities are). But the language does not preclude the possibility that the norm the language was understood to communicate is not limited *to* such citizens. As John Ely has put the point: " 'No State shall make or enforce any law which shall abridge the privileges or immunities of citizens of the United States' *could* mean that only citizens are protected in their privileges or immunities, but it surely doesn't have to. It could just as easily mean that there is a set of entitlements, 'the privileges and immunities of citizens of the United States,' which states are not to deny to anyone. In other words, the reference to citizens may define the class of rights rather than limit the class of beneficiaries."[45]

Sometimes, therefore, it will be necessary for us readers of the text of a constitutional provision to engage in a difficult historical inquiry into what norm the provision was understood to communicate by the generation of "We the people" that (through its representatives) put the provision into the Constitution. It is simply not true of every constitutional provision, even though it is true of many, that the question of the norm the provision was understood to communicate can usefully be answered by a statement of what the provision says. Referring to Article II, Section 1, of the Constitution, which states that "[n]o person except a natural born Citizen . . . shall be eligible to the Office of President," John Ely has observed that "[u]nless we know whether 'natural born' meant born to American parents on the one hand or born married parents on the other, we don't know what the ratifiers thought they were ratifying and thus what we should recognize as the constitutional command."[46]

Interpreting the text of a constitutional provision, in the sense of inquiring what norm "We the people" (probably) understood, or would have understood, the provision to communicate – and therefore what norm they meant to establish – has sometimes been confused with a different inquiry, namely, what the generation of "We the people" that established a constitutional norm would have believed to be the correct way of resolving, on the basis of the norm, a conflict that besets us today, a conflict that implicates the norm.[47] What they would have believed to be the correct way of resolving our conflict is not irrelevant, because knowing what they would have believed might help us discern better than we otherwise could the precise contours of the norm they (through their representatives) established; in particular, it might help us discern how wide their norm is, or how narrow. What finally matters, however, is not what they would have believed to be the correct way of resolving

(on the basis of their norm) our conflict, but what norm they established. After all, if "We the people" in the past would have believed X to be the correct
answer, on the basis of a norm they issued, to a conflict that besets us today,
they might have been mistaken about the contextual requirements of the
norm, just as we today might be mistaken about the contextual requirements
of a norm.

Sometimes readers of the text of a constitutional provision will have to
mine historical materials that are scant or equivocal or both in their effort
to discern what norm the provision was (or would have been) understood to
communicate by the generation of "We the people" that (through its representatives) put the provision into the Constitution.[48] As students of American
constitutional law are well aware, readers who pursue such an inquiry, even
readers who pursue it altogether dispassionately, might end up disagreeing
among themselves – *reasonably* disagreeing – about what norm the provision
was understood to communicate. There seems to be ample room, with respect
to some parts of the Constitution, for reasonable disagreement about what
norms the provisions were understood to communicate.[49] I return to this point
later (Section III.B), in discussing the Supreme Court's role in constitutional
adjudication.

Two paragraphs back, I began: "Interpreting the text of a constitutional provision, *in the sense of inquiring what norm "We the people" (probably) understood, or would have understood, the provision to communicate – and therefore what norm they meant to establish.* . . . One can "interpret" the text of a
constitutional provision in a different sense of the term, however: One can inquire what norm the provision in question is now taken to represent – or what
norm it shall hereafter be taken to represent. The conjunction of two factors
makes it virtually inevitable that the Supreme Court will "interpret" some
provisions of the Constitution in the second sense of the term rather than in
the first sense. First, there is the fact that, as I explained in Section I.C, some
premises have achieved the status of constitutional bedrock even if no generation of "We the people" meant to establish them. Second, there is the textualist sensibility of American constitutional culture, which Andrezj Rapaczynski
has described:

[J]udges sometimes admit that constitutional interpretation is sensitive to historical
evolution and that history adds a "gloss" on the text. But they never admit to deriving
the authority for their decisions from outside the constitutional text. . . . Instead, any
new result is unfailingly presented as a new and better *interpretation* of the text itself. . . . This behavior of judges is very significant because it expresses their belief
that purely noninterpretive [i.e., nontextualist] review would constitute an abuse of
their power and undermine the legitimacy of judicial review. In this belief, moreover,
they are very likely to be right.[50]

It ought not to be surprising, given the textualist sensibility of American constitutional culture, that even when the Supreme Court believes that a premise that has become constitutional bedrock for us was probably never established by any generation of "We the people," the Court will nonetheless refer the premise to some provision of the Constitution. The Court will impute the premise to some linguistically opportune piece of the constitutional text – to some configuration of words that the Court believes or hopes will bear the imputed meaning – which thereafter is taken by the Court to represent the premise. Consider a prominent example of this phenomenon: Whatever the "original" understanding of the due-process language of the Fifth Amendment, for example – whatever norm(s) the generation of "We the people" that put that language into the Constitution understood the language to communicate or establish – the language is now taken to represent (whatever else it is now taken to represent) a fundamental premise that no one, not even Supreme Court justices, can reasonably believe was any part of the original understanding of the language, namely, that whatever antidiscrimination norm is applicable to state government under the Fourteenth Amendment is applicable to the national government as well.[51]

B. Interpreting (Specifying) the Constitution$_2$

I said that interpreting the text of a constitutional provision – in the sense of inquiring what norm the provision was understood to communicate – should not be confused with inquiring what the generation of "We the people" that established a constitutional norm would have believed to be the correct way of resolving, on the basis of the norm, a conflict that besets us today. There is something else that interpreting the text of a constitutional provision should not be confused with: "specifying" (as I call it) a constitutional norm in the context of a conflict in which the norm is implicated but in which it is also indeterminate. Just as the Constitution$_1$ is not identical to the Constitution$_2$, so too constitution$_1$al interpretation is not identical to constitution$_2$al interpretation.

Assume that we agree – or, at least, that we accept for the sake of argument – that the relevant constitutional norm is X. For present purposes, it suffices to say that X is determinate in the context of a conflict that implicates it if persons who agree about both (a) what the relevant facts of the conflict – the "adjudicative" facts – are[52] and (b) what the other relevant legal norms, if any, are and what the implications of those other norms are for the conflict, cannot *reasonably* disagree with one another about how, given X, the conflict should be resolved. Similarly, X is indeterminate – more precisely, underdeterminate[53] – in the context of a conflict that implicates it if persons who agree about (a) and (b) *can* reasonably disagree with one another about how, given X, the conflict should be resolved. (Indeterminacy is not either–or; it is a matter of degree.) That X is determinate in the context of one or more conflicts does not mean that it is not indeterminate in the context of one or more other conflicts. If X is indeterminate in the context of a conflict that implicates it, then X must be "specified" in that context.

The process of "specifying," in a particular context, a norm implicated but also indeterminate in the context is the process of deciding what the norm, in conjunction with all the other relevant considerations, should be construed to require in that context. It is the process of "shaping" the norm, of rendering the norm determinate in the context of a conflict in which it is implicated but (until specified) indeterminate. Whereas the process of applying a determinate norm is basically deductive, the process of specifying an indeterminate norm is basically nondeductive. A specification "of a principle for a specific class of cases is not a deduction from it, nor a discovery of some implicit meaning; it is the act of setting a more concrete and categorical requirement in the spirit of the principle, and guided both by a sense of what is practically realizable (or enforceable), and by a recognition of the risk of conflict with other principles or values. . . ."[54] The challenge of specifying an indeterminate constitutional norm, then, is the challenge of deciding how best to achieve, how best to "instantiate," in the context of a particular conflict, the political-moral value (or values) at the heart of the norm;[55] it is the challenge of discerning what way of achieving that value, what way of embodying it, best reconciles all the various and sometimes competing interests of the political community at stake in the conflict. What Anthony Kronman has said of the process of "judgment" aptly describes the process of specifying an indeterminate norm. Such specification is a species of judgment.

Good judgment, and its opposite, are in fact most clearly revealed in just those situations where the method of deduction is least applicable, where the ambiguities are greatest and the demand for proof most obviously misplaced. To show good judgment in such situations is to do something more than merely apply a general rule with special care and thoroughness, or follow out its consequences to a greater level of detail. Judgment often requires such analytic refinement but does not consist in it alone. That this is so is to be explained by the fact that we are most dependent on our judgment, most in need of *good* judgment, in just those situations that pose genuine dilemmas by forcing us to choose between, or otherwise accommodate, conflicting interests and obligations whose conflict is not itself amenable to resolution by the application of some higher-order rule. It is here that the quality of a person's judgment comes most clearly into view and here, too, that his or her deductive powers alone are least likely to prove adequate to the task.[56]

Although courts are not the only governmental institutions that face the challenge of specifying indeterminate legal norms, courts do often face the challenge. "[A] court asked to apply a rule must decide in light of information not available to the promulgators of the rule, what the rule should mean in its new setting. That is a creative decision, involving discretion, the weighing of consequences, and, in short, a kind of legislative judgment. . . ."[57]

The fact of legal indeterminacy – and the need, therefore, for specification – is one thing, its value another: Why might a political community, or its
representatives, want to establish an indeterminate norm (a norm indeterminate in a significant number of the contexts that implicate it)? Why not issue
only determinate norms? Discussing the matter of rules – in particular, legal
rules – H. L. A. Hart emphasized that "a feature of the human predicament . . .
that we labour under whenever we seek to regulate, unambiguously and in advance, some sphere of conduct by means of general standards to be used without further official directions on particular occasions . . . is our relative ignorance of fact . . . [and] our relative indeterminacy of aim."[58] Given that
"feature of the human predicament," it makes sense that many legal (and
other) norms are relatively indeterminate.

If the world in which we live were characterized only by a finite number of features,
and these together with all the modes in which they could combine were known to us,
then provision could be made in advance for every possibility. We could make rules,
the application of which to particular cases never called for a further choice. Everything could be known, and for everything, since it could be known, something could
be done and specified in advance by rule. . . . Plainly this world is not our world. . . .
This inability to anticipate brings with it a relative indeterminacy of aim.[59]

The point is not that (relatively) determinate norms cannot be achieved.[60] The
point, rather, is that determinacy ought not always to be a goal.[61] To achieve
determinacy is sometimes "to secure a measure of certainty or predictability
at the cost of blindly prejudging what is to be done in a range of future cases,
about whose composition we are ignorant. We shall thus succeed in settling in
advance, but also in the dark, issues which can only reasonably be settled
when they arise and are identified."[62] We who "do ordain and establish this
Constitution for the United States of America" have long understood Hart's
point. Some of the norms of which the Constitution consists are "not rules for
the passing hour," as Cardozo put it, "but principles for an expanding future.
Insofar as it deviates from that standard, and descends into details and partic-
ulars, [a constitution] loses its flexibility, the scope of interpretation contracts,
the meaning hardens. While it is true to its function, it maintains its power of
adaptation, its suppleness, its play."[63]
    I now want to return to – and, against the background of what I have said in
this subsection, rehearse and amplify – a point I emphasized in the preceding
subsection: Interpreting the text of a constitutional provision – in the sense of
inquiring what norm the provision is understood to communicate – should not
be confused with inquiring what the generation of "We the people" that established a constitutional norm would have believed to be the correct way of resolving, on the basis of the norm, a conflict that besets us today. We may say,
using the language of "intention" and speaking of legal texts more broadly,

that trying to discern what norm they who enacted a legal text meant or "intended" the text to communicate – which is presumably the norm that, in enacting the text, they intended to establish – should not be confused with trying to discern how they would have resolved a particular conflict, or wanted it to be resolved, on the basis of the norm they intended to establish. How the enactors would have resolved a particular conflict, or wanted it to be resolved, on the basis of the norm they established is a different question, the answer to which is relevant only to the extent that it sheds light on the answer to the question of the norm they intended their text to communicate.[64]

Now, one might try to deflect this point by asserting that the norm they intended to establish, and the text to communicate, just *is* that each and every particular conflict be resolved *just as they would have resolved it.* Put another way, one might assert that what the enactors intended is that their enactment have just those legal effects that they would have "describe[d] [to be] the enactment's legal effects in each possible circumstance."[65] (The reference, presumably, is to what they, believing what *they* believed, mistakes included, and valuing what *they* valued, would have described to be the enactment's legal effects in each possible circumstance; if the reference were to what they, believing what *we* believe and valuing what *we* value, would have described to be the enactment's legal effects in each possible circumstance, then "they" would not be they.) In our political-legal culture, however, this is a wildly implausible construal of what those who enact legal texts often understand themselves to be doing (intending); as the statements by Neil MacCormick, Richard Posner, and H. L. A. Hart that I have quoted in this subsection illustrate, it is an implausible construal of what many legal norms are taken to be – even by those who establish the norms.[66] (This is not to deny that some legal norms – norms that are determinate in virtually every context in which the norms are implicated – can be so described. But, *pace* H. L. A. Hart, it is not plausible to describe all legal norms – least of all, all constitutional norms – that way.) "Lon Fuller, Henry Hart and Albert Sacks, and Reed Dickerson have all argued persuasively that the intended general meaning of statutory language is not reducible to the set of specifically intended applications of that statutory language."[67] Nor is it reducible to the set of applications of the statutory language that the enactors would have described to be the enactment's legal effects in each possible circumstance. "[L]egislative intent is best understood as the intent to adopt directive language with a particular general meaning and to bring about the consequences flowing from the consistent application of that general meaning in particular circumstances."[68]

None of this is to deny that the norm they intended to establish, and the text to communicate, includes at its core that one or more conflicts be resolved just as they would have resolved them. It is not to deny that a central part of what the enactors intended is that with respect to some cases – "paradigm" or "exemplary" cases – their enactment have just those legal effects that they would have "describe[d] [to be] the enactment's legal effects" in those cases. But this is a far cry from saying that the sum total of what the enactors intended is that their enactment have just those legal effects that they would have "describe[d] [to be] the enactment's legal effects" in each and every possible case that might arise and implicate their enactment. A piece of Hart's discussion is in point here:

> When we are bold enough to frame some general rule of conduct (e.g. a rule that no vehicle may be taken into the park), the language used in this context fixes necessary conditions which anything must satisfy if it is to be within its scope, and certain clear examples of what is certainly within its scope may be present to our minds. They are the paradigm, clear cases (the motor-car, the bus, the motor-cycle); and our aim in legislating is so far determinate because we have made a certain choice. We have initially settled the question that peace and quiet in the park is to be maintained at the cost, at any rate, of the exclusion of these things. On the other hand, until we have put the general aim of peace in the park into conjunction with those cases which we did not, or perhaps could not, initially envisage (perhaps a toy motor-car electrically propelled) our aim is, in this direction, indeterminate. We have not settled, because we have not anticipated, the question which will be raised by the unenvisaged case when it occurs: whether some degree of peace in the park is to be sacrificed to, or defended against, those children whose pleasure or interest it is to use these things. When the unenvisaged case does arise, we confront the issues at stake and can then settle the question by choosing between the competing interests in the way which best satisfies us. In doing so we shall have rendered more determinate our initial aim, and shall incidentally have settled a question as to the meaning, for the purpose of this rule, of a general word.[69]

I don't want to mount an argument here about how many of the norms of which the Constitution consists are indeterminate in many contexts in which they are implicated. For present purposes, I am content to observe that it is not unreasonable to believe that at least some of our most important constitutional norms are indeterminate in a significant number of the contexts that implicate them. (Recall, in that regard, Cardozo's observation that many of our constitutional norms are "not rules for the passing hour, but principles for an expanding future.")[70] Consider, for example, that part of the First Amendment that forbids government to prohibit "the free exercise of religion."[71] According to the Congress of the United States, which in 1993 passed the Religious Freedom Restoration Act, and to the president of the United States, who signed it into law, the free-exercise language was meant to communicate, whatever else it was meant to communicate, a norm to this effect: "Government shall not substantially burden a person's exercise of religion even if the burden results from a rule of general applicability, . . . [unless] application of the burden to the person (1) is in furtherance of a compelling governmental interest and (2) is the least restrictive means of furthering that compelling governmental interest."[72] There is sometimes ample room for reasonable disagreement about whether, in a particular context, a governmental interest is "compelling" – about whether, taking into account all the relevant particularities of context, the interest is sufficiently important – and even about whether a state action "is the least restrictive means. . ."

Let the European Court of Human Rights make the point in its own context. Article 10 of the European Convention for the Protection of Human Rights and Fundamental Freedoms provides in relevant part:

1. Everyone has the right to freedom of expression. This right shall include freedom to hold opinions and to receive and impart information and ideas without interference by public authority and regardless of frontiers. . . .

2. The exercise of these freedoms, since it carries with it duties and responsibilities, may be subject to such formalities, conditions, restrictions or penalties as are prescribed by law and are necessary in a democratic society, . . . for the protection of health or morals. . . .[73]

In a famous case involving a claim that the United Kingdom had violated Article 10 of the European Convention, the European Court of Human Rights stated, in a voice reminiscent of James Bradley Thayer's:[74]

48. These observations apply, notably, to Article 10 §2. In particular, it is not possible to find in the domestic law of the various Contracting States a uniform European conception of morals. The view taken by their respective laws of the requirements of morals varies from time to time and from place to place, especially in our era which is characterised by rapid and far-reaching evolution of opinions on the subject. By reason of their direct and continuous contact with the vital forces of their countries, State authorities are in principle in a better position than the international judge to give an opinion on the exact content of these requirements as well as on the "necessity" of a "restriction" or "penalty" intended to meet them. . . . [I]t is for the national authorities to make the initial assessment of the reality of the pressing social need implied by the notion of "necessity" in this context.

Consequently, Article 10 §2 leaves to the Contracting States a margin of appreciation. This margin is given both to the domestic legislator ("prescribed by law") and to the bodies, judicial amongst others, that are called upon to interpret and apply the laws in force. . . .

To say that among different states or countries, or even among persons from the same state or country, there is sometimes ample room for a reasonable difference in judgments about one or more matters that the relevant law makes determinative is not to say that anything goes; it is not to say that every difference in judgments about such matters is necessarily reasonable. Thus, the European Court of Human Rights went on to declare:

49. Nevertheless Article 10 §2 does not give the Contracting States an unlimited power of appreciation. The [European] Court [of Human Rights] is empowered to give the final ruling on whether a "restriction" or "penalty" is reconcilable with freedom of

expression as protected by Article 10. The domestic margin of appreciation thus goes hand in hand with a European supervision. Such supervision concerns both the aim of the measure challenged and its "necessity.". . .[75]

Since 1973, when the Supreme Court decided the abortion cases,[76] there has been an unending explosion of academic writing both about what it means and, especially, about what it should mean, above all for the Court, to "interpret" the Constitution.[77] Much of the writing is weakened by its failure to attend to two very different senses of constitutional "interpretation." It is marred by its failure to heed the fundamental distinction between, on the one hand, "interpreting" a constitutional *text*, in the sense of trying to discern what norm the text represents and, on the other, "interpreting" a constitutional *norm*, in the sense of determining what shape to give the norm in the context of a conflict in which the norm is implicated but in which it is also indeterminate. I argued, in Section I.A, that with respect to the Constitution$_1$, the question "What norm does this provision represent?" is often the question "What norm was this provision understood to communicate by the 'We the people' whose representatives put the provision into the Constitution?" But even if one rejects that argument, the fact remains that there is an important difference between, first, interpreting a *text* in the sense of trying to discern what norm a text represents and, second, interpreting a *norm* in the sense of determining what shape to give an indeterminate norm in the context of a particular conflict.[78] (Again, interpreting the Constitution$_1$ should not be confused with interpreting, in the sense of specifying, the Constitution$_2$.) Note that disagreement about what norm, X or Y, a provision represents can coexist with agreement about how both X and Y should be shaped (specified) in the context at hand, and that agreement about what norm a provision represents (X) can coexist with disagreement about how X should be shaped in the context at hand.

One might try to challenge, in two steps, the distinction on which I am insisting here: first, by identifying my distinction with, or by otherwise assimilating it to, the familiar dichotomy between "understanding" a law and then "applying" the law, now understood, to resolve a case; second, by responding, with Hans-Georg Gadamer, that "[u]nderstanding . . . is always application."[79] However, the distinction on which I am insisting here is not – nor does it presuppose, entail, or even track – the problematic dichotomy that Gadamer rightly challenged: the distinction between, on the one hand, understanding a legal norm and, on the other, "applying" the norm – in the sense of "bringing it to bear" – in adjudicating a particular conflict. That distinction is not my distinction. Indeed, the second half of my distinction – the act of determining what shape to give an indeterminate norm in the context of a particular conflict – presupposes that the Gadamerian insight is accurate. It presupposes that there is no difference between understanding the meaning – the contextual meaning – of a legal norm and "applying" the norm, bringing it to bear, in the case at hand; to do the latter just *is* to determine (to "specify") the contextual meaning of the norm.

The first half of my distinction – the act of trying to discern what norm a legal text represents – simply recognizes that some legal texts (not all, but some) are initially unintelligible (opaque, vague, ambiguous, etc.), in the sense that it is not initially clear to readers of the text what norm the text represents. (Like indeterminacy, unintelligibility is not either – or but a matter of degree.) If it is not clear what norm a legal text represents, a court (assuming for the moment that a court is the relevant reader of the text) must translate or decode the text: A court must identify, or try to, the norm the text represents. Before the norm that the text represents can be "understood"/"applied" – which, *pace* Gadamer, is one move, not two – the norm that the text represents must be identified. As I explained in Section I.A, it is simply not true of every constitutional provision, even though it is true of many, that the question of the norm that the provision represents can usefully be answered by a repetition of what the text says.[80]

III. Is the Supreme Court Supreme – And, If So, How Deferential Ought It to Be, If Deferential at All – in Interpreting the Constitution?

A. Is the Supreme Court Supreme?

Justice Brennan has written that "[t]he genius of the Magna Carta, as well as its longevity, lay partly in its creation of a device for resolving grievances and compelling the Crown to abide by the committee of barons' decision. Paper promises whose enforcement depends wholly on the promisor's goodwill have rarely been worth the parchment on which they were inked."[81] To be as effective as possible, the constitutional strategy for establishing norms must include one or more enforcement mechanisms. (This is especially true with respect to those norms the constitutionalization of which presupposes a realistic skepticism about majoritarian politics.) For us, a principal such mechanism has been the practice of judicial review[82] – but not because we believe what only the historically uninformed could believe, namely, that the justices of the Supreme Court of the United States, or any of our other judges, are necessarily or invariably better than any other public officials at safeguarding constitutional norms. Judicial review is simply one way, albeit a very important one, of trying to protect constitutional norms when other ways, and other officials, might have failed to do so. Sometimes judicial review itself fails.

One might want to inquire (as I have elsewhere) whether "We the people" ever established the practice of judicial review in a constitutionally ordained way.[83] But that is not, for us the people of the United States now living, a live question. Judicial review has been a bedrock feature of our constitutional order almost since the beginning of our country's history.[84] Nor is it a live question, for us, whether judicial review is, all things considered, a good idea. It would be startling, to say the least, were we Americans to turn skeptical about the idea of judicial review – an American-born and -bred idea that, in the twentieth century, has been increasingly influential throughout the world.[85] For us, the live questions about judicial review are about how the power of judicial review should be exercised. To endorse the idea and the practice of judicial review, however, is not necessarily to endorse the doctrine of judicial supremacy.

As I explained in Section II.A, there is ample room for reasonable disagreement about what norms some parts of the Constitution₁ were understood to communicate (e.g., the privileges-or-immunities language of the Fourteenth Amendment). But even if there is little if any room for *reasonable* disagreement about such a matter, there can be disagreement. As I explained in Section II.B, there is ample room for reasonable disagreement about how some of the norms of which the Constitution₂ consists should be specified in some of the contexts that implicate them. But even if there is little if any room for reasonable disagreement about such a matter, there can be disagreement. Both disagreements about what norm a provision of the Constitution₁ was understood to communicate and disagreements about how one of our constitutional norms should be specified in a particular context are disagreements about what the Constitution₂ forbids.

Article III of the Constitution anoints the Supreme Court of the United States as the arbiter of disagreements between itself and any state judiciary about what any national law, including the Constitution, forbids.[86] As a practical matter, the position of the Supreme Court about what a national law forbids will prevail over any competing position of the legislature or of the governor of any state (as well as over the competing position of the judiciary of any state) as long as the executive branch of the national government is willing to stand behind the ruling of the Supreme Court.[87] (I am assuming here that, in any such dispute, any state actor – for example, the governor – can be sued in a case that will eventually be decided, even if only on appeal, on the basis of the Supreme Court's position.) As it happens, however, the Constitution contains no norm anointing any branch of the national government as the arbiter of disagreements between itself and any other branch of the national government about what a national law – including "the supreme law of the Land" – forbids. Contrary to what many citizens might believe – and, indeed, contrary to what some justices of the Supreme Court have seemed to believe[88]

– the Constitution₁ does not state that the Supreme Court of the United States is to be the arbiter of such disagreements, nor does the Constitution₂ contain any norm to that effect.[89] Of course, a constitution could designate the judicial branch of government (or another branch) as the arbiter of some or all such disagreements, but ours does not do so.

Over time, however, an expectation has emerged, yielding a practice that has what we may call a "quasi-constitutional" status in U.S. politics: In American constitutional culture, the firm expectation is that the legislative and executive branches of the national government will each refrain from doing anything the Supreme Court says the Constitution forbids them to do, and they will each do anything the Court says Constitution requires them to do, even if they disagree with the Court's position about what the Constitution forbids (or requires).[90] Why has this expectation emerged? Certainly not because we the people of the United States believe that the position of a majority of the justices on the Supreme Court about what norm a constitutional provision should be taken to represent, or about how a constitutional norm should be specified, is necessarily or invariably superior to the position of a majority of the members of Congress or to the position of the president. Rather, this expectation has emerged mainly for two connected reasons.

First, we have come to believe that it is desirable – because less messy and more productive for our political life – that different political institutions and actors not interminably struggle with one another over their different understandings of what the Constitution forbids (or requires), some acting on the basis of one understanding, others on the basis of a competing understanding. Accordingly, we believe that, in general, one institution of government should have the power to settle, as a *practical* matter, disruptive controversies about what the Constitution forbids; one institution should have the power to determine, as a *practical* matter, what the Constitution forbids.[91] (This is not to say that one institution should have the power to determine, as an *intellectual* or *theoretical* matter, what the Constitution forbids. Practical assent – assent in practice or action – is one thing; intellectual assent is something else altogether. That there is, or might be, a need for the former does not entail that there is an equal need, or indeed any need, for the latter.)

Second, we have come to believe – at least, many of us have – that, in general, the Supreme Court is the institution least to be feared and most to be trusted in determining, as a practical matter, the minimum boundaries of what the Constitution forbids.[92]

The *minimum* boundaries, it bears emphasis, not the maximum. Again, the firm expectation that has emerged is that the legislative and executive branches of the national government will each refrain from doing anything the Supreme Court says the Constitution forbids them to do, even if they disagree with the Court's position about what the Constitution forbids. It is not inconsistent with this expectation for Congress, in enacting legislation pursuant to its responsibility under Section 5 of the Fourteenth Amendment to enforce the provisions of the amendment, to conclude that some constitutional norm forbids state government to do more than the Court says the norm does, or that some constitutional norm requires state government to do more than the Court says the norm does. Recall, in that regard, that every norm applicable to state government under Section 1 of the Fourteenth Amendment is now deemed applicable to the national government under one or another other constitutional provision. So for Congress to conclude that some norm applicable to state government under the Fourteenth Amendment forbids state government to do more than the Court says the norm does, or that some such norm requires state government to do more than the Court says the norm does, is for Congress to conclude that its own power, too, is more limited than the Court says it is, not less limited. There is certainly much less, if any, reason to fear Congress – much less, if any, reason not to trust it – when the constitutional boundaries it sets on its own power are stricter, larger, than those the Court has set. Given this, and given Congress's clear responsibility under Section 5 of the Fourteenth Amendment to enforce the provisions of the amendment, it might well be the case that Court should defer to – that it should uphold the constitutionality of – the Religious Freedom Restoration Act (RFRA).[93] (Significantly, Congress wrote RFRA to apply to the national government no less than to state government.)[94] In any event, RFRA does not violate what the Court has determined to be the minimum boundaries of what the Constitution forbids. Of course, if the Supreme Court, contrary to the decisions of three lower federal courts (so far),[95] were not to defer, were it to rule that RFRA is unconstitutional, then the Court would have said what the Constitution forbids Congress to do, namely, enact RFRA, and, given the "firm expectation" stated at the beginning of this paragraph, that would very likely be the end of the matter.

In the period since World War II, we Americans have succeeded in exporting our practice of judicial supremacy to many parts of the world. Several countries now accord their judiciaries similar supremacy in deciding what their constitutions forbid.[96] Moreover, the European Court of Human Rights is accorded supremacy in deciding what the European Convention for the Protection of Human Rights and Fundamental Freedoms forbids.[97] The belief that, on balance and in general, a well-functioning judiciary is the least to be feared and the most to be trusted – especially in deciding what the authoritative provisions regarding human rights forbid – is waxing in global influence,[98] not waning, and it seems unlikely that the belief will relax its grip, at least for long, on American constitutional culture. Nonetheless, the belief is a highly contingent one; we cannot rule out the possibility of a future in which the belief comes to seem, to a growing number of us, untenable. Indeed, the belief already seems untenable to some of us.[99]

To say that the Supreme Court serves as the arbiter of disputes between itself and one or both of the other branches of the national government about what the Constitution forbids is not to say that the Court should never conclude that the Constitution commits resolution of a conflict about what some provision of the Constitution forbids to a branch of the national government other than itself.[100] Nor is it to say that, as the arbiter of such disputes, the Court (when it does not conclude that the Constitution commits resolution of the conflict to another branch of government) should never defer to another branch's position about what the Constitution forbids. (In the next two subsections, I take up the question of the propriety of deference by the Court to another branch's judgments about what the Constitution forbids.) Moreover, nothing I have said here is meant to deny that, under the Constitution, every citizen of the United States, including every citizen who is an official of the national government or of a state government, may persist in disagreeing, as vigorously as she thinks appropriate, with a constitutional decision of the Supreme Court even long past the point where it is clear that the Court will not soon, if ever, change its mind.

Finally, it bears emphasis that neither Congress nor the president is constitutionally obligated to defer to the Court's constitutional decisions about what the Constitution forbids. The practice of deferring to such decisions is, as I said, merely "quasi-constitutional." It is best understood as a *presumptive* practice – a practice appropriate for circumstances both constitutionally and morally ordinary. In a circumstance neither constitutionally nor morally ordinary, it might be appropriate for Congress or the president (or both) not to defer to the Court. As I said earlier, to endorse the idea and the practice of judicial review is not necessarily to endorse the doctrine of judicial supremacy. When Abraham Lincoln delivered his First Inaugural Address on March 4, 1861, the circumstances were undeniably both constitutionally and morally extraordinary: "[I]f the policy of the government upon vital questions affecting the whole people is to be irrevocably fixed by decisions of the Supreme Court . . . the people will have ceased to be their own rulers, having to that extent practically resigned their Government into the hands of that eminent tribunal."[101] Lincoln had in mind, of course, the Supreme Court's infamous decision in *Dred Scott v. Sanford*.[102]

I said that the Court must decide when to defer to another branch's judgment about what the Constitution forbids. Because in a circumstance neither constitutionally nor morally ordinary, it might be appropriate for Congress or the president (or both) not to defer to the Court, Congress and the president must decide when to defer to the Court – although, again, the practice that has emerged is one of deference, a practice so long-standing and so sensible as to be, in ordinary circumstances, bedrock. (Not that the practice couldn't evolve in the direction of less deference.) As I said, the Constitution could designate the Supreme Court (or another branch) as the arbiter of some or all inter-branch disagreements about what the Constitution forbids. Such a state of affairs would be less ambiguous than the state of affairs that now prevails. But perhaps we are better off that the Constitution$_1$ does not state and that the Constitution$_2$ is not to the effect that the Court (or another branch) is to be the arbiter. Perhaps the present, less well defined arrangement – in which the Court must decide when to defer to one or both of the other branches and, as a constitutional matter, it remains open to each of the other branches to decide when extraordinary circumstances warrant its not deferring to the Court – yields constitutional decisions that are generally less divisive and destabilizing than the decisions a different, more hierarchical arrangement might yield. Perhaps.

In circumstances both constitutionally and morally ordinary, the Supreme Court of the United States serves, at least for now, as the arbiter of disagreements between itself and one or both of the other branches of the national government about what the Constitution forbids. Undeniably, this is an awesome responsibility. I said, in the preceding paragraph, that the Court must decide when to defer. How large a role ought the Court to play, or how small – put another way, how active a role ought it to play, or how passive, how deferential – in serving as the arbiter of disagreements between itself and one or both of the other branches about what the Constitution forbids?

B. How Deferential Ought the Court to Be in Interpreting the Constitution$_1$?

Again, there is ample room for reasonable disagreement about what norms some parts of the Constitution$_1$ were understood to communicate. How large a role ought the Supreme Court to play, or how small a role, when it is a party to such a disagreement; in particular, ought the Court to play a deferential role? That is, how deferential ought the Court to be in interpreting the Constitution$_1$?[103] Assume, for example, that according to a majority of the Court, the text of a particular constitutional provision was probably understood to communicate norm X, but that according to a different view that prevailed in Congress, the provision was probably understood to communicate norm Y. Ought the majority to defer to Congress's view? It is unrealistic to expect the Court to defer to Congress's view if in its opinion that view is not merely wrong but, all things considered, unreasonable. Moreover, an intellectually arrogant or politically willful justice might not be able to discern the distinction between thinking that Congress's view is wrong and thinking that it is unreasonable. Imagine, however, that in the majority's opinion, Congress's view, though wrong, is not unreasonable. Ought the Court to defer? The twofold point I want to emphasize here is that, first, it is perilous to generalize and, second, many considerations are relevant. In particular:

- How confident is the majority that it is right and Congress, wrong; that is, how close is the majority to thinking that Congress is not merely wrong, but unreasonable?
- How thoroughly has Congress considered the issue? (How has it done so – by means of what processes?) To the extent that Congress has thoroughly considered the issue, the case for the Court deferring is stronger; to the extent that it has not done so, the case is weaker.
- Is Congress's view distorted (and, if so, to what extent) by its interest in avoiding the broader limitation that norm X would place on Congress's power to act? Or, instead, does norm Y place a broader limitation on government's, including Congress's, power to act? If the former, Congress is saying that the Constitution$_2$ forbids *less* than the Court says it forbids, and the case for the Court deferring is weaker. If the latter, Congress is saying that the Constitution$_2$ forbids *more* than the Court says it forbids, and the case for judicial deference is stronger. (As I suggested in the preceding section, given Congress's clear responsibility under Section 5 of the Fourteenth Amendment to enforce the provisions of the amendment, and because Congress wrote the Religious Freedom Restoration Act to limit the power not only of state government but of the national government as well – including Congress's own power – the case for the Court deferring to RFRA is, in my view, much stronger than it would otherwise be. If Congress had written RFRA to apply only to state government, the case for the Court deferring to Congress would be weaker.)
- Which norm, X or Y, is more attractive, in the majority's view, as a matter of political morality? (Relatedly, which norm is more attractive, in the majority's view, as a matter of the judicial role that enforcement of the norm would require of the Court?)[104] If X, the case for the Court deferring is, in its view, weaker; if Y, the case is stronger.

C. How Deferential Ought the Court to Be in Interpreting (Specifying) the Constitution$_2$?

Even if the Constitution contains only a few indeterminate norms – only a few norms indeterminate in many of the contexts that implicate them – this fundamental question remains: How large a role ought the Supreme Court to play, or how small – how active a role, or how passive – in specifying indeterminate constitutional norms?[105] In particular, ought the Court to play a primary role or only a secondary, deferential role of the sort recommended by James Bradley Thayer more than a century ago?[106] That is, how deferential ought the Court to be in specifying the Constitution? (Recall here the "margin of appreciation" doctrine developed by the European Court of Human Rights.)[107] Assume, for example, that according to a majority of the Court, the best or optimal specification of a particular constitutional norm is X and that, given X, a particular national law is unconstitutional. Assume further that according to the view that prevailed in Congress, the appropriate specification of the norm is Y and that, given Y, the national law is not unconstitutional. Ought the Court to defer to Congress's view? As before, it is unrealistic to expect the Court to defer to Congress's view if in its opinion that view is not merely wrong but, all things considered, unreasonable. And as before, an intellectually arrogant or politically willful justice might not be able to discern the distinction between thinking that Congress's view is wrong and thinking that it is unreasonable.[108] Imagine, however, that in the majority's opinion, Congress's view, though wrong, is not unreasonable. Ought the Court to defer? Again, many considerations – similar considerations – are relevant.

- How close is the Court to thinking that Congress is not merely wrong, but unreasonable?
- How thoroughly has Congress considered the issue?
- Is Congress's view most likely distorted by its interest in avoiding the broader limitation that specification X would place on Congress's power to act?
- Is the norm one that Congress is arguably better positioned to specify than the judicial branch – for example, a norm establishing not a "negative" right to be free of some governmental overreaching (perhaps in conjunction with a liberty to engage in some activity) but a "positive" entitlement "to governmental assistance to meet basic material needs"?[109]
- Is the question of which specification, X or Y, is best or optimal a question that Congress's political processes can be trusted to handle fairly and well?[110] Or is it one that, perhaps because the norm is "unusually vulnerable to majority sentiment,"[111] the politically independent Court is more likely, all things considered, to handle fairly and well?

Just as it is perilous to generalize about when the Court ought to defer to Congress's or the president's view about what norm the text of a particular constitutional provision was understood to establish, it is perilous to generalize about when the Court ought to defer to Congress's view about the best or optimal specification of an indeterminate constitutional norm.[112]

We can pursue much the same inquiry – to much the same conclusion – with respect to a state law and a state legislature. The relevant considerations are the same, and it is no less perilous to generalize about when the Court ought to defer to a state legislature's (not unreasonable) view, as distinct from Congress's view, about the best or optimal specification of an indeterminate norm.[113]

Perilous though the enterprise is, I do want to gesture in the direction of one generalization. In *Democracy and Distrust*,[114] John Ely did not address the question of the role the Court ought to play in specifying indeterminate constitutional norms. Ely's concern was mainly with the different question of the unenumerated rights the judiciary – in particular, the Supreme Court – may legitimately enforce as constitutional rights (if any). Nonetheless, Ely's answer is relevant to our question. In 1991, Ely characterized the essential argument of *Democracy and Distrust* as follows: "[P]ublic issues generally should be settled by a majority vote of [sane adults] or their representatives. . . ."[115] But, Ely continued, public issues of three sorts are sensibly resolved – resolved as *constitutional* issues – principally by the judiciary:

(1) the question of whether, "where a majority of such persons [sane adults or their representatives] votes to exclude other such persons from the [political] process or otherwise to dilute their influence on it," it may do so;

(2) the question of whether, "where such a majority enacts one regulatory regime for itself and another, less favorable one, for one or another minority," it may do so; and

(3) the question of whether, where such a majority makes a political choice that implicates a "side constraint" with a certain pedigree, the choice violates the side constraint; a side constraint that, because it is "sufficiently important (and vulnerable to majority sentiment)," was designated by a supermajority "in a constitutional document and thereby render[ed] . . . immune to displacement by anything short of a similar supermajority vote in the future."[116]

Ely then explained, "[P]recisely because of their tenure, courts are the appropriate guardians of at least exceptions (1) and (2)."[117] Ely added, with respect to exception (3) – which, unlike exceptions (1) and (2), concerns enumerated rights, not unenumerated ones – that on "the supposition that no right is to be thus designated *unless it is unusually vulnerable to majority sentiment,*" courts are the appropriate guardians of exception (3) as well.[118] Finally, Ely wrote, "What does not follow from anything said above, or in my opinion from anything sensible said ever, is that judges are also to be given a license to create or 'discover' further rights, not justified by exceptions (1) or (2) nor ever constitutionalized by a supermajority, and protect them as if they had been."[119]

Whether or not one agrees with Ely's position about the (only) unenumerated rights the Court may enforce (exceptions (1) and (2)), one could agree with his position about the enumerated rights the Court may enforce (exception (3)) and yet insist that if and to the extent that any such right is indeterminate, the Court should play only a secondary role – a Thayerian role – in specifying it. One could say, in that regard, that answering the question of the best or optimal specification of an indeterminate constitutional right – the best or optimal specification, that is, of a constitutional norm establishing and protecting an indeterminate right – requires many "judgment calls" (as Ely has described them),[120] and that as long as the judgment calls implicit in the challenged governmental action are not unreasonable, the Court should defer to them. Nonetheless, Ely's argument lends support to the position that as a comparative matter, as an issue in the allocation of competences, the judiciary – not least, the federal judiciary – is institutionally well suited to play the primary role in specifying any right- or liberty-regarding norm it is charged with enforcing if our historical experience suggests that the norm is "unusually vulnerable to majority sentiment." To settle for our elected representatives, and not the judiciary, playing the primary role in specifying such a norm is probably to settle for many specifications that, even if "not unreasonable" for purposes of Thayer's minimalist approach to constitutional adjudication, are nonetheless suboptimal: specifications that fail to give the important constitutional value at stake – the value privileged by the norm – its full due.

A word of clarification is in order. My comments here are directed at the situation in which the Court faces a choice between two not unreasonable specifications of a right- or liberty-regarding norm that our history has shown to be "unusually vulnerable to majority sentiment": the Court's own, more generous specification of the norm – more generous to the principal beneficiaries of the norm – and another branch's less generous specification. It is a different situation altogether, of course, if the Court faces a choice between its own, less generous specification of a right- or liberty-regarding norm and another branch's more generous specification. That the Court should not defer, à la Thayer, to another branch's less generous specification of such a norm does not entail that it should not defer to another branch's more generous specification *if the Court concludes that that more generous specification is not unreasonable.* In particular, there might be little if any reason for the Court to insist on a specification of a right- or liberty-regarding norm less generous than the specification that Congress, in exercising its responsibility under Section 5 of the Fourteenth Amendment to enforce the provisions of the amendment, is willing to embrace. Least of all should the Court do so if both of the other two branches of the national government – Congress in enacting a law and the president in signing it – are in agreement in embracing a specification of a right- or liberty-regarding norm more generous than the specification that the Court has embraced or is inclined to embrace.

Of course, that the Supreme Court chooses to exercise the principal responsibility for specifying some indeterminate constitutional norm does not preclude the possibility that in exercising that responsibility the Court will, on occasion, act too timidly or with insufficient sensitivity or vigilance, thereby failing to give the constitutional value at stake its full due. But that possibility does not begin to support the argument that the Court should exercise only a secondary responsibility, that it should pursue only the Thayerian approach to the specification of the norm. Even if in exercising the principal responsibility the Court occasionally acts too timidly – even if usually it acts too timidly – the U.S. political community is no worse off than it would be if the Court were to exercise a secondary responsibility *as a matter of course,* habitually deferring to political judgments that, while arguably reasonable for purposes of Thayer's approach, nonetheless give the constitutional value less than its full due. The Supreme Court's sorry record of failing to take free-exercise claims very seriously comes to mind here.[121] But, as Doug Laycock has emphasized: "Some of the time, judicial review will do some good. Judges did nothing for the Mormons, but they may have saved the Jehovah's Witnesses and the Amish. If judges can save one religious minority a century, I consider that ample justification for judicial review in religious liberty cases."[122]

For a depressing example of the kind of suboptimal specification the Thayerian approach might well affirm, consider the political judgment to which Thayer's most prominent judicial disciple, Felix Frankfurter, deferred in *West Virginia State Board of Education v. Barnette,*[123] in which he, and he alone, dissented from the Supreme Court's decision striking down a public school regulation that compelled students, including Jehovah's Witnesses who conscientiously objected on religious grounds, to salute the American flag and recite the Pledge of Allegiance. It was, Frankfurter insisted, a judgment "upon which men might reasonably differ. . . . And since men may so reasonably differ, I deem it beyond my constitutional power to assert my view of the wisdom of this law against the view of the State of West Virginia."[124] As Frankfurter's Thayerian performance in *Barnette* illustrates, because legislatures so rarely make political choices about whose constitutionality men and women may *not* reasonably differ, the Thayerian approach to the specification of any constitutional norm effectively marginalizes the norm – virtually to the point of eliminating it – insofar as constitutional adjudication is concerned. It is not obvious, therefore, why one would advocate the Thayerian approach to the specification of a norm unless one thought that the norm should be marginalized.

Now, one might think that some norms should be marginalized because mechanisms other than constitutional adjudication – political as distinct from judicial mechanisms – are adequate, more or less, to the protection of the norms: namely, norms regarding the allocation of power, whether between the national government and the governments of the states[125] or between the legislative and executive branches of the national government. One might also think that some right- or liberty-regarding norms are relatively unimportant, or at least inappropriate to a constitution that is to be judicially enforced, and should therefore be marginalized. But it is not obvious why one would want to marginalize any right- or liberty-regarding norm – that is, why one would support the Thayerian approach to the specification of any such norm – that one thought was relatively important, and appropriate to a constitution, unless one concluded that, overall, political mechanisms were somehow adequate to protect the norm. However, our history suggests that such a conclusion is doubtful with respect to at least some right- or liberty-regarding norms.

Jeremy Waldron has argued that judicial review – judicial review in the sense of according the judiciary supremacy in deciding what a constitution forbids – is deeply problematic as a matter of political morality.[126] The final two paragraphs of Waldron's "right-based critique of constitutional rights" suggest the problem he sees:

> If we are going to defend the idea of an entrenched Bill of Rights put effectively beyond revision by anyone other than the judges, we should try and think what we might say to some public-spirited citizen who wishes to launch a campaign or lobby her [representative] on some issue of rights about which she feels strongly and on which she has done her best to arrive at a considered and impartial view. She is not asking to be a dictator; she perfectly accepts that her voice should have no more power than that of anyone else who is prepared to participate in politics. But – like her suffragette forbears – she wants a vote; she wants her voice and her activity to count on matters of high political importance.
>
> In defending a Bill of Rights, we have to imagine ourselves saying to her: "You may write to the newspaper and get up a petition and organize a pressure group to lobby [the legislature]. But even if you succeed, beyond your wildest dreams, and orchestrate the support of a large number of like-minded men and women, and manage to prevail in the legislature, your measure may be challenged and struck down because your view of what rights we have does not accord with the judges' view. When their votes differ from yours, theirs are the votes that will prevail." It is my submission that saying this does not comport with the respect and honor normally accorded to ordinary men and women in the context of a theory of rights.[127]

Waldron's rejection of the idea of "an entrenched Bill of Rights put effectively beyond revision by anyone other than the judges" might not be extreme in the context of, say, English political-legal culture, which has never known such a bill of rights and even now is wary about creating one. But Waldron's position *is* extreme in the context of a political-legal culture like ours, because, even though we do not always agree about what some of its provisions forbid, we generally revere our entrenched Bill of Rights.[128] (That Waldron's argument is extreme in the context of American political-legal culture does not entail that his argument is not, in that context, thoughtful or important. It is both.) Nonetheless, Waldron's argument can be borrowed to support three claims that are not extreme in the context of American political-legal culture. (That none of the three claims is extreme does not entail that none of them is controversial.)

- A constitution should contain few if any indeterminate norms.
- The appropriate *practice* of judicial review, in the case of indeterminate constitutional norms, is Thayerian.[129]
- It is a good thing that the legislative and executive branches are not constitutionally obligated to defer to the judicial branch's beliefs about what the Constitution forbids, including its beliefs about the best or optimal specification of an indeterminate constitutional norm.

That Waldron's argument lends support to these three claims does not mean that we should accept the claims. I do accept, partly on the basis of considerations like those Waldron highlights, the first and third claims. At least, I am inclined to agree both that constitution-makers should be cautious about including indeterminate norms in a constitution (which is not to say that they should never do so) and that it is a good thing that Congress and the president are, as I noted in Section III.A, constitutionally free not to defer to the Supreme Court's beliefs about what the Constitution forbids. (This is not to say that the legislative and executive branches should not accord the judiciary supremacy – i.e., *presumptive* supremacy; it is not to deny that, in circumstances both constitutionally and morally ordinary, the legislative and executive branches should defer.) But we should not accept the second claim, in my view. Neither total abstinence from the non-Thayerian practice of judicial review nor total indulgence in it is appropriate. Here, as elsewhere, there is a more moderate choice – a "middle way." In the case of at least a few indeterminate constitutional norms, the practice of judicial review should be non-Thayerian. Which norms? As I have suggested: important right- or liberty-regarding norms that our history has shown to be "unusually vulnerable to majority sentiment."[130]

Admittedly, the position I am recommending here – non-Thayerian judicial review for important right- or liberty-regarding norms "unusually vulnerable to majority sentiment" – is embedded in speculative and therefore highly contestable judgments about the likely consequences of alternative ways of allocating political power. (What position in the area is not so embedded, at least in part?) Still, in the context of the United States today, the position I am recommending here resolves any doubt about the appropriate judicial role in protecting such norms – which is, of course, an easy doubt to have, given the difficulty of the issue – in a politically realistic direction, namely, toward privileging more generous rather than less generous specifications of the norms. "Non-Thayerian judicial review for important right- or liberty-regarding norms 'unusually vulnerable to majority sentiment' " comes at least as close as any competing position to satisfying Bickel's famous criteria – or so it seems to me:

The search must be for a function which might (indeed, must) involve the making of policy, yet which differs from the legislative and executive functions; which is peculiarly suited to the capabilities of the courts; which will not likely be performed elsewhere if the courts do not assume it; which can be so exercised as to be acceptable in a society that generally shares Judge [Learned] Hand's satisfaction in a "sense of common venture"; which will be effective when needed; and whose discharge by the courts will not lower the quality of the other departments' performance by denuding them of the dignity and burden of their own responsibility.[131]

The disagreement between Waldron and American political-legal culture about whether an entrenched bill of rights is a good thing is no more susceptible to definitive resolution than the issue between a thoroughgoing Thayerian and me about how deferential a role the Court should play in connection with certain right- or liberty-regarding norms. What Bickel said about judicial review is relevant both to the difference between Waldron and American political-legal culture and to the difference between a thoroughgoing Thayerian and me: "It will not be possible fully to meet all that is said against judicial review. Such is not the way with questions of government. We can only fill the other side of the scales with countervailing judgments on the real needs and the actual workings of our society and, of course, with our own portions of faith and hope. Then we may estimate how far the needle has moved."[132]

In many constitutional cases – even cases in which the question of the norm the relevant provision represents cannot usefully be answered by a repetition of what the provision says – an identification of the norm the provision represents will be unnecessary: The Supreme Court will *already* have identified, in an earlier case now deemed authoritative, the norm the provision represents. Moreover, if the applicable constitutional norm (or norms) is indeterminate, the Court might *already* have begun, in earlier cases, the process of specifying the norm – a process that, if it has been going on for a long time, will have yielded a substantial body of constitutional doctrine, much of which will not be in question but will be deemed authoritative. In the cases in which the applicable constitutional doctrine is itself indeterminate – as, at the margin, constitutional doctrine typically is – the challenge will be to develop that doctrine further. In that sense, the challenge will be to shape further the norm that is both the warrant for and the foundation of the doctrine. The specification of an indeterminate constitutional norm is, then, a temporally extended process, the judicial version of which is analogous to the ongoing judicial development of – including the occasional revision of – the "common law." Of course, a principal aim in the judicial development of any area of law, including any area of constitutional law, is to fashion doctrine that is both internally coherent and at least not inconsistent with other doctrines of equal legal status, especially other doctrines in the same neighborhood.

IV. Concluding Comment

Again, some of the most devisive moral conflicts that have beset us Americans since the end of World War II have been transmuted into constitutional conflicts. As I said in the opening paragraph of this essay, if one wants to inquire which of those conflicts, if any, understood as constitutional conflicts, have been resolved as they should have been resolved, one must first answer, as I have done in this essay, several prior, fundamental questions that arise in connection with the Constitution. Although more must be said, in pursuit of inquiries commenced in this essay, the ideal context for doing so is an extended discussion of particular constitutional controversies. Such controversies provide the concrete detail one needs both to exemplify the constitutional-theoretical issues at stake and, then, to explicate and buttress positions on the issues. The constitutional controversies that have most engaged me – and that in subsequent work I will discuss against the background, and in elaboration, of my arguments in this essay – are those that have been decided, in the period since the end of World War II, on the basis of claims about what the Fourteenth Amendment forbids: controversies involving such deeply divisive moral issues as racial segregation, affirmative action, sex-based discrimination, homosexuality, abortion, and physician-assisted suicide.

Notes

1 Well, almost no disagreement. In 1789, Congress proposed this constitutional amendment: "No law varying the compensation for the services of the Senators and Representatives shall take effect, until an election of Representatives shall have intervened." In 1992 – more than two hundred years later! – the thirty-eighth state voted to ratify the proposed amendment, which Congress then declared "valid . . . as part of the Constitution of the United States." One may fairly wonder whether completion of the process of ratifying the (alleged) Twenty-seventh Amendment was legally valid – and whether, therefore, the Constitution₁ really contains the language of the amendment. See, e.g., William Van Alstyne, *What Do You Think About the Twenty-seventh Amendment?* 10 Constitution Commentary 9 (1993).

2 The Preamble states, in its entirety, "We the people of the United States, in Order to form a more perfect Union, establish Justice, insure domestic Tranquility, provide for the common defence, promote the general Welfare, and secure the Blessings of Liberty to ourselves and our Posterity, do ordain and establish this Constitution for the United States of America."

3 I write "We the people" rather than "We the People" because in the original text of the Constitution, which I am quoting, the first letter of "people" is lower case.

4 See Section I.C. Moreover, American constitutional history reveals that it is not only "We the people" who do in fact establish norms as constitutional. See id.

5 Steven D. Smith, *Law Without Mind,* 88 Michigan L. Rev. 104, 119 (1989).

6 Richard Kay has emphasized, over the course of several essays, much the same point I am making here:

> There may be plausible theories of government and judicial review which demote the authority of both intention and text, but it is hard to see what the political rationale would be for a theory that elevates a text for reasons unrelated to the people and circumstances which created it.

Richard S. Kay, *Adherence to the Original Intentions in Constitutional Adjudication: Three Objections and Responses,* 82 Northwestern U. L. Rev. 226, 234 (1988).

> [T]o the extent we would bind ourselves, in whole or in part, to rules inferred from mere marks and letters on paper without reference to the will of the human beings who selected those marks and letters, we enter a regime very foreign to our ordinary assumptions about the nature of law.

Richard S. Kay, *Original Intentions, Standard Meanings, and the Legal Character of the Constitution,* 6 Constitutional Commentary 39, 50 (1989).

> The influence of the Constitution is the consequence of continuing regard not for a particular assortment of words, but for the authority and sense of a certain constituent act. . . . [To deem authoritative the words of a constitutional provision] independently of the intentional act which created them is to disregard exactly that which makes the text demand our attention in the first place. That the words will bear some different meaning is purely happenstance. Without their political history, the words of the Constitution have no more claim on us than those of any other text.

Richard S. Kay, *The Bork Nomination and the Definition of "The Constitution,"* 84 Northwestern U. L. Rev. 1190, 1193 (1990).

Paul Campos's work is also relevant to the point I am making here. See his *Against Constitutional Theory,* 4 Yale J. L. & Humanities 279 (1992), *That Obscure Object of Desire: Hermeneutics and the Autonomous Legal Text,* 77 Minnesota L. Rev. 1065 (1993), and *Three Mistakes about Interpretation,* 92 Michigan L. Rev. 388 (1994).

7 The "people" who ordained and established the Constitution and Bill of Rights at the end of the nineteenth century and the "people" who amended the Constitution after the Civil War consisted mainly of white males. The question why we the people now living should accept constitutional directives issued by persons long dead as our "supreme Law of the Land" has a special urgency, therefore, for those of us who are not white males. See James MacGregor Burns, *The Vineyard of Liberty* 392 (1982): "Every new state admitted after 1819 restricted voting to whites. Only five New England states – Massachusetts, Rhode Island, Maine, New Hampshire, and Vermont – provided for equal voting rights for black and white males." Cf. id. at 364: "Some suffrage restrictions fell during the Jeffersonian era . . . and during the War with England. . . . Property requirements were replaced by taxpaying requirements, which in turn gradually faded away. . . . 'Well before Jackson's elec-

tion most states had lifted most restrictions on the suffrage of white male citizens or taxpayers.' "

8 See, e.g., *Constitutional Stupidities Symposium,* 12 Constitutional Commentary 139–225 (1995) (twenty essays on "the stupidest provision of the United States Constitution").

9 I quote Article V later in this subsection.

10 Russell Hardin, *Why a Constitution?* in *The Federalist Papers and the New Institutionalism* 100, 102, 113 (Bernard Grofman & Donald Wittman, eds., 1989).

11 Whether the processes of constitutional amendment provided for by Article V are the only constitutionally legitimate way to amend the Constitution – whether they are the only constitutionally ordained processes of constitutional amendment – is a matter of controversy. On this, and on many other interesting questions about constitutional amendment, see the rich collection of essays in Sanford Levinson, ed., *Responding to Imperfection: The Theory and Practice of Constitutional Amendment* (1995). See also Lawrence Lessig, *What Drives Derivability: Responses to "Responding to Imperfection,"* 74 Texas L. Rev. 839 (1996) (reviewing the Levinson collection); Frank I. Michelman, *Thirteen Easy Pieces,* 93 Michigan L. Rev. 1297 (1995) (reviewing the Levinson collection); and Henry Paul Monaghan, *We the People[s], Original Understanding, and Constitutional Amendment,* 96 Columbia L. Rev. 121 (1996).

It is implausible to suggest that constitutionally ordained processes of constitutional amendment are the only *morally* legitimate way to alter the Constitution. On this issue, too, see the Levinson collection. See also Richard S. Kay, *Comparative Constitutional Fundamentals,* 6 Connecticut J. International L. 445 (1991). Cf. Richard S. Kay, Book Review, 7 Constitution Commentary 434, 440–1 (1990): "No matter how far they transgress existing rules, successful constitutional conventions, like those of 1787–89, are unlikely to be perceived as outlaws. If they prosper, they will be founders."

In the conclusion to *The Constitution in the Courts,* I suggested a modification in the practice of judicial review under which the Congress and the president, acting together in their legislative capacity, would play a larger role, not in amending the Constitution, but in shaping indeterminate constitutional norms. See Michael J. Perry, *The Constitution in the Courts: Law or Politics?* 197–201 (1994). Perhaps they – and, especially, "We the people" – should play a larger role, too, in amending the Constitution, as Bruce Ackerman has suggested. See his *We the People: Foundations* 54–5 (1991) and *We the People: Transformations,* ch. 13 (draft, 1996). Or perhaps they shouldn't: "Article V is part of a Constitution that reflects a considered attempt to slow down change, and it has been so understood from the very beginning of our constitutional history. In our time, this policy may be a wise one." Monaghan, supra, this note at 177.

12 Not that there might not be costs to our doing so. A second practical reason for bowing to constitutional directives that we believe should not be a part of the Constitution, unless/until they are disestablished in a constitutionally ordained way, is that if and to the extent we were not to do so, if and to the extent we were to disestablish constitutional directives in an other than constitutionally ordained way – or if and to the extent we were to condone violations of constitutional directives – we

would risk diminishing our own power. Some day we might want to issue a constitutional directive. By maintaining a culture of fidelity to constitutional directives that have not been disestablished in a constitutionally ordained way, including directives issued by persons long dead, we make it more likely that a constitutional directive issued by *us* will be obeyed (unless/until it is disestablished in a constitutionally ordained way) even when *we* are long dead.

13 See Ackerman, supra, note 11, chs. 4–8.

14 Indeed, a constitution can forbid that one or more of its parts be amended at all. It has been suggested that the constitution of Germany, because it "declares that certain fundamental principles are immune to constitutional amendment," exemplifies "absolute entrenchment." Anupam Chander, *Sovereignty, Referenda, and the Entrenchment of a United Kingdom Bill of Rights,* 101 Yale L. J. 457, 462, and n. 30 (1991). See Bruce Ackerman, *The Future of Liberal Revolution* 110–11 (1992) (commenting on the German practice of absolute entrenchment). The constitution of Japan arguably immunizes some of its parts against amendment in providing, in Article 11, that "[t]he people shall not be prevented from enjoying any of the fundamental human rights. These fundamental human rights guaranteed to the people by this Constitution shall be conferred upon the people of this and future generations as eternal and inviolate rights." Similarly, Article 98 provides, "The fundamental human rights by this Constitution guaranteed to the people of Japan are fruits of the age-old struggle of man to be free; they have survived the many exacting tests for durability and are conferred upon this and future generations in trust, to be held for all time inviolate."

15 The "may" is the may of legality, not of politics or of morality. See supra, note 11. Cf. Chander, supra, note 14 at 462: "An absolutely entrenched [constitutional norm[is . . . (as are all other parts of an existing legal regime) vulnerable to revolution."

We might be tempted to think that the constitutional strategy for establishing a directive differs from the statutory strategy in another basic respect, in that constitutions, unlike statutes, typically declare themselves to be "the supreme law" – and that therefore to opt for the constitutional strategy is to decree that the directive is lexically prior to statutory and other nonconstitutional law, including subsequently enacted law. (Article VI of the Constitution states, "This Constitution . . . shall be the supreme law of the land. . . ." Article 98 of the Japanese Constitution states, "This Constitution shall be the supreme law of the nation and no law, ordinance, imperial rescript or other act of government, or part thereof, contrary to the provisions hereof, shall have legal force or validity.") But a legislature may decree in a statute establishing a directive that the directive is lexically prior to subsequently enacted statutory law in this sense and to this extent: "A court is not to give effect to any future statute enacted by this legislature to the extent the statute, in the court's judgment, violates the directive established by this statute, *unless such future statute explicitly states that a court is to give it effect even if in the court's judgment the statute violates the directive established by this statute.*" See id. at 463: "One common type of manner and form entrenchment requires that all contrary legislation contain an explicit declaration of its intent to override the entrenched rule." Canada has pursued, in its Charter of Rights and Freedoms, such a strategy. See Perry, *The Constitution in the Courts,* n. #, at 197–8. Even if a legislature may, in one session, enact such a decree, however, the legislature presumably may, in a later session, repeal the decree. See Julian N. Eule, *Temporal Limits on the Legislative Mandate: Entrenchment and Retroactivity,* 1987 American Bar Foundation Research J. 379. What is most distinctive about the constitutional strategy, then, is less the supremacy of constitutional law than the extreme difficulty of amending a constitution.

16 For an "outline of some of the reasons for entrenching institutional arrangements and substantive rights," see Cass R. Sunstein, *Constitutionalism and Secession,* 58 U. Chicago L. Rev. 633, 636–43 (1991).

17 See Thomas B. McAffee, *Brown and the Doctrine of Precedent: A Concurring Opinion,* 20 Southern Illinois U. L. Rev. 99, 100 (1995): "[O]ur constitutional order is based on a moral vision that humans have rights which they do not forfeit when joining civil society. At the same time, we recognize that the people are the supreme judiciary as to the content of those rights when they engage in the sovereign act of creating or amending the Constitution, a document which will in various ways define and limit those rights. There is no way out of this tension – our natural law aspirations must inevitably play themselves out through some system of human decision-making, and historically we have believed that the popular sovereignty manifest in the constitution-making process is likely to yield superior results to rule by judges or a system in which each individual becomes the judge of his own obligations to enacted law."

18 It would be especially difficult to justify the Court imposing on government, in the name of the Constitution, a norm that no one, past or present, could fairly read any language in the Constitution to represent. As Justice William Brennan explained in his Hart Lecture at Oxford: "But if America's experience demonstrates that paper protections are not a sufficient guarantor of liberty, it also suggests that they are a necessary one, particularly in times of crisis. Without a textual anchor for their decisions, judges would have to rely on some theory of natural right, or some allegedly shared standard of the ends and limits of government, to strike down invasive legislation. But an appeal to normative ideals that lack any mooring in the written law . . . would in societies like ours be suspect, because it would represent so profound an aberration from majoritarian principles. . . . A text . . . helps tether [judges'] discretion. I would be the last to cabin judges' power to keep the law vital, to ensure that it remains abreast of the progress in man's intellect and sensibilities. Unbounded freedom is, however, another matter. One can imagine a system of governance that accorded judges almost unlimited discretion, but it would be one reminiscent of the rule by Platonic Guardians that Judge Learned Hand so feared. It is not one, I think, that would gain allegiance in either of our countries." William J. Brennan, Jr., *Why Have a Bill of Rights?* 9 Oxford J. Legal Studies 425, 432 (1989).

Recalling that Chief Justice John Marshall's justification for the practice of judicial review, in *Marbury v. Madison,* appealed to the writtenness of the Constitution (see Marbury v. Madison, 5 U.S. (1 Cranch) 137, 177 (1803)), Michael Moore has commented that "[j]udicial review is easier to justify if it is exercised with reference only to the written document. . . . By now, the object of [constitutional] interpretation should be clear: it is the written document. Hugo Black was right, at least, about this. Black's Constitution – the one he was so fond of pulling out of his pocket – is our only Constitution." Michael S. Moore, *Do We Have an Unwritten Constitution?* 63 Southern California L. Rev. 107, 122, 123 (1989). See id. at 121–3. See also infra, note 50, and accompanying text.

19 I discuss the "specification" of indeterminate constitutional norms in Section II.B.

20 See, e.g., Robert Bork, *The Tempting of America: The Political Seduction of the Law* 155–9 (1989); and Antonin Scalia, *A Matter of Interpretation: Federal Courts and the Law* 139–40 (1997). But see Gary S. Lawson, *The Constitutional Case against Precedent,* 15 Harvard J. L. & Public Policy 23 (1994). For a critical comment on Gary Lawson's position, see McAffee, supra, note 17 at 101–3.

21 Or, at least, by those of us – policy-makers, religious leaders, editorial writers, politically engaged citizens, etc. – who concern ourselves with such things.

22 Cf. Frederick Schauer, *Amending the Presuppositions of a Constitution,* in Levinson, supra, note 11 at 145, 156–57 (presenting a hypothetical in which "[t]he small *c* constitution would . . . have been amended by virtue of [an] amendment to the ultimate rule of recognition, even though it could also be accurately said that the large *C* Constitution had not been validly amended according to its own terms").

23 For a complementary discussion, see McAffee, supra, note 17 at 104: "[The Supreme] Court ought to be especially reluctant to overrule precedent that is: (1) proven and long-established; (2) the product of the carefully considered judgment of all three branches of the government; and (3) based upon the fundamental values of the sovereign people. Under such circumstances, the least that can be said is that the case for the impropriety of the original constitutional judgment should be overwhelming before [the] Court should even decide whether to overrule such a precedent."

24 Bork, supra, note 20 at 158. For a thoughtful discussion, see Peter B. McCutcheon, *Mistakes, Precedent, and the Rise of the Administrative State: Toward a Constitutional Theory of the Second Best,* 80 Cornell L. Rev. 1 (1994).

25 Cf. Lawson, supra, note 20 at 33, n. 27 (wondering whether "the irrevocable enshrinement of errors through precedent should compel the self-conscious creation of errors in subsequent cases").

26 See Michael J. Perry, *The Fourteenth Amendment: What Norms Did "We the People" Establish?* (1997) (unpublished essay on file with author).

27 Cf. Charles L. Black, Jr., *"One Nation Indivisible": Unnamed Human Rights in the States,* 65 St. John's L. Rev. 17, 55 (1991): "[W]ithout such a corpus of national human rights law good against the States, we ought to stop saying, 'One nation indivisible, with liberty and justice for all,' and speak instead of, 'One nation divisible and divided into fifty zones of political morality, with liberty and justice in such kind and measure as these good things may from time to time be granted by each of these fifty political subdivisions.' "

28 The First Amendment states, "Congress shall make no law respecting an establishment of religion, or prohibiting the free exercise thereof; or abridging the freedom of speech, or of the press; or the right of the people peaceably to assemble, and to petition the government for a redress of grievances." That section 1 of the Fourteenth Amendment was meant to protect against state government the privileges

and immunities of citizens already protected against the national government by the Bill of Rights does not entail that the First Amendment was meant to protect any privileges or immunities of citizens against the national government. Jay Bybee has recently argued that the First Amendment, unlike the Second through Eighth Amendments, was not meant to protect any privileges or immunities of citizens – that is, any privileges or immunities that persons were thought to have in virtue of their status as citizens – but only to make explicit a congressional disability, a lack of legislative power on the part of Congress ("Congress shall make no law . . ."). See Jay S. Bybee, *Taking Liberties with the First Amendment: Congress, Section 5, and the Religious Freedom Restoration Act,* 48 Vanderbilt L. Rev. 1539 (1995). See also Steven D. Smith, *Foreordained Failure: The Quest for a Constitutional Principle of Religious Freedom* chs. 2–3 (1995).

29 See Perry, supra, note 26.

30 See, e.g., Bolling v. Sharpe, 437 U.S. 497 (1954).

31 See Michael J. Perry, *Discrimination and Race* (1997) (unpublished essay on file with author). By itself, the Fifth Amendment, which became a part of the Constitution in 1791, applies only to the national government. The Fourteenth Amendment, which became a part of the Constitution in 1868, applies only to state government.

32 See id.

33 Cf. McCutcheon, supra, note 24 (noting that the "unconstitutional" administrative state is now beyond judicial overruling).

34 For efforts to articulate criteria that should inform a theory of precedent, see – in addition to McAffee, whom I quote in note 17 – Michael J. Gerhardt, *The Role of Precedent in Constitutional Decisionmaking and Theory,* 60 George Washington L. Rev. 68 (1991), and Henry P. Monaghan, *State Decisions and Constitutional Adjudication,* 88 Columbia L. Rev. 144 (1988).

35 For an example of such a claim, see Planned Parenthood of Southeastern Pennsylvania v. Casey, 505 U.S. 833, 854–69 (1992).

36 I am skeptical about how accurately we can generalize either about how such "nonconstitutional" premises emerge in our constitutional law or about how, when they do emerge, some of them eventually survive to become constitutional bedrock. I suspect that we can only particularize. But cf. Ackerman's *We the People: Foundations* and *We the People: Transformations,* supra, note 11.

37 The First Amendment states, in relevant part, that "Congress shall make no law respecting an establishment of religion, or prohibiting the free exercise thereof. . . ." According to the constitutional law of the United States, however, neither any branch of the national government nor state government may establish religion or prohibit the free exercise thereof. For a discussion, see Michael J. Perry, *Religion in Politics* 10–12 (1997).

38 See, e.g., Lundman v. McKown, 530 N.W.2d 807 (Minnesota 1995). See also Caroline Frasier, *Suffering Children and the Christian Science Church,* Atlantic Monthly, April 1995, at 105.

39 Discussing "a distinction that is implicit in the idea of 'persecution' " and that the Court in *Church of the Lukumi Babalu Aye, Inc. v. City of Hialeah* (113 S.Ct. 2217 (1993)) "repeatedly tried to articulate," Steve Smith has explained, "The distinction is between measures that 'target' a religion *on religious grounds* and because

it is objectionable *as* a religion and, on the other hand, measures that 'target' a religion only by prohibiting a practice of the religion that is objectionable *on independent or nonreligious grounds.*" Steven D. Smith, *Free Exercise Doctrine and the Discourse of Disrespect,* 65 U. Colorado L. Rev. 519, 563 (1994). See id. at 563–8.

40 For an extended presentation and defense of the latter position, see Michael W. McConnell, *The Origins and Historical Understanding of Free Exercise of Religion,* 103 Harvard L. Rev. 1309 (1993); McConnell's historical argument has been criticized. See Gerard V. Bradley, *Beguiled: Free Exercise Exemptions and the Siren Song of Liberalism,* 20 Hofstra L. Rev. 245 (1991), and Philip A. Hamburger, *A Constitutional Right of Religious Exemption: An Historical Perspective,* 60 George Washington L. Rev. 915 (1992). However, Peter Braffman has presented a powerful argument that McConnell's position is closer to the truth than are the views of those who have criticized his position. See Peter A. Braffman, *The Original Understanding of the Free Exercise Clause* (May 1995) (unpublished ms.). According to Braffman, "Protecting 'free exercise of religion' meant protecting those religiously motivated actions which did not disrupt the public peace." Id. at 81. Braffman elaborates: "The public peace did not refer to all laws of the land, but rather to a limited category of laws which prevented overt acts of violence that disrupted civil society. As such, religiously motivated conduct could conflict with – and be exempted from – general laws so long as that conduct did not violate the peace." Id. at 96. See also Kurt T. Lash, *The Second Adoption of the Free Exercise Clause: Religious Exemptions Under the Fourteenth Amendment,* 88 Northwestern U. L. Rev. 1106 (1994).

41 In *Employment Division, Oregon Department of Human Resources v. Smith,* Justice Scalia wrote, for himself and four other members of the Court, that "if prohibiting the exercise of religion . . . is . . . merely the incidental effect of a generally applicable and otherwise valid provision," the free-exercise norm, without regard to whether the refusal to exempt the religious practice in question serves an important public interest, has not been violated. Employment Division, Department of Human Resources of Oregon v. Smith, 494 U.S. 872, 878 (1990). Three members of the Court joined a statement by Justice O'Connor that the accommodation position should not have been rejected by the majority. See 494 U.S. at 892–903. The majority's position provoked so many interested persons off the Court that an unprecedented alliance of groups, from the American Civil Liberties Union on the one side to the so-called religious right on the other, joined forces to lobby Congress to undo the decision. The alliance was successful. Congress enacted, in 1993, the Religious Freedom Restoration Act, Public Law 103–41, 42 U.S. Code 2000bb. Section 3 of the act states, "Government shall not substantially burden a person's exercise of religion even if the burden results from a rule of general applicability, [unless] . . . it demonstrates that application of the burden to the person (1) is in furtherance of a compelling governmental interest; and (2) is the least restrictive means of furthering that compelling governmental interest." (After the Court's decision in *Smith,* which involved Oregon's failure to exempt the religious use of peyote from its ban on the ingestion of hallucinogenic substances, Oregon passed a law making it lawful to use peyote in connection "with the good

faith practice of a religious belief" or association "with a religious practice." Oregon Revised Statutes §475.992(5)(a)&(b) (1991).)

On the Religious Freedom Restoration Act, see Thomas C. Berg, *What Hath Congress Wrought? An Interpretive Guide to the Religious Freedom Restoration Act,* 39 Villanova L. Rev. 1 (1994); Scott C. Idleman, *The Religious Freedom Restoration Act: Pushing the Limits of Legislative Power,* 73 Texas L. Rev. 247 (1994); Douglas Laycock and Oliver S. Thomas, *Interpreting the Religious Freedom Restoration Act,* 73 Texas L. Rev. 209 (1994); *Symposium: The Religious Freedom Restoration Act,* 56 Montana L. Rev. 1–294 (1995).

In June 1997, the Supreme Court ruled that in enacting the Religious Freedom Restoration Act, Congress exceeded the scope of its power under Section 5 of the Fourteenth Amendment. See City of Boerne v. Flores, 65 LW 4612 (1997). Three lower federal courts had ruled to the contrary. See Flores v. City of Boerne, Texas, 73 F.3d 1352 (5th Cir. 1996); Sasnett v. Sullivan, 65 USLW 2115 (7th Cir. 1996); Belgard v. Hawaii, 883 F.Supp. 510 (D Hawaii 1995). At the time of the Court's ruling, scholarly opinion was divided. Those who argued that RFRA is unconstitutional include: Bybee, supra, note 28 at 1624–32; Daniel O. Conkle, *The Religious Freedom Restoration Act: The Constitutional Significance of an Unconstitutional Statute,* 56 Montana L. Rev. 39 (1995); Christopher L. Eisgruber and Lawrence G. Sager, *Why the Religious Freedom Restoration Act Is Unconstitutional,* 69 New York University L. Rev. 437 (1995); Eugene Gressman and Angela C. Carmella, *The RFRA Revision of the Free Exercise Clause,* 57 Ohio State L. J. 65 (1996); Marci A. Hamilton, *The Religious Freedom Restoration Act: Letting the Fox into the Henhouse under Cover of Section Five of the Fourteenth Amendment,* 16 Cardozo L. Rev. 357 (1994); and William W. Van Alstyne, *The Failure of the Religious Freedom Restoration Act under Section 5 of the Fourteenth Amendment,* 46 Duke L. J. 291 (1996). For arguments that RFRA is constitutional, see Douglas Laycock, *RFRA, Congress, and the Ratchet,* 56 Montana L. Rev. 145, 152–70 (1995), and Bonnie I. Robin-Vergeer, *Disposing of the Red Herrings: A Defense of the Religious Freedom Restoration Act* 69 Southern California L. Rev. 589 (1996). In my view, Laycock's and Robin-Vergeer's arguments are persuasive.

A full treatment of the issue of the constitutionality of RFRA would have to deal with the establishment clause claim on which Justice Stevens relied in concurring in the Court's ruling of unconstitutionality. See 65 LW at 4620. See also Christopher L. Eisgruber and Lawrence G. Sager, *The Vulnerability of Conscience: The Constitutional Basis for Protecting Religious Conduct,* 61 U. Chicago L. Rev. 1245 (1994). I have addressed the claim briefly. See Perry supra, note 37 at 25–30. See also Robin-Vergeer, supra, this note at 754–6. A full treatment would also have to address the federalism problem that several scholars have raised. See, e.g., Van Alsyne, supra, this note at 315–18, 322–3. Both Laycock and Robin-Vergeer have addressed the problem. See Laycock, supra, this note at 157–65; Robin-Vergeer, supra, this note at 756–64.

42 This was the position of the majority in the *Slaughter-House Cases.* See Slaughter-House Cases, 83 U.S. (16 Wall.) 36 (1873). But see Richard L. Aynes, "Constricting the Law of Freedom: Justice Miller, the Fourteenth Amendment, and the

Slaughter-House Cases," 70 Chicago-Kent L. Rev. 627, 627 and n. 4 (1994) (noting that "everyone agrees" that the majority's position in the *Slaughter-House Cases* was wrong).

43 I address all these questions elsewhere. See Perry, supra, note 26.

44 I address these questions, too, in id.

45 John Hart Ely, *Democracy and Distrust: A Theory of Judicial Review* 25 (1980). I address the who-is-protected question in Perry, supra, note 26.

46 Ely, supra, note 45 at 16.

47 For a discussion of the confusion, see Perry, supra, note 11 at 42–6.

48 For a helpful discussion of how – on the basis of what sources – to pursue such an inquiry, see Steven G. Calabresi and Saikrishna B. Prakash, *The President's Power to Execute the Laws,* 104 Yale L. J. 541, 550–9 (1994).

49 Consider, for example, the vigorous debate about what norm the free-exercise language of the First Amendment was understood to communicate. See, on one side of the debate, McConnell, supra, note 40 at 1409, and *Michael W. McConnell, Free Exercise Revisionalism and the Smith Decision,* 57 U. Chicago L. Rev. 1109 (1990). McConnell acknowledges, however, that the historical record does not speak unequivocally. See his *Origins and Historical Understanding* at 1511–13, and *Free Exercise Revisionism* at 1117. Indeed, one could plausibly conclude, as some scholars have, that McConnell's position is wrong. See, e.g., William P. Marshall, *The Case Against the Constitutionally Compelled Free Exercise Exemption,* 40 Case Western Reserve L. Rev. 357, 375–9 (1989–90); Gerard V. Bradley, *Beguiled: Free Exercise Exemptions and the Siren Song of Liberalism,* 20 Hofstra L. Rev. 245 (1991); and Philip A. Hamburger, *A Constitutional Right of Religious Exemption: An Historical Perspective,* 60 George Washington L. Rev. 915 (1992). According to Peter Braffman, McConnell's position is closer to the truth than is that of his opponents. See Braffman, supra, note 40.

50 Andrezj Rapaczynski, *The Ninth Amendment and the Unwritten Constitution: The Problems of Constitutional Interpretation,* 64 Chicago–Kent L. Rev. 177, 192 (1988). See supra, note 18.

51 See supra, note 30.

52 By "adjudicative" facts, I mean the facts of the case (e.g., who did what, and where and when she did it), as distinct from "legislative" facts, that transcend the case (e.g., what will most likely happen to our society if we let this kind of speech go unregulated).

53 See Lawrence B. Solum, *On the Indeterminacy Crisis: Critiquing Critical Dogma,* 54 U. Chicago L. Rev. 462 (1987).

54 Neil MacCormick, *Reconstruction after Deconstruction: A Response to CLS,* 10 Oxford J. Legal Studies 539, 548 (1990). Where I have used the term "specification," MacCormick uses the Latin term *determinatio,* borrowing it from John Finnis. "John Finnis has to good effect re-deployed St Thomas' concept of *determinatio;* Hans Kelsen's translators used the term 'concretization' to much the same effect." Id. (citing J. M. Finnis, *On the Critical Legal Studies Movement,* 30 American J. Jurisprudence 21, 23–5 [1985], and Hans Kelsen, *The Pure Theory of Law* 230 [1967]).

55 Put another way, it is the challenge of deciding how best to avoid the political-moral *disvalue* at the heart of the norm.

56 Anthony T. Kronman, *Living in the Law,* 54 U. Chicago L. Rev. 835, 847–8 (1987).

In *The Federalist,* No. 37, James Madison commented on the need, in adjudication, for specification: "All new laws, though penned with the greatest technical skill and passed on the fullest and most mature deliberation, are considered as more or less obscure and equivocal, until their meaning be liquidated and ascertained by a series of particular discussions and adjudications." *The Federalist Papers* 229 (Clinton Rossiter, ed., 1961). Cf. Kim Lane Scheppele, *Legal Secrets* 94–5 (1988): "Generally in the literature on interpretation the question being posed is, What does a particular text (or social practice) *mean?* Posed this way, the interpretive question gives rise to an embarrassing multitude of possible answers, a cacophony of theories of interpretation. . . . [The] question that (in practice) is the one actually asked in the course of lawyering and judging [is]: what . . . does a particular text mean *for the specific case at hand?*"

In *Truth and Method* 275 (1975), Hans-Georg Gadamer commented on the process of specification both in law and in theology: "In both legal and theological hermeneutics there is the essential tension between the text set down – of the law or of the proclamation – on the one hand and, on the other, the sense arrived at by its application in the particular moment of interpretation, either in judgment or in preaching. A law is not there to be understood historically, but to be made concretely valid through being interpreted. Similarly, a religious proclamation is not there to be understood as a merely historical document, but to be taken in a way in which it exercises its saving effect. This includes the fact that the text, whether law or gospel, if it is to be understood properly, i.e., according to the claim it makes, must be understood at every moment, in every particular situation, in a new and different way. Understanding here is always application."

57 Richard A. Posner, *What Am I? A Potted Plant?* New Republic, September 28, 1987, at 23, 24. Cf. Benjamin N. Cardozo, *The Nature of the Judicial Process* 67 (1921): "[W]hen [judges] are called upon to say how far existing rules are to be extended or restricted, they must let the welfare of society fix the path, its direction and its distance."

58 H. L. A. Hart, *The Concept of Law* 128 (2d ed., 1994).

59 Id.

60 They can. One way to do so, Hart writes, "is to freeze the meaning of the rule so that its general terms must have the same meaning in every case where its application is in question. To secure this we may fasten on certain features present in the plain case and insist that these are both necessary and sufficient to bring anything which has them within the scope of the rule, whatever other features it may have or lack, and whatever may be the social consequences of applying the rule in this way." Id. at 129.

61 This is not to say that determinacy ought never to be a goal: "To escape this oscillation between extremes we need to remind ourselves that human inability to anticipate the future, which is at the root of this indeterminacy, varies in degree in different fields of conduct. . . ." Id. at 130–1. See id. at 130 et seq.

144   MICHAEL J. PERRY

62 Id. at 129–30.

63 Cardozo, supra, note 57 at 83–4.

64 See Richard Kay, *"American Constitutionalism,"* in *Constitutionalism: Philosophical Foundations* (Lawrence A. Alexander, ed., forthcoming): "Since the principal feature of constitutionalism is its employment of fixed, a priori rules, constitutional interpretation cannot be a direction to decide individual controversies over the use of public power in whatever way is thought would be most congenial to the constitutional enactors. Such disputes are to be resolved, rather, by reference to the constitutional *rules*. Once the intended scope of the rules is decided, however, the relevance of the original intentions is exhausted."

65 Larry Alexander, *All or Nothing at All? The Intentions of Authorities and the Authority of Intentions,* in *Law and Interpretation: Essays in Legal Philosophy* 357, 370 (Andrei Marmor, ed., 1995). But see supra, note 64.

66 Much of the discussion in Alexander's essay, id., seems to me to proceed on the basis of this implausible construal.

67 Patrick J. Kelley, *An Alternative Originalist Opinion for* Brown v. Board of Education, 20 Southern Illinois U. L. Rev. 75, 76 (1995).

68 Id. Kelley continues: "Thus, although the intended general meaning is fixed by legislative action and does not thereafter change, the set of factual applications of that fixed general meaning may expand or contract with the application of the fixed general meaning to changed circumstances. New situations, unheard of at the time the statute was enacted, may fall squarely within the fixed intended meaning. Later changes in the institutions existing at the time the statute was enacted may alter the later application of the fixed statutory meaning to those institutions. So the fact that no one at the time it was adopted thought that the Fourteenth Amendment affected segregated public schools is not controlling in the two-step process of first, determining the intended general meaning of constitutional language; and second, applying that fixed general meaning to particular current factual situations." Id. It is doubtful that "no one at the time it was adopted thought that the Fourteenth Amendment affected segregated public schooling." See Michael W. McConnell, *Originalism and the Desegregation Decisions,* 81 Virginia L. Rev. 947 (2995), and Michael W. McConnell, *The Originalist Justification for* Brown: *A Reply to Professor Klarman,* 81 Virginia L. Rev. 1937 (1995).

69 Hart, supra, note 58 at 129. Cf. Paul Brest:

The extent to which a clause may be properly interpreted to reach outcomes different from those actually contemplated by the adopters depends on the relationship between a general principle and its exemplary applications. A principle does not exist wholly independently of its author's subjective, or his society's conventional exemplary applications, and is always limited to some extent by the applications they found conceivable. Within these fairly broad limits, however, the adopters may have intended their examples to constrain more or less. To the intentionalist interpreter falls the unenviable task of ascertaining, for each provision, how much more or less.

What of a case where the adopters viewed a certain punishment as not cruel and unusual? This is not the same as saying that the adopters "intended not to prohibit the punishment." For even if they expected their laws to be interpreted by intentionalist canons, the adopters may have intended that their own views not always govern. Like parents who attempt to instill values in their child by both articulating and applying a moral principle, they may have accepted, or even invited, the eventuality that the principle would be applied in ways that diverge from their own views. The adopters may have understood that, even as to instances to which they believe the clause ought or ought not to apply, further thought by themselves or others committed to its underlying principle might lead them to change their minds. Not believing in their own omniscience or infallibility, they delegated the decision to those charged with interpreting the provision. If such a motivation is plausible with respect to applications of the clause in the adopters' contemporary society, it is even more likely with respect to its application by future interpreters, whose understanding of the clause will be affected by changing knowledge, technology, and forms of society.

The Misconceived Quest for the Original Understanding, 60 Boston U. L. Rev. 204, 216–17 (1980) (paragraphs rearranged).

70 See supra, note 63. Cf. Richard A. Posner, *The Problems of Jurisprudence* 131 (1990): "In many cases the conventional materials will lean so strongly in one direction that it would be unreasonable for the judge to go in any other. But in some they will merely narrow the range of permissible decision, leaving an open area within which the judge must perforce attempt to decide the case in accordance with sound policy – in those grand symbolic cases that well up out of the generalities and ambiguities of the Constitution . . . – while paying due heed to the imprudence of trying to foist an idiosyncratic policy conception or social vision on a recalcitrant citizenry."

71 The First Amendment states, in relevant part, "Congress shall make no law respecting an establishment of religion, or prohibiting the free exercise thereof. . . ." This and the other commands of the First Amendment are now taken to apply not only to the legislative branch of the national government, but also to the executive and judicial branches. Moreover, the commands are understood to apply not only to the national government, but also to state government. See Perry, supra, note 37 at 10–12.

72 See supra, note 41.

73 In its entirety, Section 2 of Article 10 states: "The exercise of these freedoms, since it carries with it duties and responsibilities, may be subject to such formalities, conditions, restrictions or penalties as are prescribed by law and are necessary in a democratic society, in the interests of national security, territorial integrity or public safety, for the prevention of disorder or crime, for the protection of health or morals, for the protection of the reputation or rights of others, for preventing the disclosure of information received in confidence, or for maintaining the authority and impartiality of the judiciary." For the European Convention, see Ian Brownlie, ed., *Basic Documents on Human Rights* 326 (1992).

74 See James Bradley Thayer, *The Origin and Scope of the American Doctrine of Constitutional Law,* 7 Harvard L. Rev. 129 (1893). See generally *One Hundred Years of Judicial Review: The Thayer Centennial Symposium,* 88 Northwestern U. L. Rev. 1–468 (1993).

75 Handyside Case, European Court of Human Rights, 1976, Ser. A, No. 24, 1 EHRR 737. The European Convention on the Protection of Human Rights and Fundamental Freedoms contains several provisions with provisos substantially identical to Article 10 §2. See Article 8 (protecting one's "right to respect for his private and family life, his home and his correspondence"), Article 9 (protecting "the right to

freedom of thought, conscience, and religion"), and Article 11 (protecting "the right to peaceful assembly and to freedom of association with others").

Similar examples can be drawn from the international law of human rights. (A national political community can agree to remove certain choices or options from the agenda of its politics by ratifying legal norms established in conventional international law.) For example, Article 18 of the International Covenant on Civil and Political Rights provides in relevant part: "Everyone shall have the right to freedom of thought, conscience, and religion. This right shall include the freedom to have or adopt a religion or belief of his choice, and freedom, either individually or in community with others and in public or private, to manifest his religion or belief in worship, observance, practice or teaching." Article 18 further states: "Freedom to manifest one's religion or beliefs may be subject only to such limitations as are prescribed by law and are necessary to protect public safety, order, health, or morals of the fundamental rights and freedoms of others." There is sometimes ample room for reasonable disagreement about what, in a particular context, "the public morals" require – or about what, in a particular context, is "necessary to protect public safety, order, health, or morals." (For the ICCPR, see Brownlie, supra, this note at 125. The United States ratified the ICCPR, including Article 18, in 1992.)

On the "margin of appreciation" doctrine in the European Convention system, see Henry J. Steiner and Philip Alston, eds., *International Human Rights in Context: Law, Politics, Morals* 626–36 (1996).

76 Roe v. Wade, 410 U.S. 113 (1973); Doe v. Bolton, 410 U.S. 179 (1973).

77 This book continues my contribution to the enterprise. My other (and, in some cases and to some extent, recanted) contributions include *The Constitution, the Courts, and Human Rights* (1982); *The Authority of Text, Tradition, and Reason: A Theory of Constitutional "Interpretation,"* 58 Southern California L. Rev. 551 (1985); *Morality, Politics, and Law,* ch. 6 (1988); and *The Constitution in the Courts: Law or Politics?* (1994).

78 Philip Bobbitt's presentation of six types of constitutional argument implicitly collapses the important difference between discerning what norm the text of a constitutional provision represents and deciding what shape to give an indeterminate constitutional norm in a particular context. See his *Constitutional Fate: Theory of the Constitution* (1982) and *Constitutional Interpretation* (1991). The same thing is true of Richard Fallon's presentation of "the five types of argument that generally predominate in constitutional debate." See his *A Constructive Coherence Theory of Constitutional Interpretation,* 100 Harvard L. Rev. 1189 (1987). (The quoted language appears at 1194.) Although Richard Posner, too, ignores the distinction between discerning what norm a constitutional norm represents and deciding what shape to give an indeterminate constitutional norm in a particular context, Posner's writings in support of a "pragmatist" approach to constitutional adjudication are best understood, in my view, as supporting a pragmatist approach to the question of what shape to give, in a particular context, an indeterminate constitutional norm – or, at least, to the question of what shape to give an indeterminate constitutional doctrine (indeterminate in the context at hand) that is the yield of earlier judicial efforts to give shape to such a norm. See, e.g., Richard A. Posner,

Bork and Beethoven, 42 Stanford L. Rev. 1365 (1990), and Richard A. Posner, *What Has Pragmatism to Offer Law?* 63 S. California L. Rev. 1653 (1990). (On the relation between an indeterminate constitutional norm and the judicial development of constitutional doctrine, see Section III.B.)

79 Gadamer, supra, note 56 at 275. The complete passage in which Gadamer's statement appears is also in note 56.

80 See Perry, supra, note 11 at 34–5.

81 Brennan, supra, note 18 at 426.

82 "Judicial review" is the name for the judicial practice of inquiring if an act or failure to act violates the Constitution (the Constitution$_2$) of the United States. On the origins of the term "judicial review," see Robert Lowry Clinton, *Marbury v. Madison and Judicial Review* 7 (1989): " 'Judicial review,' as a term used to describe the constitutional power of a court to overturn statutes, regulations, and other governmental activities, apparently was an invention of law writers in the early twentieth century. Edward S. Corwin may have been the first to coin the phrase, in the title of an article in the 1910 *Michigan Law Review.*" Clinton's reference is to Edward S. Corwin, *The Establishment of Judicial Review,* 9 Michigan L. Rev. 102 (1910).

83 See Perry, supra, note 11 at 24–7.

84 See Charles L. Black, Jr., *Structure and Relationship in Constitution Law* 71 (1969): "[J]udicial review of Acts of Congress for federal constitutionality . . . rests also on the visible, active, and long-continued acquiescence of Congress in the Court's performance of this function. The Court now confronts not a neutral Congress nor a Congress bent on using its own constitutional powers to evade the Court's mandates, as some state legislatures have tried (and as Congress very clearly could succeed in doing, in many cases, if it were so minded), but rather a Congress which has accepted, and which by the passage of jurisdictional and other legislation has facilitated, this work of the Court." See also Sylvia Snowiss, *Judicial Review and the Law of the Constitution* x (1990): "I do not offer this [historical] reinterpretation as a way of attacking or defending the [modern] institution of judicial review. I share the prevailing view that judicial authority over legislation has by now generated sufficient support to be unaffected by assessments of original intent."

85 Consider, to cite but one, very important example, the European Court of Human Rights. For recent developments, see Anthony Lester, *Radical Reform of the Enforcement Procedures of the European Convention,* 8 Interrights Bulletin 25 (1994), and Jeremy McBride, *A New European Court of Human Rights,* 8 Interrights Bulletin 47 (1994).

86 For the argument, which invokes Article III of the Constitution, see Justice Story's persuasive opinion for the Court in Martin v. Hunter's Lessee, 14 U.S. (1 Wheat.) 404 (1816). Cf. Alexander M. Bickel, *The Least Dangerous Branch: The Supreme Court at the Bar of Politics* 12–13 (2d ed., 1986).

Article VI of the Constitution states that it "shall be the supreme Law of the Land; and the Judges in every State shall be bound thereby, any thing in the Constitution of Laws of any State to the Contrary notwithstanding." But this provision leaves room for a state judiciary to oppose its own view of what the Constitution$_2$ forbids to the Supreme Court's view (even if the Court's view is endorsed by one or even by both of the other branches of the national government). The state judiciary's view will not stand, because, under Article III of the Constitution, the Supreme Court gets to reverse any state judiciary's interpretation of national law it believes to be incorrect.

87 See supra, note 90.

88 See, e.g., Cooper v. Aaron, 358 U.S. 1, 18 (1958) (unanimous op'n). For a persuasive critical comment on the relevant aspect of the Court's opinion in *Cooper v. Aaron,* see Robin-Vergeer, supra, note 41 at 643–50.

89 See Michael Stokes Paulsen, *The Most Dangerous Branch: Executive Power to Say What the Law Is,* 83 Georgetown L. J. 217 (1994), and Gary Lawson and Christopher D. Moore, *The Province and Duty of the President: The Executive Power of Constitutional Interpretation* (unpublished ms., 1995). See also Robin-Vergeer, supra, note 41. But cf. Van Alstyne, supra, note 41.

90 Similarly, the firm expectation, in American constitutional culture, is that the executive branch of the national government will stand behind a constitutional ruling of the Supreme Court – even one with which the officers of the executive branch, including the president, might disagree – that is being resisted by the state against whom the ruling has gone. In *Cooper v. Aaron,* supra, note 88, the justices of the Court understood this.

91 For an interesting elaboration of the point, see Larry Alexander and Frederick Schauer, *On Extrajudicial Constitution Interpretation,* 110 Harvard L. Rev. 1359 (1997).

92 Cf. Christopher L. Eisgruber, *The Most Competent Branches: A Response to Professor Paulsen,* 83 Georgetown L. J. 347, 371 (1994): "Considerations related to stability, individual rights, and judicial competence provide compelling justification for much (though not all) of the respect routinely accorded the judiciary. In particular, Paulsens' Euclidean logic supplies no ground for doubting two core tenets of the modern doctrine of judicial supremacy: the states may not flout the Supreme Court's interpretations of the Constitution, and the President is almost always (perhaps simply always) bound to comply with and enforce judicial mandates rendered in good faith."

93 See generally Robin-Vergeer, supra, note 41. On RFRA, see supra, note 41.

94 The constitutionality of RFRA as applied to the laws and acts of the national government is beyond serious dispute. See Equal Employment Opportunity Commission v. Catholic University of America, 1996 WL 246568 (D.C.Cir.) – 83 F.3d 455 – (D.C. Cir. 1996).

95 See supra, note 41.

96 See David M. Beatty, ed., *Human Rights and Judicial Review: A Comparative Perspective* (1994).

97 See supra, note 41.

98 Cf. Jon Elster, *Majority Rule and Individual Rights,* in *On Human Rights: The Oxford Amnesty Lectures, 1993* 175 (Stephen Shute and Susan Hurley, eds., 1993).

99 See, e.g., Allan C. Hutchinson, *Waiting for Coraf: A Critique of Law and Rights* (1995), and Robert F. Nagel, *Judicial Power and American Character: Censoring Ourselves in an Anxious Age* (1994). Cf. Mary Becker, *Conservative Free Speech and the Uneasy Case for Judicial Review,* 64 U. Colorado L. Rev. 975 (1993).

100 On the so-called political question doctrine, see Louis Henkin, *Is There a "Political Question" Doctrine?* 85 Yale L. J. 597 (1976); Martin H. Redish, *Judicial Review and the Political Question,* 79 Northwestern U. L. Rev. 1031 (1985); and Robert F. Nagel, *Political Law, Legalistic Politics: A Recent History of the Political Question Doctrine,* 56 U. Chicago L. Rev. 643 (1989).

101 Abraham Lincoln, First Inaugural Address (March 4, 1861), reprinted in *Inaugural Addresses of the Presidents of the United States from George Washington 1789 to George Bush 1989,* S. Doc. No. 10, 101st Cong., 1st Sess. 133, 139 (1989).

102 19 How. 393 (1857). See Don E. Fehrenbacher, *The Dred Scott Case: Its Significance in American Law and Politics* (1978).

103 For further discussion, see Perry, supra, note 11 ch. 4.

104 See id. at 84–6 (discussing the influence of Justice Scalia's conception of proper judicial role on his interpretation of the free-exercise language of the First Amendment).

105 I have discussed this issue at length elsewhere. See id. ch. 6.

106 See supra, note 74.

107 See supra, note 75 and accompanying text.

108 Of course, different persons – different judges – might well draw the boundaries of "the reasonable" in different places. What I am referring to here is not an algorithm of choice, but a judicial stance, a judicial attitude. Although, at the limit, some judge might always or almost always draw the boundaries of "the reasonable" so that they are substantially congruent with "what I, the judge, believe," I think most of us recognize the arrogance, the dogmatism, in that. There will be some occasions, perhaps many, on which we want to say to our interlocutors: "I disagree with you. I think you are wrong. Nonetheless, I have to admit that your position is not unreasonable."

109 In commenting on the suggestion that the Constitution be read "to recognize that governmental assistance to meet basic material needs is a constitutional right," Terrance Sandalow writes: "I have already suggested that there is little in our constitutional tradition to warrant such a reading and much to argue against it. Even if that difficulty is waived, however, the question remains whether courts are competent to undertake the responsibility that Sager would assign them. Governmental budgets call for the resolution of intractable issues, requiring not only choices from among the innumerable demands upon the public fisc, but judgments about the levels of taxation the citizenry will accept and the economic effects of both taxation and the proposed expenditures. Responding to these issues requires access to technical resources unavailable to judges and a breadth of perspective that judges, just because they are politically unaccountable, necessarily lack. The demands upon the treasury that Sager would authorize judges to make, to put the latter point somewhat differently, would necessarily be the product of tunnel vision." Terrance Sandalow, *Social Justice and Fundamental Law: A Comment on Sager's Constitution,* 88 Northwestern U. L. Rev. 461, 467 (1993).

110 Herbert Wechsler's argument about "the political safeguards of federalism" is relevant here. See his *The Political Safeguards of Federalism,* in *Herbert Wechsler, Principles, Politics, and Fundamental Law* 49 (1961). See also Jesse H.

Choper, *Judicial Review and the National Political Process: A Functional Reconsideration of the Supreme Court,* ch. 4 (1980). For a fundamental and vigorous dissent from the position defended by Wechsler and the kindred position defended by Choper, see Steven G. Calabresi, *"A Government of Limited and Enumerated Powers": In Defense of United States v. Lopez,* 94 Michigan L. Rev. 752 (1995).

111 See supra, note 117 and accompanying text.

112 For one who accepts an "originalist" approach to constitutional interpretation, the question of whether the judiciary should play a primary role or only a secondary, Thayerian one in cases arising under the United States Constitution could be answered by the Constitution$_2$. Listen, in that regard, to Gary Lawson, who wrote in his review of my book: "[W]hile Professor Perry is entirely correct that originalism and minimalism are logically distinct concepts, he does not explore the possibility that originalism can resolve the minimalism/nonminimalism debate. Does 'the judicial power of the United States,' as originally understood in 1789, carry with it an understanding of the judicial role that compels either minimalism or nonminimalism as a strategy for [the specification of indeterminate constitutional norms]?" Gary Lawson, *Recommended Reading: Michael J. Perry's "The Constitution in the Courts: Law or Politics?" Federalist Paper,* July 1994, at 9–10. Gary has raised a fair question and identified an important inquiry. Let me just say that I remain deeply skeptical about whether a constitutional consensus was ever achieved concerning the best answer, all things considered, to the minimalism/nonminimalism question.

113 Is there, with respect to state action, a need for a nationally uniform specification of any indeterminate norm that is part of the Constitution of the United States? I don't see it. Imagine this scenario: At Time 1, the legislature in State A declined to enact a law, because it believed that the law would be inconsistent with the best or optimal specification of a relevant but indeterminate norm in the United States Constitution; at Time 2, the legislature in State B enacted the law that the legislature in State A declined to enact, because, unlike the legislature in State A, the legislature in State B believed that the law would not be inconsistent with the best specification of the norm in question; at Time 3, the Supreme Court, on the ground that State B's specification was not unreasonable, declined to invalidate State B's law; at Time 4, the legislature in State A, after reconsidering the matter, reaffirmed its original view and so declined to enact the law. Why is the persistence of a disagreement between the two state legislatures, about the best specification of the norm in question, a problem – much less a problem the Court needs to resolve?

114 See supra, note 45.

115 John Hart Ely, *Another Such Victory: Constitution Theory and Practice in a World Where Courts Are No Different from Legislatures,* 77 Virginia L. Rev. 833, 834 n. 4 (1991).

116 Id.

117 Id.

118 Id. at 834 n. 4 (emphasis added).

119 Id.

120 Ely, supra, note 45 at 103.
121 See John T. Noonan, Jr., *The End of Free Exercise,* 42 DePaul L. Rev. 567 (1992).
122 Douglas Laycock, *The Benefits of the Establishment Clause,* 42 DePaul L. Rev. 373, 376 (1992).
123 319 U.S. 624 (1943).
124 319 U.S. at 666–7 (1943).
125 See supra, note 109.
126 See Jeremy Waldron, *A Right-Based Critique of Constitutional Rights,* 13 Oxford J. Legal Studies 18 (1993), and Jeremy Waldron, *Freeman's Defense of Judicial Review,* 13 Law & Philosophy 27 (1994). See also Jeremy Waldron, *Precommitment and Disagreement,* in Alexander, ed., supra, note 64.
127 Waldron, *A Right-Based Critique of Constitutional Rights,* supra, note 125 at 50–1.
128 Cf. Mark V. Tushnet, *Red, White, and Blue: A Critical Analysis of Constitutional Law* 4 (1988): "Judicial review is an institution designed to meet some difficulties that arise when one tries to develop political institutions forceful enough to accomplish values goals and yet not so powerful as to threaten the liberties of the citizenry."
129 Cf. Jeremy Waldron, Book Review, 90 J. Philosophy 149, 153 (1993) (reviewing Bruce Ackerman, *We the People: Foundations* [1991]): "Even if one concedes the superior authority of Ackerman's higher law making, one is left unsure why it should be the special function of the courts to interpret that legislation. Judicial review becomes politically most important in cases where citizens disagree among themselves about the best way of understanding some constitutional provision. . . . [W]e were all enthusiastically in favor of the free exercise of religion, [for example,] but now in the cold light of morning we have to work out how it is to fit in with public-education policy. Surely on Ackerman's account, this is a problem for normal politics – the phase of the democratic process that alone is capable of working out how various aspects of public policy fit together. . . . Once the people begin disagreeing among themselves about how to interpret their own past acts of higher law making, it is unclear why any particular interpretation of that heritage should be able to trump any other simply because it is endorsed by five judges out of nine. Ackerman asks, "Isn't it better for the Court to represent the *absent* People by forcing our elected politicians/statesmen to measure their statutory conclusions against the principles reached by those who have most successfully represented the People in the past? But that game is up once there is disagreement about the meaning of those principles: then all we have is our present legislation, measured against two or more contrary interpretations of our past.
130 My point is not that, with respect to every other indeterminate constitutional norm, the practice of judicial review should always by Thayerian. As I said, it is perilous to generalize. My point is only that, with respect to certain norms, the practice should always be non-Thayerian.
131 Bickel, supra, note 86 at 24.
132 Id.

4

On the Authority and Interpretation of Constitutions: Some Preliminaries

JOSEPH RAZ

I. What Kind of Constitution?

The writings on constitutional theory fill libraries. They are often presented as, and almost invariably are, writings on the constitutional practice of one country or another. Whether they offer an analysis of current practices, doctrines that may justify them or critiques of these practices, and suggestions for their improvement, they are valid, if at all, against the background of the political and constitutional arrangements of one country or another, valid for the interpretation of the constitution of one country or another. Few writings on constitutional interpretation successfully address problems in full generality; that is, few offer useful lessons regarding the nature of constitutional interpretation as such. In part this is explained by the ambition of writers on interpretation. Whether or not they mean their writings to provide an account of current interpretive practices in their countries, they almost invariably aim to provide an account of how constitutional interpretation should be carried out, an account of the correct method of constitutional interpretation. They also aim to present their conclusions in a form that will be usable by lawyers and judges, and therefore in a form that shuns very abstract formulations which presuppose much for their interpretation and application. They aspire to help with the solution to important constitutional problems facing their countries, and these aspirations limit the relevance of their conclusions to one jurisdiction, or a few similar ones.

But possibly it is not their underlying aspirations that limit the validity of most writings on constitutional interpretation. Possibly there is no room for a truly universal theory of the subject. After all, the law, including constitutional law, can vary from country to country, and from period to period even in one country. Even the most basic understanding of the constitution and its role in the life and law of a country may be different in different countries. How can there be a theory of constitutional interpretation that spans all these differences?

Up to a point these doubts are well founded. A powerful case can be made to the effect that a substantive theory of constitutions and of constitutionalism has limited application. Its application is to some countries and to some constitutions only. One reason is that the notion of "a constitution" is used in legal discourse sometimes in a thin sense and sometimes in a variety of thicker senses. In the thin sense it is tautological that every legal system includes a constitution. For in that sense the constitution is simply the law that establishes and regulates the main organs of government, their constitution and powers, and ipso facto it includes law that establishes the general principles under which the country is governed: democracy, if it establishes democratic organs of government; federalism, if it establishes a federal structure; and so on.

The thick sense of "constitution" is less clear, and probably there are several such senses in use in different legal cultures. For the purposes of the present discussion I will regard constitutions as defined by a combination of seven features.

First, incorporating the thin sense, the constitution defines the constitution and powers of the main organs of the different branches of government. (This feature identifies the constitution as *constitutive* of the legal and political structure which is that legal system.)

Second, it is, and is meant to be, of long duration: It is meant to serve as a stable framework for the political and legal institutions of the country, to be adjusted and amended from time to time, but basically to preserve stability and continuity in the legal and political structure, and the basic principles that guide its institutions. (The constitution is *stable,* at least in aspiration.)

Third, it has a canonical formulation. That usually means that it is enshrined in one or a small number of written documents. It (they) is (are) commonly referred to as the constitution. (The constitution – we say when referring to this feature – is *written.*)

Fourth, it constitutes a superior law. This means that ordinary law which conflicts with the constitution is invalid or inapplicable. (The constitution is *superior law.*)

Fifth, there are judicial procedures to implement the superiority of the constitution, that is, judicial processes by which the compatibility of rules of law and of other legal acts with the constitution can be tested, and incompatible rules or legal acts can be declared inapplicable or invalid. (The constitution is *justiciable.*)

Sixth, while there usually are legal procedures for constitutional amendment, constitutional amendments are legally more difficult to secure than ordinary legislation. (The constitution is *entrenched.*)

Seventh, its provisions include principles of government (democracy, federalism, basic civil and political rights, etc.) that are generally held to express the common beliefs of the population about the way their society should be governed. It serves, you may say, not only as a lawyers' law, but as the people's law. Its main provisions are generally known, command general consent, and are held to be the (or part of the) common ideology that governs public life in that country. (The constitution expresses a *common ideology.*)

This characterization of a constitution (in the thick sense) yields a vague concept. Each one of the seven criteria is vague in application. To give but one example: Is it a condition of a country having a written constitution (condition 3) that there cannot be an "unwritten" part of the constitution – for example, a part that is "customary law"? And if the written-constitution condition is compatible with part of the constitution being unwritten, does it follow that Britain has a written constitution? Remember that while some of its constitution (in the thin sense) is customary or common law, part of it (e.g., the Bill of Rights of 1689, the Act of Union between England and Scotland of 1706, the European Communities Act of 1971) is written law. We know that in the relevant sense Britain does not have a written constitution. But that does not clearly follow from the characterization given, which is vague on the point.

But then the characterization is not meant to draw borderlines, but to focus discussion. Its purpose is to highlight the central features of constitutions – in (one) thick sense – features that explain why (some) constitutions (i.e., constitutions in this thick sense) give rise to theoretical questions that do not apply, at least not to the same degree, to other law. This essay will consider some questions relating to constitutions in this sense. Some of the questions, even some of the answers, apply to constitutions that meet only some of the specified conditions, or meet them only to some degree. Indeed, some of them apply to ordinary (i.e., nonconstitutional) law as well. But it is useful to discuss them in the constitutional context, and we will not be concerned with the degree to which the problems or their solutions apply elsewhere.

There would be little point in investigating in general terms thick constitutions wherever they are were it not the case that they play a major role in the life of more and more countries. Clearly, not all countries have a constitution in this sense. Britain today and the Roman Empire of old are but two examples of countries that do or did not. The absence of a constitution (in the strong sense) may be due to a variety of factors. One is that the country enjoys a level of political consensus that makes a constitution unnecessary. Such consensus means that everyone knows and accepts the framework of government, the distribution of powers among its organs, and the general principles guiding or constraining the exercise of governmental powers. These are, if you like, matters of understood conventions, with no mechanisms for their enforcement. A consensus of this kind can exist in a small country with a relatively homogeneous and stable population, enjoying relative equality of status and a stable economy. But it can also exist in a large country with a diverse population marked by considerable social and economic stratification if it is based on a culture of deference and enjoys stable social, demographic, and economic conditions.

Constitutions in the strong sense tend to exist in societies that enjoy relative stability within diversity and change. Such societies must have stability and a sense of a common identity sufficient to ensure the durability and stability of the constitution itself. But being large-scale societies, with many divisions of, for example, religion, class, and ethnic origin, they need the assurance of publicly accountable government, guided by openly administered principles, to strengthen the stability of the political structures and the authority of their legal institutions. A tempting suggestion is that the way to construct a theory of the authority and the proper interpretation of the (thick) constitution is to explore further the social, cultural, and economic conditions that justify it. Surely they hold the clues to an understanding of the nature and function of the constitution and therefore to its authority and interpretation. But the suggestion is misguided. No doubt such an inquiry will be very valuable. It will not, however, yield the hoped-for results. It assumes that the law, constitutional law at the very least, develops exclusively in response to the relatively stable aspects of the social conditions of the country to which it applies. As we know, this is far too rationalistic a view of the development of the law. Much of it depends on the ambitions of powerful personages, the political convenience of the hour. Fluctuating public moods and even temporary economic turns can lead to changes that remain in force many years after the conditions that led to them are forgotten.

Nor are matters any different with constitutions. The thought that their "higher status" and their propensity for longevity make them responsive only to fundamental and lasting social conditions or social trends is mistaken. In 1995, to give but one example, influential voices in the British Labour Party called on it to put constitutional reform at the center of its platform, because the economic situation in the country seemed to be improving and might favor the Conservative government in the forthcoming election. Similarly, it is arguable that the courts in Britain would not have been so active between the late 1980s and the mid-1990s in developing new doctrines in public law, leading to a series of humiliating defeats for the government, but for the fact that the Conservatives had been in power for seventeen years, meeting very little effective parliamentary opposition. Constitutional politics may not be the same as parliamentary politics, but they are not altogether separate either. Similar examples can be found in the history of other countries, including those with a constitution in the strong sense. Moreover, in our ever-contracting world the adoption of constitutions, and the way they develop, often owe more to fashion than to principle. Certain ways of understanding the constitution become fashionable, perhaps because of the prestige of the country that initiated them. It becomes politically expedient to follow fashion. More than we often like to admit is owed to this factor.

It may be objected that none of these facts matters to constitutional theory, which is a normative theory and therefore unaffected by mere contingencies. In a sense to be explored, a constitutional theory is normative. But that does not mean that it is or should be blind to the basic realities of life. That the adoption and development of constitutions are affected by a variety of short-term factors is no mere aberration in the life of one country or another. It is a universal feature of the political life of all countries with a constitution. Constitutional theory had better allow for that. A theory that condemns all such influences as aberrations to be avoided is too remote from this world to be much use in it.

We will have to come back to this point and explore it further. While the main exploration will have to await a more detailed discussion of the normativity of constitutional theory, we can begin here by making one relevant observation: A good deal of legal development (and this includes constitutional development) is autonomous. This means that its traditions crystallize into practices that are followed in decisions which develop constitutional law. These traditions may be informed by valid considerations, such as concern for the efficiency of government, or for the dignity of individuals, or for the relative autonomy of different regions. But the crucial point is that these considerations do not determine the outcome of the decisions they influence. These considerations will be respected by a variety of constitutional decisions. The decision actually taken is chosen out of habit, or out of respect for the constitutional practices and traditions of that country.

If that is right, and if the autonomous legal traditions of different countries rightly play a major part in determining their constitutional development, then a theory of the constitution cannot be based on social or economic or cultural factors. It cannot be derived from extraneous circumstances. It must allow a major role to internal legal considerations. Therefore, the reflections on a constitutional theory offered here proceed by examining the abstract central features of a constitution, the seven enumerated earlier and some of their implications. The theory abstracts from the possible impact of social conditions, for I assume that they will differ from country to country. I hope, however, that a theory of the constitution will provide the theoretical framework within which the effect of diverse social conditions can be assessed.

I believe that most of what needs saying about the nature of constitutions has already been said. This does not mean, of course, that matters are relatively clear and settled. The problem is not so much that the truth is elusive or obscure and has not yet been seen by anyone, as that a variety of misleading analogies helped lend plausibility to some misguided ideas. I will spend much of this essay trying to explain why we should not listen to some false sirens.

We can start, though, by recalling one principle that seems to be common ground to many approaches to constitutional studies: Constitutional theory comprises two major parts, an account of the authority of constitutions and an account of the way constitutions should be interpreted. The first explains under what conditions the constitution of a country is legitimate, thus fixing the condition under which citizens have a duty to obey it. In doing that, it provides an account of the principles of political morality that underpin the constitution, in that they justify and legitimize its enforcement, if it is indeed justified. The theory of constitutional interpretation explains the ways the principles of constitutional interpretation in different countries are determined. A principle of constitutional theory that commands widespread support says that the principles of constitutional interpretation depend in part on the theory of constitutional authority. In determining the conditions for constitutional legitimacy, the theory of the authority of the constitution contributes to the determination of principles of interpretation. Unfortunately, this sound principle is also the source of many false analogies motivated by attempts to assimilate the authority of the constitution to that of other parts of the law.

PART I: THE AUTHORITY OF CONSTITUTIONS

II. The Authority of the Constitution and the Authority of its Authors

It is tempting to think that the authority of law, of any law, derives from the authority of its maker. Customary law is allowed to be a puzzling exception. But consider enacted law – that is, law whose validity derives from the fact that it was made by a legitimate legal authority acting with the intention to make law. The paradigm example of this kind of law is statutes. They are valid because they were passed by a body authorized in law to pass them. If, for example, the legal validity of a regulation is impugned on the ground that the body that enacted it had no legal power to do so, the charge cannot be repulsed by a claim, however justified, that the rule the regulation embodies is nevertheless legally binding because it is a good rule, one that it would be sensible to follow. This does not mean that the merits of rules are irrelevant to legal reasoning. In appropriate contexts, such considerations can guide the interpretation of a statute or regulation whose legal validity is established on other grounds. In some contexts, the merits of having a rule of a certain kind may also justify the courts in adopting it and basing their decision on it, even if this requires overriding existing legal rules. The merit of a rule may also be grounds for giving it binding force, either through the courts, by turning it into a binding precedent, or by legislation. But the merit of a rule is not the sort of consideration which can establish that it is already legally binding.

I belabor this familiar point to bring out the fact, itself obvious, that the identity of the lawmaker is material to the validity of the law, at least in the case of enacted law. It is plausible to think that only if the identity of the lawmaker is the reason for the validity of the law can one make sense of this feature of enacted law. The fact that the law was made by that person or institution provides, on this view, the justification (at least at one level of justification) for holding the enacted rule to be valid in law. That means that with enacted law the authority of the law derives from the authority of its maker.

This is a powerful argument for the claim that the authority of constitutions derives from the authority of their makers. The argument is not that there is no other way in which law can have authority. Customary law shows that there are other ways of establishing the authority of law. Nor is the argument that anything which was made with the intention to make law must, if it is legally valid at all, derive its authority from the authority of its maker. That is not so either. In Britain, to mention just one example, a regulation laying down a rule may be *ultra vires,* in that the body which adopted it had no power to make law on that matter, and yet the rule which the regulation embodied may be valid, since it also happens to be a long-established common law rule. The argument lies elsewhere: Unless the authority of the constitution derives from the authority of its makers, there is no explaining the fact that it matters that it was made by one body rather than another. But surely it makes all the difference in the world that the constitution was adopted by those who did adopt it, and not by others. It is, we want to say, valid because it was so adopted. Does it not follow, by the force of the argument above, that its authority derives from the authority of those who made it?

As is so often the case, the short answer is both yes and no. To explain it, a longer answer must be given. But first we must dispose of a false answer waiting in the wings. Its interest lies not so much in itself, but in bringing us face to face with one aspect of the perennial question of the relations between law and morality. It may be claimed that the authority of constitutions cannot derive from that of their makers, for their makers, standing at the birth of their states, cannot have authority themselves. All authority derives from the constitution that they themselves made without prior authority to do so.

A. *The Nature of the Authority of the Makers of an Originating Constitution*

To be taken seriously, this argument has to be confined to the few constitutions that can be called "originating" constitutions. Most constitutions are not like that. They are made by legitimate legal authorities as part of a process of legal reform. Even constitutions that stand at the birth of a new independent country are often made in pursuance of legal authority conferred on their makers by the previous legal order in force in these countries, often a colonial regime. This is the way most of the countries of the British Commonwealth acquired their independence. But is not the argument cogent regarding those constitutions to which it applies? It is not.

The argument assumes that only those on whom authority has been conferred by preexisting law can have legitimate authority. That is not, nor can it be, the case. Legal authority is itself a form of claimed moral authority.[1] The point is sometimes lost to sight, for legal structures transmit the authority to make law from one body to another. We are familiar with the fact that the law is a structure of authority, in which each legal authority derives its power from laws made by another. We rely on the authority of one to justify the authority of another. Only infrequently do we appeal to moral reasons to justify a claim to legal authority. This gives discourse about legal authority an appearance of being autonomous, technical, legal discourse. In a way it is. If the constitution and the other rules that establish legal authorities are morally justified, so are the authorities that they establish, and the laws made by those authorities are morally binding. This means that once the moral justification of those ultimate legal rules (i.e., those whose legal validity does not presuppose that of any other law) is established, or assumed, the moral justification of the rest of the law is – up to a point – established by technical legal argumentation. (This is so up to a point only, because, as was noted, the interpretation of the law may well involve further moral or other nonlegal considerations.) Since much of the time legal argument is addressed to legal officials who accept the moral validity of the ultimate laws, and much legal argument explains (to clients or lawyers, or to any individual) what is the position in law – on the supposition that it is morally legitimate – regarding one matter or another, much legal argument is technically legal.

None of this denies the fact that the law claims to be morally binding and that on the whole only people who accept that claim, people who accept at least that it is morally permissible to apply the law (to tax people, to determine their property rights, or their right in and to employment, to imprison them, etc.), serve in the authorities that make and apply the law. A theory of law is, therefore and among other things, a theory of the conditions, if any, under which the law is morally legitimate and of the consequences that follow from the assumption that it is morally legitimate. That is also the nature of our investigation into the authority of the constitution. If the constitution is not an originating constitution, if it has been made by a body on which some other law (perhaps an earlier constitution) bestowed power to enact a constitution, then it may be morally legitimate if the law that authorized it is morally legitimate. But if it is an originating constitution, then the question of its moral legitimacy cannot turn on the legitimacy of any other law. It must turn directly on moral argument.

It follows that the argument that an originating constitution cannot derive its authority from the authority of its makers for they had no such authority is invalid. It is true that the makers of the constitution had no authority bestowed on them by other laws. But it does not follow that they had no authority, nor that the authority of the constitution cannot rest on their authority. They may have moral authority, and it may be the reason for the authority of the constitution.

One may reply that, true as my observations are, they miss the point of the argument they were meant to refute. That argument, it may be said, is about the *legal* authority of originating constitutions, not about their moral authority. In a sense it is true that their framers did not have legal authority. (It is misleading to put the point in this form, but the technical considerations involved need not detain us here.)[2] The crucial point is that our interest in legal authority lies in how it establishes the moral authority of the law, or of parts of it. We are interested in the authority of law, if any, in order to establish whether we have an obligation to respect and obey it.[3] Moreover, the grounds for the authority of the law help to determine how it ought to be interpreted. Judges, perhaps more than anyone else, follow the law because they believe they are morally required to do so. There can be no other way in which they can justify[4] imprisoning people, interfering with their property, jobs, family relations, and so on, decisions that are the daily fare of judicial life.

It may be worth repeating that none of this implies that there is no room for more narrowly focused legal reasoning about whether any institution meets the purely legal conditions for the possession of authority. My claim is only that such an inquiry is of interest because it is embedded in a wider inquiry into the moral legitimacy of that institution's power. Nor do I claim that in any chain of reasoning about legal authority there will be a stage in which the moral considerations affecting legitimacy will be confronted directly or explicitly. Very often they are taken for granted. Nor is it, of course, my claim that whenever the legal conditions for legitimacy are met so are the moral conditions.

B. The Argument from the Rule of Recognition

This may be an appropriate place to clear out of the way another misguided argument for the independence of the authority of the constitution from that of its authors. Some theorists who broadly follow H. L. A. Hart's theory of law think that the constitution of a country is its rule of recognition, as that term is used by Hart.[5] Since the rule of recognition exists as a practice of the legal officials, it is, as it were, a living rule, a rule sustained by *current attitudes and conduct,* and not by what happened at the point it came into being. Hence, since the constitution is the rule of recognition, the constitution's authority derives from the current practice of the officials, and not from the authority of its makers.

This argument is easily refuted. For one thing, its conclusion can be turned around and used as a ground for rejecting its central premise: If the constitution is the rule of recognition, then its authority does not derive from the authority of its authors; since its authority does derive from the authority of its authors, it follows that the constitution is not the rule of recognition. There is no reason to prefer the argument to this reversal of it. This lands us in a tie. Fortunately, there are plenty of independent reasons which establish that constitutions are not the rules of recognition of their countries. No constitution can be, if that term is understood in the thick sense in which it is used here. For example, most constitutions may be amended or even repealed and replaced by others in accordance with procedures that they themselves provide. This means that they can be amended or repealed by enactment. The rule of recognition cannot be repealed or amended by an enactment. It can change only as the practice that it is changes. Customary law can be repealed and replaced by statute. There is nothing in the nature of custom to prevent it from being changed by legislation. But once that happens, the law on the point is no longer customary. It is statutory. The rule of recognition, on the other hand, cannot give way to statutory law. It is and always remains customary.

Not only is it a mistake to identify constitutions with rules of recognition, but rules of recognition do not play the legitimating role that constitutions can play.[6] The rule of recognition is unlike the rest of the law. It is the practice – that is, the fact – that the courts and other legal institutions recognize the validity, the legitimacy, of the law, and that they are willing to follow it and apply it to others. As such it is unlike any other legal rule, including other customary legal rules. It is the point (one such point) at which – metaphorically speaking – the law ends and morality begins. It is the fact that enables us to separate legal from moral facts. If the rule of recognition exists – that is, if the appropriate practice of recognition is followed by the courts – then the law exists. But only if they are right in so conducting themselves is the law actually legitimate and binding, morally speaking.

Put it in different terms: Because we can identify a social fact of the judicial recognition of the law by the courts, we can establish that there is a law in a certain country and establish its content even if it is a morally bad and illegitimate system of law. The rule of recognition, being a social fact, enables us to identify the law without recourse to morality. But that is (by and large) all it does. It cannot be sensibly regarded as a conventional rule – that is, we cannot assume it to be a necessary truth that when a judge follows the practice of, let us say, applying acts passed by the Queen in Parliament as binding, he does so because all the courts do so, or because they all hold themselves duty-bound

to do so (even though they do). He may do so because Acts of Parliament enjoy democratic legitimacy, or for some other reason. The rule of recognition
constitutes a normative practice, but not a conventional practice.

C. The Argument from Consent

Some people think that the only way in which some people can have authority
over others is through the others' consent.[7] Since the constitution is the source
of legal authority in the state, its own authority must arise from the consent of
the governed. If consent is the source of all authority, then this consent must
be the consent of the living, the consent of those subject to the law as it is
from time to time. Those who think that consent is the foundation of authority
cannot tolerate the supposition that the current generation is subject to the law
because it enjoyed the consent of the population living two hundred years
ago. Hence, even if a constitution was adopted by a referendum, it is valid not
because of the process by which it was adopted originally but because it commands the consent of the public as it is from time to time.

Some variants of this argument modify it to accommodate two objections:
First is the fact that some people may refuse their consent by whim in a totally
arbitrary or irrational way. When this happens, those who refuse their consent
will not be subject to the law of the state. They can break the law with impunity. It seems implausible that it is that easy to escape the authority of the
law, that people can escape its authority at will. Second, many people are
never actually called upon to give their consent to the constitution. Many may
have failed to consent to it simply because it never occurred to them that they
should. Again it seems implausible that they will be exempt from the authority of the law. Both objections can be circumvented if one stipulates that the
consent that gives rise to the authority of the constitution is not necessarily
the actual consent of the governed. Rather, at least regarding those who did
not in fact consent, it is the fact that they would have consented – had they
been reasonable and rational people (but not necessarily exemplary moral
people) – if they had been invited to do so. These variants regard authority as
arising out of the hypothetical consent of the governed.

This is not the place to engage in a comprehensive discussion of the weaknesses of consent accounts of authority.[8] Suffice it to say that while in the respects mentioned accounts based on hypothetical consent are stronger than
simple consent-based accounts, in others they are weaker: There is some normative force to the fact that one gives one's free and informed[9] consent to an
arrangement affecting oneself, which hypothetical consent does not have.
Consent, whether wise or foolish, expresses the will of the agent concerning
the conduct of his own life. Whatever mess results from his consent is, in part
at least, of his own making. Since his life is his own, it is relevant whether it is

under his control or not, and consent shows that it is. So even if real consent is a source of authority, it is far from clear that hypothetical consent is. I know of no argument which shows that it is.[10]

In any case, *this* relevance of consent is not of a kind that can establish the legitimacy of any authority. Not being able to argue the case in full, let me give an analogy: Suppose that I consent to a boxing match with an opponent of far superior strength and skill. I am simply mad at him and lose my head in my desire to fight him. That I consented is relevant to what I can say later, when nursing my wounds. It affects the sort of complaints I can make (I can say to my friends, "Why didn't you stop me?" but I cannot say to my enemy, "Why did you fight me?"). It also affects any reasonable judgment of my character. But it does not necessarily establish that my enemy was right to fight me. He should have known that boxing is immoral and that my consent does not make it otherwise. He should have known that the fight will not be fair, given his superiority (he was not fighting in self-defense; it was an arranged fight). You may disagree with the judgments I am relying on here. Even so, you should agree that if they are true then my consent did not make my enemy's action right. The case of legitimate government is similar: My consent can bar me from certain complaints and can be material to judging my character. But it cannot endow the government with a right to govern if it did not have it – unless consent is relevant to its right in a way that is different from the one I was commenting on earlier. I will assume in the sequel that that aspect of consent is not relevant to our issue.

It is plausible to suppose that whatever merit there is in hypothetical-consent accounts derives from the fact that the kind of hypothetical consent they involve captures whatever it is that matters in real-consent accounts – for example, that it represents the true will of the agent. To that extent they suffer from some of the limitations of real-consent accounts – that is, those which affect not only the form of consent, but its underlying rationale. An important aspect of consent, as of all human action, is that it is given for a reason – that is, a reason the agent regards as a good reason, in light of all the considerations, moral considerations included, that apply to the case. The reasons agents believe in may not be good reasons, or not adequate to the task, and the agents may even know this and give their consent out of weakness of the will. However, I know of no consent-based account of authority that does not assume that the reasons for the consent are cogent and adequate. Indeed, it would be impossible to base authority on consent that is misguided and ill-founded – again, I am afraid, not a point that can be established here. But if so, then the consent is given in the true belief that there is adequate reason to recognize the authority of the institutions, or principles, in question. The question arises whether these considerations are not enough to establish the authority of those bodies or principles, independently of the consent.

Obviously, in many cases consent is required for one to have an obligation. But typically these are cases in which the wisdom of the consent is not in question (e.g., with few exceptions, a promise is binding whether or not one's reasons for making it are good reasons). It is equally clear that not all obligations arise out of consent or undertakings (e.g., the obligation to keep one's promises does not depend on consenting to do so). Nor do all our obligations to accede to the will of others arise out of consent (e.g., we have an obligation to accede, within bounds, to the will of our parents, which – at least in the conditions prevailing in some societies – extends beyond childhood and applies to the relations between adults and their parents as well). So the question arises: If consent to authority is effective only when based on adequate reasons to recognize the authority, why are these reasons not enough in themselves to establish that authority?

This is a serious question, not a rhetorical one. We can well imagine answers which would show that in certain matters no one can have authority over another except with that person's consent. Such may be the case in matters that relate to what we call "private" areas of life. What is much more difficult to imagine is that no political authority can be legitimate without consent – that is, that there is no area over which an authority may have legitimate power independently of consent. Many areas of governmental action (e.g., determining the relative contribution of individuals to the maintenance of essential common services or securing that those who injure others compensate them for the harm caused, when fairness or justice require that they do so) are matters of setting up schemes to facilitate conformity with precepts of justice and morality, and these are typical of matters where obligations that are not voluntary abound.

Assuming that in many areas authority need not depend on consent makes it more likely that in these matters at least consent is not a way of establishing authority at all.[11] For it seems reasonable to suppose that, regarding such matters, the only reasons which justify consent to authority also justify the authority without consent.

If the sketch of the argument offered here can be fleshed out to make a sound argument, then consent is not at all an important way of establishing legitimate political or legal authority. This puts an end to the consent-based argument to show that the authority of constitutions cannot derive from the authority of their authors.

D. The Dead Hand of the Past

We should turn to the best-known and most powerful argument aiming to sever the authority of constitutions from that of their authors. No one, the argument goes, can have authority over future generations. Therefore, the authority of a constitution cannot rest on the authority of its makers. Let us examine it.

First, a couple of obvious qualifications: The argument does not apply to new constitutions. But constitutions are meant to last for a long time, and it is fair to concentrate on older constitutions, as all constitutions are meant to be one day. Equally obviously, at least prima facie, the argument applies equally to old statutes. There may be differences between constitutions and ordinary law, arising out of the differences in their content, which affect the argument. But these remain to be argued for. Neither of these points substantially affects the force of the argument.

The way the argument works is this: We are looking for the conditions under which constitutions can be justified, can enjoy legitimate (moral) authority. Whatever they are, it cannot be the case that the authority of an old constitution can derive from the authority of its authors. For there is no reasonable way of justifying the authority of any institution that allows it to have authority stretching long into the future. How much into the future can authority stretch? Does the power of an authority die with it? And if so, what is the lifetime of an institutional authority (is it the period between elections, does the U.S. Congress change every two years or every six years, or is it a continuous body that will die only with a fundamental change in its constitution)? Or should we think of the lifetime of an individual authoritative decree, the lifetime of each individual statute or regulation, or that of every constitutional provision? The second seems the more reasonable approach.

The authority of institutions to issue binding decrees is limited in various ways: Some institutions have authority to lay down binding rules about the way banks should be run; others may have authority to direct the running of schools. Possibly, no institution can have unlimited authority regarding all subject matters. Similarly, the authority of any institution is limited by the range of people subject to it. Some have authority over people in Kansas, others over people in France, and so on. The considerations that limit the authority of others over us are, roughly speaking, of the same order as those that establish the immorality of slavery. They set limits to subjugation, to the subordination of one person to the will of another. Just as they do that by setting limits to the subject matter regarding which different authorities can have power and to the range of people over whom their power extends, so those very same considerations limit the temporal validity of their directives. Just as the range of subject matter and people will vary from case to case, so the temporal duration of an authoritative directive will vary depending on the circumstances. But it is reasonable to think, say, that none will be valid one hundred years after its passing. That is, if it were still valid at that time, that would not be due to the authority of its original author.

It is tedious to spell out the argument to this conclusion in full detail. But it may be helpful to provide some pointers to the sort of considerations involved. They come at two levels: (a) the types of factors that determine whether laws are good or bad and (b) the factors that determine the competence of political authorities to achieve worthwhile goals, which thereby both establish and limit the scope of their legitimate powers. Considerations of both levels must be combined to establish the boundaries of political authorities.

I will illustrate the first level by mentioning two categories (simplified for the purpose of the present discussion):

1. Some law, if it is good law, directly[12] implements unconditional moral imperatives. Here one may mention the basic legal protection of personal safety in the criminal law and (to a certain degree) tort law. Some civil rights, like freedom of religion or of thought, are often thought to belong to this category.
2. Much law, if it is good law, reflects a fair distribution of opportunities, resources, and amenities among members of the population, given their actual or likely needs, goals, and aspirations, the existing technological and economic resources, and the existing social organization. Laws whose value is to be judged by these criteria should be subject to continuous review, as the factors that make them satisfactory at any time are subject to frequent and significant changes. These include all welfare law, planning and zoning laws, consumer protection legislation, safety regulations, health provisions, education law, and much else.

It may be thought that laws belonging to the first category do not require frequent adjustment. They incorporate into law immutable moral principles. Therefore, it may be argued, the authority of lawmakers to make these kinds of law is long-lasting. But the argument fails on both counts. First, while arguably the moral precepts that these laws are there to enforce are immutable, it does not follow that so are the laws that protect and enforce them. Take a simple example: The moral wrong committed by rape may involve the violation of a universal moral principle. But the legal regulation of rape may rightly vary from place to place and from time to time. To go no further, it is far from a universal principle that rape should constitute a separate offense rather than be assimilated to serious assault. There is no generally cogent reason for there being a one-to-one correlation between type of moral wrong and type of offense. Whether and when a sexual motive should determine the character of the offense, rather than be relevant to the sentence only, whether or when penetration should single out some sex offenses from others, whether or when violence matters or not (it is not a necessary ingredient of rape, according to most jurisdictions) – all these are questions sensitive to social conditions, to perceived social meanings, to the informal consequences of criminal convictions, and to many other factors that are as variable as any. Hence, the first step in the argument for a long-lasting authority regarding laws directly implementing universal moral principles of conduct is unsound.

The second leg of the argument is no more sound. To see that, let us waive the objection I raised in the preceding paragraph. Let us assume that there is a category of laws whose validity is as timeless as that of the universal moral principles from which they derive. Would that show that long after their enactment the authority of these laws rests on the authority of their makers? Far from it. This may be the case should the authority of the laws derive from the authority of their makers. But the very fact that they have, as we suppose, timeless authority militates against that view. The timeless authority of these supposed laws depends on their content. If they are timelessly valid, that is because they express universal moral principles. They are not timelessly valid because they were enacted by a fallible social institution or approved by a referendum. For an authority to be able to pass timelessly valid laws of this kind it must be counted as an expert on morality – that is, as having a significantly superior grasp of abstract moral principles than do the people who are bound by its laws. While there seem to be people who acquire moral expertise in some specialized problems of applied morality (e.g., the knotted issue of consent to medical experimentation), there is no reason to think that anyone or any institution can claim expertise in the very abstract basic principles of morality. Therefore, the authority of laws that express such principles cannot derive from that of their authors at all. As I indicated in my comment on the first step of the argument, in fact the authority of the law can be said to derive from that of its author at least inasmuch as the laws determine the temporary, and socially sensitive, way in which moral principles are to be enshrined into law. But that does not help show that anyone can have lawmaking authority to make laws that last for very long.

On the whole the case for the temporally limited authority of institutions regarding laws of the second kind – those that allocate resources, burdens, and opportunities fairly among people – is easier to establish. It seems impossible to formulate these laws in ways that do not necessitate frequent revision. Given that lawmakers cannot make laws that remain good for long, their authority cannot be the reason for the authority of old laws that they made.

To see this point more clearly we need to turn to the second level of considerations, to the factors that determine the competence of institutions to function well and, therefore, to be legitimate authorities. These have been touched upon in the preceding few paragraphs but deserve separate consideration, however brief.

Broadly speaking, political authority can be based on one or more of three types of considerations: expertise, coordination, and symbolic value. Considerations of expertise underlie, for example, much consumer protection law, safety at work law, and most other safety regulations. They are also relevant to many laws that implement direct moral imperatives. Medical expertise is relevant to the definition of death, as well as health, illness, injury, and the like. Psychological expertise is relevant to many aspects of family law, and so on. To assume that expertise gives lawmakers timeless authority is to assume that either no advance in knowledge in the relevant area or no advance in its spread is likely, or both. Such advances would negate the expertise of the old lawmakers relative to new experts (new advances in knowledge) or relative to the population at large (the spread of knowledge). Either would denude them of legitimate authority insofar as it is based on expertise.

Much law is a matter of securing social coordination. Securing coordination predominates when the law aims to secure social conditions whose achievement depends on the conduct of a number of people, and when, should enough of them not behave in a way conducive to the achievement of the desired conditions, there is no reason (or no sufficient reason) for others to behave in that way either.[13] The law can help to secure coordination, and in fulfilling these functions it can achieve a variety of goals, including all those that fall into the second category listed earlier. Inasmuch as forms of coordination have to be adjusted or replaced by others in changing circumstances, and inasmuch as there is a limit to anyone's ability to provide for such changes in advance, there is a limit, a temporal limit, on the laws they have power to make.

The third factor that can endow institutions with authority is the symbolic value of their position as legal authorities. Here we have to distinguish between the value of an office and the value of having a certain person, or group of people, holding the office. Some people qualify for positions of high authority in having become symbols of their nations in periods of transition or struggle. The position of Vaclav Havel in the years immediately following the democratization of Czechoslovakia (and later in the Czech Republic) is an instance of that, and there are many others. Our concern, however, lies in the less common, or at least less easy to document, case in which an institution has acquired symbolic value. Arguably, the Crown has such a position in the United Kingdom. It expresses and symbolizes the unity of the country (which is not a nation-state). The symbolic meaning of an institution is itself reason to recognize it as enjoying morally legitimate standing. While the symbolic value of giving office to certain people does not affect the theory of authority, the fact that an institution has symbolic value may feature in an argument establishing its legitimate authority. But it is unlikely to affect it in a timeless way. After all, there is prima facie reason for not accepting laws as valid unless they are the sorts of laws one should have. That the institution making them is of value does not show that the laws it has enacted are good. Even if the value of the institution may nevertheless provide an argument for recognizing its authority, it is not likely to extend to endowing it with timeless authority.

I have rehearsed these familiar considerations because they are of the kind that tends to establish that no human institution has authority to make laws which last forever, or for a very long time. It follows that even if new constitutions may derive their authority from the authority of their makers, old constitutions, if morally valid at all, must derive their authority from other sources. While with new law the authority of the law derives from the authority of its makers, the authority of old law must rest on other grounds.

III. Principle and Practice in Justification

A. *Difficulties about Facts and Norms*

This conclusion is liable to appear paradoxical on a number of grounds. It may be thought to give rise to a paradox of change: The constitution that is valid in the United States today is the one that came into force in 1789 and has been amended a few times since, most importantly between 1865 and 1870. But if my conclusion is right, some may object, then sometime after its adoption the constitution lapsed and a new different constitution came into place. But this is a simple misunderstanding. My argument is not that the constitution changed, but that the reasons for its validity did. The same law can be valid for a variety of reasons, and these may change without the law changing.

There may be a deeper worry in the background, which I am groping to identify. One strand in it arises out of the worry that my argument leaves unexplained the full role of the original constitution-makers and their importance in the life of some countries. It is not exhausted by their role in the early life of the constitution. There are countries where respect for the authors of the constitution is very much a living political force long after the validity of the constitution has ceased, according to the argument of the preceding section, to depend on their authority. But that need not be an obstacle to accepting the argument. The authors of a constitution, especially the authors of a country's first constitution, sometimes become political symbols, people respect for whom unites the country and appeal to whose wisdom becomes the common currency of political argument. Such political facts – justified or otherwise – need have no bearing on the narrower issue of the grounds for the legitimate authority of constitutions, where they have such authority. Nor is the fact that the wisdom of the founding fathers, and so on, is appealed to in interpreting a constitution an objection to the argument, for, as will be seen later, local interpretive practices are to a degree self-legitimating.

But these are not the only worries the argument of the preceding section gives rise to. It also raises new questions about the relations between law and morality. We recognize the dual character of the law. On the one hand it is a social rather than a moral fact that the law of one country or another is so and so, and no different. This aspect of the law derives from several features fundamental to our understanding of its nature: First, it explains how there can be not only good and bad law, but also law and governments lacking all (moral) legitimacy, as well as those that are (morally) legitimate.[14] Second, it explains why we cannot learn what the law in a certain country, or on a certain matter, is simply by finding out what it ought to be. Third, it explains how two people, one believing the law to be legitimate and the other denying its legitimacy, can nevertheless agree on what it is. What accounts for these and other simple but deep features of the law is that it is a social fact, which means that its existence and content can be established as social facts are established, without reliance on moral arguments.[15] On the other hand, the law has a different, normative aspect. It aims to guide people's conduct and it claims moral authority to do so. And while it may fail to enjoy such authority, it must be in principle capable of making its claim good. That is, the law is a social institution that claims moral authority over its subjects and is in principle, by its nature, capable of enjoying such authority.

A theory of law must explain this dual nature of the law, as fact[16] and as norm. The doctrine that the (moral) authority of all law derives from the (moral) authority of its authors provides an easy way of doing so. There are, according to the simple version of this explanation, two steps in establishing the moral validity of the law. First, one has to establish the moral authority of the lawmakers to make law, and then one has to establish as a matter of social fact alone that those lawmakers made this particular law – that is, a law with this particular content. The two aspects of the law are thus separated into these two stages in establishing the legitimate authority of the law. According to this explanation, the moral authority of the law, if it has any, derives in part from its factuality. That it consists in such and such social facts becomes the core of the moral argument for its authority: When these facts are of such and such character, moral arguments endow the law with moral legitimacy, but when they have this and that character, there is no moral argument that can legitimate the law. This explains why the content of the law can be established independently of any issues regarding its moral legitimacy. Here morality follows the facts: It applies to independently established facts.

But all this presupposes that legislators, in the form of social institutions, mediate between law and morality. They provide the factual anchor of the law; they are part of its factual aspect, which is then submitted to moral scrutiny. Much in this simple picture is correct, but it unnecessarily focuses on legislation as the one feature that allows for an account combining the two aspects of the law. An adequate account of the dual nature of the law along the suggested lines[17] requires (a) that the content and existence of the law be determined by social sources and (b) that the moral argument for the authority of the law depends on the actual nature of the social sources. It does not require that the social sources take the form of legislation. They can be custom, common law, juristic opinions, and much else.[18]

It may help clarify the picture to reflect on the implications for the relations between law and morality of the dual aspect of law. The two aspects of the law are reconciled by the fact that the application of morality to our conduct is mediated by its application to norm-making social facts. This is a special kind of mediation. It is not surprising that our moral rights and duties depend on how things are with us and with the world in which we live: "I should not take this or that action, for there are people around who may get hurt by it." "I should offer assistance to this person, for he fell down and needs help." "I should give the car to my neighbor next week, for I promised to do so." These are common instances of the way the implications of morality depend on facts. But none of them are norm-creating facts.

Not so in its relations to the law. Here morality applies by sanctioning (or condemning) norms generated by the social facts of legislation, custom, and so on. Why must it be mediated in this special way when it comes to law? Not because all moral considerations have to be mediated by socially generated norms. The reasons for this are, at least in part, well understood. The law can help in securing social coordination and in bringing to people the benefits of information that is not generally available. The ability to benefit from such information and to secure social coordination is often advantageous or even necessary to achieve valuable goals, and even for compliance with moral requirements. But why cannot people coordinate their actions or share information without the mediation of legal norms? If moral norms are enough to justify coordination and sharing of information, why do not people act to achieve these goals simply because they are aware of the moral reasons for doing so? Sometimes they do, and when they do legal mediation is not necessary. But sometimes they do not, and for all too familiar reasons. Among the reasons that have attracted much attention in recent writings are (a) the fact of disagreement about which goals one has good (moral) reasons to pursue, (b) collective action problems, and (c) the indeterminacy of moral reasons. These factors make it sometimes difficult to secure coordination and sharing of information, except through the intervention of social or legal authorities whose legitimacy is acknowledged and who possess enough power to enforce a reasonable degree of compliance by those who doubt their legitimacy or who might otherwise be tempted to free-ride and so on.

Perhaps the last factor mentioned is the least familiar.[19] The underlying thought is simple: Barring ignorance and disagreement about moral goals or the best ways of implementing them, and barring backsliding, free riding and their like, were moral considerations to indicate how things should be arranged in society in a univocal way then people would follow these considerations. But when moral considerations underdetermine the goals to be pursued or the ways to pursue them, there may be additional difficulties in securing coordination, and to overcome them the mediation of the law is sometimes helpful, and in some cases necessary. Think of a hypothetical example: Assume that the theory of democracy yields only a general principle – for example, that a democratic government is one where there are formal legal mechanisms making the content of policies and the identity of those in charge of implementing them sensitive to the wishes of the governed, in a way that as far as possible does not give any individual greater political power than that enjoyed by any other. It follows that there can be in principle many morally legitimate ways of organizing democratic governments: federal republics and unitary constitutional monarchies, single-member constituencies, and proportional representation systems, parliamentary government and elected presidential systems, and so on. All these radically different systems would be adequate democratic systems of government. Possibly, the circumstances of one country or another will make one or more of them inadequate for that country. But – that is the assumption underlying the example – such considerations will not reduce the number of acceptable systems to one.

In such circumstances mediation through law serves the role of concretizing moral principles – that is, of giving them the concrete content they must have in order for people to be able to follow them. In our example a country must have one or another system of democratic government. So the law determines which one it has. Of course, to do so the law itself must be a matter of social, not moral, fact. Its point and purpose, as far as this example goes, is to supplement morality. To do that, its content cannot be determined by moral considerations. It must reflect social practices or traditions or some other social facts.

These considerations show how the fact that the content of the law is determined by facts and not by norms not only explains the fundamental truisms about the law that I stated earlier, and others like them, but also contributes to an account of how the law is capable of discharging some of its basic functions (such as tackling disagreements about morality and concretizing moral principles). The very same considerations explain how sometimes it is advantageous, morally speaking, for the mediation to be through legislation, whereas in other circumstances it is better for it to be through other means. Legislation would be the preferred method of mediation when changes in the law become desirable frequently, or suddenly, and when the adjustments to the law that become desirable can be worked out through deliberation or negotiation. But other forms of mediation are preferable when the adjustments to the changes can be slow and gradual, when neither deliberation nor negotiation is of much help, and especially when it is important to secure continuity, to discourage premature or hasty change, to deny interest groups the possibility of blackmailing (or twisting the arms of) the rest of the community into agreeing to change, and so on. In brief, mediation should not be carried out exclusively through legislation when the matter is of constitutional importance, that is when it should form part of an entrenched constitution.

B. *Legitimacy through Practice*

The discussion of the relations between norm and fact is instructive. But the conclusion it points to may seem problematic. Let me put it in the most paradoxical form: Constitutions, at least old ones, do not derive their authority from the authority of their authors. But there is no need to worry as to the source of their authority. They are self-validating. They are valid just because they are there, enshrined in the practices of their countries.

Obviously to put it thus is to misrepresent the conclusions that the preceding discussion yields. A most important qualification should be added to them: *As long as they remain within the boundaries set by moral principles,* constitutions are self-validating in that their validity derives from nothing more than the fact that they are there. It should be added that this conclusion follows *if morality underdetermines* the principles concerning the form of government and the content of individual rights enshrined in constitutions. I have said nothing in support of the underdetermination thesis, nor will I do so in this essay. However, since I believe this to be the case,[20] I will explore here some implications of this position.

The main implication is that within the broad bounds set by moral principles, practice-based law is self-vindicating. The constitution of a country is a legitimate constitution because it is the constitution it has. This conclusion has to be explained and elaborated before we can accept it.

First, the fact that moral principles underdetermine the content of the constitution does not mean that the people or institutions who adopt constitutions or amend them do not do so for reasons, or that they cannot have adequate reasons for their decisions. It only follows that their reasons are not ones of moral principles (i.e., not the moral principles that determine which constitution is legitimate and which is not). For example, a government may support a change in the constitution that is not required by principled moral grounds for the reason that it is popular with the electorate or for the reason that it will offer some advantage to a group that is currently resentful and alienated and will thus help reconcile it to the state, or to the larger society. Alternatively, such a change may recommend itself simply because it is a change, and a change will infuse a new spirit in a society that has grown moribund and stagnant, or because every change leads to some people losing power and others gaining power, and it is good to reduce the power of the people or groups who currently hold power in the country.

Such reasons and many others are in a sense moral reasons, and they can be perfectly adequate reasons for adopting changes in a constitution. The point is that none of them is what I will call a"merit reason"; none derives from the moral desirability of any constitutional provision. I will call reasons that bear on the merit of being subject to a particular constitutional provision "merit reasons," to distinguish them from reasons for adopting a constitutional provision or for amending it that do not derive from the good of being subject to it. On the contrary, they are all examples of how constitutional amendment may be justified by reasons that do not bear on the merit of the constitutional change they justify. In that, they are also examples of how ordinary political concerns, even relatively short term political concerns, can have a legitimate role in the politics of the constitution.

The self-legitimating aspect of practice is not negated by the fact that action for and against constitutional reform may be taken for good reasons. Because reasons of the kind just illustrated are not merit reasons and do not bear on the merit of the content of the constitution, they do not bear on its legitimacy. That is determined primarily by merit reasons that show the content of the constitution to be morally acceptable, and nothing in the examples undercuts the claim that merit reasons typically greatly underdetermine the content of the constitution, leading to the conclusion that within the boundaries they set, constitutions are legitimated by their existence.[21]

C. Stability and Continuity

I introduced the idea of self-legitimation, of the legitimating effect of practice through reflection on the fact that moral principles underdetermine the content of constitutions, and practice takes on the slack. But as is well known, the self-legitimating power of practice is not confined to this. Conventions are, perhaps, the most familiar example. Conventions illustrate a larger category in which behavior is justified if, and normally only if, a general practice exists: One should not cross the lawn if there is a general practice not to do so. That things happen in a certain way makes it right, or good, that they should continue to happen in that way.

An important concern of a similar nature is the concern for stability. The need to secure stability is in itself indifferent to the content of the constitutional practices prevailing in any time or place. Whatever they are, the concern for stability indicates that they should be perpetuated. Stability is not always an advantage. In the preceding subsection I noted that shaking things up can be desirable when it can change a moribund or corrupt power structure, infuse a country with a sense of energy and hope, and so on. However, stability is often desirable, and for many reasons. Remember that here as before the reference to the "self-legitimating" character of the "constitution" is not to the formal legal existence of the constitution but to the constitution as it exists in the practices and traditions of the country concerned. Constitutions are meant to provide a framework for the public life of a country, giving it direction and shape. For this to be achieved, widespread knowledge of the constitution has to be secured. This requires knowledge not only of the text but of its significance – that is, knowledge of the constitutional practices in the country. Until people absorb and adjust to it, a radical constitutional change upsets these practices. It has ramifications regarding different aspects of public life, and there is bound to be a temporary uncertainty regarding the way the reform or change will affect various aspects of constitutional practice. The uncertainty affects people's ability to function. It is made worse if it generates fear of continuous change, leading to a sense of dislocation and loss of orientation.

These are some of the many, mostly familiar reasons for preferring stability to instability. They do not amount to a rejection of change, but they create a reason to prefer continuity to change, unless there are really good reasons for the change. They add to the main and powerful conservative argument: While it is possible to predict the direct consequences of small changes in legal and social practices, changes that take place within existing frameworks and do not upset them, it is impossible to predict the effect of radical, large-scale changes. They are liable to affect the legal and social framework, which constitutes the background conditions that make predictions of social events possible. Hence, while radical reform may be inspired by cogent reasons to bring about different social conditions, there is no adequate advance reason to believe that it will bring about the hoped-for consequences. In itself this is no argument against radical reform and change. It does not show that radical change is likely to be for the worse. But it does undercut many reasons that people often advocate in pressing for radical change. Taken together with the advantages of stability, it adds to a certain conservative attitude sometimes expressed by saying that in relatively stable and decent societies there is a presumption in favor of continuity against which all proposals for change should be judged.

Broadly speaking, the argument for stability and the underdetermination of constitutional principles by morality combine to establish the self-legitimating aspect of constitutional practices and traditions.[22] Yet lumping them together like this runs the risk of obscuring the two fundamental differences between them.

In the first place the underdetermination argument means that within broad boundaries set by moral principles the very existence of a constitution establishes that it is a good constitution for the country in question. Others would have done, but given that they were not adopted, not they but the one enshrined in the practices of that country is its legitimate constitution. The desirability of stability does not establish that the constitution is legitimate. It applies even to illegitimate constitutions. The drawbacks of instability apply there too, though they are overcome by other considerations.

Second, while the argument from underdetermination allows that, within bounds, existing constitutions are self-legitimating, it does not constitute a reason for not changing the constitution. The constitution is legitimate, but so would be many alternatives we might have in its place. The arguments for stability, on the other hand, while they do not establish the legitimacy of the existing constitution, establish the existence of reasons for not changing an existing constitution.

Things are different if the constitution is morally legitimate – that is, if it instantiates one of the permissible forms of government, if it lies within the permissible as determined by moral considerations. When this is so, the arguments from underdeterminacy and from stability combine to legitimate the constitution and provide a reason for keeping the constitutional tradition going as it is.

What role if any do the authors of the constitution play in providing it with legitimacy? Their role can be of enormous practical importance, though it is a secondary role, from a theoretical point of view. Basically they help launch the constitutional tradition, and sometimes their reputation helps to keep it going. They may endow it with authority in its early years, and the respect in which they are held may be of great importance in determining the willingness of the population, and its politically active groups, to abide by it. This willingness is crucial both to the survival and to the legitimacy of the constitution. But it is so to the extent that it helps to bring the constitution within the bounds of the morally permissible.

PART II. INTERPRETING CONSTITUTIONS

IV. Interpreting the Constitution: On the Nature of Interpretive Doctrines

We can take constitutional interpretation as an established practice and confine ourselves to studying how it is conducted in different countries. Such a study would not be without interest, but from a theoretical point of view its benefits would be limited. A study based on this kind of survey and classification of interpretive techniques would yield an unwieldy plethora of interpretive styles and techniques, varying within countries as well as between countries and changing over time. It would also reveal large disagreements among judges about the proper methods and techniques of constitutional interpretation. Finally, it would show that not infrequently what judges say is one thing and what they do is another. The practice of some judges does not accord with their more general statements about the nature of constitutional interpretation.

Perhaps in part for these reasons, many legal philosophers have either shied away from writing about interpretation or offered normative accounts of interpretation generally and of constitutional interpretation in particular. Does this betray the task of explaining the law as it is rather than as it ought to be? Not necessarily. First, legal interpretation is much more than a method of establishing what the law is. When used by courts and by lawyers, or commentators and academics who focus on the interpretations that courts should adopt, legal interpretation is also a tool for developing the law, changing and reforming it. Second, while it is generally accepted (for reasons that will emerge in the sequel) that there is a point in following established interpretive methods, to the extent that they exist, it is also generally accepted that interpretations are subject to objective assessment, that some are defensible and others are not.[23] Moreover, it is part of the practice of legal interpretation as it is in many countries that courts are not bound to follow past interpretive techniques if they can be shown to be mistaken or less desirable than some alternatives. They can modify them or replace them with better ones. This is the case, for example, in all common-law jurisdictions. In such countries the study of sound interpretation is also part of the study of the law as it is. But it is a study of a very special aspect of the law, one that demarcates some of the lawmaking powers of the courts and the circumstances for their legitimate use.

Therefore, when reflecting on constitutional interpretation, we should start not from the fact that certain methods of interpretation are used, and others not, but from the question: Why is interpretation so central to constitutional adjudication? The answer, as always when there is reason to resort to interpretation, turns on a combination of reasons for respecting the constitution as it exists and reasons for remaining open to the possibility that it is in need of reform, adjustment, or development in order to remove shortcomings it always had or shortcomings that emerged as the government or the society that it governs changed over time.

It may be worth emphasizing that this Janus-like aspect of interpretation (that it faces both backward, aiming to elucidate the law as it is, and forward, aiming to develop and improve it) is not special to legal interpretation. It is the mark of interpretation in general that it aims to be true to an original that is being interpreted and to be open to innovation. In the performing arts such as the theater, for example, good performances interpret the text and in doing so they often express the views of the performers at the same time. This does not mean that all good interpretations are innovative, merely that interpretations can be innovative and therefore are ever open to this possibility. This is not the place to consider the nature of interpretation in general.[24] But we should reflect on the reasons why constitutional interpretation should be double-sided.

The reason for the backward-looking aspect of constitutional interpretation takes us back to the principle with which we started. The doctrines of constitutional interpretation, it was our assumption from the beginning, are based, at least in part, on the doctrine of sources of the authority of constitutions. Since the authority of a long-established constitution rests primarily on the desirability of securing continuity, the same desirability should inform constitutional interpretation as well. To secure continuity the interpretation should be backward-looking. It should be faithful to the constitution as it exists at that time. If so, should not this consideration dominate constitutional interpretation to the exclusion of all else? The moral importance of the issues decided upon in constitutional cases would not allow this to happen. Courts whose decisions determine the fortunes of many people must base them on morally sound considerations. Nothing else could justify their actions. If we admit that, does it not follow from the preceding argument that the morally correct decision is the one which is purely backward-looking – that is, which does nothing more than set out the content of (the relevant parts of) the constitution as it is at the time? This may be the right course for them to take, but only when it would be morally required, or at least morally reasonable, to rely on considerations of continuity above all else.

In other words, given the impact that constitutional decisions, like many other legal decisions, have on people's lives, they are justified only if they are morally justified. As we saw, considerations of continuity are of great moral importance, and they are the primary considerations determining the continuous legitimacy of the constitution. But they are hardly ever the only moral considerations affecting an issue. When they are not, courts should try to reach decisions that satisfy as much as possible all the relevant considerations, and when it is impossible to satisfy all completely, they should strive to satisfy them as much as possible, given their relative importance. Hence, while on occasion the desirability of continuity in the matter concerned will prevail over all else, often this will not be the case, though even when continuity does not override all else, it should still be taken into account as much as possible. Hence, in such cases, while the courts should still interpret the constitution, for they are still rightly moved by considerations of continuity, they should also give weight to other moral considerations. That is, their interpretation should also be forward-looking. None of this should be taken to imply that all defects in a constitution can be put right through ingenious interpretation. All I am saying is that sometimes this is possible.

Yet again, an objection that this view is misconceived for it overlooks the fact that the doctrine of constitutional interpretation is a *legal,* not a moral, doctrine is bound to occur to some. Whatever the moral merit of my observations, the objection goes, it is irrelevant to an understanding of constitutional interpretation. That doctrine is a legal doctrine and there is nothing judges may do other than follow the doctrines of interpretation that are binding on them according to the law of their own country. Let me concede right away that there is something to the objection. Judges who follow the views on interpretation developed here may find themselves morally obliged to disobey the law of their country. That is the result of the fact that I am developing an approach to constitutional interpretation that, for lack of a better word, we may call a moral approach. The law of any country may be at odds with morality in a variety of ways. One of them is the existence of locally binding rules that prohibit the courts from following any morally acceptable interpretation.

I am not proposing the observations in this essay as a substitute for an examination of the rules and doctrines of interpretation prevailing in this country or that. That is clearly an important task for those interested in the law of the countries concerned. Nevertheless, it would be false modesty to say no more than that the topic of my discussion is different. I am also making claims for its importance. Let me first recapitulate: First, while there is every reason for people interested in this or that legal system to study the rules of interpretation binding in it, there is no universal theory of interpretation that applies to all law, except as a normative theory – that is, of what interpretation should be like. Second, whether they like it or not, courts face moral problems and should behave in a way sanctioned by morality. This may bring them into conflict with the law. Third, quite often the proper ways of interpreting constitutions are controversial. Fourth, typically courts have power to adopt new ways of interpreting the law and to revise established ones when they have good reason to do so.

The last two points are interconnected, and both stem from a fact not yet mentioned: At the most basic level there are not, nor can there be, specifically legal ways of interpretation. Of course, most legal systems have rules of interpretation laid down in legislation or precedent that are special to them. But most interpretation does not, cannot, depend on them. This is not only, not primarily, because rules of interpretation themselves often require to be interpreted. It is primarily because problems of interpretation are rarely problems of the meaning of one term or phrase. They are more often than not questions of the interpretation of sentences, or of articles in statutes or in constitutions, or of moral and political doctrines. And they can arise in unexpected places. No set of explicitly articulated rules of interpretation can deal with all of them. The same is true of rules of interpretation implied in a legal culture, rather than explicitly articulated in its laws. Such rules cannot settle all possible issues of interpretation. All too often interpretation is just a matter of reasoning to a reasonable view on the basis of a variety of considerations, some reinforcing each other, some clashing. There is no way of reducing such reasoning to the application of rules, or other norms, nor is there any way of eliminating the need and the desirability of interpretation that consists in and results from such reasoning.

This explains why the law of interpretation, meaning the rules and doctrines of interpretation in force in any given country, useful as they may be, cannot contain all that can and need be said in an account of legal or constitu-

tional interpretation. Ultimately an account of constitutional interpretation
has more to do with understanding legal or constitutional reasoning than with
understanding any legal doctrine specific to this or that country. Reasoning
that aims to establish the meaning of a law, a work of art, literature, religion,
or anything else and that combines respect for its original expression or its
traditional or current meaning with openness to innovation is interpretive. For
the reasons already given, constitutional reasoning is to a considerable degree
interpretive reasoning. But accounts of reasoning are accounts of rationality
in belief, and they are universal normative accounts, specific to any locality
or subject matter only in the details of their application.

All this was said to explain the importance of a normative account of constitutional interpretation, an account that goes over and above the study of the
rules and doctrines of interpretation established in one country or another. But
the drift of these remarks raises a different objection to the thought that there
can be a general study of constitutional interpretation. If the study of interpretation is just the study of reasoning that is constrained by the condition specified earlier, and if the study of constitutional interpretation is just the study of
such reasoning when applied to constitutions, can anything specific be said
about it beyond the unhelpful but sound advice that in interpreting constitutions one should reason well? There may be a general account of reasoning,
and perhaps even a general account of interpretive reasoning. But once one
has mastered those is there anything more that is special to constitutional interpretation and that is not merely an application of the general account of interpretive reasoning to the content of the constitutions of specific countries?

This revives the doubt about the possibility of a general theory of constitutional law raised at the outset, but this time addressed specifically to issues of
interpretation. As I explained there, I believe that there is much truth in the
doubt. There is no general theory of constitutional interpretation if that is
meant to be a general recipe for the way such interpretation should be conducted that is set out in some detail in order to guide the interpreter every step
of the way with practical advice. There is little more that one can say other
than "reason well" or "interpret reasonably." What little there is to say consists mainly of pointing out mistakes that have been made attractive by the
popularity they enjoy among judges, lawyers, or academic writers.

V. Fidelity and Innovation

Interpretation, it was suggested, lives in spaces where fidelity to an original
and openness to novelty mix. It exists in a dialectical tension, as some might
say. The reason we find this tension in reasoning about constitutional law, I
claimed, is that constitutional decisions are moral decisions that have to be
morally justified, and the moral considerations that apply include both fi-

delity to the law of the constitution as it is, arising out of concern for continuity, and openness to its shortcomings and to injustices its application may yield in certain cases, which leads to openness to the need to develop and modify it.

Two opposing mistakes are invited by this fact. The first is to think that because a good interpretation may combine both elements, the distinction between the constitution, and more generally the law, as it is and as it ought to be is illusory. Constitutional interpretation, one argument runs, establishes the meaning of the constitution. That is, there is no sense in talking of the content of the constitution except as it is determined by a process of interpretation. Since interpretation mixes fidelity and innovation, it undermines both notions. It breaks down the distinction between them, for fidelity assumes that the content of the constitution, to which one is supposed to be faithful, can be established independently of interpretation and, by the same token, so does innovation, since it is identified as deviation from pure fidelity. Without an interpretation-independent identification of the content of the constitution, we cannot tell fidelity from innovation, and since the content cannot be identified independently of interpretation, it follows that there is no coherent meaning to the notion of fidelity to the constitution and none to constitutional innovation either.

This argument fails. I intimated earlier that not all explanations of meaning are interpretations. But we need not rely on this in refuting the argument. It overlooks the fact that the reason fidelity and innovation are often mixed is that we often have reasons to interpret in ways that mix them. But this is not always the case. Sometimes we have reason to interpret the constitution in ways that simply elucidate its content at the moment, warts and all. Such an interpretation, I call it "a conserving interpretation," will be successful if it is true to the existing meaning of the constitution. It will include no mixing of conflicting elements. It will display no dialectical tension, and it will establish the benchmark by which we can measure other interpretations to see whether they are more or less innovatory.

The failure of the preceding argument does not mean, of course, that there are no other better ones. But I do not know of any successful argument to the same conclusion. It does not follow that in every case we can establish what the law is. The evidence may be incomplete. Moreover, it is not the case that we can establish the legal answer regarding any legal question, since the law is often indeterminate on various issues. As a result, when the constitution is interpreted with the goal of establishing just what it is at a given moment in time the interpretation will show it to be vague and indeterminate. Granted all these points, it is still the case that when the evidence is available it is possible to establish what the law is, and therefore to distinguish between innovatory and conserving interpretations. I suspect that one reason which encourages people to assume that it is impossible to interpret the law, to establish its meaning at any given time without changing it at the same time, is the following sort of argument: (a) Courts can always change the law that is relevant to the case in front of them. (b) Courts can change the law only when it is indeterminate. (c) It follows that the law is indeterminate on all issues. (d) Therefore, no interpretation can simply establish what it is without changing it. The argument is invalid, for from the claim that the law is indeterminate on all issues it does not follow that an interpretation cannot merely describe it without changing it. All that follows is that such an interpretation will describe it as indeterminate. More important, the second premise is simply false. Courts can develop the law even when it is determinate. They can and often do simply change it.

This brings us to the second mistake one should avoid, which in some ways is the opposite of the first. Some may think that if there is a distinction between a conserving interpretation that merely states the law as it is and an innovatory one that develops and changes it, then it must be possible to take any interpretation and point to where it stops merely stating the law as it is and starts developing and changing it. It must, in other words, be possible to separate the descriptive and the innovative elements in every interpretive statement. The thought that this is so is encouraged by the fact that sometimes such a separation is indeed possible. But these occasions are relatively rare, and it certainly does not follow from the previous observations that it is ever, let alone always, possible. In clearing the first mistake, I argued for the possibility of comparing different interpretations by their degree of novelty and of distinguishing innovative interpretations from conserving ones. (There could be several of them, since one can provide interpretations that restate the law as it was at different points in time.) That thought is very different from the suggestion that within each interpretation one can separate the elements that are true to the law as it is from those that are innovative. All that my position implies is that when thinking of the reasons that justify an interpretation one can distinguish those which suggest that the interpretation should be faithful to existing law from those which suggest that it should develop or even change the law.

Having cleared these two theoretical mistakes out of the way, we can face one of the main mistakes to which theories of constitutional interpretation are liable. Having established in the preceding section that constitutional interpretation has to answer to a variety of reasons, some urging fidelity to existing law, others urging its development, change, and adaptation, it is natural to expect that the central task of a theory of constitutional interpretation is to spell out the right proportions of innovation and conservation in constitutional interpretations, or to tell one how to determine how much of each to allow in each case. But this is a misconception, which if not checked is bound to breed many false theories. It overlooks the fact that there is no one reason to develop and change constitutional law. When it is adequate to its tasks and to the situation in the country, there is no need to change or to develop it. Modification of the law is called for either when it is undetermined on the issue the court has to decide or when it is less than adequate. In those cases the court should take notice of the reasons for having the law take one shape or another. But those are enormously varied both in nature and in importance. Any moral reason whatsoever can figure in the considerations of a constitutional court on these occasions. There cannot be a general answer to the question of how much importance reasons for change should have in their conflict with reasons for continuity.

Of course, there are certain generalizations one can safely put forward. For example, it is generally (but not universally) the case that the greater are the defects in the constitutional law concerned, the less important is it to preserve continuity and the more important is it to change it. We can also emphasize that sometimes it is possible to reconcile continuity with change, by introducing changes in the law that deviate little from it, especially in matters where established expectations led people to make plans on the basis of existing law. This is particularly true of cases in which the need to resolve legal indeterminacy on this issue or that is the only reason for deviation from existing law. In such cases, it may be that no expectations have been generated, and resolution of the case need not affect stability. One can continue in this vein to offer more helpful generalizations. But they will not amount to a general answer to the question of what is the right mix of innovation and preservation in constitutional decisions.

VI. Considerations of the Moral Merit of the Constitution and of Institutional Role

So far I have argued for four main conclusions: First, there is no real theory of constitutional interpretation, in the sense of a set of principles that when applied to an interpretive question yield the correct interpretation of the constitutional provision concerned. All a philosophical discussion of interpretation can do is explain the nature of the activity and its main parameters, and help one to avoid some mistakes. Second, there is a cogent way of distinguishing between innovative and conserving interpretations, and often between more or less innovative (less or more conserving) interpretations. Third, interpretation is central to legal reasoning because in legal reasoning fidelity to an original competes with, and has to be combined with, reasons for innovation. Constitutional interpretation is central to constitutional adjudication because courts are faced with conflicting moral considerations, some militating for continuity, and therefore for giving effect to the constitution as it is at that moment, and some pointing to the need to develop and improve it. Fourth, it makes no sense to ask in general what is the right mix of conservation and innovation in constitutional interpretation.

To help us make further progress with the argument, we need to retreat and consider an objection to the third conclusion – that whatever the merit of innovative interpretations in literature, history, and elsewhere, judicial interpretations of the constitution should be purely conserving. Earlier I argued against this view on the ground that (a) courts are faced with moral issues and should make morally justified decisions, and (b) the moral considerations they face often point not only to the advantages of continuity, but also to the desirability of modifying and improving the constitutional provisions concerned. My imaginary objector agrees to both premises but denies that the conclusion follows. It seems to follow, he points out, only because I disregarded altogether the importance of institutional considerations to legal decisions. Over and above the moral considerations I gestured toward stands the doctrine of the role of the courts, which says that their job is exclusively to apply the law as it is.[25] Others have the responsibility to improve it. Therefore, the fact that there are good reasons for dissatisfaction with the law as it stands is no justification at all for judicial "activism." It is not the courts' business. They have a job to do and they should confine themselves to doing it and no more.

The value of this objection is that it reminds us of the importance of institutional considerations in justifying political and legal actions. The objection relies on a doctrine of division of labor among various organs of government. But behind it are additional complex considerations of institutional design, relative advantage in performing one task or another, and others necessary for its justification. Philosophers are sometimes prone to let institutional considerations drop out of their sight. I suspect that contributing to this is the fact that institutional considerations do not mark one outcome as better than others. They merely indicate that the court is or is not an appropriate body to adopt one interpretation or another, not that it is better for the law to be this way or that. In other words, institutional considerations do not contribute to showing which result is best. They do, however, show which decision is justified. They act something like side constraints, though they are not necessarily exceptionless.[26]

The objection is that my argument overlooks the effect of institutional constraints and that once the omission is repaired we can see that the courts may not modify the law. Is this really the sole role of the courts? My earlier argument that since the courts have to take a moral decision they have to reach the best moral result was too simple-minded. It took too simple a view of who the agent is. The courts do not act in their own name. They act as organs of the political society, that is – to simplify – of the state. It is the state that has the responsibility to reach the right result. It does not automatically follow, and that is what the institutional objection points to, that it should do so through its courts. The state has other organs, and possibly the courts should always simply apply existing law, and if that is not the right result, that is, if the law should be modified, then it falls to other state organs to modify it.

How, then, are we to determine the responsibility of different organs of state? In the first instance by examining the structure of state organs and the division of powers enshrined in the constitution. But beyond that, we need to examine the moral soundness of that structure. It is not morally sound if following it is not a good way to make sure, inasmuch as that is possible, that the state reaches the right outcome in each case. In that case it falls to each state organ to consider whether it would not be morally right for it to deviate from existing law in order to secure the best outcome. It ought, of course, to weigh the reasons, of continuity, separation of powers, and others, against doing so. But it cannot avoid facing the question of the desirability of change seriously. There is no need here to explore the structure of that kind of reasoning. The important lesson is that the issue of the relative role of institutions is itself, like all the other issues we have encountered, a moral issue, and the courts have to act on moral considerations that apply to division-of-labor questions.

The salient fact for our concern is that whether or not in this state or that the role of the courts includes responsibility for improving the constitution is a question of the doctrine of constitutional interpretation in force in it. As I observed earlier, in most countries issues of interpretation at this level of generality tend to be subject to dispute and disagreement. Since in such countries there is no established practice on the issue, there is in them no settled law about it, and there is nothing to stop the courts from giving effect to the view of their own role that is morally compelling.

Is that the view which confines the courts to merely applying existing law?[27] That would be their role if and only if there were other state organs fully able to engage in improving the law when necessary. The more entrenched the constitution is, the less likely is it that there are such alternatives.

But does not the fact that constitutions are entrenched show not that there are inadequate means of amending them but rather that it is undesirable that they be amended in ways other than the procedures provided? It may mean that this is what their authors intended, but it does not follow that their view is sound. This is yet another debate that can only be touched upon here. There is a strong case for separating constitutional development and adjustment from the course of ordinary politics. In most circumstances it is advantageous to secure the stability and durability of the framework of governmental institutions and the fundamental principles of their operation from short-term political pressures. But the case for separation is not a case for making it difficult to change constitutional provisions. It is merely a case for a special process controlling their change. The argument against easy changes is the case for stability and continuity in constitutional law. But that case has complex conclusions. It establishes that radical changes in the structure of the constitution should not be easy to effect. Their adoption should require extensive publicity, wide-ranging public debate, and substantial and durable consensus. There is no objection to regular development of the law within existing frameworks. Such modifications do not undermine continuity. By and large they tend to enhance it. So far I have not distinguished between stability in the law – that is, the absence of change in the law – and stability in the social or economic effects of the law. Since the two often go hand in hand, there was no need to distinguish between them. But they go hand in hand only as long as the underlying social, political, or economic conditions do not change. When they do, the law may have to change if it is to continue to have the same social or economic effects. In such a case innovative interpretations that modify the law prevent it from ossifying and getting progressively less and less adequate to its task and requiring major reform. Of course, the cumulative effect of small-change reform may well amount to a radical change in constitutional law over the years. But stability is consistent with slow change, whatever its cumulative effect. Therefore, entrenching the constitution may be justified in that it secures extensive debate and solid consensus behind radical constitutional changes. But it also means that it falls to the courts to take charge of continuous improvements and adjustments within existing structures. The institutional argument against innovative constitutional interpretations by the courts fails.

VII. Moral and Legal Considerations: Where the Law Is Autonomous

In the preceding discussion it was assumed that there are two anchors to constitutional interpretation. On the one hand, reasons for continuity militate in favor of conserving interpretation.[28] On the other hand, imperfections in the law militate in favor of innovative interpretation that will develop and modify the constitution. Conserving interpretations articulate or restate the current meaning of the constitutional provisions in question. That means that they aim to capture the meaning these provisions have in current constitutional practice. In the early days of a constitution this will be the meaning intended by its authors, inasmuch as it was expressed in its text as understood given the conventions of meaning and interpretation of the time.[29] In later years this meaning will be gradually overlaid by layers of interpretive decisions and by the way the relevant provisions have come to be understood in the practices of the legal institutions of that country and by its population. Naturally, quite often the constitution so understood will be vague and indeterminate on many issues. How does moral and legal underdetermination affect interpretation?

Indeterminacy in constitutional provisions will favor innovative interpretations. As long as they merely make determined what was underdetermined, they cannot offend against stability. Whatever moral reasons apply to improve the constitutional provisions involved can be given effect. Sometimes, however, there will be indeterminacy both in law and in morality. Nevertheless, the matter must be decided, and the constitutional position has to be settled. How is the court to proceed then?

A distinction introduced in Section III is relevant here. I distinguished there between merit reasons, which bear on the merit of a constitution and its provisions, and reasons for amending a constitution, or some of its provisions, which have no bearing on the merit of those provisions. The need for a change to infuse a spirit of optimism in a new future, or in order to win the support or allegiance of some segment of the population, were examples of the second type of reason. When addressing the consequences of the incommensurability of reasons, we need to distinguish between incommensurability of all the reasons bearing on a decision and incommensurability in some class of reasons.

Merit reasons which show that one interpretation, innovative or not, makes the constitution better than its alternatives take pride of place in constitutional interpretation. This is not because the balance of these merit reasons always defeats all other reasons with which they may conflict. This is not so. Other reasons may rightly defeat merit reasons on various occasions. The court may, to mention but one familiar consideration, adopt an interpretation that renders the constitution inferior to what it would be on one or more alternative interpretations in order to placate a hostile legislature or executive, which may otherwise take action to limit the power of the courts or to compromise their independence. Merit reasons are the primary reasons because they define the task of the courts in constitutional interpretation: Their task is to apply the constitution when it is adequate to its task and to improve it when it is wanting. Their success, and therefore the merit of maintaining the existing system of constitutional courts, depends on their being good at this task. If in the long run the constitutional courts are not good at performing their task (i.e., not as good as some alternative might be), then one should reform them or assign some of their functions to another institution. But, to repeat, the fact that merit reasons are primary does not mean that they are the only reasons constitutional courts can take account of, nor that they are always decisive.

In Section III it was argued that when we consider the legitimacy of a constitution as a whole, merit reasons often underdetermine the verdict. Often the constitution we have is legitimate not because it is superior to any alternative we may have, but because we have it, and there is nothing fundamentally wrong with it; that is, it lies within the bounds of the morally permissible. It would be a mistake, however, to think that it *follows* that if the constitution is legitimate then considerations of merit play no role in constitutional interpretation. Given that a country has a legitimate constitution and that it developed institutions and practices to fit its constitution, many considerations of merit apply that would not have applied otherwise. For example, given that in democracies a major consideration in defining the reach of the doctrine of freedom of expression is the importance of the freedom for democratic politics, the boundaries of the right to free expression will inevitably depend in part on the powers of government, in all its branches. Roughly speaking, the more wide-ranging are the powers of the government, the more extensive is the right to free expression.

Merit reasons also depend on other aspects of the economic, social, and legal life of a country. Compare two examples, both relating to the proper balance between freedom of expression and the protection of the administration of justice from undue influence by the media. First, this balance depends on the conduct of the media in the country. When good sense prevails in practice, freedom of the press can and should be wider than when the conduct of the media is careless of the need to protect the administration of justice from its influence. Second, the balance also depends on whether trials and other legal proceedings take place before juries or before professional judges sitting without lay jurors. In the second example the doctrine of freedom of expression is affected by merit reasons that depend on another aspect of the constitution; in the first example it is affected by social practices that are not enshrined in law. In both cases merit reasons have considerable weight even though the constitution the provisions of which are litigated is not the only morally good one, but merely a morally permissible constitution legitimated by practice.

Having said that, I should add that while merit reasons are central to constitutional adjudication they will often be incommensurate. They will fail to determine which constitutional provision is better. As was anticipated earlier, this does not mean that there will be no sound reasons for establishing that the courts should prefer one interpretation over others. For the most part, however, these reasons are particularly time-bound and agent-bound. That is, they may be reasons that apply at a particular point in time but lapse fairly quickly, and they may be reasons for the courts to interpret the constitution one way or another, without being reasons for other agents to do so. My example of the way the scope of freedom of expression depends on how mindful the media are of the need to protect the administration of justice illustrates the familiar point that the temporal relativity of reasons for a constitutional interpretation affects merit reasons as well as others. The way non–merit reasons may be relative to the interpreting agent is illustrated by the example of a preference for an interpretation that will not trigger action by the legislature against the courts. Suppose an individual relies in her dealings with an agency belonging to the executive branch of government on the interpretation that, were it adopted by the courts, would offend the legislature. The executive and its agencies cannot legitimately refrain from accepting the validity of the interpretation because of these considerations. The supposition is that only the courts are in disfavor with the legislature. Organs of the executive should, therefore, adopt the interpretation supported by merit considerations. Unfortunately, if they refuse, the individual may not find relief in the courts, which may be rightly inhibited from adopting the "best" interpretation.

Much more can be said about the relative role of merit and other considerations. But we have to turn back to the issue of incommensurability. Let me summarize the points made so far: (a) Moral reasons motivate all interpretive decisions, both conserving ones and innovative ones. (b) Merit considerations may justify an innovative interpretation even when a conserving interpretation is possible, that is, even when the issue is settled by the constitution as it is. That would be the case when the need to improve the law is greater than the need for continuity on the point, and when there is an interpretation that improves the law. (c) When the constitution is underdetermined on the issue in question, the need for improvement exists and meets no direct opposition from considerations of continuity. (d) The fact that the constitutional scheme as a whole is legitimated by practice, and is merely permissible, does not mean that merit considerations are exhausted. (e) While merit reasons are the primary reasons for innovative interpretations, they are not the only relevant ones. There are sound interpretive reasons that are not merit reasons and that compete with them. (f) Those other reasons can determine the right interpretation to adopt even when both the constitution as it is at the time and the merit reasons fail to resolve the issue at hand. The question is: How are courts to decide cases in which these reasons also fail to resolve the issue and determine the outcome of the case?

Why is this a problem? Rational action is action for a reason that is reasonably thought to be undefeated. It is not action for a reason that defeats all those which conflict with it.[30] We have no difficulty in choosing which orange to pick from a bowl of oranges just because there is nothing to choose between them. Of course, incommensurable reasons are not reasons of equal strength. But the fact that no one incommensurable reason defeats the others should not present a mystery about how we manage to choose what to do when facing incommensurable reasons.

Incommensurability of reasons is pervasive, and while we are far from having a satisfactory philosophical explanation of all its aspects, it does not pose a difficulty in explaining how we can act without belief that the act we perform is supported by stronger reasons than all its alternatives. Yet there is a problem here. It is a problem specific to law and to other public actions. It arises not from a difficulty of squaring incommensurability of reasons with a theory of rational action or rational choice, but from a principle of political morality, namely the principle of the public accountability of public actions. This principle directs not only that courts should take their decisions for cogent reasons and that they should avoid irrelevant reasons, but also that as far as possible the fact that no irrelevant considerations affected the decision should be publicly visible. This principle makes it inappropriate for the courts to act as people do when confronted by incommensurability of reasons for the options facing them. People's choices are in part not dictated by any reason. They reveal dispositions and tastes they have that may or may not be important in their lives, but are nonrational in nature. It is important for institutions acting for the public not to take decisions the explanations for which are the nonrational dispositions or tastes of the people who hold office in them. Public institutions should develop or adopt distancing devices – devices they can rely on to settle such issues in a way that is independent of the personal tastes of the judges or other officials involved.

The need for this distancing is one of the reasons why many judges persist in arguing that at no point did they rely in their decisions on anything other than a conserving interpretation of the law and that there is only one such true interpretation. But the law can and should provide them with genuine distancing devices. Elsewhere I have suggested that legal doctrine can and does play such a role.[31] Legal doctrine can be, of course, no more than what morality dictates. But notoriously doctrine can take a life of its own, detached from moral considerations. This tendency in legal thought is often decried as formalism, conceptualism, or essentialism, and often it deserves the criticism. But criticism is deserved – in constitutional law – only in cases where relying on formal legal reasoning prevents a court from adopting an innovative interpretation that could improve the constitution. In cases where reasons for the two or more best interpretations are incommensurate, reliance on formal legal reasoning is justified; it serves as a distancing device.

I am not arguing, of course, that such distancing devices are always available in the law. On the contrary, I asserted earlier that often they are unavailable and the law is indeterminate. I am simply pointing out the desirability of having them available. We can now return for the last time to the argument expounded earlier in this part that it is frequently appropriate for courts to adopt an innovative interpretation even when there is a conserving interpretation they could adopt instead. Some legal doctrines and methods of interpretation fall into my category of formal doctrines – ones that are not justified by moral value or whose application to the case at hand cannot be so justified. Formal legal doctrines, I have been arguing, are valuable. But they should not be used to stop the courts from resorting to moral considerations to develop and improve the law.

They should be brought into play only once moral resources have been exhausted, when the courts need to resort to distancing devices to justify their choice between otherwise incommensurate interpretations.

VIII. Coda: But Is It the Same Constitution?

Possibly this doubt is not yet laid to rest. If the courts make the constitution, does it not follow that many people who believe that, let us say, they are living under a constitution adopted two hundred years ago are mistaken? Is it not the case that if people like me are right then the constitution has been made and remade many times since, and we are not now living under the constitution then adopted? It has to be admitted that people who do not realize that the law of the constitution lies as much in the interpretive decisions of the courts as in the original document that they interpret, and who deny that courts are entitled to adopt innovative interpretations, are making a mistake. But it is not the mistake of thinking that it is the same constitution. It is still the constitution adopted two hundred years ago, just as a person who lives in an eighteenth-century house lives in a house built two hundred years ago. His house had been repaired, added to, and changed many times since. But it is still the same house and so is the constitution.

A person may, of course, object to redecorating the house or to changing its windows, saying that it would not be the same. In that sense it is true that an old constitution is not the same as a new constitution, just as an old person is not the same as the same person when young. Sameness in that sense is not the sameness of identity (the old person is identical with the young person she once was). It is the sameness of all the intrinsic properties of the object. Sometimes there are good reasons to preserve not only the same object but the same object with all its intrinsic properties intact. In the case of constitutions, such reasons are moral reasons. When they prevail, only a conserving interpretation is appropriate. Like many others, I have pointed out a range of reasons for thinking that they do not always prevail. The point of my coda is to warn against confusing change with loss of identity and against the spurious arguments it breeds. Dispelling errors is all that a general theory of the constitution can aspire to achieve.

Notes

1 See, for an extended discussion, Joseph Raz, *The Morality of Freedom* (Oxford: Oxford University Press, 1986), Part 1, and Joseph Raz, *Ethics in the Public Domain,* rev. ed. (Oxford: Oxford University Press, 1995), Essays 9 and 10.

2 I discussed some of them in *The Concept of a Legal System,* 2d ed. (Oxford: Oxford University Press, 1980), 29–32.

3 The question of the authority of law does not exhaust the issue of political obligation, but it is a major part of it.
4 Possibly, some hold judicial office for reasons of personal advantage even when
   they believe that it is morally wrong for them to do so. In some oppressive regimes
   we can imagine judges and other officials perpetrating immoralities out of fear for
   their life or the life of their families. In such circumstances it may be morally ex-
   cusable to act as they do. But these are likely to be the exception, and I will disregard such cases in the present discussion.
5 See H. L. A. Hart, *The Concept of Law,* rev. ed. (Oxford: Oxford University Press,
   1961, rev. ed. 1994).
6 The views expressed in this paragraph and the next are at variance with Hart's own
   interpretation of the rule of recognition, as explained in the postscript to the revised edition of *The Concept of Law.*
7 Other variants of the argument relate it to democracy rather than consent. The considerations advanced against the version considered in the text have to be adapted
   to apply to other variants of the argument.
8 I have discussed them in "Government by Consent," *Ethics in the Public Domain,*
   355.
9 Meaning not that consenting was rational given the information, but that – judged
   in light of the information generally available at the time – the information known
   to the agent presented roughly a true picture of the (nonevaluative) features of the
   situation, inasmuch as they were relevant to his decision.
10 This is not to deny that arguments which are not consent-based cannot be presented as relating to hypothetical consent: Suppose you have an obligation deriving from whatever source whatsoever to recognize the authority of certain governments. It follows trivially that if you know your obligations you would consent
   that you have an obligation to recognize the authority of such governments.
11 Or that it plays only a secondary role in establishing authority over such areas.
12 The directness is important here. Ultimately all moral principles either are or derive from universal principles. The laws belonging to this category are justified by
   direct reference to universal principles of conduct, without the mediation of complex arguments regarding the way these apply to social and economic conditions.
13 This notion of coordination captures, I believe, the natural meaning of the term as
   used in political discourse. I have used it in this sense in writing about the justification of authority. Consequently it varies from the artificial sense given the term
   in game theory.
14 Bad laws, i.e., laws that should be repealed or amended, can have moral legitimacy; that is, one may have a moral obligation to apply them or to obey them.
15 As is well known, this claim needs careful statement that may include clarifica-
   tions we need not enter into here. It may, for example, be the case that only creatures having a capacity for moral knowledge, and moral life, can have the ability to
   identify and understand social facts.
16 For reasons of convenience I follow the convention of contrasting fact with norm,
   or with morality or value. I do not mean to imply that there are no moral facts.
17 And there are possible alternatives that deviate from the simple way in which fact
   and norm are neatly separated into two distinct stages, and allow some mixing in
   certain circumstances.

18 Not every social fact can be a source of law. It must satisfy other conditions that need not concern us here.

19 In recent times its importance has been emphasized by J. Finnis, *Natural Law and Natural Rights* (Oxford: Oxford University Press, 1996).

20 The fact that morality underdetermines the content of the constitution seems to follow from the thesis that moral values are extensively and significantly incommensurable. I have explored this view in several publications, especially in *The Morality of Freedom,* ch. 13, and "Incommensurability and Agency," in R. Chang (ed.), *Incommensurability, Incomparability and Value* (Cambridge, Mass.: Harvard University Press, 1998).

21 This conclusion can be strengthened. Even when an alternative constitution is somewhat better than the one we have, the fact that this is the one we have makes it legitimate. The considerations that support this conclusion and give it more precise meaning arise out of the cost of change and the conservative presumption. These are discussed later.

22 One should always remember, but I will not repeat the point again, that the self-legitimating aspect of constitutional practices is subject to their falling within what is morally acceptable.

23 As is clear, this does not imply accepting that for any question about the interpretation of the law there is only one acceptable answer.

24 For the reasons for denying that every time we understand something we interpret it see A. Marmor's application of Wittgenstein's position in *Interpretation and Legal Theory* (Oxford: Oxford University Press, 1994). For my own stab at a general account of interpretation see "Interpretation without Retrieval," in A. Marmor, ed., *Law and Interpretation* (Oxford: Oxford University Press, 1996), 155–76.

25 We can imagine a more moderate objector who allows the courts creative functions in special circumstances. I am using the extreme position as a way to explain my argument.

26 A notion introduced by Robert Nozick in *Anarchy, State and Utopia* (New York: Basic Books, 1974). His notion is of exceptionless side constraints, except *in extremis*; see 28ff.

27 I am overlooking here the objection to this position that challenges its intelligibility and claims that whatever the courts' intentions they cannot but engage in developing and modifying the law, at least on occasion. The argument in the text goes a long way beyond that conclusion and establishes that there are occasions when courts should engage in innovative interpretation even when they can avoid doing so.

28 But remember the distinction between continuity in the law and continuity in its effects introduced earlier. The first is needed typically only when it is necessary for the second.

29 This formula is meant to capture the conclusions of my essay "Intention in Interpretation," in R. P. George, ed., *The Autonomy of Law* (Oxford: Oxford University Press, 1996), 249–86.

30 I am relying here on my analysis in "Incommensurability and Agency."

31 Joseph Raz, "On the Autonomy of Legal Reasoning," in *Ethics in the Public Domain,* 326.

5

Legitimacy and Interpretation

JED RUBENFELD

I. Introduction: Foundations

To seek the foundations of what is itself supposed to be foundational is – a delicate proposition. This book, if true to its name, would uncover constitutional law's philosophical foundations. But suppose that the law which founds a legal system is founded on nothing – not on philosophy, not on a revolutionary founding moment – but its own future. Suppose that a constitution will have been well founded only if it brings about, over time, those future-perfect conditions of community and authority, those practices of reason-giving and reason-accepting, within which alone its particular rendition of morality, justice, and legitimacy becomes meaningful. We ask after the law's foundations in philosophy; perhaps we should be asking after philosophy's foundational debt to the laws.[1]

But what is meant by foundations here? American constitutionalism raises two foundational questions. There is first the question of legitimate authority, and second that of interpretive method.

A. Legitimacy

How can a two-hundred-year-old legal text, enacted by a series of majority votes under conditions very distant from our own, exert legitimate authority in the present? How can it possibly bind a majority today? A constitution of this sort is a scandal. It is an offense against reason, against democracy – against nature herself.

Or so we are told. In Chapter 4, this volume, Joseph Raz reiterates the position that the makers of an old law cannot reasonably claim legitimate authority over anyone today. In Chapter 2, Frank Michelman wrestles with the ultimate groundlessness of any law that attempts to find a purchase in the past. Indeed, for a good century, whose beginning we could mark with the publication of Tiedeman's *Unwritten Constitution* in 1890,[2] almost every "philosophical" inquiry into the United States Constitution has begun or ended by confronting the seemingly antidemocratic nature of constitutional law.[3]

Now, why exactly is old law vulnerable to this sort of attack? The basic thinking, in one form or another, is as follows. Who alone has the legitimate, final authority to make the decisions by which we live? We do. We *here and now*, in other words, could in principle govern ourselves. Doing so might be difficult; it might even be conceivable only as a regulative ideal. (We might have to deliberate with one another in certain ideal ways; the relevant "we" might have to be constructed as an ideal community or as an ideally free set of individuals; we might have to reason under conditions of ignorance; and so on.) But however the necessary conditions of self-governance are worked out, it is evident that a people cannot govern itself by *having* given itself law a century or two ago. A written constitution is a thing of the past; self-government belongs to the present.

Some Americans saw this difficulty from the beginning. "The earth belongs in usufruct to the living," wrote Jefferson. "The dead have neither power nor rights over it."[4] Thus, a constitution that did not lapse every generation was unnatural: "[B]y the law of nature, one generation is to another as one independent nation to another."[5] Nor were late-eighteenth-century Americans the first to question how an expression of sovereign will today could claim sovereign authority tomorrow. (They were only the first to solve this problem, in a particular way, as we shall see.) As Stephen Holmes observes,[6] the same problem had already been articulated by many others, including Hobbes:

The Soveraign of a Common-wealth, be it an Assembly or one Man, is not Subject to the Civill Lawes. . . . For he is free, that can be free when he will: Nor is it possible, for any person to be bound to himself; because he that can bind, can release; and therefore, he that is bound to himself onely, is not bound.[7]

No sovereign self can bind himself "to himself" – so argued not only Hobbes, but also Bodin, Pufendorf, and Rousseau.[8] All the authorities agree: The day that the sovereign people sought to bind itself to itself was a dark day. American written constitutionalism is contradictory. By purporting to bind the sovereign popular will tomorrow, the Constitution violates the very principle of self-government on which it stakes its claim to legitimate authority in the first place.

Let us call this conundrum the constitutional problem of time. With us, certain superficial answers to it are well known. Thus, the Constitution escapes the snare of time (it is often said) by the simple expedient of providing for its own amendment. Through Article V, which sets out an amendment procedure available to the people at any moment, the Constitution disclaims "perpetual" authority. It never purported to bind subsequent generations or even the same generation at a later point in time. It does not bind the sovereign, only the politicians. Citizens can amend whenever they choose, and the conundrum thereby disappears.

But citizens cannot amend the Constitution whenever they choose. As everyone knows, amendment is very difficult. Article V imposes stringent supermajority requirements and onerous procedural obstacles before it permits amendment. As a result, constitutional law in the United States does in fact override popular will on any given day. That is part of its point. When it comes to certain elemental matters of political power, justice, and liberty, we are in fact governed, and designedly so, by reference to a text enacted generations ago as interpreted by a judiciary insulated from popular will.

Another tempting escape from the problem of time is to declare, all the same, that the majority of Americans today consent to being ruled by the Constitution in this way.[9] Hence, there is no true temporal conflict after all. As long as the Constitution retains current majority consent, all the temporal difficulties again disappear.

But this is no answer. Assuming a tacit-consent claim in this context could overcome the weaknesses common to all such arguments,[10] the claim still would not answer the problem of time. By locating legitimate authority in present majority will, the tacit-consent position tacitly consents to the following. If today's majority genuinely, deliberately wanted to establish a church or enslave a minority, there would be no reason of political principle why this majority shouldn't have its way. But American constitutionalism stands precisely for the principle that there *is* a reason why such a majority shouldn't have its way. It would be in violation of the Constitution. American constitutionalism affirms that there are limits *legitimately and rightfully* imposed on majority will by virtue of a certain kind of democratically enacted text until that text is amended through appropriate (onerous, supermajoritarian) procedures. The problem of time is nothing other than the problem of explaining how majorities today and tomorrow can rightfully and legitimately be bound by limits on their power enacted generations ago. Invoking current majority consent as the source of the Constitution's legitimacy does not save constitutionalism from the problem of time. It repudiates constitutionalism, implicitly conceding that the problem of time is insuperable.

In other words, if we say that a constitution can escape the problem of time just insofar as it continues to comport with present majority will, we are saying that a constitution remains fully legitimate only to that extent. But a fully legitimate constitution, so defined, could not fully function *as* a constitution. It could, to be sure, impose restraints on local or individual actors who acted contrary to the present will of the national majority. But it could not perform at least one definitive constitutional function. It could impose no restraints on governmental action that accurately represented deliberate national majority will. If the Constitution's purchase on legitimacy depends on its conformity with present majority will, the price of attaining this legitimacy would be constitutionalism itself.[11]

Thus emerges what appears to be a fundamental antithesis between constitutionalism and democratic self-government. For some time now, American constitutional theory has expressly embraced this antithesis as its starting point, usually under the name of the "counter-majoritarian difficulty."[12] But the embarrassing conclusion is that constitutional theory has never solved the constitutional problem of time that Hobbes and others identified long ago. As a result, American constitutional law has no account of its own legitimacy.

B. Interpretation

The second foundational question of constitutional law is that of interpretation. Embarrassing conclusion number 2: Constitutional law in the United States has no very good account of its own interpretive method. Here all the authorities disagree. There is no consensus on some of the most basic questions concerning what counts as a proper method of constitutional interpretation.

There are several plausible sources of guidance in constitutional interpretation, all of which flourish in the general American practice of constitutional argument. For example, in roughly ascending level of breadth, interpretive guidance is sought in the "plain meaning" of the text, the "original understanding," precedent, Anglo-American traditions, contemporary consensus, consequentialist considerations, and general moral or philosophical argument about "fundamental" values such as liberty or justice. None of these sources of constitutional meaning is authoritatively accepted as dispositive; some of them are not authoritatively accepted even as *relevant*.

This malady may not be the fault of constitutional law. A number of disciplines today seem to suffer from a kind of hermeneutic neurasthenia. Perhaps what constitutional law needs, on this score, is no different from what literary criticism needs: a general theory of interpretation. Reflecting this sort of thinking, recent legal scholarship includes a number of efforts to articulate a general theory of interpretation that is supposed to tell us what all interpretation properly consists of and hence what constitutional interpretation ought to consist of. There is, for example, a universal intentionalist position, according to which all interpretation (and therefore constitutional interpretation) properly consists of determining the original intentions of the speaker(s) or author(s) at issue.[13] There is also a vulgar deconstructive position, according to which all interpretation actually consists of readers reading their own constructions into the interpreted object.[14] And Ronald Dworkin has suggested that all interpretation properly consists of striving to make the interpreted object "the best it can be."[15]

This turn to hermeneutics to solve the riddles of legal interpretation might come as a surprise to hermeneutics itself, which not long ago turned to law to solve the riddle of interpretation as such.[16] But according to a growing body of thought, constitutional law must be rooted in a general philosophy of interpretation, which, at least initially bracketing all questions of political philosophy, is said to dictate in broad outline the proper interpretive method for constitutional law.

C. Legitimacy and Interpretation

I submit that this approach to constitutional interpretation is quite mistaken. In the first half of the remainder of this essay, I address those approaches to constitutional interpretation that seek to bracket the distinctive problems of political theory – and particularly the problem of legitimacy – that constitutionalism raises. I argue that such approaches cannot succeed. In constitutional law, legitimation precedes interpretation.

In the second half of the essay, I propose a solution to the constitutional problem of time and hence to the countermajoritarian difficulty. I then sketch out an interpretive method that would be consistent with this solution. These modest aims are motivated by the hope that a distinctive understanding of the foundations of written constitutionalism – foundations found neither in a timeless philosophy nor in an authoritative foundational moment, but in the Constitution's own temporal extension – lies at the heart of both the Constitution's legitimacy and its proper interpretation.

II. Methodologies of Constitutional Method

In constitutional law today, there is a surfeit of interpretive approaches: originalist, literalist, activist, passivist; moral-philosophical, structural, law-and-economical; precedent-based, process-based, tradition-based, justice-based; and more besides. Some of these converge in any given dispute; others conflict. We could tell ourselves that this multiplicity of method is inevitable, that it is even desirable. Our cup runs over; let's go bobbing for arguments as suits the case.

If, however, it seems unappealing to make method the handmaiden of result, then we are obliged to think about what sort of argument would have to be made in order to establish that a given method of constitutional interpretation was the proper one. In other words, the question for constitutional interpretation has today become: Is there an appropriate method for determining the appropriate method of constitutional interpretation?

We can distinguish three possible answers to this question: three methodologies of constitutional method. The first I shall call the methodology of universal hermeneutics; the second, that of the concept of law; the third, which I will advocate, that of legitimation.

A. *Universal Hermeneutics*

Suppose we said that interpretation is interpretation. What constitutional law needs is not political theory, but interpretive theory. It needs only to understand what is true of all interpretation. It needs a universal hermeneutics.

This remarkable ambition – to understand constitutional interpretation in light of a unified account of all interpretation – is pursued in several quarters today. As already noted, the three most prominent such efforts are intentionalism, vulgar deconstruction, and Dworkin's best-it-can-be interpretivism. What these approaches have in common is that they all endeavor – at the stage of the inquiry that specifies the appropriate contours of interpretive method – to begin with interpretive theory, confronting only later, if at all, the difficulties of political philosophy, and especially political legitimacy, raised by constitutional law. Thus, universal intentionalism differs from familiar originalism in an important respect. The familiar originalist freely concedes the existence of a variety of forms of textual interpretation; as far as he is concerned, there is no objection to the interpretation of (say) poetry in nonintentionalist fashion. But when it comes to constitutional law, he will say that originalism is the only democratically *legitimate* interpretive method that judges may engage in.[17] By contrast, the universal intentionalist says that originalism is the only *possible* or the only *conceptually tenable* mode of interpretation, whatever text is to be interpreted.[18]

What should we make of these universal hermeneutic strategies? One option would be to join the debate they open up. In other words, we could try to ascertain for ourselves the best theory of interpretation. I will not do so. Instead, I want to explore a much narrower observation. In all three of the positions described, a certain fatal incompleteness – a self-referential incompleteness – is inherent in the argumentation. In every case, this incompleteness leaves open a kind of window. It leaves open the possibility of another mode of interpretation, one that was supposed to have been ruled out by the universal hermeneutics but that turns out to be necessary to sustain the universal hermeneutic position itself. And through this window escapes the hope of pinning down a single proper method for constitutional interpretation.

The Self-referentiality Problem. Take the claim that all interpretation is intentionalist, and suppose that a judge is attempting to read a text using a methodology that he says is nonintentionalist. Perhaps he is seeking to make the text the best it can be. Perhaps he is seeking to arrive at the reading that will best further justice. Or perhaps he just skips every two words and makes the best sense he can of what is left over.

The universal intentionalist must respond in one of two ways. He could say that every one of these manners of reading a text, along with every other imaginable way of reading it, is in fact intentionalist. That claim would keep his thesis intact, but render it trivial. Or he could argue that nonintentionalist readings are possible but that they are not "interpretation" at all, properly understood. This is just what Stanley Fish, in his universal intentionalist mode, says:

[S]omeone committed to the distinction between intentionalist and nonintentionalist interpretation might reply . . . that one can always find meanings in a text other than the ones intended by the author. This statement is undoubtedly true, but the question is, in what sense would that action be an instance of interpreting? Suppose, for example, my method of interpreting a text consists of taking every third word of it and seeing what patterns of significance then emerged. . . . I am playing with the text. . . . I am not trying to figure out *what it means* but trying to see what meanings it *could be made to yield.* I have no necessary quarrel with those who want to do that . . . , but *I do not think it should be called interpreting.*[19]

There is a difficulty in this passage. What we are reading seems itself to be an interpretation – of "interpretation" – and it is not an intentionalist one.

Here is what it means to "interpret" a text, we are told, but the *here* is not located in any particular speaker's intentions. Here is what it means to say of a text "what it means." This is not a claim about what you or I or any particular author intended when using the word "interpretation." Nor is Fish saying merely, "This is what *I* intend when *I* say 'interpretation.' " We are told rather what interpretation *really* means: what conduct should be counted as "interpretation," properly so called. For the universal intentionalist, therefore, all instances of proper interpretation are intentionalist – but one.

Perhaps this incompleteness may seem at first a technicality, a small logical hitch that should not affect the rest. But it is no technicality. If "interpretation" has a true or proper meaning, regardless of what any given user of the term intends or intended, then why not the "freedom of speech" or "the equal protection of the laws"? Universal intentionalism, through its own propositions, opens up at least one mode of interpretation that is not intentionalist. And this other mode of interpretation happens to be one that has traditionally opposed itself to originalist constitutional interpretation.

There are roads that universal intentionalism might pursue to extricate itself from this self-referential difficulty. I will get to them presently. First, let us observe a similar problem in vulgar deconstruction and in best-it-can-be interpretation.

In vulgar deconstruction, the claim is that there can be no true or correct meaning of a text (nor a true or correct fact about the world) against which we could measure our interpretations, because any statement of the text's true or correct meaning (or any statement about the world) would itself have to be an interpretation. Hence, there is no such thing as a right or wrong interpretation at all. Textual meaning is always a meaning constructed by readers, and all the world's a text. Thus, of poems: "[R]eaders do not decode poems; they make them."[20] Of texts in general: "[A]ll readings are misreadings."[21] The claim here is *not* that intended meaning ought merely to be deprivileged; it is that we cannot even say of an interpretation that it gets the intended meaning right or wrong, because what we deem to be the speaker's or author's intention is just another interpretive construct. "[A]uthorial intent" is not "a positive entity that preexists" interpretation, against which interpretation could be measured; it is "a construct of interpretative activity, rather than a ground for the activity."[22] (These are the claims that differentiate vulgar deconstruction from the work of Jacques Derrida.)[23]

The self-referential difficulty here is obvious. In fact, it is a double difficulty. One who makes these claims tells us what he means to say so that we can correctly interpret his text. For example, he insists that we would misunderstand him if we took him to be denying the existence of reality, because his thesis is merely that what we think of as "reality" is an interpretive, linguistically mediated construct.[24] But part of what he means to say turns out to be that a text cannot be correctly interpreted by reference to what its author means to say (which, as a piece of interpretively constructed reality, cannot serve as a "ground" on which to rest interpretation). In other words, he is both (a) declaring that, in reality, whatever we say or think about it, there can be no reality known by us other than what we say or think about it, and (b) asking us to understand him for what he means to say, which happens to be that an author cannot be understood for what he means to say.

There must be one set of statements that exceed the reach of vulgar deconstruction: namely, the propositions of vulgar deconstruction itself. To understand these propositions as their proponent would have us understand them, we must both take them for what he means to say and take them as an effort to get interpretation right.[25] This means that vulgar deconstruction cannot make itself understood without establishing at least the possibility of a form of reading – perhaps two forms of reading – that its putatively universal hermeneutics was supposed to have ruled out.

The same is true of Dworkin's account. He wants to collapse the distinction between an interpretation of what something really is and an interpretation that makes the interpreted object the best it can be. An interpretation is correct (it gets the interpreted object right) if it makes the interpreted object the best it can be. To collapse this distinction is intelligible, provided that an exception is made in one case – the case of interpreting interpretation itself.

For if there were no exception in that case, then Dworkin would be saying that his interpretation of interpretation is correct *because* it makes interpretation the best it can be. But even if Dworkin's interpretation of interpretation *did* make interpretation the best it could be, his interpretation of it could not claim correctness on this ground. That would make the argument circular.

To see this circularity, consider the following argument about the nature of interpretation. "Interpretation properly consists of treating every text or practice as something whose principal purpose is to reveal the nature of God. To interpret something correctly just is to interpret it as having this purpose. How do I validate this assertion? Nothing could be easier: This interpretation of interpretation makes interpretation a practice whose principal purpose is to reveal the nature of God. Therefore, it is the correct interpretation of interpretation." Or: "Interpretation properly consists in making the interpreted thing the worst it can be.[26] To interpret something correctly just *is* to interpret it in such a way as to make it the worst it can be. How do I validate this assertion? Nothing could be easier: This interpretation makes our practices of interpretation the worst they can be. Therefore, it is the correct interpretation of interpretation, don't you see?"

To validate his interpretation of interpretation, Dworkin cannot *merely* say that it makes interpretation the best it can be.[27] He must also say: and (not *hence*, but *and*) this is the *right* interpretation of interpretation. He must invoke, implicitly or explicitly, some criteria of rightness that identify the right interpretation of interpretation *as* the one that makes it the best it can be, standing independent of whatever argument he would use to show that his interpretation of interpretation *is* the one that makes it the best it can be. In other words, to validate his interpretation of interpretation, he must rely on supplemental criteria of interpretive correctness independent of those given by his theory of correct interpretation. In Dworkin's writings, these independent criteria appear in the form of broad-brush empirical claims, suggesting that when we interpret things, we do in actual fact try (whether we know it or not) to make the interpreted object the best it can be.[28] He claims, in effect, to have found the actual purposive structure underlying most (perhaps all) of our practices of interpretation.

But precisely by purporting to identify the actual purposive structure underlying interpretation, Dworkin necessarily opens up another possibility of interpreting rightly independent of striving to make the interpreted object the best it can be. He opens up the possibility of interpreting a practice by reference to its actual purposive structure, regardless of whether so interpreting it makes it the best it can be. Of course, "actual purposive structure" is my phrase, not Dworkin's. But whatever they are, the criteria of right interpretation to which Dworkin must have recourse in order to validate his interpretation of interpretation will also be applicable to other objects of interpretation. Dworkin may try to suppress these independent criteria of right interpretation, but he cannot rule them out, unless he wishes to leave his entire theory of interpretation bottomed on pure circularity (the circularity of saying that the best-it-can-be interpretation of interpretation is the right interpretation of interpretation because it makes interpretation the best it can be). In other words, to make his own point, Dworkin must open up the possibility of a mode of interpreting rightly that his universal hermeneutics was supposed to have ruled out.

A Way out of Self-referentiality? There is an escape route through which a unified field theorist of interpretation might avoid the self-referentiality problem that we have found in each of the three universal hermeneutic positions just canvassed. In each of these three cases, self-referentiality became a problem because the would-be universal theory of interpretation was treated as itself an instance of interpretation (an interpretation of interpretation). But a theory of interpretation need not be, at least on its own terms, an instance of interpreting at all.

A theory of interpretation could instead take the position that it was offering an account of what interpretation *is,* not what it *means.* A scientist who propounds a theory of gravity is not (it might be said) offering a theory of gravity's meaning. He is trying to discover what gravity is. He is trying to describe the relevant phenomena and concepts accurately. Similarly, a theory of interpretation may be said to be an attempt to describe accurately the phenomena and concepts actually involved in the practice of interpretation, not an inquiry into interpretation's meaning. And this same theory of interpretation might hold that interpretation is always an inquiry into meaning, so that an account of what interpretation is (rather than what it means) is not an instance of interpreting.

Observe that this line of argument is not available either to vulgar deconstruction or to Dworkin, because according to the express premises of both, their accounts of interpretation *are* instances of interpretation. (They purportedly do not allow for the adoption of an "Archimedean" perspective from which one might say what interpretation is, as opposed to offering an interpretation of it.) But a version of this reply is available to the universal intentionalist. Universal intentionalism (it might be said) tells us what textual interpretation is, not what any text means.[29] Thus, there is no self-referentiality problem.

This reply, whatever its merits, does not eliminate the difficulty I am trying to bring out. The universal intentionalist's position is now: When a text comes into play, interpretation must be intentionalist; but interpretation itself, standing (as it were) outside a text, can be taken to refer to certain concepts and phenomena whose content does not depend on any particular speaker's intentions. In other words, to make good on the claim that he is telling us what interpretation is, rather than what it means, the universal intentionalist is obliged to say that the word "interpretation" here serves as a label for certain concepts and phenomena (or a "practice") whose content may be determined nonintentionalistically.

But this means that the universal intentionalist has acknowledged a nonintentionalist mode of understanding language: understanding words, that is to say, by analyzing the actual content of the concepts or phenomena to which they are said to refer. In this way, universal intentionalism has once again been obliged to recognize two distinct modes of understanding language, one intentionalist, the other nonintentionalist. And as it happens, both ways of understanding language may be applicable when we are confronted with a norm-prescribing text like the Constitution. Thus, if the concept or practice of "interpretation" can be determined in nonintentionalist fashion, so too could the "equal protection of the laws." We could endeavor to say what equal protection *is,* in the same sense that the universal intentionalist says he is telling us what interpretation is. Of course, the intentionalist might say that, unlike interpretation, the equal protection of the laws is not the sort of thing of which one can say what it is (as opposed to what it means). But in this reply the intentionalist would in fact only be giving us his account of what equal protection is.

The intentionalist at this point might reply, "Very well, you could try to determine what equal protection is, rather than what it means, in the same way that I have determined what interpretation is. But in that event just don't say that you're interpreting. Just don't call what you're doing interpretation of the constitutional text."

This claim, however, no longer has the force the intentionalist wants it to have. As we saw earlier, when the universal intentionalist initially said to nonintentionalists, "Just don't call what you're doing 'interpreting,' " his charge was that nonintentionalist readers were merely *"playing with the text";* that they were merely seeing what meanings a text *"can be made to yield."*[30] But the story is different now that the intentionalist has conceded that he himself engages in a nonintentionalist process of understanding a word *x* (consisting of determining the actual content of *x,* rather than the intended meaning of *x*) and that a nonintentionalist reading of the Constitution's words could engage in the same process. For if the intentionalist is not playing with "interpretation" when he tells us what it really is – if he is not merely seeing what meanings "interpretation" can be made to yield – then neither is one who tries to say what equal protection really is. If he can say *definitively* what "should be called interpreting,"[31] why can't someone else say definitively what should be called the equal protection of the laws? Hence, when the universal intentionalist now says, "Just don't call what you're doing 'interpretation,' " he no longer means, "Just admit that you are playing with the text." He has now said nothing more than "Just don't call what you're doing 'intentionalist.' " And with that, there need be no disagreement.

What there *would* be disagreement over is which method of reading is appropriate when we are confronted with a text like the Constitution. Someone might object that judges have no proper authority to take the "equal protection of the laws" the way universal intentionalism takes "interpretation": as the label for a concept or practice the contents of which are to be determined through ahistorical, nonintentionalist analysis. (Or the objection might be that such an analysis would be permissible only if the founders intended it.) But this objection would entail a very different defense of intentionalism – a defense of intentionalism based on a theory of political legitimacy, not a theory of interpretation.

B. The Concept of Law

Suppose we abandoned the ambition of deriving constitutional method from a unified theory of interpretation. We might still say that constitutional interpretation has no need to launch itself into theories of democracy or political legitimacy. We might say instead that the Constitution is *law*. Legality is the feature of the Constitution dispositive of its proper interpretation. Never mind legitimacy; leave that to politicians and political theorists. All a constitutional judge needs to know is how to interpret law.

This strategy – of finding a unified interpretive method applicable to all law and hence applicable to the Constitution – which in its scope and ambition is only a little less remarkable than the first one, also has its adherents. For example, in *The Tempting of America,* Robert Bork offers an argument that the Constitution's status as law dictates originalist interpretation:

When we speak of "law," we ordinarily refer to a rule that we have no right to change except through prescribed procedures. . . .

What is the meaning of a rule that judges should not change? It is the meaning understood at the time of the law's enactment. . . .

If the Constitution is law, then presumably its meaning, like that of all other law, is the meaning the lawmakers were understood to have intended. . . . There is no other sense in which the Constitution can be what Article VI proclaims it to be: "Law."[32]

Here is a defense of originalism that once again eschews the more familiar, legitimacy-based line of argument (although in other passages Bork pursues this line as well). The claim is not that the Constitution must as a matter of popular sovereignty be enforced according to the will of those who ratified it. The claim is that the very concept of law mandates originalism.

There is at least one pretty good objection to Bork's syllogism: Its major premise is manifestly false. It is not the case that the meaning of all law – not even of "all other law" than constitutional law[33] – is "the meaning the lawmakers were understood to have intended" "at the time of the law's enactment." The law of custom, the oldest law of all, is not enacted by any lawmakers and cannot possibly be said to mean what the "lawmakers were understood to have intended" "at the time of . . . enactment." Moreover, the common law, even beyond its consuetudinary origins, was and is characteristically distilled from a series of judicial opinions. If the meaning of cases A, B, and C, handed down at disparate times by different judges, is given (at a still later time) by a process of reconciling the holdings of these cases while taking into account diverse elements of legal policy and principle, how can we say that the meaning of A is that which the "lawmakers," whoever they might be, were originally understood to have intended? Even in the case of statutes, while intentionalism is certainly a dominant interpretive approach, the law's meaning is frequently developed in altogether nonintentionalist fashion. A statute's meaning may have accreted through case law (a famous example in the United States being the development of the Sherman Antitrust Act). Or a statute's meaning may have developed through the pragmatic interpretation of administrative officers charged with its implementation.

In other words, even if we limited ourselves to our own legal system, and even if we excluded constitutional law itself from the analysis, it would still be utterly impossible to conclude that the meaning of all law is the intentionalist meaning that Bork describes. Some law in our system is interpreted in accordance with original intentions. But there are far too many kinds of legal practices, with far too many modes of meaning-production, to support an account that purports to specify any single methodology as the methodology by which all law receives its meaning.

This is why one finds the argument from law being deployed so variously in constitutional scholarship. Here are Charles Black's conclusions, in a book on constitutional judicial review, about the nature of law:

> [L]aw is also insight and wisdom and justice. We have always intuitively known this. . . . Who ever felt comfortable about a judge, however learned and upright, who had no common sense and no . . . deep feeling for the goals after which the law is questing?
>
> . . . Underneath all I have said is the conviction that "decision according to law" can be a meaningful phrase, even if the decision in question is made by something other than a machine. . . . If [this] is not true, then there is no substance in our philosophy of government – or, indeed, of law itself.[34]

This is another appeal to law, but with a profoundly different apprehension of what law is. As a result, Black demands in the name of the law what Bork rejects in the name of the law: the introduction of the judge's own wisdom and sense of justice in constitutional adjudication.

Or consider Herbert Wechsler's well-known endeavor (aped by none other than Robert Bork) to make the demand for "neutral principles" the operative basis for constitutional interpretive method.[35] He too understood his position to be grounded in the proposition that courts must function as "courts *of law.*"[36] Yet he concluded that the "main qualities of law, its generality and its neutrality," furnished a ground for rejecting those interpretive methods that regard constitutional provisions as bearing a "fixed 'historical meaning,' " a meaning "fixed by the consensus of a century long past."[37]

The examples could be multiplied. The concept of law has been invoked on behalf of a commanding principle of stare decisis in constitutional interpretation; it has been invoked in defense of judicial restraint; it has been invoked to justify adherence to the "plain meaning" of the constitutional text.[38] Not that any of these arguments is mistaken. The diverse predications of law on which they rest are all imaginable and defensible within the confines of our own legal system. As a result, however, the concept of law does not choose among them.

To state what should be obvious: I am not saying that there can be no unified theory of law, and I am not saying that the Constitution's status as law is irrelevant to constitutional interpretation. The point is simply that the Constitution's status as law is consistent with most of the interpretive methods advocated in the field today, and that a unified theory of law, if there were such a thing, could not both cover the territory and dictate a single method of legal interpretation.

To be sure, the fact that a variety of forms of legal interpretation exists in our system is not an argument that it ought to exist. The diversity of our actual legal interpretive traditions does not preclude the search for a unified normative theory of law, and such a theory could certainly purport to dictate a single method of legal interpretation. Austin's command theory of law is perhaps an example of such a theory; as a systematic will-based account, it might (if it had been successful) have had strong interpretive implications, broadly suggestive of intentionalism as the proper interpretive method throughout the legal system. Joseph Raz's moral theory of law is perhaps another example; as a systematic reason-based account, it might also (if successful) have strong interpretive implications, broadly suggestive of an approach in which judges seek to formulate rules on the basis of "right reason,"[39] mindful of the law's proper "social functions."[40]

Without entering into the merits of any such theories of law, we can say this much: A theory of law must either take the law as it is or tell us what it ought to be (or both). To the extent that a tendentious thesis about the nature of law is made (like Bork's) on the basis of nothing more than a descriptive slap at the actual legal scene, it must accept the variety of legal interpretation in our system and must therefore leave us with an open question when it comes to selecting the form of legal interpretation appropriate to constitutional law. To the extent that a more sophisticated jurisprudence offers a thoroughgoing normative vision of law, and calls for a single interpretive method, it must select one such method from the still-greater variety of actual and imaginable legal forms. But this it cannot do on the basis of the concept of law alone.

The contrast between Austin and Raz (which mirrors, at a deeper level, that between Bork and Black) bears this out. Legal interpretation, for all that the concept of law requires, can be organized at a minimum in two profoundly different ways. It can be organized around the determination of a sovereign's will, and it can be organized around the pursuit of reason, justice, wealth maximization, or some other criterion of the right thing to be done. These two possibilities are instinct in the concept of law. Law has an irreducibly double nature: Law is the word of the sovereign, and law is also the right.

This double nature does not imply a "fundamental contradiction." It does not mean that law cannot integrate these two aspirations. And doubtless it could be said that the rule of law imposes inherent limits barring a system of legal interpretation from gearing itself excessively toward either sovereign will or the right. But it remains the case that a system of legal interpretation can be substantially oriented toward either pole – and still qualify as law. Nothing prevents the constitutional rules of a legal system from opting for either approach.

This means, however, that when it comes to the interpretation of the constitutional rules themselves, the status of the Constitution as law cannot itself dictate a particular interpretive method. There will always be at least two interpretive methodologies available: The Constitution could be read according to the will of the sovereign agents (whoever they are said to be), or it could be read according to the right (whether the right is understood in terms of reason, justice, economic efficiency, or something else again). If someone says that only one of these two overarching interpretive methodologies will permit constitutional law to qualify legitimately as law, what must be meant by such an assertion is that the insisted-upon interpretive method is necessary to make constitutional law legitimate, not to make it law.

C. Legitimation

The lesson of the preceding two sections is that constitutional interpretation cannot be derived from the bare fact that the Constitution is an object of interpretation, or from the only slightly less bare fact that the Constitution is law. We are obliged, instead, to say what mode of interpretation is appropriate to this particular kind of text, this particular kind of law, this world-changing practice brought into being in the United States in the late eighteenth century. The thought that constitutional interpretation must respond to the unique position of constitutional law underlies the third methodology of constitutional method. This is the methodology of legitimation. It demands that judges select an interpretive method for constitutional law in accordance with the requirements of legitimacy that pertain to the extraordinary position of an unelected judge applying a written constitution in a democratic polity. This approach to interpretation is perhaps the most widespread of all in American constitutional practice, if we count not only the thoughtful body of work that has grappled with the "counter-majoritarian difficulty," but also the whole, less thoughtful debate about judicial "activism." The antiactivist argues against certain interpretive methods on the ground that they change the meaning of the Constitution or otherwise result in judge-made constitutional law that cannot legitimately be imposed on the nation. The antiactivist argument is, therefore, a legitimacy argument.

Those who make this argument, however, have invariably neglected to explain why a judge who follows their preferred interpretive method (typically originalism of some form) will produce law that *can* be legitimately imposed on the nation. In other words, antiactivists make claims about the requirements of legitimacy that apply to constitutional judges without ever confronting the problem of legitimacy that applies to constitutional law as such (the constitutional problem of time). Former judge Bork is a prime example. He has recently confounded many by suggesting that judicial constitutional decisions be subject to legislative override.[41] How could such a devotee of the Founding suddenly become a partisan of legislative supremacy? The answer is that Bork has merely worked out the logic of his own position: However shrill was his condemnation of the illegitimacy of nonoriginalist interpretation, he never had anything like an adequate account of why originalist constitutional law *would* have been legitimate. On the contrary, precisely that which permitted him to call judge-made law a species of tyranny (its imposition of law on the nation contrary to present majority will) left him with no real defense and no true understanding of constitutional law at all.

So we might say that the methodology of legitimation demands, when fully thought through, a confrontation with the constitutional problem of time (a confrontation whose outcome is, of course, not guaranteed). What grounds this approach? Why should legitimation precede interpretation? The answer is twofold: There is an answer internal to the institution of constitutional law, and there is an answer from the perspective of political theory as a whole.

The internal answer is that constitutional interpretive method has a duty to find a way to respond to the distinctness of the Constitution – a way to preserve it as the extraordinary thing that it is. This internal duty is expressed in canonical form when judges remind themselves "that it is *a constitution* we are expounding."[42] And what is this revolutionary thing that Americans learned to call a constitution? A written constitution of the American variety presents itself fundamentally as two things: (a) as an act of the people and (b) as foundational law. In other words, it presents itself as – it is supposed to be – an act of popular self-government and an act of law that establishes the foundational institutions and constraints within which the (democratic) political-legal order is to operate.

Now, if interpretation could preserve constitutional law exactly as the law intended by the relevant people at the moment of ratification, the Constitution would become, as time passed, less and less recognizable as an act of popular self-government today. (It would appear to be more and more an act of imposition by one "generation," as Jefferson said, upon successive ones.) But if interpretation could preserve constitutional law as an exact expression of popular will today, then the Constitution would become in an important sense inoperative as foundational law. (It would cease to impose constraints on majoritarian action.) Solving the constitutional problem of time is nothing other than finding a way to allow the Constitution to be *a constitution* – in the American sense.

From the external point of view of political theory, the reason that constitutional interpretation must follow from a theory of constitutional legitimacy is that *all* law ought to be interpreted in accordance with the grounds of its legitimate authority. For if law is otherwise interpreted, then it loses its claim to legitimate authority. Legitimacy is obviously not the only desideratum of law. Let us say that it is a necessary condition of law's acceptability. But no unified method of legal interpretation follows from this observation. There is no reason why the legitimate authority of different kinds of law must all rest on identical grounds. Quite the contrary.

The authority of a judge's decision might rest principally on judicial impartiality and reason. That of an administrative regulation might rest principally on the agency's superior technical knowledge. That of a statute, on its representing the will of a majority of representatives accountable to electoral majorities. Each of these different grounds of legitimate authority might in turn generate different interpretive practices (e.g., respectively, a jurisprudence of common-law reasoning, of deference to administrative agencies, or of adherence to legislative intent). But ultimately the legitimate authority of all these genuses of law will have to back up upon that of the basic constitutional order, which calls for the election of the legislators and executive officers, who enact the statutes, commission the regulators, appoint the judges, and so on. Everything will depend upon the legitimacy of the system's constitution, and in the case of a written constitution, none of the relatively simple grounds of authority just mentioned can apply. Instead, to preserve constitutional law's legitimate authority, constitutional interpretation would have to answer a very difficult question. In the American case, it would need an account of how a two-hundred-year-old text, enacted by past democratic majorities, could possibly continue to exert legitimate authority over democratic majorities in the future. Constitutional interpretation must solve the constitutional problem of time.

III. Demo-graphy in America

Let us try, then, to solve it. The constitutional problem of time arises from a very particular conception of self-government. Solving the problem requires that we identify this conception and replace it with another.

A. *Popular Voice, Constitutional Text*

Self-government, as we almost invariably understand it, consists ideally of government by the will or consent of the governed. This holds for the most cynical as well as the most romantic depiction of self-government. We might, in other words, conceive self-government in terms of atomic individuals or in terms of an organic community, but still we would begin with the premise that true self-government (whether we are thinking of the government of each individual or the government of all by the general will) consisted of government by the self's own will. This way of thinking has a particular temporal orientation. Whether we understand the will of the governed through a hyperdisintegrative lens such as public choice or through a hyperintegrative lens such as fascism, in either case, and in all the intermediate cases, we begin by understanding self-government as, ideally, government by the will of the governed *here and now*.

Rousseau expressed this ideal in exacting terms: "Now the general will that should direct the State is not that of a past time but of the present moment, and the true characteristic of sovereignty is that there is always agreement on time, place and effect between the direction of the general will and the use of public force."[43] Aside from the mysteries of Rousseau's "general will," this idea has been everywhere in evidence across a wide terrain of modern political thought. The same insistence on present will was in play when Hobbes and other classical jurists said that the sovereign will could not bind itself to itself, when Jefferson said that each generation stood to the next as one foreign nation stands to another, and when Professor Bickel wrote of the "counter-majoritarian difficulty."[44]

I call this conception of self-government speech-modeled. One reason is that in all its widely different forms, it tends to express itself in a language of speech, voice, conversation, dialogue, and so on.[45] And the reason for this language of speech is in turn the temporal orientation that we just observed. If present sovereign will is what ought to govern, the ideal political desideratum is never an authoritative text (at best a recordation of a past will), but rather an authoritative voice. If the governed are to govern themselves here and now, then somehow or other, the people must speak.

Now, the central problem for every conception of self-government based on the ideal of government by present popular will has always been that of fundamental rights. To be sure, the prevailing understanding of democracy embraces the idea that certain fundamental rights – of conscience and speech, of equality before the law, of property, and so on – are beyond the reach of majority will. Textbook definitions of democracy invariably include such rights. The point, however, is that the textbooks cannot explain how these fundamental rights sit with the majority-will conception of self-government that exists alongside them.[46] How can any political actor in a speech-modeled system enforce fundamental rights against popular will without arrogating to himself dictatorial powers? Without acting fundamentally illegitimately? The prevailing understanding of democracy has no good answer to this question, which is why a political scientist as thoughtful as Elster finds himself obliged to define democracy as "simple majority rule, based on the principle 'One person one vote' " – period. The crucial normative problem for every speech-modeled conception of democratic self-government has always been that of explaining the legitimate foundation of constitutional rights.

There is a well-known and well-worked repertoire of possible solutions to this problem. Very broadly speaking, we may categorize this repertoire as follows. Within a conception of self-government based on the will or consent of the governed, only a limited number of moves – four, to be precise – can be made to legitimize fundamental rights. Either there must be an appeal to timeless, pre-political rights superior in authority to all temporal exercises of power, or else there must be an appeal to the past, present, or predicted will of the governed. These are the only sources to which the speech-modeled conception can turn for ultimate normative authority. The appeals to pre-political rights and to past will are illustrated by the earliest and most primitive solutions to the fundamental-rights problem: natural law and social contracts. The appeals to present and predicted popular will are illustrated in the latest and most sophisticated solutions, which argue for fundamental rights as the necessary conditions of deliberative democracy in the present,[47] or as the rights that would be consented to by rational persons under hypothetical conditions.[48]

These four moves or solutions, not coincidentally, appear over and over in constitutional thought. They underlie the major schools of constitutional interpretation.[49] Appeals to pre-political or timeless rights, more prominent in an earlier era than they are today, still flourish in the area of constitutional law called the right of privacy.[50] The appeal to past will underlies originalism and "plain-meaning" jurisprudence.[51] The present-tense approach is visible in the contemporary-consensus and process-based schools.[52] And predicted will is exactly what Bickel in *The Least Dangerous Branch* (and others later) concluded should guide the Supreme Court in constitutional adjudication.[53]

The point is that all of these various strategies are committed to the same starting point: a presumptive antithesis between constitutional rights and the ideal of self-government (understood as government by the will or consent of the governed). Solutions to this antithesis may be possible, but they necessarily distort the situation of constitutional rights in the United States, because the entire problematic within which they operate misunderstands American written constitutionalism. American constitutionalism broke – sharply and self-consciously – from the confines not of democratic self-government, but of speech-modeled self-government. American constitutionalism models self-government not as government by popular will or voice, but as government by popular authorship. Because of the emphasis on popular authorship, I will call the American conception of self-government *democracy as demo-graphy*.

B. *Committed to Writing*

What does it mean to break with the idea that self-government ideally consists of government by the self's own present will or consent? It means, among other things, that if we could imagine the entire American people made equal, if we could imagine this people assembling in one body at one time, deliberating with ancient wisdom, and ultimately declaring in one voice its sovereign will – if we could even imagine this supreme voice being instantaneously followed, its will translated immediately into governance in every particular – we still would not have imagined self-government.

To say so is to suggest a relationship between time and freedom very different from what is conceivable on the model of speech. The speech-modeled conception of self-government punctuates time, crystallizing legitimate authority in the will of a single privileged moment (whether past, present, or predicted). This punctuated temporality is inadequate to capture the dimension of temporal extendedness integral to our moral and political lives. (It is because of this inadequacy that speech-modeled thought finds itself drawn to solutions that flee time altogether.) An alternative conception of the ideal relation between time and freedom would imagine self-government as a temporally extended project.

Here, in broad brush, is the starting point of this alternative conception. Of all animals, only humans make history; only humans make themselves over time. Extended temporality is a constituent part of our being. To be a person takes time. A person, we might say, does not exist at any given time. This means that freedom is possible only over time. To be free in the human sense, it is not sufficient to act on one's will at each successive moment. That is animal freedom. Human freedom requires a relationship of self-making to one's life as a whole: It requires individuals to give their temporally extended being a shape or purpose of their own determination.

Now, the capacity of humans to relate to themselves over time has a condition: the capacity to write. (Some animals speak; only humans can write.) Humans relate to themselves over time through writing. Autonomy is therefore always autobiography: not in the sense of writing a life after the large facts, but before and during those facts. Every exercise in human freedom is an exercise in self-life-writing. It is an exercise in living out commitments of one's own making. Freedom in the human sense requires that we give our lives purpose, meaning, something at which to aim. We must give our lives, in two words, a text.

Similarly, to be a people takes time; it takes generations. To realize within a polity a new set of foundational principles may take a century – or two or more. To be self-governing, a people must attempt the kind of self-government that takes place over generations. It must attempt the reins of time.

American constitutionalism was revolutionary because it made this attempt. It opened up, in place of democracy organized around the vox populi, an inscriptive and temporally extended democracy. American constitutionalism opened up the possibility of democracy as demo-graphy: of a people writing down its foundational commitments and living under these commitments for generations to come. Written constitutionalism denies the desirability (and perhaps the possibility) of self-government *at any given time*. It rather embraces the struggle for self-government *over time*.

We can therefore summarize democracy as demo-graphy in three theses. The first has to do with peoples:

> *(1) The Popularity Thesis.*   A people, considered as a collective
> and temporally extended agent, is a proper subject or "self" in the
> project of democratic self-government.

The popularity thesis ("popularity" referring to the condition or status of being a people) does not claim that peoples are just like persons. But it does assert that there is such a thing as a people, that a people exists over time, and that it must be recognized as a collective subject for some political purposes.

One could object to this thesis on a number of grounds. The word "people," it might be said, is pure reification except when used as the plural of "person." Or the only proper subject of self-government is the individual. Or even if popular self-government were an admissible concept, it would not apply to U.S. history, because Americans cannot be said to make up a single people, and surely the American people that made the Constitution cannot be said to be the same people as the one that exists today.

These are serious objections, one and all. To say that the Constitution's legitimacy depends on rejecting them hardly offers a refutation. But it is so. If the Constitution legitimately binds us today, it does so insofar as we are members of the same people that gave itself this law.

Doubtless the idea of a people persisting over time romanticizes. But so does the idea of a person persisting over time. Without even attempting to argue for the thesis here, I will say only that, ultimately, I don't think the obstacles to regarding political communities as persisting agents over time are greater than the obstacles to regarding persons as having a persisting identity over time. What must be avoided at all costs is the notion that we are speaking here of a "collective will," an "organic" group, a "moral person" whose identity, once established, would transcend and supplant that of its constituents. What must be avoided is the old duality in which we are asked to view a people as either a solid particle of personhood (with a will of its own) or else an epiphenomenal wave (in which case the real entities are the "atomic" individuals).

This is the duality in which the feckless quarrel between liberalism and republicanism runs its entire course. Liberalism believes in individuals and insists that the very idea of collective subjectivity threatens individuality, whereas republicanism believes in the political nature of human identity and insists that the very idea of individuality threatens community. But both parties agree on the need to choose between these two poles of subjectivity in thinking through self-government. Either self-government must consist of government by a "common will"[54] or else self-government must exclusively be a matter of each individual governing himself.[55] Can we never move beyond this outdated political physics?

The idea of recognizing the agency of both peoples and persons in self-government could be put as follows. Humans cannot meaningfully achieve self-government as individuals. Not because our identity is essentially communal, rather than individual, so that self-government could intelligibly exist only at the communal level. The reason is simpler. We live in societies. We interact. If the basic rules and long-term consequences of these interactions are to be governed at all, they must be governed by law. No individual but a king (and perhaps not even he) can live under law of his own making. But a polity can live under law of its own making. In this simple but decisive sense, self-government is attainable for individuals only through their membership in a political community that gives itself its own law. At the same time, self-government is not attained for individuals, but obliterated, if the law prohibits them from exercising their own capacity for self-life-writing.

But what is a people? How are we to understand popularity in a way that does not make the subjectivity of a people exclusive of or antithetical to that of individuals? Suppose we just say that a people consists of the set of persons who are members of a particular society, and suppose we define a society as a set of persons living under a particular political-legal system. (This means that citizens of the United States are to be differentiated from Canadians not by reference to some uniquely American (as opposed to North American) values or attributes, but by reference to the legal boundary between the two countries. It also means that there may be subpeoples within a larger, national people, because there may be subsidiary political-legal systems within a larger one.) Because this people is not imagined as some sort of organic body in mystic terms, we need not attribute to it any collective will. But this people would be romanticized just enough to imagine it as capable of having commitments. This capability would only mean, however, that the persons who are members of this people are able to share in great numbers important convictions on the basis of which they are prepared to act. These convictions can be the basis of popular commitments.

I will not try to defend this notion of popularity here (even though I recognize that saying a little about matters such as these is probably worse than saying nothing at all). Instead, having raised the subject of popular commitments, let me turn to the second thesis of democracy as demo-graphy:

> *(2) The Commitment Thesis.*   Self-government is achieved not
> when a self is governed by its own will or consent, but when a self
> lays down and lives up to its own commitments over time.

The significance of the commitment thesis lies in recognizing commitment as a moral or normative operation that is profoundly different from the classically liberal operations of consent or choice. The latter are the proper normative operations if the agent's normative authority over himself (his ability to bind himself) is to be crystallized in the exercise of a single moment's will. (As a result, consent and choice necessarily call up an endless conflict among past, present, and predicted will.) By contrast, commitment is the normative operation a temporally extended subject engages in when, without entering into an agreement with another, he imposes temporally extended obligations on himself. Here are some of the differentiating characteristics of commitment.

An act of consent or will is completed at a single moment, but a commitment is not made at any particular moment. It takes time to commit oneself. Saying that one is committed to something – even saying it sincerely, even saying it in writing, even promising it – doesn't make it so. One can *decide* to commit oneself at a given moment, but being committed requires more.

Every commitment requires at a minimum a commitment of time: a commitment of some portion of one's precious time on earth.

The obligations perfectly entailed by an act of consent or choice are in principle reducible to those the self intends to be imposing on itself. To the extent that we hold a consenting party to a nonintended obligation, it is either because we have implicitly moved from the domain of consent to that of commitment or because we are appealing to other, nonconsensualist grounds: reliance, assumption of risk, public policy, and so on. A commitment, by contrast, is always an engagement not only with an uncertain future, but with an object at least in part external to self: a principle, a relationship, an institution, a cause, a goal. The object of the commitment will have its own, independent requirements.[56] And although these requirements will invariably be subject to interpretation, the obligations of a commitment cannot as a result be measured by or reduced to a mental state of the committing party at any particular time – past, present, or predicted. Interpreting a commitment cannot be reduced to a determination of intentions. To live up to a commitment, one cannot ask merely: What did I intend at the moment when I made this commitment (or what do I will now, or what will I will at some predicted moment)?

On the other hand, the obligations of a commitment are not to be regarded as purely external either. Interpreting a commitment is not only a matter of thinking through the requirements entailed by the object of the commitment. One must also think through: What am *I* committed to in being committed to this object? For one person's commitment to a principle, a purpose, a relationship, and so on may be different from another's. At stake in interpreting a commitment is an interpretation of one's own life: a re-collection of one's temporally disparate experiences.

Finally, we can know the entailments of our commitments only by living them out. We cannot know in advance what our deepest commitments will turn out to require of us. This is so because with principles, institutions, relationships, or other objects of deep commitment, moral knowledge requires more than speculation. It requires a period of living with and living under. Those, for example, who memorialized the U.S. Constitution's commitment to the equal protection of the laws could not know in advance what all the requirements of this principle would be, precisely because no one then had ever lived with or under it. What they did know – and what can never be forgotten – will be considered shortly.

The combination of the first two theses produces a third:

> *(3) The Constitutionalism Thesis.* A people attains self-government not by perfecting a politics of popular voice, but by way of an inscriptive politics, through which the people struggles to

memorialize in foundational law, and to live out over time, its own foundational commitments.

For a people to be self-governing, there must be more than a politics permitting citizens to give voice to their will. There must be an inscriptive politics at the foundation of the legal order. This inscriptive politics would include institutions through which the polity could memorialize, preserve, interpret, enforce, and rewrite its fundamental political commitments over time. The first freedom of a self-governing people is not, therefore, the freedom of speech. It is the freedom to write: to give oneself a text. A fully self-governing people must be the author of its own constitution.

If constitutional law embodies this inscriptive politics, then there is no countermajoritarian difficulty. Why? Because the countermajoritarian difficulty is more (it must be more) than a claim that judicial review sometimes produces countermajoritarian results. The *difficulty* referred to is not countermajoritarianism as such; the difficulty, as Bickel observed, is that this countermajoritarianism makes constitutional law "undemocratic."[57] It makes constitutional law "a deviant institution" in "American democracy."[58] The countermajoritarian difficulty, in other words, is a formulation of the antithesis between constitutionalism and democracy with which speech-modeled thinking begins. It holds only if democracy is equated with some version of present-tense, speech-modeled self-government.[59] But written constitutionalism is not antithetical to democratic self-government. It *is* democratic self-government, over time.

To illuminate the view I have just outlined, let me point out differences between it and some of the prominent, prevailing efforts within constitutional thought to conceptualize written constitutionalism within a democratic polity. To begin with, the demo-graphic perspective explains originalism's utter failure. Originalism seeks to reduce the nation's temporally extended commitments to a moment's act of will; it seeks to read the written Constitution as an expression of popular voice. By contrast, processualism (which invites us to understand constitutional guarantees as the necessary conditions of the process of forming and effectuating *present* popular will) fails to capture the historicity of constitutional law. On the processualist view, all constitutions ought to provide the same rights; the particular constitutional struggles of a given nation's history are incidental. Processualism has no place for a politics of constitution-writing or for the substantive constitutional commitments that emerge from it.

One account that does capture the importance of constitutional politics and constitutional history is Professor Ackerman's, which brings back a much-needed emphasis on higher lawmaking into American constitutional thought.[60] But Ackerman still conceptualizes this higher lawmaking in terms of time-punctuated moments ("constitutional moments")[61] and hence in terms of the model of speech. What results is an insistence on popular will and voice[62] that culminates in a stunning disparagement of constitution-writing and constitutional text. The "commanding voice of the People"[63] is so triumphant here that Ackerman ends by arguing for constitutional amendments never written or enacted, which have (apparently) superseded provisions that a less rigorously speech-modeled reader might have supposed were still part of the operative text.[64]

Ronald Dworkin, important as he has been to jurisprudence in general, has not yet been as influential in the domain of constitutional thought. Nevertheless, his approach has the virtue of capturing the normative openness of constitutional law and of avoiding fixation on any particular moment of democratic will. Dworkin's constitutionalism, however, is so systematically ahistorical that it is almost atemporal. Indeed, with the exception of those few still openly advocating natural law, Dworkin's constitutionalism comes closest today to the wholesale flight from temporality mentioned earlier. For him, constitutional rights are those rights that a philosopher-god would announce if called on to make the Constitution the morally, legally, and politically best constitution it could be.[65] Demo-graphy is (if only just slightly) more modest. It insists that the Constitution be understood and preserved as the law that a particular people, with a particular history, gave itself – whether or not this makes the Constitution the best it could be. These remarks return us to the problem of interpretation.

C. Interpretation: The Paradigm-Case Method

If we took the demo-graphic view of the Constitution, what would our interpretive method look like? I will call demo-graphic interpretation *reading the Constitution as written*.

Here are the constraints: Reading the Constitution as written (resting on a theory of self-government through exercise of the freedom to write) must take text seriously. More than this, it must give a privileged position to the "Founding" in the following sense. It must give privileged significance to the particular, historical struggles of constitution-writing on which demo-graphy depends and with which it begins. In some special, privileged fashion – which we will have to specify carefully – reading the Constitution as written must preserve our constitutional commitments as the original commitments the people gave itself. On the other hand, reading the Constitution as written cannot reduce constitutional meaning to the democratic will of the "founding moment" or any other moment – past, present, or predicted. For that would destroy constitutional law's claim to legitimate authority, by subjecting a temporally extended people to the (putatively) democratic will of a given moment. A commitment, as we have seen, if it is to be honored at all, must be honored even though what it requires is contrary to the will of the committed party at any particular moment. To read the Constitution as written, then, is to honor the constitutional commitments the United States gave itself in its actual, historical struggles of constitution-writing (there can be no recourse here to timeless or pre-political rights), while never reducing these commitments to the democratic will of any particular moment. How can this be done?

There is an interpretive method that satisfies these requirements: the paradigm-case method. It may or may not be the only way to read the Constitution as written. But if constitutional method does not at least look greatly like the method I am about to describe, it is difficult to believe that the requirements specified earlier will be fulfilled.

In the paradigm-case method, the initial question in interpreting a constitutional right is always this: What are the core historical applications of this right? In particular, what were the abuses of power that those who fought for this right fought most centrally to abolish? This is a question of fact, and it will in general be an answerable question of fact. If we inquire into the general principles originally understood to lie behind a constitutional provision, we may find vast disagreement. If we inquire into the original (ratifiers') intent concerning most of the myriad specific constitutional controversies that arise today, we are likely to find no answer at all. But we are much more likely to find positive answers if we ask instead, Was there a set of core applications of this right, were there circumstances to which all or almost all of those who fought for this right would have agreed that it applied, were there one or two or three prohibitions that they would have overwhelmingly agreed on?

These core applications are a constitutional provision's foundational paradigm cases. They are inviolable, because they define the provision. They create the paradigm(s) through which it is to be interpreted. Any interpretation of a constitutional right under which the right would not prohibit the core abuses it was enacted to prohibit is categorically wrong.

Why? Suppose that Mississippi passed a statute barring blacks from serving on juries or making it a crime for blacks to behave insolently toward whites. And suppose the Supreme Court upheld this statute, changing its equal protection framework to require only that legal classifications be rationally related to legitimate state interests. What is so wrong with the Court's decision? What entitles us to say categorically that the decision is a constitutional outrage?

Well, one thing we could say is that the Court's decision is indefensible on its own terms (and therefore hypocritical, irrational, etc.). There is no conceivable legitimate state interest, we might say, to which Mississippi's statute could possibly be rationally related. But suppose Mississippi offers empirical proof that discriminating against blacks in this way will on the whole create a net gain in overall social utility. Is increasing social utility an illegitimate state interest? Does the Mississippi statute stand or fall on the correctness of the state's empirical claim?

Another thing we might say is that the Mississippi statute flies in the face of contemporary national norms. But would this response mean that if enough states passed the same law, then it would be constitutional (or less categorically unconstitutional)? Does it mean that if Congress passed the same law, the federal statute would not be (categorically) unconstitutional?[66]

Shall we say, then, that the Court's decision is categorically wrong because it contravenes original intent? The Court's decision certainly does depart from the original understanding of the Fourteenth Amendment, but if modern equal protection doctrine is not to be rejected wholesale, that fact alone cannot be enough to reject what the Court has done. For the Court's desegregation decisions also departed from the original intentions, and so did the Court's decision to strike down sex discrimination under the equal protection clause. If Mississippi's hypothetical statute is categorically unconstitutional, it had better not be because Mississippi has not obeyed the original intentions underlying the Fourteenth Amendment.

But perhaps someone dedicated to justice-based constitutional interpretation (Lawrence Sager, Chapter 6, this volume, provides an excellent illustration) will have a very different answer. "The Mississippi statute is grossly unjust," he might say, "regardless of original intentions and regardless of where the nation currently stands on the issue. That is why it is categorically unconstitutional." But not everything unjust (as even Professor Sager acknowledges) violates the Constitution. "All the same," it might be said, "the question posed was 'What is so wrong with the Court's decision?' and the correct answer to that question is that the decision is monstrously unjust."

Putting the wrongness of the Court's decision on this footing alone is not satisfactory. It misses the fact that the justices have violated a primary duty of constitutional interpretation. The justices have done something not only unjust, but interpretively illegitimate: They have allowed a state to do exactly what a state was supposed to be prohibited from doing as a result of the enactment of the Fourteenth Amendment. They have in one stroke of "interpretation" excised from constitutional law the heart of the struggle that culminated in the Fourteenth Amendment. They have erased the American people's actual, historical act of constitution-writing through their putative interpretation of the constitutional text.

On what basis do I say so? The Southern black codes – imposing certain legal disabilities on blacks alone, including precisely the kind of provisions reenacted in Mississippi's hypothetical statute – were the Fourteenth Amendment's paradigm cases. They were the core abuses the amendment was enacted to abolish. This is what entitles us to say categorically that the Court's decision was wrong, no matter what one's ideology, no matter what views of justice one holds, no matter what position a current national majority takes. Black codes are in this sense definitive of the Fourteenth Amendment. If it means anything, the Fourteenth Amendment means that such laws are unconstitutional. Paradigm cases, we might say, represent facts about constitutional meaning, facts that precede all interpretation. Judges are without authority to "interpret" a provision of the Constitution contrary to its paradigm cases. Judges who do so have not interpreted the Constitution at all; they have rewritten or unwritten it.

This is not originalism. Core foundational prohibitions are privileged, but the original understanding is privileged no further. Deciding on everything *else* (beyond the paradigm cases) that the Fourteenth Amendment may or may not prohibit remains a matter of interpretation. For example, even if every framer and ratifier of that amendment intended it to permit race-segregated schooling, *Brown v. Board of Education*[67] would be nonetheless defensible. For the paradigm cases of a constitutional right consist (as already stated) only of that which the right was intended at its core to *prohibit*. The original understanding of what a constitutional right *permitted* has no such foundational standing.

Why exactly is the intent to prohibit privileged in this decisive way over the intent to permit? Constitutional law begins with constitution-writing, and the latter begins with a never-again. When a right is written, the constitutional change that occurs does not consist of setting in stone the power of government to do this or that. Such a commitment to governmental power is perfectly possible; the United States Constitution contains many power-granting provisions. (I will return to them in a moment.) But a commitment of power to a particular governmental body is not what is effected by a constitutional right limiting that body's actions. The constitutional change effected by a right consists, rather, of setting in stone what some actor or actors shall never do again. "*This* shall occur here no more" is the meaning of a constitutional right. Reading the Constitution as written requires that the core of this never-again – written, perhaps, in blood – must always be honored. To be sure, if the legitimate authority of constitutional law hung on the consent of the governed, there would be as good a reason to preserve the original understanding of what a right was to *permit* as there would be to preserve what the right was to *prohibit*. But commitment is not consent. Those who make commitments may always be in for more than they originally foresaw.

To repeat, commitments come fully into being only as they are lived out. Their true entailments cannot be known by ex ante or a priori philosophizing. One can know them only by living with or under the principles, institutions, or whatever else one has committed oneself to. I have already observed one reason for this: the necessity of lived experience for the moral knowledge of a commitment. The other reason is the human capacity for hypocrisy and rationalization. Moral astigmatism is general in man. We all know what it is to decry injustice in a neighbor's house, while failing to observe the same injustice at home. But when that neighbor's injustice is given a name and when its abolition is committed to writing, there can only be a short time before what has been invisible begins to demand recognition. Time has a way of embarrassing those of us who proclaim dedication to a principle. It has a way of revealing our shortcomings – and as a result, of making it possible for us to be truer to our commitments.

Thus, the original intent to permit can never be accorded foundational status in the interpretation of a constitutional right. A commitment to a principle of justice or liberty is a commitment to see that principle through, even if it requires one to give up practices that seemed perfectly reasonable, perfectly natural, at the time one embarked upon the commitment. No matter how widely held, and no matter how intensely felt, was the original understanding that the Fourteenth Amendment permitted discrimination against women, this understanding deserves no deference in Fourteenth Amendment interpretation. It was an instance of a failure to live up to principles, just as slaveholding was for those who subscribed to the Declaration of Independence. What *else* a right prohibits (beyond its core applications) is a matter of interpretation, reserved for the future to decide.

I have so far been referring to the foundational paradigm cases: those that actually motivated the struggles of constitution-writing. Supplementing the foundational paradigm cases are additional ones established by precedent. The paradigm cases set up by precedent can be of greater or lesser entrenchedness. They can even attain coequal status with the foundational paradigm cases, but they can never attain a higher status.

The case-by-case work of constitutional interpretation consists of formulating and applying principles and rules of application that capture the paradigm cases. This means three things. First, these principles and rules must cover – be consistent with – the paradigm cases.[68] Second, they must explain the paradigm cases as cases of the actual textual proposition. (The following rule for equal protection law – any state statute that singles out blacks for adverse treatment is unconstitutional as long as it was passed by a state below the Mason–Dixon line – would cover the paradigm cases, but would not capture them as cases of the prohibition set forth in the text.) There must, in other words, be a return to the text in the effort to formulate principles and rules of application on the basis of paradigm cases. Interpretation must always make sense of the text; it must be consistent at a minimum with the words used. The return to the text may not be a stringent requirement, but it is not toothless. Current Eleventh Amendment law, for example, covers the paradigm cases but fails the return to the text.[69]

Finally, not only must interpretation be consistent with the paradigm cases, it must take its shape from them. They must be at the heart of the constitutional rules and principles, just as they were of the constitutional enactment itself. In other words, rules and principles of application must emerge from consideration of what the paradigm cases stand for. Interpretation must answer the question of what it means for the nation to be committed to these paradigm cases.

With respect to constitutional grants of power (as distinct from rights), the only difference in interpretive method is that here the paradigm cases consist of that which the constitutional provision was centrally intended to *permit*. The reasoning is the same. The constitutional change effected by a power-granting provision is to establish permission for some actor or actors to do something. Hence, the paradigm cases of this constitutional transformation are the core cases of what was to be permitted. What else the grant of power allows is a matter of interpretation.

Perhaps it will be objected that rights and powers differ in a critical respect that has not been accounted for. A right does not grant government any power whatsoever. Constitutional rights do not in any way expand or create governmental power; they merely limit powers already there. But the reverse (it might be said) is not true of powers. The enumeration of Congress's powers, in particular, was specifically and centrally intended to limit governmental power even as it created such power. Constitutional grants of power therefore have a double function – to permit and to limit – whereas the function of constitutional rights is solely to limit. It follows that the distinction between prohibitory and permissive intention cannot apply to powers as it does to rights. In the case of powers, paradigm cases of the intent to *prohibit* must be recognized as on a par with paradigm cases of the intent to *permit*.

But it is not true that grants of power have a double aspect not present in the case of rights. Commitments of power and commitments to rights share the identical logical and normative structure. To be sure, those who framed and ratified the Constitution's grants of congressional power centrally intended these powers to be limited in scope. But those who framed and ratified the Bill of Rights also centrally intended them to be limited in scope. A right in the Bill of Rights of universal scope would have been as utterly unthinkable as a universal grant of power in Article I (indeed, it would have been more so).

Moreover, constitutional permissions (grants of power) and limitations (rights) are equally subject to shortsightedness. If we commit ourselves to a particular institution, how do we respond when that institution makes a claim on us that extends beyond the reach we supposed it originally to have? Of course, we may always repudiate the commitment, but if we want to take it seriously, we cannot unreflectively hew to our original understanding of the institution's role in our lives. Rather, we will confront a question of interpretation, which will in turn depend in an important way on the experience we have had of living under that institution. In resolving this question of interpretation, when we reflect on the essential or paradigmatic kinds of claim that we permit the institution to make on us, we may find that, properly understood, our commitment extends beyond our original understanding, imposing on us obligations both onerous and unexpected.

Consider the power granted to Congress under Article I to regulate commerce among the states. It was surely a clear and central understanding of most of the founders that this power did not permit Congress to ban slavery. Modern commerce clause doctrine, however, permits Congress to regulate employment and labor relations within the states. Is modern doctrine wrong because it countenances exercises of congressional power clearly understood in 1789 to be beyond Congress's reach?

Some believe the answer to this question is yes. Justice Thomas so indicated in a recent opinion.[70] Others have said that the anti-intentionalist aspect of modern commerce clause doctrine (its permitting what was clearly understood originally to be prohibited) may not make modern doctrine wrong, but at least requires us to regard modern doctrine as an example of constitutional amendment through transformative judicial opinions.[71]

The paradigm-case method rejects both these conclusions. Interpretation is no more bound by the original understanding that the commerce clause would not permit Congress to regulate slavery than it is bound by the original understanding that the equal protection clause would not prohibit a state from banning women from the professions. To vest a central government with the authority to regulate commerce (even "among" states) is an awesome commitment of power. It is a commitment that, consonant with its paradigm cases, can quite properly be found to reach beyond specific late-eighteenth-century expectations.

Obviously I am not saying that it is somehow impossible for constitution-makers to put an exercise of power outside the national government's reach. Far from it. All they have to do is commit that limitation of power to writing.[72] All the United States has to do, in order to vest the states with a substantive domain of exclusive power, is to commit itself to this power in writing. It never has.[73] Any substantive commitment of exclusive power to the states *would* require judges to preserve the paradigm cases of that commitment, prohibiting Congress from trespassing on the paradigmatic instances of state power. But in the absence of such a substantive commitment to exclusive state power, when judges interpret an Article I grant of power such as the commerce clause, they appropriately shape their rules and principles of application around what Congress is *permitted* to do under that clause (by reference to the foundational paradigm cases and to the precedent, at least if the precedent is not itself in question).

That is an outline of reading the Constitution as written. Its method demands and leaves considerable room for normative judgment in constitutional law. The paradigm cases will very rarely dictate a single possible set of principles or rules of application. They can be expected to rule out a great number of potential interpretive solutions, but they cannot generally be expected to rule in only one. As a result, judges will be obliged to consider a wide variety of factors – ranging from justice in the largest sense to administrative workability – in deciding among competing alternatives. A great deal will depend on the judges' constitutional instincts: their ideology, their sympathies, their qualities of feeling. Ultimately, however, the question judges must answer is interpretive: They must offer an interpretation of why a particular historical struggle merited a constitutional transformation. Implicitly or explicitly, their answer to this question will determine the shape of their constitutional adjudication.

IV. Conclusion

Illustrating how the paradigm-case method applies to concrete constitutional debates would be the best way to explain what in practice I mean by reading the Constitution as written. But doing so would require entire essays. The interested reader can find one such illustration elsewhere;[74] others are forthcoming.

Let me conclude instead with a word about constitutional amendment. There has never been a very good explanation in principle of a supermajoritarian amendment process. There are splendid pragmatic explanations – organized around the need for long-term stability – but no one has ever quite managed to explain why, if a political community is to govern itself, past-enacted law can deny to a current majority of voters, but grant to a supermajority, the right to alter or abolish that law as it pleases.

Demo-graphy can. If a majority could for one sublime moment have its way on all things – so that the perfect Rousseauian moment were attained, with complete agreement between present popular will and the exercise of state power – self-government would not have been achieved. A people is always free to tear down its monuments and repudiate its prior commitments. But a people does not attain political freedom by exercising this freedom to repudiate. Self-government takes time. Supermajoritarian requirements exist to ensure that when a people sets down foundational commitments, it does so through a process that ensures that the people is prepared to live by them for some extended period of time.

If written constitutionalism, together with its amendment process, were understood in the temporally extended fashion described here, we would be obliged to start thinking about self-government more historically than we do today. Indeed, we would be obliged to think differently about "thinking historically," with far more emphasis placed on authorship of the future. What ambitions, other than enhancing the usual economic indicators, do we have for our polities over the next fifty years? Over the next five? As the millennium breaks upon us, we find ourselves with unprecedented power to make our societies embody our dreams – if only we had dreams. Self-government requires an active, affirmative engagement with the future, despite all the risks that such engagements entail. We must commit ourselves to be free.

Notes

1 As Socrates asked, when making ready to die. See Plato, *Crito*, in *Plato: Collected Dialogues* 27 (E. Hamilton & H. Cairns, eds., 1961). See also Jacques Derrida, *Force of Law: The "Mystical Foundation of Authority,"* 11 Cardozo L. Rev. 919, 992–7 (1990).

2 Christopher, Tiedeman, *The Unwritten Constitution of the United States: A philosophical Inquiry into the Fundamentals of American Constitutional Law* (1890).

3 Tiedeman, for example, wrote that "the binding authority of law . . . does not rest upon any edict of the people in the past." Id. at 122. Judges, he argued, had to de-sacralize the framers and "recognize the present will of the people as the living source of law." Id. at 154. Three years later, Thayer wrote his famous essay counseling judicial restraint in the name of the virtues of self-government. See James B. Thayer, *The Origin and Scope of the American Doctrine of Constitutional Law,* 7 Harv. L. Rev. 129 (1893). The Civil War and its aftermath were evidently decisive in this regard: Constitutionalism had not seemed problematically undemocratic to, say, Lincoln or Cooley. (For an excellent overview, see Paul Kahn, *Legitimacy and History* ch. 3 [1992].) But the theme has been ineradicable for us ever since, highlighted in the first decades of this century by Holmes (and in a different way by Beard), in the 1930s and 1940s by the fight over the New Deal, in the 1950s by Hand (see Learned Hand, *The Bill of Rights* [1958]), in the 1960s by Bickel (see Alexander Bickel, *The Least Dangerous Branch: The Supreme Court at the Bar of Politics* [1962]), in the 1980s by Ely (see John H. Ely, *Democracy and Distrust: A Theory of Judicial Review* [1980]), and in this decade by too many to name.

4 Thomas Jefferson, 5 *The Writings of Thomas Jefferson, 1788–1792* 116 (1895). See also, e.g., Thomas Paine, *The Rights of Man,* in *The Life and Major Writings of Thomas Paine* 251 (P. Foner, ed., 1961) ("Every age and generation must be free to act for itself, *in all cases,* as the ages and generations which preceded it") (original emphasis).

5 Thomas Jefferson, *Letter to James Madison* (September 6, 1789), in 15 *The Papers of Thomas Jefferson* 392, 392 (J. Boyd et al., eds., 1958). Webster expressed the same view. "[T]he very attempt," he warned, "to make perpetual constitutions, is the assumption of the right to control the opinions of future generations; and to legislate for those over whom we have as little authority as we have over a nation in Asia." Noah Webster, *On Bills of Rights,* 1 Am. Mag. 13, 14 (December 1787);

see Gordon Wood, *The Creation of the American Republic: 1776–1787* 379 (1969).

6 See Stephen Holmes, *Precommitment and the Paradox of Democracy,* in *Constitutionalism and Democracy* 200, 207–12 (J. Elster & R. Slagstad, eds., 1988).

7 T. Hobbes, *Leviathan* pt. 2, ch. 26 at 204 (1965).

8 See J. Bodin, *Six Bookes of a Commonweale* bk. I, ch. 8 at 91–9 (1962); S. Pufendorf, *De Jure Naturae et Gentium* bk. 1, ch. 6. sec. 7 at 94; bk. 7, ch. 6, sec. 8 at 1064 (C. H. & W. A. Oldfather, trans., 1934); J.-J. Rousseau, *Sur le gouvernement de Pologne,* in 3 *Oeuvres Complètes* 981 (B. Gagnebin & M. Raymond, eds., 1964).

9 See, e.g., Robert H. Bork, *Neutral Principles and Some First Amendment Problems,* 47 Ind., L. J. 1, 3 (1971) ("Society consents to be ruled undemocratically within defined areas by certain enduring principles . . . placed beyond the reach of majorities").

10 The putative grounds of implied consent are typically failure to amend, failure to leave the country, or failure to take up arms. It is not hard to show that each of these "failures" is a very weak reed on which to sustain a legitimate inference of present majority consent. But the point is not worth arguing. Suppose we grant that, as a matter of fact, a majority of Americans today, in an up or down vote on the Constitution as a whole, would vote in favor of it. I hope and expect they would (although the artificiality of the choice between the Constitution and nothing, together with the high likelihood of suppressed Condorcet paradoxes, would significantly weaken any effort to say that such a vote proved much about majority will). The real question is whether the existence of current majority consent to the Constitution somehow does away with the constitutional problem of time. For the reasons that follow in the text, it does not.

11 The same trap ensnares those who believe that the answer to the problem of time is to facilitate the amendment process. Professor Amar, for example, has argued for a majoritarian amendment process on the ground that it alone could justify an inference (from failure to amend) of present majority consent. See Akhil R. Amar, *Philadelphia Revisited: Amending the Constitution Outside Article V,* 55 U. Chi. L. Rev. 1043, 1064–6 (1988). Professor Amar's reasoning is correct, but the vision of up-to-date amendments that make the Constitution conform perfectly to majority will does not solve the problem of time. It once again concedes that problem's insuperability and, in doing so, surrenders the very heart of American constitutionalism itself.

12 See Bickel, supra, note 3 at 16–17.

13 See, e.g., Stanley Fish, *There's No Such Thing as Free Speech* ch. 12 (1994); S. Knapp and W. Michaels, *Intention, Identity, and the Constitution,* in *Legal Hermeneutics* 187 (G. Leyh, ed., 1992); P. Campos, *Against Constitution Theory,* 4 Yale J. L. & Hum. 279 (1992).

14 No one is a self-proclaimed vulgar deconstructivist. But for citations to work that falls at least on occasion into vulgar deconstruction, see notes 21 and 22 below.

15 Ronald Dworkin, *Law's Empire* 53, 228–32, 380 (1986).

16 See Hans-Georg Gadamer, *Truth and Method* 324–30 (1994). Describing the "exemplary significance of legal hermeneutics," Gadamer finds in legal interpretation

"the model for the relationship between past and present that we are seeking." *Id.* at 324, 327–8.

17 See, e.g., Richard Posner, *Law and Literature* 228–9 (1989).

18 See, e.g., S. Knapp and W. Michaels, *Intention, Identity, and the Constitution*, in *Legal Hermeneutics* 187 (G. Leyh, ed., 1992). Of course, to make sense at all, the universal hermeneutic approaches to constitutional law must start with the premise that judges are to *interpret* when deciding constitutional cases – a premise that may itself depend on claims about political legitimacy. But the point is that once it is settled that judges are to interpret, the universal hermeneutic approaches take the position that they can work out in general terms what constitutional interpretation must look like or must aspire to solely by reference to a theory of interpretation as such.

19 Fish, supra note 13 at 185 (emphasis added). I have omitted sentences in which Fish considers the possibility that the every-third-word reader imagines his author as having written in an every-third-word code. Id. As Fish observes, on that supposition, the every-third-word reader engages in a straightforwardly intentionalist decoding. Id.

20 Stanley Fish, *Is There a Text in This Class* 327 (1980).

21 Jack Balkin, *Deconstructive Practice and Legal Theory*, 96 Yale L. J. 743, 774–5 (1987) (quoting Jonathan Culler, *On Deconstruction: Theory and Criticism after Structuralism* 176 [1982]).

22 Gary Peller, *The Metaphysics of American Law*, 73 Calif. L. Rev. 1152, 1188 (1985).

23 Here is Derrida: "[H]ow surprised I have often been, how amused or discouraged . . . by . . . the following argument: Since the deconstructionist (which is to say, isn't it, the skeptic-relativist-nihilist!) is supposed not to believe in . . . intention or "meaning-to-say," how can he demand of us that we read *him* with pertinence, precision, rigor? How can he demand that his own text be interpreted correctly? . . . The answer is simple enough: this definition of the deconstructionist is *false* (that's right: false, not true) . . ." (J. Derrida, *Limited, Inc.* 146 [S. Weber., trans., 1988] [original emphasis]). Derrida specifically rejects the idea that all interpretation is misinterpretation. "I do not think nor have I ever said that 'any interpretation is inevitably a false interpretation, and any understanding a misunderstanding.' " Id. at 157 n. 9. If one attends to Derrida's own readings of others' texts, the central role accorded not only to intentionality but to right intentionalist interpretation is unmistakable. To give just one of many examples: Criticizing Michel Foucault's reading of a certain passage in Descartes, Derrida not only repeatedly refers to Foucault's "intentions," but bases his entire reply on the claim that Foucault mistook what Descartes "said and meant." J. Derrida, *Cogito and the History of Madness*, in *Writing and Difference* 31, 32 (1978) ("[H]as what Descartes said and meant been clearly perceived?").

24 See, e.g., Peller, supra, note 22 at 1170.

25 Note that vulgar deconstruction cannot take the position that it too is merely another ideological construct, making no claim whatsoever to truth or to rightness. For then vulgar deconstruction would be saying nothing at all. As if someone should say, "The sun will go out tomorrow – but by the way, what I say makes no claim to truth or to getting anything, including my own beliefs, right."

26 Worst-it-can-be interpretation is quite conceivable. A person could mount a version of *The Merchant of Venice* that deliberately rendered it as viciously anti-Semitic as possible, conceding that his interpretation made it a worse play – dramatically or morally – than other interpretations would. (He might say that his interpretation revealed the truth about the play more effectively than would an interpretation that makes the best play.) If Dworkin answered that *The Merchant* was here being made into the best anti-Semitic play it could be, either he would have trivialized his claim that interpretation should strive to make the interpreted object the best it can be, or else he would simply have shifted all the interesting problems to the stage of the inquiry at which one decides what sort of thing the interpreted object "is" (an "anti-Semitic play") so that interpretation can then make it the best exemplar of that sort of thing it can be.

27 Obviously, to avoid self-contradiction, Dworkin must claim that his interpretation of interpretation *does* make interpretation the best it can be. This requirement he recognizes. See Dworkin, supra, note 15 at 49 ("[A]ny adequate account of interpretation must hold true of itself"). He apparently thinks that this requirement exhausts the self-referentiality problem. It does not.

28 See, e.g., id. at 53 ("Understanding another person's conversation requires using devices and presumptions, like the so-called principle of charity, that have the effect in normal circumstances of making of what he says the best performance of communication it can be"), 63 (the possibility that interpreting "social practices" might properly consist of determining actual intentions of participants is "ruled out by the internal structure" of the practice, within which "the claims and arguments participants make, licensed and encouraged by the practice, are about what *it* means, not what *they* mean") (emphasis in original).

29 For a very good example of this line of reply, see Larry Alexander, *All or Nothing at All?* in *Law and Interpretation* 357, 362 n. 12 (A. Marmor, ed., 1995).

30 Fish, supra, note 13 at 185 (original emphasis in the first case, added in the second).

31 Id.

32 Robert Bork, *The Tempting of America* 143–4 (1991).

33 Id. The first half of Bork's book is an effort to show that constitutional interpretation has been significantly antioriginalist from just about the beginning. It is not clear to me why, given this showing, constitutional law itself does not count as a sufficient counterexample to the assertion that the meaning of law is necessarily the originalist meaning. I would be surprised to learn that the United States had never had any constitutional *law*, but evidently it must be so.

34 Charles Black, *The People and the Court* 182 (1960).

35 See Herbert Wechsler, *Toward Neutral Principles of constitutional Law*, 73 Harv. L. Rev. 1 (1959). For Bork's use of Wechsler, see Bork, supra, note 9.

36 Id. at 12, 19 (emphasis added).

37 Id. at 16, 19.

38 See, e.g., Casey v. Planned Parenthood, 505 U.S. 833 (1992); Robert Post, *Constitutional Domains* ch. 1 (1995); Antonin Scalia, *The Rule of Law as a Law of Rules*, 56 U. Chi. L. Rev. 1175 (1989).

39 Joseph Raz, *The Morality of Freedom* 262 (1988).

40 Joseph Raz, *The Authority of Law* ch. 9 (1979). Raz himself believes that his account of law generally warrants intentionalism. This is, I think, a point he may wish to reconsider. Raz may have an argument for *individuals* to follow legislative intent, but within Raz's framework *judges* do not seem at all forbidden (they may even be required) to come to their own best judgment of how the parties before them ought to act, according (in Raz's special use of the terms) to the reasons applicable to those parties. (The question would be whether judges could do so better than could the legislature, which is presumed to be able to do so better than could the individuals themselves.) Cf. Andrei Marmor, *Interpretation and Legal Theory* 176–84 (1992) (arguing that Raz's account warrants intentionalism in some but not all contexts). But if Raz's account of law does not warrant an open-ended "right reason" style of interpretation, it is sufficient for present purposes to observe that others' (say, Dworkin's) would.

41 See Robert H. Bork, *Slouching Towards Gomorrah: Modern Liberalism and American Decline* 117 (1996).

42 McCulloch v. Maryland, 17 U.S. (4 Wheat.) 316 (1819) (original emphasis) (Marshall, C. J.).

43 Jean-Jacques Rousseau, *On the Social Contract, or Essay about the Form of the Republic (Geneva Manuscript),* in *On the Social Contract* 157, 168 (R. Masters, ed., J. Masters, trans., 1978).

44 See Bickel, supra, note 3 at 16–18 (constitutional review "thwarts the will of representatives of the actual people of the here and now"; that is why constitutional law can be called "undemocratic").

45 This usage cuts across such dividing lines as republican, liberal, or fascist. Thus, Rousseau insisted that a people could not be free unless it spoke a "tongue" with which one could "make oneself understood to the people assembled." Mill warned that popular assemblies ought not to try to "govern and legislate," but to do only what they were properly constituted to do – "talk." And Carl Schmitt wrote that the "natural way in which a People expresses its immediate will is through a shout of Yes or No by an assembled multitude." (For citations and further examples, see Jed Rubenfeld, *Reading the Constitution as Spoken,* 104 (Yale L. J. 1119, 1123–34 [1995].) These statements are not merely metaphoric. In every case, acts of speech – *literal* acts of speech – are said to be the necessary, proper, or natural medium of popular will formation and will expression.

46 Consider these remarks from the definition of democracy in one venerable textbook:

> [T]here must necessarily be some formula or mechanism for the making of decisions or the selection of policies. In a democracy this formula is majority rule. . . . But democracy has to recognize that a majority can become a tyranny which may ruthlessly destroy the rights of minorities temporarily at its mercy. . . . Thus there must be a balancing of majority power and minority rights. This is the most difficult issue facing any democratic society. . . . For one thing, there is a certain logical dilemma to overcome here. No political philosopher and no constitution-makers have ever quite succeeded in explaining away this dilemma.
>
> R. Carr, M. Bernstein, D. Morrison, R. Snyder, and J. McLean, *American Democracy in Theory and Practice* 29–30 (rev. ed., 1956).

47 Jon Elster, Introduction to *Constitutionalism and Democracy* 1 (J. Elster & R. Slagstad, eds., 1993).
48 See, e.g., Robert A. Dahl, *Democracy and Its Critics* ch. 12 (1989); Jürgen Habermas, *Between Facts and Norms* (W. Rehg, trans., 1996); Stephen Holmes, *Passions and Constraint: On the Theory of Liberal Democracy* (1995).
49 See, e.g., John Rawls, *A Theory of Justice* (1971).
50 See Griswold v. Connecticut, 381 U.S. 479 (1965); Planned Parenthood v. Casey, 505 U.S. 833 (1992).
51 The role of past will in originalism is obvious. Past will undergirds the "plain meaning" approaches insofar as what is sought under the label of "plain meaning" is the meaning that would have been understood by those who ratified the Constitution.
52 For the contemporary-consensus treatment see, e.g., Robert Post, *Theories of Constitution Interpretation,* 30 Representations 13, 30 (1990) ("fundamental ethos of the contemporary community"), and Harry H. Wellington, *Common Law Rules and Constitution Double Standards: Some Notes on Adjudication,* 83 Yale L. J. 221, 310 (1973) ("commonly held attitudes"). John Ely's *Democracy and Distrust* (1980) has been by far the most influential processualist treatment of constitutional law. Ely argues that judicial review draws its democratic legitimacy from its serving to safeguard the democratic representative process.
53 Bickel ended that book by calling upon judges to "declare as law only such principles as will – in time, but in a rather immediate foreseeable future – gain general assent." Bickel, supra, note 3 at 239. For an example of a Rawlsian approach to constitutional law see Professor Michelman's influential *Property, Utility, and Fairness: Comments on the Ethical Foundations of "Just Compensation" Law,* 80 Harv. L. Rev. 1165 (1967).
54 See, e.g., Jürgen Habermas, *The Theory of Communicative Action* 81 (Thomas McCarthy, trans., 1987) (a democratic politics must strive toward implementation of a "common will, communicatively shaped and discursively clarified in the political public sphere"). For Habermas's own efforts to move beyond the choice between individual and collective subjectivity, and hence beyond the choice between liberalism and republicanism, see his *Between Facts and Norms,* supra, note 47, esp. 287–314.
55 See, e.g., John Stuart Mill, *On Liberty* 3 (Oxford 1946). Rawls's spectacular *Theory of Justice,* it should be noted, was not a repudiation of these two poles of subjectivity, but an effort to have both at once. For Rawls, each individual is to decide for himself and yet all are to end by speaking with a single voice. Hypothetical consent theories of this sort either are not consensualist at all or else are another version of the basic speech-modeled ideal: The ideal polis or town meeting is still alive, if only in the mind of political philosophy.
56 Professor Cover made a similar point, also in the context of constitutional law, fifteen years ago. See Robert Cover, *Nomos and Narrative,* in *Narrative, Violence and the Law* 93, 144–6 (M. Minow et al., eds., 1995).
57 Bickel, supra note 3 at 17.
58 Id. at 17–18.
59 Bickel's version ran as follows: "[D]emocracy does not mean constant reconsideration of decisions once made," but it "does mean that a representative majority has the power to accomplish a reversal." Id. at 17.

60 See Bruce Ackerman, *We the People: Foundations* (1991).

61 Id. at 51, 262–4.

62 Id. at 49, 171 ("rare periods of constitutional creativity, when the People mobilize and speak with a very different voice"), 183 (distinguishing between politicians who do and do not "speak" in "the *genuine* voice of the American people") (original emphasis), 264 ("At such moments, the Supreme Court should bend to this new expression of constitutional will"), 286 ("the living voice of the People").

63 Id. at 185.

64 Professor Ackerman claims that the Constitution was amended some time in the 1930s or 1940s by transformative judicial opinions (responding to decisive elections) that codified New Deal principles of activist government and unlimited federal legislative subject-matter jurisdiction. See id. at 40–57, 105–30.

65 I note for the record that Dworkin insists his approach is not open-ended philosophy, but rather interpretation of actual constitutional text and practices. For example, judges are not free on his account (he says) to enforce unenumerated rights. Ronald Dworkin, *Freedom's Law* 80 (1996). But rights that have seemed unenumerated to some seem to Dworkin to follow from express guarantees. See id. at 87–107 (defending the Supreme Court's abortion decisions as an interpretation of the religion clauses).

66 The United States Constitution's equal protection clause applies only to states; the Court has, however, read an equal protection guarantee against the federal government into the Fifth Amendment's due process clause. See Bolling v. Sharpe, 347 U.S. 497 (1954). But it should be observed that the Fourteenth Amendment's citizenship guarantee makes all persons born in the United States citizens of the United States. U.S. Const., Amdmt. XIV §1. And the status of citizens may, properly considered, include a certain right of equal treatment. In any event, for present purposes, we can put aside questions that might be raised about *Bolling*.

67 347 U.S. 483 (1954).

68 Constitutional law has in fact almost always adhered to this cardinal rule. But see Home Building & Loan Assoc. v. Blaisdell, 290 U.S. 231 (1934).

69 The Eleventh Amendment, enacted in 1798, provides that the federal judiciary shall have no jurisdiction over suits brought "against one of the United States" – i.e., a state – "by Citizens of another State, or by Citizens or Subjects of any Foreign State." U.S. Const., Amdmt. XI. The Supreme Court reads this language to bar federal jurisdiction over any suit commenced against one of the United States even by citizens *of that same state*. See, e.g., Seminole Tribe v. Florida, 116 S. Ct. 1114 (1996).

70 See his concurring opinion in United States v. Lopez, 115 S. Ct. 1624 (1995).

71 See Ackerman, supra, note 59 at 43–4, 51–2, 283–4.

72 There is no such thing as an unwritten commitment in written constitutionalism. Nevertheless, I believe there is a narrow but important place for unwritten rules of constitutional law within written constitutionalism. They are to be distinguished from commitments, however, and they can be legitimately enforced only when there is a case to be made that they are necessary conditions for the entire project of written constitutionalism. This is a matter worthy of much more attention, which I cannot devote to it here.

73 With small exceptions, the Constitution's demarcation of the states' domain of ex-

clusive power is done purely by negative implication. See, e.g., U.S. Const., Amdmt. X ("[P]owers not delegated to the United States by the Constitution . . . are reserved to the States").

74 See Rubenfeld, supra, note 44 at 1179–84 (takings clause).

6

The Domain of Constitutional Justice

LAWRENCE SAGER

I. The Idea of a Domain of Constitutional Justice

In this essay I explore the idea that constitutional justice has a domain – a general area of concern that can be described with sufficient clarity to aid in understanding the Constitution generally and in resolving more specific problems of interpretation as well. This could be true in two different senses. In the weaker sense, constitutional justice would have a domain if we could establish that the justice-bearing provisions of the Constitution are not appropriately understood as isolated dots, but must be interpreted with regard to each other as a more or less coherent whole; in the stronger sense, we would conclude that the liberty-bearing provisions of the Constitution not only are connected to each other in this way, but have some important, nonarbitrary connection to the role of constitutions in general and to the role of the United States Constitution in particular. I will argue for a domain of constitutional value in this deeper sense.

Whether this is an interesting or even a meaningful question will depend upon what more general view we hold of our constitutional practice, how we explain the puzzle of our constitutionalism. My purpose in exploring the issue is twofold and reciprocal. First, I think that the best view of our constitutional practice makes the question of the domain of constitutional justice salient; and second, I hope to use the inquiry into the question of the domain of constitutional justice as a way of presenting important and interrelated features of what I take to be the best view of our constitutional practice.

II. Two Accounts of Our Constitutional Practice

The idea that there is a distinct and describable domain of constitutional justice is more or less congenial, depending on one's general understanding of the purpose and nature of the Constitution – more precisely, of the purpose and nature of our constitutional practice as a whole. That practice includes the written Constitution itself, our relatively robust tradition of judicial decision-making that names the Constitution as its warrant, and our legacy of popular constitutional decision-making in which amendment has been infrequent and constitutional language – I refer here to the liberty-bearing provisions of the Constitution – is typically both general and abstract. It includes as well the broad acceptance in our political culture of constitutional discourse as a legitimate and often preferred means of resolving fundamental questions of political justice.

Our constitutional practice concedes authority over an important set of questions – questions addressing the basic structure of both governmental authority and individual liberty – to an odd, transtemporal partnership. One partner consists of persons in the founding or amending generations who participate in the utterance of the Constitution's text. The other partner consists of political actors – most prominently but not exclusively judges – who participate in the interpretation of that text. There are familiar reasons for questioning the credentials of each: The drafting partner most likely comprises persons who lived a century or two ago, not those of us who soldier on today; and the interpreting partner prominently features judges past and present, wise or unwise, most of whom are in any event unelected. Ongoing popular political processes have their say, of course, but they are largely squeezed aside: The Constitution is notoriously difficult to amend; and justices of the Supreme Court often surprise the presidents who nominate them and the senators who acquiesce in their appointment.

While the sentiment is far from unanimous, many observers of our constitutional institutions are strongly inclined to see the insulation of constitutional judgment from ongoing popular politics as a virtue, not a liability – strongly inclined, that is, to credit rather than fault the combined effect of an obdurate text and a life-tenured judiciary. How can we explain this aspect of ourselves to ourselves? A satisfactory account of our constitutionalism will be a crucial term in any thoughtful discussion about the division of constitutional labor among judges, legislators, and citizens; likewise, it will be essential to the process of resolving contested readings of the general and specific content of the Constitution. (By "account," I mean an understanding of these features of our actual political life that explains why, if at all, we should regard them as valuable and how we should shape them to make them as valuable as possible.)[1]

We can begin by contrasting two very different sorts of accounts of our constitutional institutions: historicist and justice-seeking. Historicist accounts see the content of the Constitution as laid down at identifiable moments in the past by popular political events of particular sorts, and see the job of giving meaning to the Constitution as one of recovering or excavating material deposited in these past constitutional moments. Historicist accounts are open to contemporary reflection on the advantages and limitations of our constitutional institutions, but the normative content of these reflections does not bleed into the interpretation of the Constitution itself. The only link between contemporary normative judgment and the protocol of constitutional interpretation recognized by historicist accounts is in this sense self-denying: A historicist might well argue that it is undemocratic for judges to permit their own values or judgments to determine the outcome of constitutional controversies and that judicial inquiry must for precisely that reason confine itself to the enterprise of deciphering past constitution-making events.[2]

In historicist accounts, constitutional architecture is elementary. We can imagine the universe of possible collective, political decisions. All of these decisions are in a sense made under the aegis of the Constitution, but most are commended by the Constitution to various more or less popular political entities. Some of these entities (like Congress) are created by the Constitution itself; others (like the states and their political institutions) are inherited or incorporated by the Constitution. Many of these entities are open to change by other state or federal political processes in ways that are largely unrestricted by the federal Constitution. In all, most of the matters that attract our collective attention are left open by the Constitution, and constitutional justice is nothing more or less than the comparatively small subset of political matters concluded by the historical Constitution.

For the historicist, constitutional justice comprises just those matters that the framers (or, somewhat more plausibly, the framing generation) took up and resolved, and constitutional interpretation is the backward-looking enterprise of decoding the text and the circumstances of its authorship to reveal the meaning lodged there. Constitutional justice picks up and leaves off just as and because the framers took up and left off, whatever the cause: arbitrary choice, oversight, political pressure, or simple fatigue. The domain of constitutional justice, on this view, is described by whatever unifying themes we might or might not be able to extract from a historicist dig into our constitutional past, full stop. Failure to establish the existence of such a domain would not necessarily be a cause for regret; it would become so only if our ability to retrieve the message of the past fully and accurately was impeded by the absence of a grasp of a set of unifying themes. Indeed, from the historicist perspective, the discovery of and reliance upon a domain of constitutional justice would be somewhat suspect as an abstract intellectual construct capable of deflecting attention away from the concrete grit of text and history.

But there are good reasons to see the Constitution in terms very different from the historicist model. The Constitution is not written like a tax code and has not been interpreted like one. Particularly in its liberty-bearing provisions, the Constitution offers broad structural propositions and moral generalities, and the judiciary has by and large accepted the obligation to fill in these general stipulations with concrete applications, to fashion workable and defensible conceptions of the Constitution's moral concepts. To be sure, this broad concession of responsibility to the judiciary requires explanation and justification. But without this understanding of the judicial role, our constitutional practice would make very little sense. If the Constitution were only a piece of legislation elevated by its status to be primary over conflicting sources of law, we would have a hard time explaining why one generation's legislative impulses should govern persons living a century or two later and why, further, we choose to interpose the effort and imperfection of historical reconstruction between a people and their laws. On the historicist account, parliamentary democracy would seem to have considerable advantage over constitutionalism with its historical encumbrances.

To make sense of our constitutional practice, we have to see it as justice-seeking – that is, as serving the end of making our political community more just. Central to our constitutional practice is the partnership between the popular constitutional drafter who typically paints with broad strokes and the judicial constitutional interpreter[3] who is concerned with bringing rich content and close detail to the general principles announced in the text. The justice-seeking view of our constitutional institutions depends upon the belief that the judiciary – guided only broadly by the text of the Constitution – is a reasonably good guide to the most critical requirements of political justice.[4] It bears emphasis that this is a pragmatic judgment: The requirements of political justice are themselves matters of principle and often are best expressed or reflected upon in abstract terms, but the ability or tendency of real-world institutions to make decisions in conformity with those requirements is an exquisitely practical matter.

In the end, confidence in this aspect of our constitutional practice may depend upon an assessment of our actual national experience in comparison with the experience of other nations. But several features of constitutional adjudication hold out promise ex ante. First, the constitutional judiciary is specialized and redundant, like a quality-control inspector. Judges are steeped in the tradition of constitutional discourse, and their job is pointed toward the evaluation of governmental conduct against the norms of the Constitution. Second, the coherence-driven protocol of adjudication is well suited to normative reflection. In the course of deciding a case before them, judges are responsible to both past decisions and future possibilities; they must test the principles upon which they are tempted to rely against these other outcomes, real and imagined. The enterprise of adjudication thus embodies a kind of institutional reflective equilibration. Third, judges are obliged to give each other and the broader audience of their opinions reasons for their decisions, and these reasons are of a special sort: They are in principle publicly accessible and publicly defensible; they are exemplars of what some philosophers have called "public reason."[5] Fourth, these features of constitutional adjudication are strongly reinforced by the collegial, deliberative nature of constitutional tribunals in our legal system – most particularly, of the Supreme Court itself. Fifth, constitutional adjudication is reflective of what we might call the egalitarian logic of democracy: Every claimant before a court stands on equal footing; the force of her claim is the force of reason – the strength of its connection to an articulated scheme of principle – not her wealth, popularity, or social stature.

III. The Justice-Seeking Constitution and the Domain of Constitutional Justice

A. *The Moral Shortfall of the Constitution*

The justice-seeking account of constitutionalism invites speculation and concern about the domain of constitutional justice. This is so in an obvious sense: The justice-seeking account recognizes that our constitutional practice is in important respects forward- rather than backward-looking and that constitutional judges have important contemporary judgmental authority and responsibility; naturally, we hope that justice-seeking judges do the best possible job of fulfilling that responsibility. If the connections among the precepts of constitutional justice, the role of constitutions generally, and the shape and logic of our constitution in particular can usefully guide their decisions, we obviously want our judges to have the benefit of that guidance. We hope, in other words, that our constitutional judges seek and find the boundaries of the domain of constitutional justice.

The justice-seeking account calls attention to the possibility and importance of a domain of constitutional justice in another, less obvious way. Justice-seeking theorists have the burden of explaining why the Constitution seems to stop so far short of its target. Constitutional law plainly does not address all of political justice. Consider, for example, these two claims: that members of our political community are entitled to economic arrangements that offer them minimally decent material lives in exchange for hard work on their own behalf, and that government is obliged to make reasonable efforts to undo structurally entrenched social bias against vulnerable racial groups and women. Neither of these principles – the right to minimum welfare or the obligation to reform entrenched bias – has now or has ever had any apparent life in constitutional doctrine. This is not hard to explain on the historicist account: Constitutional law runs out because the moral imagination or generosity of the founding and amending generations ran out, and there would be nothing more to explain. But if we understand the Constitution to be justice-seeking, then we have to explain how judicial implementations of it have failed to seriously approach – much less secure – what many of us would regard as important and unduckable requirements of political justice.[6]

The justice-seeking view of the Constitution acknowledges the guidance of constitutional text, history, and established doctrine, of course, and it might be in these conventional legal constraints that a partial explanation for the moral shortfall of constitutional law is to be found. But the sharp refusal of constitutional law to embrace claims like the right to minimum welfare and the obligation to reform entrenched bias is too durable, too widely endorsed, and insufficiently founded on the dictates of text and history to be accounted for on these grounds alone.

B. Distinguishing Between the Constitution and Its Judicial Enforcement

An important part of the moral shortfall of our constitutional law can be explained by the gap between the Constitution proper and the adjudicated Constitution. The Constitution is underenforced by the judiciary, and for good reason. Some principles of political justice are wrapped in complex choices of strategy and responsibility that are properly the responsibility of popular political institutions. When tangled in principles of this sort, the judiciary justifiably declines to enforce the Constitution to its full margins and defers – at least in the first instance – to the political branches of the state and federal governments.

The right to minimum welfare and the obligation to reform structurally entrenched social bias are, in fact, two good examples of precepts of political justice that are justifiably underenforced by the judiciary. Consider just one component of the right to minimum welfare, minimally adequate medical care. Recent national experience stands as a reminder of the questions that implementation of such a right would entail: What level of medical care is minimally adequate? How should such care be provided – by general financial support, single-payer or managed-competition insurance, medical vouchers, or clinics for the poor? What level or levels of government should be responsible for the design, oversight, and support of the program? How should the financial burden of such a program be distributed, and how should the distribution of this burden be implemented? All of these decisions of strategy and responsibility remain on the table even after we have accepted the basic norm of a right to minimum welfare and identified medical care as one of its critical components.

These are powerful reasons why the judicial enforcement of the Constitution stops short of affirmative ingredients of justice like the right to minimum welfare and the obligation of government to reform entrenched racial and

gender bias. They are not good reasons for supposing that the Constitution itself – as opposed to the adjudicated Constitution – similarly falls short of addressing these fundamental elements of political justice. A justice-seeking account of constitutionalism that acknowledges a gap between the scope of
judicial enforcement and the scope of constitutional obligation can better
serve these distinct conceptual masters than one that insists on linking them.[7]

Only when we recognize the existence of a gap between the adjudicated
Constitution and the Constitution itself – when we recognize, in other words,
the judicial underenforcement of the Constitution – can we explain a number
of important but otherwise anomalous doctrines and developments. Thus,
while the Supreme Court has never been much tempted to confront head-on
questions of the distribution of material well-being in the United States, it has
for many years been acutely alert to categorical exclusions from educational
opportunities, even when orthodox constitutional doctrine was unavailable to
support its concern; the Court's insistence that Texas permit the children of illegal immigrants to attend its public schools is a striking example of that preoccupation.[8] And thus, while the right to a hearing in noncriminal matters has
not in general been appealing to the Court, it famously recognized such a
right when the claimant's entitlement to basic welfare grants is at stake,[9] and
even held that a ten-day suspension from the public schools required a prior
hearing.[10] Why these pockets of judicial softheartedness? If we suppose that
there is indeed a constitutional right to minimum welfare, then these decisions make good sense. The right to minimum welfare is not in the first instance judicially enforceable, for the reasons that we have seen; but once government has put in place public education and basic welfare problems and
thus resolved the questions of strategy and responsibility that elude judicial
competence, the picture changes. Now the Court can play its constitutional
part by policing these public programs for unjust categorical exclusions or arbitrary individual deprivations.[11]

Or consider another important and apparently anomalous line of Supreme
Court decisions. The Thirteenth and Fourteenth Amendments each confer on
Congress the authority to "enforce this article by appropriate legislation."[12] In
the case of the Thirteenth Amendment, the abolition of slavery is commended
to Congress's enforcement authority; in the case of the Fourteenth Amendment, the salient provisions prohibit states from denying due process or equal
protection. Given the structure of these grants of federal legislative authority,
one might well suppose that the Court's view of what was barred by the substantive provisions of the amendments would in turn determine the scope of
Congress's legislative authority, authority that would largely entail the implementation of remedial or enforcement schemes. But Congress's authority
goes considerably further than that. While the Court has held that only inden-
tured servitude as such is directly barred by the Thirteenth Amendment, it has

also held that the amendment empowers Congress to root out the "badges" or "incidents" of slavery, in the name of which enterprise Congress can make illegal virtually any form of private racial discrimination.[13] Similarly, if somewhat less dramatically, the Court has held that, in the name of enforcing the Fourteenth Amendment, Congress can make illegal conduct that the Court would approve as consistent with the amendment.[14] How are we to understand this rather surprising deference to congressional readings of the liberty-bearing provisions of the Constitution? Once again, the underenforcement thesis is clarifying. If we recognize that government is constitutionally obliged by the Thirteenth and Fourteenth Amendments to redress structurally entrenched social bias against vulnerable racial groups and women, we confront another constitutional obligation that is encumbered by questions of strategy and responsibility of the sort that do not sit comfortably with the constitutional judiciary. Under these circumstances, it is appropriate for the judiciary to endorse legislative authority to do what the Constitution requires, even while withholding judicial vindication of the constitutional obligation in the first instance.

C. The Continuing Need for a Domain of Constitutional Justice

The distinction between the scope of the Constitution itself and the scope of the adjudicated Constitution explains some of the most prominent lapses in the moral reach of constitutional law. But even after we take judicial underenforcement of the Constitution into account, there remain good reasons for supposing that the Constitution itself addresses only a subset of justice. First, a satisfactory account of our constitutional practice must recognize and respond to our deep commitment to popular political institutions and our durable understanding that these institutions have broad leeway in managing our political affairs. Second, important to our judgment that there exist constitutional principles that elude judicial enforcement is the existence of trace elements of these judicially unenforceable principles in the ore of otherwise anomalous judicial doctrine. The right to minimum welfare and the obligation of redress are in this way embedded in the corpus of adjudicated constitutional law. But there are important elements of full political justice that are not similarly reflected in the corpus of constitutional law. This is true, for example, of economic justice once we leave the narrow compass of the right to minimum welfare. Third, our general sense of the realm of constitutional principle is that it is relatively narrow and relatively coherent as it stands. This sense survives the addition of important but judicially unenforceable constitutional norms like the right to minimum welfare and the obligation to reform entrenched bias, but other possibilities – like the obligation to pursue full economic justice – seem to fit poorly with the extant mix.

Very few constitutional observers believe that the Constitution requires perfect economic justice, whatever that might be. This is no small enclave around which the Constitution skirts. The area left untouched is a catchall that includes just about every aspect of distributive justice that is not marked by the extreme and enduring vulnerability of a limited set of victim groups. The right of minimum welfare and the obligation to redress entrenched bias seem to fit with the limited set of distributive concerns recognized by the Constitution precisely because they deal with the extremity of circumstance faced by the victims of grinding poverty or entrenched bias. Debates on the frontier of constitutional law – like the question of the rights of homosexuals to be free from discrimination – do not put this basic shape of the Constitution's concerns at contest; rather, they are debates about whether the circumstances that surround homosexuality in our culture conform to the limited range of the Constitution's concerns. Outside a handful of cases of special vulnerability, distributional matters of every kind – ranging from the use of one's land to the use of one's time and work in a profession, to the apportionment of taxes and the disgorgement of public benefits – fall into the capacious, ruthlessly aconstitutional category of economic justice. What stops our constitutional tradition from pressing ahead to some or all of these questions?

It might be tempting to answer that constitutional justice implicates only the behavior of government and that the salient features of our economic arrangements are private. But, as the Court in *Shelly v. Kramer*[15] famously discovered, there is a conceptual continuum between that which the state actively does, that which it endorses, and that which it merely tolerates. In economic matters in particular we understand that the extant distribution of wealth and opportunity is critically connected to the state's regime of law, to the decisions explicitly or tacitly made by state actors in their solemn official capacities.[16] There are, of course, matters so private that a constitution should protect them from its own reach as well as the reach of legislation and common-law supervision, *as a matter of justice*. This is neither paradoxical nor particularly hard to grasp. But that is not the view we take of our economic arrangements. Our repudiation of the tradition of *Lochner v. New York*[17] was based not on the idea that economic transactions are beyond the reach of the state – that would be nonsense, given the state's involvement everywhere in commercial affairs – but on the insistence that the state can pursue a variety of economic approaches and employ a wide range of economic regulatory mechanisms without transgressing constitutional constraints.

The underenforcement thesis takes us some distance to understanding the limited scope of the adjudicated Constitution, but this sweeping truncation of constitutional justice goes considerably further – deeper – than the question of judicial enforcement. We are, therefore, back to the question of the domain of constitutional justice itself. Indeed, when we recognize that adjudication does not exhaust the authoritative reach of the Constitution, the enterprise of identifying the distinct domain of constitutional justice becomes both more difficult and more useful. If the adjudicated Constitution were the whole of the Constitution, there would be two immediate guides to the boundaries of constitutional justice: The pattern of adjudication over time would offer a good picture of this domain for us to interpret; and insights about the limits of judicial competence would offer a conceptual basis for the drawing of that domain's boundaries. When we admit underenforcement into the picture, our inquiry is more difficult. It is also more useful, of course: An understanding of the reach of constitutional justice will be an important guide to the content of the judicially unenforceable portion of the Constitution.

D. The Architecture of Constitutional Justice

All this leaves us with a rather complex picture of constitutional justice. Constitutional justice sits between all of political justice, on the one hand, and the much narrower substance of the adjudicated Constitution, on the other. We can expect constitutional justice to draw from political justice and to be reflected in turn in the substance of the adjudicated Constitution, but it occupies its own domain, narrower than the former and broader than the latter. The conceptual boundaries of that domain are the object of our inquiry.

IV. Democratarian Theories of the Domain of Constitutional Justice

There is a somewhat common modern view of our constitutional practice that accepts – and, indeed, depends upon – the idea that there is a domain of constitutional justice of the sort we are after. A number of commentators see the project of constitutional justice as that of perfecting democracy, of bringing our public institutions and projects closer to the democratic ideal. These theories span a substantial range of ideas about just how demanding the ideal form of democracy is. John Hart Ely's well-known treatment of this theme in his book *Democracy and Distrust*[18] is often characterized as majoritarian, and indeed it does emphasize the procedural dimensions of democracy, especially freedom of expression and the satisfactory alignment of the franchise, broadly understood. Even Ely, however, is anxious to defend the centerpiece of the Warren Court's constitutional lessons, the protection of African-Americans against discriminatory treatment; this important substantive commitment does not comfortably fit Ely's process-based understanding of the domain of the Constitution. Still, Ely's attachment to process has real consequences in his theory. The possibility of constitutional independence – for example, the recognition in *Griswold v. Connecticut*[19] of a right to privacy broad enough to protect married persons' decisions to buy and use contraceptive devices – does not enjoy a place at Ely's democracy-perfecting table. At the other end of the spectrum is Ronald Dworkin.[20] His idea of constitutional democracy is keyed to the question of what circumstances make it possible for self-determination in the personal sense to coexist with self-determination in the public, democratic sense. The result is an account of democracy that is broad and encompasses many substantive features, including any aspect of liberty Dworkin might otherwise be tempted to award constitutional status. Somewhere between Ely and Dworkin is (or at least at one point was) Frank Michelman, who argued that some liberties – like the right to pursue one's gay sexual orientation openly – are connected to democracy, because they make it possible for citizens to find and fulfill their true identities and hence participate more authentically as citizens in the political process.[21]

As a corollary to their insistence that the domain of constitutional justice is confined to the improvement of the conditions of democracy, these theories – we can call them democratarian theories – claim for themselves a particular conceptual advantage. They claim to ameliorate significantly, or even eliminate, the tension between our constitutional practice and democracy. If the job of the Constitution and our constitutional institutions is to improve the circumstances of democracy, democratarian theorists argue, then they can hardly be faulted on the grounds that they are undemocratic. Judicial intervention in the name of democracy is pro-democratic, not counterdemocratic. This putative advantage of democratarian accounts of the Constitution, in fact, is often offered as an important reason for identifying the improvement of democracy as the exclusive domain of constitutional justice.

Democratarian accounts have considerable intuitive appeal. They also have a number of difficulties. We will consider their liabilities first and then consider what sustains their appeal. We can begin by observing that the conceptual judo of these accounts, which seem to turn the force of democratic objections to robust adjudication against themselves, is much overstated. To see why this is so, let us consider a spectrum of political states of affairs, running from a radically deficient state, democratic in form only, at one end to a perfect democracy at the other. When the affairs of a political community are sufficiently close to the awful end of this spectrum, there is little or no reason to prefer the results from the badly deformed popular process simply because it has the form of a majoritarian institution over the studied judgment of the constitutional judiciary. Fair enough. But at some point along the spectrum, moving toward the perfect end, there will be a point where political arrangements satisfy the requirements of what we might call a working democracy: The franchise is reasonably well distributed, the channels of political expression are open, and there is no gross distortion of the political process. At this point, there *could* be real cost in displacing the judgments of the ordinary political process. From this point forward, progress toward perfection is likely to be controversial among well-intentioned observers. The judiciary may surely be making what it regards as improvements in democracy, but reasonable persons may well disagree, and the question will become who should decide what qualifies as an improvement in democracy. Now, the voice of the people speaking through reasonably well formed popular political institutions has a claim to authority that cannot be dismissed out of hand.

By most accounts, the United States is a working democracy. The constitutional judiciary plays an important role in our political life as a justice-seeking mechanism and can be defended – indeed, welcomed – on that ground; but judicial intervention in the name of the Constitution is not necessarily cost-free in the way that democratarian theorists suggest, even if the judiciary confines itself to perfecting the democratic process.

Or perhaps it would be more accurate to say this: If judicial intervention in the name of the Constitution is cost-free, it is not cost-free for the reason that democratarian theorists give. I offer this alternative formulation because I think the view that some cost is paid whenever an important public decision is taken out of the hands of the popular political process is itself doubtful. If a democratic people live with a set of political institutions and practices that include a justice-seeking constitution and a responsible constitutional judiciary, it is far from clear that there is even a prima facie cost in terms of democratic choice. If there is a broad popular domain in which choices are made by reasonably well designed popular political institutions, and a constitutional domain in which an important but narrow set of precepts of political justice is well-tended by a robust judiciary, there may be no such loss. This is a matter of some complexity, and I do not mean to lay it to rest here. The important point is that democratarian judicial restraint is not the talisman. If there is a cost in placing constitutional choices in the hands of the transtemporal partnership between founding generations and judges, democratarian restraint does not cancel it; alternatively, if there is no such cost, democratarian restraint is not the reason.

By putting so much emphasis on an open-textured concept like democracy as the lamp for the constitutional genie, democratarian accounts are prone to distortion in one of two offsetting directions. If the concept of democracy is held stable and relatively narrow, democratarian accounts truncate the reach or distort the motivation of constitutional justice – hence, the idea that gays and lesbians owe their right to live within their sexual identities to their ultimate service as voters, or even that they have no such right at all. Alternatively, democratarian accounts can put inappropriate weight on artful understandings of the requirements of democracy and create the sense that democracy is being used as a shell for claims of justice that belong elsewhere, or at least that too much is being made to turn on whether a particular claim of constitutional justice is inside or outside democracy as appropriately understood.

But democratarian accounts have considerable appeal, and we can learn from them. Part of what makes them attractive is the sense, latent in their insistence on democracy as the object of constitutional justice, that the Constitution is meant to prepare the field and set the ground rules for popular politics, not replace those politics as the primary mechanism of public choice. But understood in this way, democracy is merely a placeholder for this basic sense. Even as democratarian accounts remind us that constitutional justice should play this general role in our political life, they mislead by equating that insight with the stipulation that only that which composes democracy is a proper object of constitutional attention.

Democratarian accounts are attractive for two other reasons, both particularly congenial to our inquiry. First, democratarian accounts proceed from a justice-seeking view of our constitutional practice: Democracy enters the democratarian story in the right way, as part of a reflection on the question of what understanding of the liberty-bearing provisions of the Constitution will best serve political justice; and even comparatively bare-bones democratarians like John Hart Ely insist that there must be considerable room for the independent, justice-seeking judgment of constitutional judges. Second, democratarian accounts do not posit arbitrary or happenstantial limits to the scope of constitutional justice; they point to limits that can be explained with regard to the Constitution as a whole and, more generally, with regard to the role of a constitution in a liberty-loving political community. Democratarian accounts describe and undertake to defend constitutional justice as commited to a subset of the principles of political justice; they point to a domain of constitutional justice in the stronger sense that we named as our goal at the outset of this inquiry.[22]

V. Justifying and Constraining the Disappointments and Burdens of Membership in a Political Community

A. *The Urgent Concerns of the Members of a New Political Community as a Guide to the Domain of Political Justice*

So we turn at last to sketch the domain of constitutional justice. I propose that we begin by considering what would worry persons like those who shaped the founding and the refounding (or the completion of the founding represented by the Reconstruction amendments) of the Constitution – what the most urgent fears of the soon-to-be members of our political community would have been. This may seem a benign enough starting point, but even this modest formulation of the question raises some difficulties that we would do well to address at the outset.

When we set out to determine the domain of constitutional justice, our inquiry straddles the local and the global. On the one hand, we are trying to understand the Constitution and our constitutional practices, and the question of the domain of constitutional is in this way inspired by, particular to, and subject to the limitations of our constitutional experience. On the other hand, what we wish to know is whether our constitutional commitments connect in a nonarbitrary way to what makes constitutions valuable to political societies in general, and what makes ours valuable to us in particular. We can answer that question (even in its more particularized form) only by making judgments about what makes a constitution valuable to a people like us, who value the core elements of political justice – to a people, that is, who value democracy, equality, and liberty. A successful account of our constitutional practice, accordingly, will necessarily draw our attention to universal features of constitutionalism and, it is to be hoped, will inform not only persons interested in evaluating and shaping our constitutional institutions but those whose concerns are with the direction of constitutional development in other countries. The local–global dualism of our inquiry is reflected in the form of the question I have just put, which asks after the concerns of "persons *like* those who shaped the founding . . . of the Constitution."

Asking what would urgently worry persons joining a political community may seem an oddly constricted and negative lens through which to approach the question of the domain of constitutional justice. After all, people who form or reform political communities have many positive hopes and ambitions, ambitions for a more perfect – read peaceful and prosperous – union. They want their government to make wise and decisive choices, to conduct itself effectively in international affairs, to manage the domestic economy successfully, and so on. All this was certainly true of the persons who founded our constitutional community. And while their diverse concerns may come freighted with greater or lesser passion and urgency, there is no reason to suppose that they parked their lesser concerns at the Constitution's door.

But our concern is with constitutional *justice*. In general, justice is concerned most clearly and centrally with avoiding various nasty states of affairs – prominent failures to treat individuals and groups fairly. This focus on the negative, and further on the urgently negative, is especially apt to *constitutional* justice. Constitutional precepts have to be durable, spare, and capable of reasonably clear application and judgment; constitutional justice, accordingly, should narrow its focus to extreme and rather clear breaches of political justice.

The need for the Constitution to speak with a parsimonious, focused clarity may not be obvious, especially in a conceptual environment that recognizes that the judicially enforced portion of the Constitution does not exhaust the whole. If we were operating on the understanding that the judiciary is empowered and obliged to enforce the whole of the Constitution, there would be a more obvious need for constitutional parsimony, since to place a matter under the aegis of the Constitution would be to commend it to the authority of the constitutional judiciary, and we have already encountered good reasons for thinking that some aspects of political justice are not well suited to judicial enforcement. But we have also concluded that the Constitution reaches further than its judicial enforcement – why a narrowed constitutional focus under these circumstances?

There are two important and closely related reasons for maintaining a narrowed constitutional focus. First, while we have been at pains to resist the democratarian impulse to confine constitutional justice to the limits of a stipulated conception of democracy, no one can doubt that a comparatively robust commitment to democratic rule is an important part of political justice in general and of constitutional justice in particular. Constitutional justice thus carries the seeds for its own substantive restraint, since the concern for democracy insists that whatever values of constitutional justice lie outside democracy not unduly congest the field over which democratic choice can operate.

This concern obviously extends to those political decisions that are *preference-driven,* that is, to those questions – like the choice between museums and playing fields – the best answers to which are constituted or at least inflected by the distribution of preferences among the members of our political community. Less obvious, perhaps, but no less important, the concern for democratic choice also extends to many questions that are *judgment-driven* – questions the best answers to which are constituted by concerns of justice independent of the distribution of preferences and ideally are chosen rather than constituted by the weight of popular judgment. For example, decisions about the environmental legacy of our generation or the perpetuation of the national debt or the waging of morally contestable wars may be properly understood as judgment-driven, but they belong to the people, not to the Constitution. It bears emphasis that democracy enters our story here not as distinct from or prior to constitutional justice, but rather as an important – albeit nonexclusive – requirement of constitutional justice itself.

The second reason for maintaining a narrowed constitutional focus is more overtly pragmatic. Suppose we were able to agree – more or less – on the underlying principles of distributive justice applicable to a modern society. Even given this heroic assumption, there would remain staggering issues of strategy, priority, and timing. Imagine that we have something like a comprehensive picture of the way in which our society – now and projected forward in time – fails to satisfy the requirements of distributive justice. That picture will suggest an enormous range of hard choices. Whose legitimate complaints do we address first: the worst off or the larger group (we imagine) who are quite badly but not worst off? By what arbitrage do we adjust the unrequited claims of present members of our political community against the competitive claims (again, we imagine) of members yet to be born? Fundamental structural features of our economy – for example, whether it is market-driven or centrally managed – and fundamental directions of culture and enterprise – for example, whether we are to be an agrarian or industrial society – will have immediate and long-term consequences for distributive justice; these fundamental features and directions also have enormous consequences on many other fronts. To what degree does distributive justice govern or prevail against other strong reasons we have for making these fundamental choices? When and to what degree is it appropriate to defer present justice in favor of greater future justice? These are just an arbitrary few of the questions that flood forward even after agreement on basic principles. The picture, I mean to suggest, is like the game of Go, exaggerated many times over and in many dimensions. In Go, there are many small skirmishes all over the board between the protagonists; the great difficulty for each player lies in choosing where to fight and for how long.

And this dizzying picture, bear in mind, is drawn on the hypothesis that we could reach broad agreement on the underlying principles of distributive justice applicable to a modern society. These principles, even in the abstract, are notoriously open to disagreement. They are also unusually prone to confusion of a particular sort, namely the confusion between basic and enduring principles and more transitory or passing concerns that may connect for a time with, and be mistaken for, those deeper precepts.

The point is emphatically not that conscientious political decision-makers should ignore the broad concerns of justice; the point is that, to be effective, a constitution must be more focused and more insistent than general principles of justice that by their nature are radically open to contest, offset, and temporizing. A constitution can significantly enhance political judgment over the concerns of justice only if it restricts itself to demands so basic and so durable that they can generally and reasonably function as dominant and non-negotiable. This, if anything, is the more true of constitutional precepts that elude judicial enforcement. If the judicially unenforced portions of the Constitution were swamped with the broad and undifferentiated concerns of distributive justice, it would lose the capacity to offer a firm and unduckable basis for challenge and debate.

We can see the important connection between these two points by considering an objection that could be raised to the first. The objection goes as follows. Surely all political choices should acknowledge the demands of justice, broadly conceived; democracy does not imply a freedom from responsible judgment; accordingly, there can be no democratic harm in calling all the requirements of justice "constitutional," as long as that label does not always imply that the judiciary is entitled to second guess the "constitutional" decisions of popular political entities.

But this objection overlooks the interaction of the claim from democracy with the claim from constitutional efficacy. The bite – the value and real-world significance – of judicially unenforced constitutional rights depends upon a variety of related circumstances. First, it is important that the judiciary be able to police such rights as their substantive, procedural, and institutional margins. Second, in order both to enable this policing and to guide popular political choice, it is important that judicially unenforced constitutional rights be recognizably of a piece with the adjudicated Constitution. And third, it is important that judicially unenforced constitutional rights be able to speak with what at least approaches uncompromising authority over the competing concerns of our political community. By now the reader may have guessed where this is leading: If judicially unenforced constitutional rights acquire significance as a result of their categorical authority, oneness with the material of the adjudicated Constitution, and reinforcement by the judiciary in its role as supporting political actor, then they will constrict popular choice. That, after all, is precisely what we would hope of them.

Only by restricting itself to urgent and non-negotiable requirements that are fundamentally of a piece with the articulate principles of the adjudicated Constitution can the judicially unenforced Constitution deliver on the promise of being the durable conscience of democratic politics – hence the need for triage, for focusing on the most urgent concerns of political union.

B. *The Burdens of Membership in a Political Community*

So the worries of persons like those who shaped the Constitution: For the members of any political community there is the certainty that some questions of considerable importance will be decided against their interests. That is the situation even in a democracy, of course, where someone has to lose elections and lose votes in the legislative assembly. No political community can avoid the prospect of disappointment, and that is an important part of what potential members of a community must consider when contemplating the structure of that community. Disappointment for these purposes includes not just failures to prevail as to goals, priorities, and strategies on matters of public policy, but the imposition of various burdens of membership that may seem unnecessary or arbitrary or, worse, unjust or oppressive. Membership will always entail burdens, even to those who do prevail; this is true, for example, of reasonable taxes levied in pursuit of the very projects one has sponsored or endorsed. But the burdens of membership will not always be welcome in this way, or reasonable. They have the potential to be of such magnitude or so constricting of individual choice as to diminish the quality of one's life radically.

This point is sometimes sharpened and redirected by a play on words. The problem for a democracy, it is sometimes said, is how to reconcile two states of affairs, both of which are highly esteemed: self-rule (or self-determination) in the sense of an individual's control over her own life, and self-rule (or self-determination) in the group sense of democratic rule. The two are obviously in tension. Every individual gives up some control to the political community of which she is a part, even in the best of circumstances; and the democratic insistence of self-government at the group level seems to imply the absence of precisely the sort of restraint or intervention in the majoritarian process that is required to preserve important elements of individual self-rule. Those who are inclined to see the problem in these terms are apt offer solutions of the following form. If the members of a political community have the proper relationship to their community, it is appropriate to regard their individual choices as subsumed within the group choices of the community as a whole.

There are several respects in which this seems to make the problem too fine and the solution too grand. Self-government in the personal sense is never anything like fully possible. We simply cannot all be dictators to the whole, and many of us will fail to prevail with regard to some or even many public decisions, some or many of which in turn will be important to us. There surely is an important connection between self-rule writ small for the individual and large for the community: If individuals within a community do not in some meaningful sense enjoy the capacity to reflect upon and choose among values, commitments, and projects for themselves and their community, then it is hard to see why "self-determination" at the community level is a meaningful or valuable commodity; conversely, the capacity to maintain one's independence is surely prominent among the conditions that make the burdens of membership tolerable. But it is not the case that the disappointments or burdens of membership can be made to disappear, that the individual can be made to own or identify with the decisions of the group in such a way that no disparity between the group and the individual exists. Nor is it the case that protecting individual choice against group domination is the only legitimate and urgent concern about the burdens of group membership.

Justifying and constraining the disappointments and burdens of membership in a political community is the crucial project of constitutional justice. Under the circumstances of the constitutional founding and refounding of our political community, this project was of particular importance. (We should note, however, that this is a common feature of constitutional foundings.) At the Founding, the transfer of a substantial but necessarily unknown degree of governmental authority from the states to the national government was the occasion for sharp attention by a plural people to constitutional constraints on the burdens of membership. Membership in the national political community involved giving over potentially significant aspects of one's welfare and destiny to a national process of political choice over which one's friends and familiars could exert only limited influence – hence the firm insistence on a national government of limited powers, on the state-centered composition of the Senate, and, ultimately, on a Bill of Rights preoccupied with liberty-bearing restraints on the national government.

During Reconstruction, the structure of constitutional concern was different, but the basal substance of that concern was not. Now the project was that of extending true membership in our political community to those who had borne the grotesque burdens of slavery and of placing the responsibility and authority for securing the privileges and immunities of that membership into the hands of the only government that seemed trustworthy in the service of that undertaking. It was, accordingly, the distribution rather than the terms of membership that was the primary focus of the Reconstruction amendments.

What would or (should) persons in the circumstances of those who founded and refounded our political community have been at pains to secure through the mechanism of their constitutional arrangements in order to constrain and justify the burdens and disappointments of membership in our political community? I think that these four broad concerns are good candidates, that each person or group in our political community had and has good reason to insist on this much: first, that their interests and concerns be treated with the same respect as the interests and concerns of all other groups and persons (we can call this *equal membership*); second, that the processes of government be fair to them and open to their participation and voice (we can call this *fair and open government*); third, that matters in the community be arranged so as to offer them the opportunity to secure materially decent lives (we can call this the *opportunity to thrive*); and fourth, that they have the opportunity to form judgments about their lives and the government under which they live and reasonable latitude in leading the lives they choose to lead (we can call this *independence*).

Equal membership, fair and open government, the opportunity to thrive, and independence: These are the basic, urgent concerns of political membership for a plural people whose life projects are at once important to them and the source of much of their plural division. These concerns are not meant to be read as immediate propositions of constitutional justice. The pursuit of some substantive principles (like the principle of free speech and its entailments) is demanded by these concerns, and some institutional arrangements (like particular distributions of authority across branches or between federal layers) may be favored by them. But these concerns are signposts to the neighborhood of constitutional justice; they describe its domain, not its axiomatic content.

It may be useful to compare this characterization of the domain of constitutional justice with the idea of political legitimacy. Views about the preconditions of a legitimate government vary considerably, so this is a bit of a moving target. Still, these observations may help: If legitimacy is taken seriously and literally, it has to be understood to comprise rather weak conditions, lest the vast bulk of world governments past and present be pronounced illegitimate; we may need to save that unfortunate verdict for extreme cases. Full realization of each of the concerns within the domain of constitutional justice may thus be a standard more demanding than political legitimacy; but, if so, this is more a matter of the frailty of our (species-wide) capacity to make and abide by satisfactory collective arrangements and commitments than it is a case of setting our constitutional sights too high. As a bottom line: No modern government could legitimately renounce any one of these concerns; the failure of a government to meet these concerns fully, while possibly inevitable, is nonetheless deeply regrettable; and the chronic and blatant failure to meet any one of these concerns should cast doubt on the legitimacy of the government in question.

The United States Constitution – and we can expect this of constitutions generally – is in this sense aspirational but not utopian. The Constitution aims not at a hopelessly artificial state of perfection, but at a not fully obtainable state in which the most critical, baseline demands of political justice are met. If men and women were angels, we would not need governments; and if governments were fundamentally just, we would not need constitutions.

These concerns clearly do not exhaust the requirements of political justice. We could imagine states of affairs, for example, that fully satisfied the requirement that circumstances in the political community be so arranged as to give each member of the community the opportunity to live a materially decent life, but that fell significantly short of a just allocation of opportunity and resources.

C. A Defense of the Opportunity to Thrive

I have not offered an extended defense of these four concerns here, but I expect them to be generally well received, in light of our actual constitutional experience (about which more will be said in the next section) and in light of our common instincts about what it is that wary members of a political community would and should worry about. I imagine, however, that readers may have doubts about the opportunity to thrive, which can be described as the opportunity of hardworking persons to provide themselves and their families with decent material lives.

Complaints, I think, could come in two flavors. First, the objection might be that the insertion of material well-being into the list of urgent concerns about the disappointments and burdens of political membership requires a special defense. Second, the objection might be that the kind and level of material well-being stipulated by the opportunity to thrive seem inappropriately arbitrary or simply wrong.

The inclusion of some concern for material well-being is not hard to justify, either as a general concern of membership in a political community or in the particular circumstances of the Founding and Reconstruction. Our revolution, like most revolutions, was prompted in significant part by economic injustices, like the famous complaint against taxation without representation. Ours was an economic constitution, with the amalgamation of the states into an open and unified national economic regime being high or highest on the list of reasons for replacing the Articles of Confederation. Not surprisingly, the principal divisions at the constitutional convention were closely associated with concerns for the material circumstances of economic life. During Reconstruction, the prosperity of the emancipated slaves was an important part of the concern for justice in the Fourteenth Amendment, with the national legislation retroactively authorized by the amendment conspicuously granting equal rights to contract and to hold and enjoy real property, and with the amendment itself announcing concern for deprivations of property without due process of law. So too, modern civil rights legislation has been heavily preoccupied with material well-being, attacking discrimination in housing, employment, and education. There is nothing unique about the materiality of these constitutional events. We would be astonished to learn that a new constitution in South Africa, Latin America, or Eastern Europe had been enacted without serious attention to economic concerns.

The more serious complaint is that I have arbitrarily and conveniently given the constitutional concern for material well-being the particular size and shape of the opportunity to thrive. Why, for example, not insist on broad economic justice, or stipulate the rough content of economic justice in a manner consistent with our long-standing commitment to a market economy, or demand something like the opportunity to prosper according to one's talents and capacities? Or why not read into constitutional justice a general predisposition to Locke and his proviso? Or why not see only a concern with certain forms of pernicious discrimination? Why this moderate and vague opportunity to lead a materially decent life?

The complaint that the opportunity to thrive is an arbitrary cut at the material dimension of constitutional justice could rest on one of three claims. The first form of the objection would deny that the opportunity to thrive is itself a part of or is subsumed within the critical material requirements of political justice. The second form of the objection would deny that the opportunity to thrive is appropriately concrete and immediate in its entailments to qualify as a constitutional concern. The third form of the objection would agree that the material dimension of constitutional justice should in one way or another encompass the opportunity to thrive, but would argue for inclusion in the constitutional canon of more robust (and possibly more philosophically complete) requirements of distributional justice.

The view that political justice does not include the opportunity to thrive simply is not plausible. To be locked in grinding poverty is an awful form of human existence. For those who suffer that state, the promise of equal membership, fair and open government, and independence is empty and meaningless. A society that organizes its affairs in a way that fails to provide the opportunity to thrive can hardly have regarded the interests of those who lack such an opportunity with the same respect as the interests and concerns of other groups and persons (equal membership); in no meaningful sense are the processes of government fair to persons who are locked in poverty, or open to their participation and voice (fair and open government); and no group has a lesser opportunity to form judgments about their lives and the government under which they live and less latitude in leading the lives they choose to lead (independence). For a prosperous society in normal times – even for a society deeply wed to free markets as, inter alia, the basis of that prosperity – it cannot be just to maintain economic arrangements that fail to provide its citizens with the opportunity to thrive.

The suggestion that the opportunity to thrive is not appropriately shaped to qualify as a constitutional requirement – that it is not sufficiently concrete and immediate to be effective in this role – appeals to our earlier observation about the need for parsimonious clarity in constitutional precepts. In thinking about this objection, we must observe two distinctions. The first is between a concern within the domain of constitutional justice itself and the more precise principles or precepts that the concern may sponsor or entail; the second is between the question of whether a principle or precept is enforceable by the judiciary and the question of whether it is sufficiently urgent, concrete, and focused to function as an immediate, more or less non-negotiable demand of constitutional conscience.

With these distinctions in mind, let us consider the right to minimum welfare, which we defined earlier as the entitlement of members of our political community to economic arrangements that offer them minimally decent material lives in exchange for hard work on their own behalf. The right to minimum welfare, as we discussed, is not enforceable by the judiciary in a full and direct sense (although the judiciary can and does police it at its substantive and procedural margins); it is, however, urgent, concrete, and focused. In a prosperous political community that recognizes the right to minimum welfare as a requirement of justice, the right has the shape and form necessary to function as a more or less non-negotiable demand of constitutional conscience.

The right to minimum welfare is somewhat narrower and more precise than the opportunity to thrive, which we described as the requirement that matters in a political community be arranged so as to offer the community's members the opportunity to secure materially decent lives. This reflects a certain tension latent in our analysis to this point, which I would like to take a moment to discuss directly. On the one hand, I have suggested that the concerns that compose the domain of justice are more basic and general than would be the operative principles – the axioms and postulates, if you will – of a scheme of constitutional justice. In this vein, I have talked about the entailments of these concerns. We could not, for example, treat seriously the concern for fair and open government without a commitment to a robust principle of free expression, and we could not treat seriously the concern for the opportunity to thrive without a commitment to the right to minimum welfare. On the other hand, I have suggested that a principle of parsimony attaches to the domain of constitutional justice because, to be effective, a constitution must make immediate and essentially non-negotiable demands. The reader might well wonder whether and why the more general concerns that comprise the domain of justice have to be limited if it is the entailments of these concerns that are operational, that have to do the categorical work.

The point is this: Our central inquiry in these pages is about the shape of the domain of constitutional justice and its justification. That shape, I have argued, is best understood as reflective of the most urgent and durable concerns of the members of a political community. The liberty-bearing facets of a constitution must be so confined, in important part, because only then can the constitution function appropriately and effectively as the political conscience of an ongoing democratic community. In practice, this means that the concerns taken up by a constitution must give on to substantive constitutional principles that have the right sort of bite. "Must give on to" is an intentionally soft phrase. Roughly, I have this in mind: A constitutional concern should clearly point toward one or more operational constitutional principles compliance with which would go a substantial distance toward the satisfaction of the underlying concern. A well-shaped and robust doctrine of free speech, for example, would be part of a set of operational principles that, if complied with, would go a substantial distance toward satisfying the underlying concern of fair and open government; the right to minimum welfare bears this same relationship to the opportunity to thrive.

Finally, let us consider the third form of the complaint that the opportunity to thrive represents an arbitrary cut at the material requirements of political justice. This form of the complaint agrees that the material dimension of constitutional justice should in one way or another encompass the opportunity to thrive, but argues for inclusion in the constitutional canon of more robust requirements of distributional justice. In responding, I want to agree that it is neither crucial to the analysis of this essay nor possible to defend the precise formulation of either the opportunity to thrive or the right to minimum welfare that we have taken it to spawn.[23] Still, there are important advantages to these or to roughly comparable formulations; a review of those advantages will not only explain my formulation but suggest what would make alternative formulations roughly comparable.

First, there is the point upon which we rested earlier. To be effective, constitutional concerns have to embody or give on to durable, concrete, gripping, essentially non-negotiable claims of constitutional conscience; broad commitments to economic justice of many stripes will flunk this requirement. Second, there is the question, to which we will turn more fully in the next section, of the fit of the concern for material well-being with our constitutional experience. The emphatic repudiation of *Lochner* in that tradition, and the limited exceptions to that repudiation that can be read from the trace elements of the right to minimum welfare, argue strongly for a modest rendition of the constitutional concern for material well-being. Third, the four concerns of constitutional justice that we have identified must be read in relation to each other. Equal membership, fair and open government, and independence are consistent with the opportunity to thrive and its instantiation in the right to minimum welfare; indeed, they require the satisfaction of these precepts for their own fulfillment. But a significantly more robust concern for material well-being as a constitutional precept might well be inconsistent with the confluence or union of these three concerns. For example, the diversity of life projects characteristic of a plural society that respected these three nonmaterial concerns would most likely be reflected in democratically contested disagreements about the desired course of economic development. Fourth, flexibility in the arrangement of the economy is crucial for prosperity over time, and a concern for material well-being in an enduring constitution must be appropriately adaptable; the opportunity to thrive and the right to minimum welfare it brings with it leave most of the details of the economy unspecified and are themselves softly indexed to prevailing expectations and material circumstances.

VI. The Domain of Constitutional Justice and Our Extant Constitutional Tradition

Does this description of the domain of constitutional justice fit our actual constitutional experience? What we have described as making up the domain of constitutional justice includes four interrelated concerns. It does not count as a demerit on grounds of fit that there is no simple, straightforward correspondence between these concerns and the specific clauses of the Constitution or the formal conceptual structure of constitutional doctrine. The question is whether the jurisprudence of the liberty-bearing features of our constitutional tradition can be fairly understood as reflecting the pull of these basic concerns.

The point that there need be no one-to-one or nominal correspondence between the concerns that make up the domain of constitutional justice and the textual or doctrinal packages of our liberty-bearing constitutional tradition for there to be a good fit between that tradition and the domain of constitutional justice requires some elaboration. The reader may worry that I have ignored an important distinction between the content and the purposes of a constitution. We can imagine, for example, a constitution that by its terms addressed only the durable, structural features of government and made no textual reference to principles of liberty or equality. We can imagine further that the constitutional judiciary has read this *constitution lite* as raising only questions of governmental structure but that, in resolving such questions, the judiciary invokes the ideas of liberty and equality as important goals of the constitution's structural stipulations, and therefore as important guides to the best interpretation of those stipulations. Under these circumstances, ideas of political justice would figure in the best understanding of the constitution as the purposes against which its interpretation should be judged, but they would not be part of the constitution; they would operate at an instrumental remove from the substance of the constitution. If the connection between the concerns that make up the domain of constitutional justice and the substance of our constitutional tradition were like that, then of course there would be a discontinuity between the two. If the connection were like that, however, much of our earlier discussion about the domain of constitutional justice would seem to have missed the point: The idea that constitutional concerns have to be immediate and non-negotiable to be effective, for example, would be inapt if these concerns were meant to function only in the background of the Constitution.

But the connection between the domain of constitutional justice and the substance of our constitutional tradition is not like that. To be sure, our constitutional text and jurisprudence respond in part to concerns of political justice by architecting and protecting structural features of government – the horizontal separation of powers and the vertical distribution of authority within a federal structure. (James Madison was being neither disingenuous nor hopelessly naive when he initially favored governmental structure over the inclusion of a bill of rights in the nascent Constitution as the means of protecting liberty.) But we also have a liberty-bearing constitutional text and a relatively secure tradition of wide-bodied judicial interpretation of that text. Without undertaking an elaborate survey here, let me say that I think the most active and secure ingredients of our liberty-bearing constitutional jurisprudence fit handsomely and recognizably with the broad concerns of equal membership, on the one hand, and fair and open government, on the other. The Supreme Court's preoccupation with racial and gender justice is clearly in the service of its vision of equal membership and so too, correctly understood, is much of the work of the modern Court in the area of religious liberty.[24] Many aspects of constitutional doctrine – ranging from the dominant themes of freedom of expression to the varied facets of voting rights and ballot access that have figured prominently in modern adjudication – reflect the Court's understanding of fair and open government.

An abiding concern with independence per se is somewhat less clearly manifest in our adjudicated constitutional tradition. In part, this is because our strong constitutional commitments to equal membership and fair and open government overlap with independence and obscure its discrete role in constitutional thought. In part, this is because aspects of independence lend themselves poorly to the categorical firmness of constitutional judgment. We have described independence as having a judgmental face (the opportunity of members of a political community to form judgments about their lives and the government under which they live) and a behavioral face (the reasonable latitude of those members to lead the lives they choose). The judgmental face of independence is protected in an important way by aspects of our jurisprudence of free expression, especially in those contexts where the stakes most clearly comprise the judgmental autonomy of the audience rather than the interests of the speaker or the political life of the community in any direct sense. More directly, there is a strong constitutional right of persons to believe what they choose to believe, sometimes assigned (misleadingly, in view of the precept's breadth) to the religion clauses. Less obviously, perhaps, our abiding reluctance to turn complete control of education over to the state is reflective of our commitment to judgmental independence.

To a greater degree than we realize, we depend upon the manifest restraint of legislative bodies in the United States for the maintenance of a broad sphere of independent conduct. Apart from a general avoidance of overreaching by legislatures – a strong reluctance, for example, to tell people what to wear, what to read, how to decorate their houses, with whom to associate in their homes, whom to hire for their personal guidance, and so on – there are specific legislative berths for discordant behavior that reflect a sensitivity to the concerns of independence. So-called Mrs. Murphy exemptions from antidiscrimination laws come to mind as an example. The Court, for its part, has policed untoward interference with behavioral independence in both acute and chronic circumstances. The acute cases involve intrusions that pass the ordinary and seem to direct people in their intimate lives. The ability of seven justices in *Griswold v. Connecticut* to surmount the extreme and widely shared conceptual allergy to Lochnerizing[25] and strike down Connecticut's silly and pernicious law is an example of the Court in its acute independence mode. The chronic cases involve situations where there are more general structural grounds for judicial concern. Part of our tradition of religious liberty is an example: The sense shared by legislatures and courts that there is a core of religious activity – worship – that is beyond governmental interference in any but the most extreme circumstances is best understood as a reflection of the distinct structure of organized religious practice in which deeply personal matters are conducted in an open and public space.[26] Part of our tradition of free expression may also be best understood as a chronic concern with behavioral independence. When we consider our general reluctance to tolerate the suppression of the arts, we stand at the juncture of concerns with free and open government, judgmental independence, and behavioral independence.

In all, equal membership, fair and open government, and independence are robust and recognizable themes in our constitutional tradition. Further, our rather straightforward reading of the domain of constitutional justice that centers on these themes is superior on grounds of fit to most democratarian views of the domain of constitutional justice. As I intimated earlier, these views characteristically secure fit at some expense to either the foot or the shoe: John Hart Ely has trouble with the religion clauses, has to smuggle in a substantive commitment to equal membership by treating lapses from that standard as failures of rationality, and has nothing to offer to account for our durable post-*Griswold* tradition of a right to "privacy";[27] Frank Michelman in his democratarian phase argued for the rights of gays and lesbians on the ground that people who had realized their sexual identities were better voting citizens;[28] Ronald Dworkin's view of democracy is sufficiently capacious to avoid these difficulties of fit, but his approach deflects attention to a controversial concept of democracy and makes these broad concerns dependent upon their connection to that view of democracy in a way that is both somewhat strained and unnecessary.[29]

The issue of fit is more problematic in the case of the opportunity to thrive and its more pointed entailment, the right to minimum welfare. Here, there is both a paucity of adjudicated constitutional outcomes that directly respond to material well-being and good reason to conclude that the judiciary is institutionally unfit to be the primary protector of this dimension of constitutional justice. The question then becomes where one looks for fit. We have already seen a part of the answer: There are important threads of Supreme Court doctrine that seem awkward and anomalous on first encounter; they make good sense, however, when we posit the existence of the right to minimum welfare that is supported but not directly enforced by the constitutional judiciary.

But there is more to say about the question of fit in this connection. Were it the case that our polity regularly acted in a manner deeply and self-consciously inconsistent with the right to minimum welfare, there would be an objection on grounds of fit to the claim that this is an aspect of the domain of constitutional justice. Having concluded that primary responsibility for the maintenance of constitutional guarantees like the right to minimum welfare must lie with our popular political institutions, it is important that we look in part to those institutions in considering the issue of fit. Despite our rather bad job of living up to our commitments in this regard, I think there is evidence that we acknowledge the existence of a right to minimum welfare as a matter of political justice, the Constitution aside. These may seem somewhat hazardous times to make even modestly optimistic statements about the enduring commitments of our political community to the minimum welfare of its members. We are in the midst of "reforms" of social welfare programs that seem heartless and unjust in their consequences for some persons in our society – especially children and the disabled – and political sentiment appears coldly indifferent. But two things blunt the force of these contemporary political currents. First, the worst fears about the impact of recent legislation concern the circumstances that may obtain some years from now, and it is certainly to be hoped that true welfare reforms will be put in place to ensure the opportunities of those willing to work hard on their own and their families behalf and to protect the innocent young whose opportunities depend on a future they may not otherwise come to enjoy at all. Second, if this hope is not realized, the burden of our discussion is that we will then be acting in stark contradiction to an important constitutional norm. A constitutional norm is not voided by passing misbehavior; it is violated.

These immediate times aside, we have at least aspired to secure the right to minimum welfare. There has been a pervasive social and political recognition of the need for a safety net, as well as efforts to implement a base of public support that satisfies the limited promise of that metaphor. Public or publicly supported education has not flourished in our time, but neither, emphatically, has it perished; we would, I strongly hope and believe, never retreat from our sustained commitment to a free basic education. Even in the face of our inability to rationalize the distribution of medical care, most if not all urban centers provide a network of public hospitals or some other mechanism by which the most urgent medical needs of the poor are met.

This focus on the pattern of popular political judgment raises the question of whether there is a negative question of fit lurking in our enduring economic arrangements, whether a view of the material dimension of constitutional justice that goes no further than the opportunity to lead a materially decent life is underinclusive of our actual constitutional commitments. The claim that this is so would invoke the durability of certain features of the economic landscape in the United States. We have, for example, consistently maintained a market economy. Does this suggest that our commitment to a market economy has constitutional dimensions and, in turn, that we have understated the material dimensions of the domain of constitutional justice? It does not, for this simple reason: Durable practices do not, without more, acquire constitutional tenure. However wise or foolhardy, the imposition of a flat tax would certainly be revolutionary; it would not, for that reason, be unconstitutional. We approached the point of asking whether our polity has acted in a manner that affronts the right to minimum welfare from the opposite direction. That is, we began with a freestanding argument in favor of recognizing the opportunity for a materially decent life as part of constitutional justice; then we observed not only that our constitutional jurisprudence on the best understanding is consistent with the recognition of the right to minimum welfare as an instantiation of that concern, but that important cases call for such an explanation. Then we asked, by way of a possible veto, in effect, whether our ongoing legislative practices are deeply inconsistent with the existence of that right as a matter of constitutional justice.

VII. Two Looks Back

A. *Another Look at the Universal and the Particular, and the Worry That the Picture Is Too Tidy*

As we observed in passing, the attempt to offer an account of our constitutional practice necessarily puts the universal and the particular in some tension with each other. When we ask what a people like ourselves should most urgently worry about as members of a political community, or what general shape constitutional concerns must assume to function effectively as the conscience of a democratic people, or what the advantages of a constitutional practice like ours might be, we are addressing questions of an apparently general character. When, on the other hand, we ask whether the justice-seeking account of our constitutional practice or our description of the domain of constitutional justice fits our constitutional experience, we are addressing questions of an apparently local character. It is in the nature of an interpretive enterprise like this, however, that the general inquiry into justification and the particular inquiry into fit have substantial influence over each other: Our justifications, while appealing to general propositions of political justice or practice, are shaped to our particular practice, and we view our actual practice through the lens of our justifications for that practice. If we have been successful – if we have fashioned an attractive and plausible account of our constitutional practice – then we have made the ends meet, more or less.

This may inspire in the reader doubts that things have been made too tidy, too rosy. Suddenly we may seem to be portraying ourselves as possessed of the best of all possible modes of governance; that portrayal, of course, has not been defended, and almost certainly is indefensible. But that worry would overread what I mean to argue here. The strongest claims that I would make are that (a) the account we have traced of a justice-seeking, judicially underenforced, domain-of-constitutional-justice-restricted constitution is the best available account of our actual constitutional practice, and (b) a modern society like our own would find the important project of doing justice among a plural democratic people reasonably well served by adopting a constitutional practice that shared the core features of our own. To believe that the themes or concerns of equal membership, fair and open government, the opportunity to thrive, and independence are firmly represented in our constitutional jurisprudence and/or political practice is not to believe that we have satisfied these concerns. These are targets, and on the whole we seem in good faith to aim at them, but we have often missed, sometimes by a mile. This is perhaps most clearly true of our political practice, in which we have fallen measurably short of realizing the opportunity to thrive or even of fairly satisfying the more pointed right to minimum welfare, but it is also true of our constitutional jurisprudence, which, we can safely assume, will always need improvement.

For all of this, I do not want to concede the field to localism or to glum fallibility. At its inception, our constitutional project was plagued by the twin debilitating flaws of slavery and the immunity of state and local governments from the reach of most of the Constitution's liberty-bearing provisions. Once those flaws were rectified, our experiment in justice-seeking constitutionalism could be properly launched. In all, I think that experiment has been an important success. And I think that other national political communities can learn and have learned from its example.

To the extent that our experiment has been a success – to the extent that we have directed ourselves to the concerns that comprise the domain of constitutional justice and have done a reasonably good job of satisfying those concerns – our success is connected in an important way to the design of our constitutional practice. We have alluded to the form of the partnership between the framing constitutional generations (speaking at a high level of moral generality or abstraction in the liberty-bearing provisions of the Constitution) and the constitutional judiciary (whose independent moral judgment is required to provide concrete and detailed operational consequences from these general commitments). But the complete picture is more complicated. For example – though I do not intend to make the case here – the Constitution's general obduracy to amendment and particular insistence on broad geographic support for amendment is an important part of our constitutional machinery; together, they inspire a generality of perspective and generosity of spirit that are conducive to sound constitutional decision-making by the framing generations of popular constitutional decision-makers.

B. *What We Understand When We Understand the Domain of Constitutional Justice*

It is time to take stock. If we agree that there is a domain of constitutional justice in the strong sense, then we already agree on something important. There are good reasons for seeing our constitutional practice as justice-seeking and significantly forward-looking, rather than as historicist and dominantly backward-looking. But our constitutional tradition seems firmly limited in its moral reach in a way that calls for an explanation. On the historicist account, the limits of constitutional justice can be as arbitrary as the limits of a particular political generation's imagination, will, and insight. The justice-seeking account, in contrast, requires a nonarbitrary explanation for this moral shortfall – an explanation that connects the limits of constitutional justice to the enterprise of securing political justice. To agree that there is a domain of constitutional justice in the strong sense is to agree that there is an explanation for the limits of constitutional justice of precisely this sort.

There are good reasons for pulling apart the questions of what is required ·by constitutional justice and what is enforceable by the constitutional judiciary. Some precepts of political justice come entwined with questions of strategy and responsibility that are outside the competence of the judiciary, but this does not disqualify them from inclusion within the canon of constitutional justice. We can make the best sense of adjudicated constitutional outcomes if we recognize that constitutional justice is and should be underenforced by the judiciary. But, even taking judicial underenforcement of the Constitution into account, there remain good reasons for thinking that the domain of constitutional justice stops well short of exhausting all political justice.

If we agree on this much, we then need to consider the nature of the connection between the limits of constitutional justice and the broader enterprise of securing political justice. Democratarian theories see constitutional justice as limited to the project of perfecting democracy, and see that limitation as exempting our constitutional practice from the charge that it is inconsistent with democracy. I have argued that democratarian theories claim too much, that – under the circumstances of a reasonably well functioning ("working") democracy – constitutional practices that take judgments about perfecting democracy out of the hands of popular politics do not enjoy the special exemption they claim. But if democratarian theories claim too much, they also restrict too much. Bereft of their underlying justification, they con-

tinue to insist that all of constitutional justice must be an elaboration of the requirements of democracy, a demand that risks either the artificial truncation
of constitutional justice or the artificial expansion of the requirements of
democracy.

In the justice-seeking account, the limits of constitutional justice are explained by the related concerns that democratic politics not be unduly con-
gested and that constitutional precepts function effectively as restraints on
popular will. To function effectively as the conscience of a democratic people, constitutional justice must comprise durable, immediate, essentially non-
negotiable (the adjective "categorical" comes to mind) precepts. This imposes
on the domain of constitutional justice the need for parsimonious clarity. The
domain of constitutional justice, accordingly, is confined to the most urgent
and fundamental concerns that members of a political community should have
about the magnitude and fairness of the burdens that may accompany their
membership.

If we agree on all this, we share an important understanding of constitutional practice, including the structure of constitutional justice – whether or
not we agree on the concerns that should be taken to constitute constitutional
justice. I have offered four: equal membership, fair and open government, the
opportunity to thrive, and independence. Of these, the opportunity to thrive is
likely to be the least obvious, but not the least important, especially given the
dependence of the other three concerns upon the satisfaction of this crucial,
material fourth.

What have we gained toward the decision of actual cases by mapping the
domain of constitutional justice? Consider the right to minimum welfare. The
recognition of such a right, albeit judicially unenforceable in the first instance, has real-world consequences. It should both explain past constitutional decisions in the way that we have observed in passing and drive future
decisions to which the existence of this right is relevant in the same secondary
way. It should also influence the way we as citizens call upon one another and
upon our elected representatives to confront the injustice of grinding, un-
abated poverty.

One standard form of objection to the acknowledgment of such a right is
that it does not belong in the Constitution in some deep sense, that it is not
within the domain of constitutional justice. Such an objection might come
from someone who held a democratarian view of the domain of constitutional
justice, or perhaps from someone who insisted on the basis of a less fully developed view that the right to minimum welfare was simply made of the
wrong stuff to be part of the Constitution. The idea underlying such objections, the idea that constitutional justice has a somewhat restricted domain, is
entirely correct and we cannot satisfactorily explain our constitutional experience without reference to such a domain. But fundamental justice demands

the opportunity to secure for oneself and one's family a materially decent life and the exclusion of that concern from the domain of constitutional justice would require an explanation not offered by the mere observation that there is such a domain.

We do not have the best of all possible constitutions, and surely we do not inhabit the best of all political worlds. We do have a good constitution, however, one that insists that we honor the fundamental demands of political justice. When we understand that, we can get down to the business of understanding more concretely what constitutional justice requires of us as a political community.

Notes

1 I am not interested here in more general disputes over the nature of interpretation, but Ronald Dworkin's characterization of interpretation well describes my effort and the efforts of others to offer an account of constitutional practice. See Ronald Dworkin, *Law's Empire* 45–86 (Cambridge, Mass.: Harvard University Press, 1986).

2 The point can be put more strongly: To be at all persuasive, a historicist account of our constitutional practice must be founded on a view of political justice. Historicists have to jump into the political justice soup with the rest of us; they cannot conceptually afford to remain outside of and skeptical of such matters.

3 Our focus here is on the judiciary, but the justice-seeking account depends upon other constitutional interpreters as well. This should become clear in our discussion of judicial underenforcement of the Constitution, in Section III.B.

4 For a justice-seeking account of our constitutional practice that focuses upon history and the principle of constitutional supremacy rather than on the pragmatic promise of constitutional adjudication, see Sotirios A. Barber, *On What the Constitutional Means* chs. 3–4. (Baltimore: Johns Hopkins University Press, 1984).

5 John Rawls both employs the idea of public reason and argues that the judiciary's public-reason-giving practice is an important credential in constitutional decision-making. See John Rawls, *Political Liberalism* 216 (New York: Columbia University Press, 1993).

6 Not all accounts of our constitutional practice map neatly onto the historicist/justice-seeking dichotomy. One group that does not is composed of what we might call *reluctant judgment* accounts. Reluctant judgment theorists, at least on the surface, are aspirationally historicist; that is, if the historical Constitution offered a stable and applicable mandate that judges could access without bringing to bear their independent moral judgment, these theorists would regard that circumstance as preferable. Unfortunately, these theorists observe, things are not like that. To be faithful to the mandate of the Constitution, judges need to bring some independent moral judgment to bear. This might be so because the mandate uttered in one era has to be translated in a modern milieu where many things have changed, including the conceptual paradigms by which we understand our world. Or it might be so

because – appropriately understood – the Constitution contains broad, partially conflicting mandates, which must be reconciled or synthesized by judges committed to taking their instructions from the Constitution. The process of translation or synthesis on these views necessarily involves the exercise of judges' independent moral judgment. I understand Lawrence Lessig, *Fidelity in Translation*, 71 Tex. L. Rev. 1165 (1993), and Bruce Ackerman, *We the People: Foundations* 142–62 (Cambridge, Mass.: Harvard University Press, 1993), to be examples of this general view.

There is no sweeping answer to the question of whether, for the purposes of our discussion, we should regard reluctant judgment accounts as more like historicist or justice-seeking accounts of our constitutional practice. The more room a particular reluctant judgment theorist makes for independent judicial judgment, the more like a justice-seeking theorist she becomes for these purposes. That is, the more open to challenges about the moral shortfall of the Constitution she is, and the more interested in the question of the domain of constitutional justice she should be.

While this is not the place to consider at length the conceptual contest between reluctant judgment and justice-seeking views of our constitutional practice, I cannot resist this passing observation: Reluctant judgment theorists offer a grudging justification for the independent moral judgment constitutional judges in fact exercise, but they do not offer us a reason to favor the constitutional practices that put judges in the position of having to exercise such judgment; they do not, in other words, explain why we are advantaged by the partnership of popular and judicial decision-making that is characteristic of our constitutional practice, why we would not be better off with parliamentary government or a more concrete and detailed constitution, or some other set of institutional arrangements that obviated the broad need for the independent exercise of judicial judgment. I discuss these themes in *The Betrayal of Judgment*, 65 Fordham L. Rev. 1545, 1546–53 (1997).

7 I explore the underenforcement thesis in Lawrence G. Sager, *Justice in Plain Clothes: Reflections on the Thinness of Constitution Law*, 88 Nw. L. Rev. 410, 419 (1993), *Fair Measure: The Legal Status of Underenforced Constitutional Norms*, 91 Harv. L. Rev. 1212 (1978).

8 Plyler v. Doe, 457 U.S. 202, 102 S.Ct. 2382, 72. L.Ed.2d 786 (1982).

9 Goldberg v. Kelly, 397 U.S. 254, 90 S.Ct. 1011, 25 L.Ed.2d 287 (1970). Subsequently, in *Matthews v. Eldridge*, the Court held that a disabilities benefit claimant is not similarly entitled to hearing as a precondition of the termination of her benefits. The Court distinguished *Goldberg* on the ground that basic welfare recipients are on the very margins of subsistence (424 U.S. at 340) and that the likely stakes of terminating their benefits would be the very means by which to live (id., quoting *Goldberg*, 397 U.S. at 264).

10 Goss v. Lopez, 419 U.S. 565 (1975).

11 Frank Michelman, an early and important advocate of the constitutional right to minimum welfare (see his *The Supreme Court 1968 Term – Foreword: On Protecting the Poor Through the Fourteenth Amendment*, 83 Harv. L. Rev. 7 (1969), and *In Pursuit of Constitutional Welfare Rights*, 121 U. Pa. L. Rev. 962 (1973), was subsequently drawn to something like this view of the Court's role with regard to

such rights. See Frank Michelman, *Welfare Rights in a Constitutional Democracy*, 1979 Wash. L. Q. 659, 660–5, 679–80.

12 This is the text of Section 2 of the Thirteenth Amendment. Section 5 of the Fourteenth Amendment actually reads in relevant part, "to enforce, by appropriate legislation, the provisions of this article."

13 The foundational case is Jones v. Mayer, 392 U.S. 409, 88 S.Ct. 2186, 20 L.Ed.2d 1189 (1968).

14 Here the foundational case is Katzenbach v. Morgan, 384 U.S. 641, 86 S.Ct. 1717, 16 L.Ed.2d 282 (1966). Recently, in City of Boerne v. Flores, 117 S.Ct. 2157 (1997), the Court endorsed the outcome in *Katzenbach* but gestured toward what might be a narrowed view of congressional authority under Section 5 of the Fourteenth Amendment. Under the best reading of the *Boerne* case, however, Congress retains considerable authority to overreach the Court. See Christopher L. Eisgruber and Lawrence G. Sager, *Congressional Power and Religious Liberty after City of Boerne v. Flores*, Supreme Court L. Rev. (forthcoming).

15 334 U.S. 1, 68 S.Ct, 836, 92 L.Ed. 1161 (1948). In *Shelly,* the Supreme Court held that the judicial enforcement of private, racially restrictive subdivision covenants constituted state action, and was thus subject to the Fourteenth Amendment.

16 I take this to be the starting point of Cass Sunsten's sustained attack on "status quo neutrality." See his *Lochner's Legacy,* 87 Colum. L. Rev. 873 (1987), and *The Partial Constitution* 50 (Cambridge, Mass.: Harvard University Press, 1993).

17 198 U.S 45 (1905). *Lochner* struck down New York legislation specifying maximum hours for bakery workers, and is commonly identified as launching a period of three decades in which the Supreme Court acted to strike down economic regulations that it deemed inconsistent with free market outcomes.

18 John Hart Ely, *Democracy and Distrust* (Cambridge, Mass.: Harvard University Press, 1980).

19 316 U.S. 479 (1965).

20 Ronald Dworkin, *Freedom's Law: The Moral Reading of the American Constitution* 15–26 (Cambridge, Mass.: Harvard University Press, 1996).

21 Frank Michelman, *Law's Republic,* 97 Yale L. J. 1493, 1535–6 (1988). In conversation, Professor Michelman has expressed some doubts about this aspect of his argument, which is why I am reluctant to assume his ongoing commitment to it.

22 A democratarian account of the Constitution need not equate the whole of the Constitution with the adjudicated Constitution; such an account could include judicial underenforcement of the Constitution. With the addition of this movable part, a democratarian account could be refined in several directions. Such an account, for example, might confine only judicial enforcement of the Constitution to the perfection of democracy and leave unadjudicated portions of the Constitution less fettered; or – more conventionally – it might maintain democratarian limits on the whole of the Constitution and distinguish between the judicially enforceable and judicially unenforceable portions of the Constitution on grounds of the likelihood that popular political institutions will arrive at constitutionally accepted outcomes. Admitting judicial underenforcement into the democratarian picture improves that picture, but the continued insistence on the hegemony of popular politics still causes difficulty. Confining *either* the reach of constitutional justice *or* constitu-

tional adjudication to the perfection of democracy requires a justification that does not, I believe, exist – unless democracy is defined so broadly as to embrace the full concerns of constitutional justice.

23 Alternative formulations of the material dimension of constitutional justice surely merit attention. Prominent among the possibilities is a shift of focus away from minimum welfare per se and toward the opportunity to work and earn a decent wage. Sotirios Barber, for example, sees material well-being as a historically derived constitutional end that includes the individual's capacity to choose among vocations that promise income sufficient for decent housing, adequate nutrition, health care, education, and a secure old age. Sotorious Barber, *Welfare and the Instrumental Constitution,* Am. J. Jurisprudence 42–5 (forthcoming). Kenneth Karst has insisted on the material dimensions of constitutional justice in a number of illuminating essays; his most recent claim is for a judicially nonenforceable "right of access to work." Kenneth L. Karst, *The Coming Crisis of Work in Constitutional Perspective,* 82 Corn. L. Rev. 523 (1997).

24 Correctly understood, our constitutional tradition of religious liberty centers on the project of protecting minority religious views from devaluation or discrimination, of ensuring the equal regard of all citizens whatever their religious commitments. See Christopher L. Eisgruber and Lawrence G. Sager, *The Vulnerability of Conscience: The Constitutional Basis for Protecting Religious Conduct,* 61 U. Chi. L. Rev. 1245 (1994); Christopher L. Eisgruber and Lawrence G. Sager, *Unthinking Religious Freedom,* 74 Tex. L. Rev. 577, 600–14 (1996); and Eisgruber and Sager, supra, note 14.

25 Infamy is almost always involved when the name of a person or a case becomes a verb.

26 The Constitution does not privilege religious commitment; it protects religious commitment from devaluation and discrimination. Organized religious commitments, however, do have the unusual feature of placing intensely private acts and relationships in a public structure; they enjoy protection because of their private substance, and hence are examples of the chronic protection of independence in our constitutional tradition. See supra, note 24.

27 See Section IV, text accompanying notes 18 and 19.

28 See Section IV, text accompanying note 21.

29 See Section IV, text accompanying note 20.

7

Precommitment and Disagreement

JEREMY WALDRON

I. Democracy and Popular Sovereignty

The British are contemplating constitutional reform. Among the changes under consideration is the enactment of a bill of rights enforced, if necessary, by the judicial review of legislation, along lines well established in the United States.[1] The radical change in British law that this would involve provides us with an opportunity to reflect more expansively than American constitutional scholars often do on the nature and purpose of constitutional constraints and their relation to the democratic principles often taken to be embodied in the "sovereignty" of a Westminster-style legislature. The conclusions of such reflection will be relevant to the debate in the United Kingdom of course, but they will be relevant not only there. They may be helpful to us too, for we can often learn about our own constitution by comparing it with other constitutions,[2] and we often learn how to understand the characteristics of our own constitution by imagining them abroad as serious objects of political choice, rather than as features we were taught to revere in elementary school. Certainly to the extent that the political dramatics of judicial review are bound up with the self-image and self-importance of American lawyers and law professors, it may be easier to persuade them to consider the institution carefully, critically, and impartially when what is at stake are the role and image of lawyers and judges somewhere else.

On the other hand, the debate in other countries may be responsive to features that are not present in the American case. It is arguable, for example, that in the United Kingdom the institution of a bill of rights with judicial review will not be subject to the "counter-majoritarian difficulty" often associated with the American version.[3] For if these changes take place, they will not have been undemocratically imposed upon the British people; nor will they be something the British have inherited because they seemed like a good idea to a bunch of slave-owning revolutionaries living on the edge of an undeveloped continent at the end of the eighteenth century. If a bill of rights is incorporated into British law in the next few years, it will be because Parliament or perhaps the British people in a referendum have voted for incorporation on the understanding that they will be changing the British constitution by establishing a practice of judicial review. Indeed, far from posing a countermajoritarian difficulty, this will be one of the first opportunities the British people have had to control major aspects of their constitution by explicit majority decision.

Ronald Dworkin once argued that this alone is sufficient to dispose of the objection that the institution of such constraints is contrary to the spirit of democracy. On his view, the democratic objection to a bill of rights with judicial review is self-defeating because polls reveal that more than 71 percent of people believe that British democracy would be improved, not undermined, by the incorporation of a bill of rights.[4]

The objection cannot be disposed of quite so easily. The fact that there is popular support, even overwhelming popular support, for an alteration in the constitution does not show that such an alteration would make things more democratic. Certainly, a radical democrat is committed to saying that if the people want a regime of constitutional rights with judicial review, that is what they should have; that is what democratic principles require, as far as constitutional change is concerned. But we must not confuse the reason for carrying out a proposal with the character of the proposal itself. If the people voted to experiment with dictatorship, principles of democracy might give us a reason to allow them to do so. But it would not follow that dictatorship is democratic. (This is just another way of saying that it is not conceptually impossible for a democracy to vote itself out of existence.)

Let me put the matter more theoretically. There is a distinction between democracy and popular sovereignty. The principle of popular sovereignty – basic to liberal thought – requires that the people should have whatever constitution, whatever form of government they want. But popular sovereignty does not remove or blur the differences that exist among the various forms of government on the menu from which the people are supposed to choose. John Locke and Thomas Hobbes both believed in popular sovereignty. They argued that the people – acting by majority decision – had the right to vest legislative authority in a single individual or small group of individuals (thus constituting a monarchy or an aristocracy) or alternatively in an assembly comprising the whole people or in a large representative institution (thus constituting a direct or an indirect democracy).[5] But although this decision was to be popular and majoritarian, and in that sense democratic, it was at the same time a significant choice between democratic and undemocratic options. Hobbes believed that the people would be making a mistake if they vested sovereignty in a democratic assembly;[6] Locke, on the other hand, credited the people with thinking that they "could never be safe . . . till the Legislature was placed in collective bodies of Men, call them Senate, Parliament, or what you please" and he thought it important for that collective body to be the "Supream Power" of the commonwealth.[7] Neither of them thought a constitution became more democratic simply by being the upshot of popular choice.

There may be a connection the other way. It may be easier to establish that a polity is based on popular sovereignty if it is in fact democratically organized. We can see this if we reflect a little on the artificiality of the Hobbes–Locke model. The distinction between a democratic method of constitutional choice and the democratic character of the constitution that is chosen is clearest when we can point to a founding moment in the life of a political society (a moment of constitutional choice) and distinguish between the decision procedures used at that moment and the decision procedures which, at that moment, it was decided to employ in all subsequent political decision-making. But in the real world, the formation of a new political order is seldom so tidy.

Often the decisions that determine the shape of a society's constitution are entangled with or woven into the fabric of ordinary political life.[8] As they occur they may be indistinguishable – in time, solemnity, or any other respect – from the ordinary run of political decision-making. Often, for example, we will not know whether a different way of doing things (in some run-of-the-mill case or even in some crisis that is not evidently or on its face a *constitutional* crisis) is going to "stick" – that is, whether it is going to become established as a rule or practice governing the conduct of political life, or whether it will turn out to be just an aberration, consigned to the minutiae of history. Even in the United States, where there is a full written constitution and an established tradition of interpreting it, an event that has fundamental significance for the basis on which political life is conducted may not advertise itself as "constitutional."[9] Certainly in the United Kingdom and elsewhere, understanding the formation and growth of the constitution is often a matter of studying apparently routine political events, to discern which of them have and which of them have not acquired normative significance as far as the conduct and organization of other political events are concerned.[10]

An attribution of popular sovereignty to a political system is therefore a matter of theoretical judgment. It requires us to figure out which decisions count as constitutive of the political system in question and to venture a certain explanatory hypothesis to account for the constitutional significance of those decisions – a hypothesis to the effect that they "stuck" or became established as constitutional practices because they were acceptable as such to most of the ordinary members of the society. Obviously this will be easiest to justify in a society whose ordinary workings are democratic, because the events we adjudge "constitutional" will be part of that ordinary working.

The argument is not cast-iron, however. It is one thing for a particular decision to be made democratically; it is another thing for it to sustain the same

popular support under the description that it is setting a constitutional precedent. The people may support the ratification of an important treaty in a referendum, but some of them might have voted no if they had thought their support was going to be regarded as effecting a change in the rule requiring that
treaties be ratified by a vote in the Senate, not by a vote among the people.[11]
Thus, the events that amount over time to a change in the constitution may be
democratic events without its being proper to describe that constitutional
change as democratic.

II. Precommitment

Still, suppose that a bill of rights together with American-style judicial review
is chosen by the British people and supported by a majority in full awareness
that this amounts to a reform of the constitution. Then, it may be said, even if
we cannot infer that judicial review is democratic, we have surely nevertheless answered the democratic objection. The existence of written constitutional constraints and the courts' power to interpret and apply them – these
would not be products of judicial usurpation. Rather they would be mechanisms of restraint that the British people have deliberately and for good reasons chosen to impose upon themselves.

Why would they do this? What makes this sort of self-restraint intelligible?
The answer is that everyone knows that majoritarian legislation can be unjust;
everyone knows that popular majorities can sometimes be driven by panic to
pass measures that harm or discriminate against minorities who are powerless
politically to resist them. Elsewhere I have argued that respect for individual
rights is not compatible with a purely predatory image of legislative majorities, for majorities are made up of individual rights bearers and part of what
we respect in individuals is their ability as rights bearers to figure out respon-
sibly what they owe to others.[12] But of course this argument does not require
us to think that rights bearers are always angels or to deny that, acting individually or en masse, they are sometimes capable of rights violations. It requires us to say, rather, that although rights bearers may on occasion be rights
violators, they are not always themselves indifferent or partial to that possibility. To the extent that they foresee it, they have as rights bearers the moral
capacity to condemn it in advance and take precautions against the temptations that may trigger it. Constitutional constraints and mechanisms of judicial review may be viewed, then, as precautions that responsible rights
bearers have taken against their own imperfections. It follows that such precautions do not involve any fundamental disrespect for the people, individually or collectively, or for their capacities of self-government; on the contrary,
taking such precautions represents the epitome of the exercise of those capacities in a troubled and complicated world.

I shall call this the "precommitment" view of constitutional constraints, and much of the rest of this essay will be devoted to a critique of it. For the moment, however, let us consider it in the best possible light. In the words of one of its most persuasive proponents, the view presents the constitutional arrangements we have been discussing as "a kind of rational and shared precommitment among free and equal sovereign citizens at the level of constitutional choice."[13] Its effect can be summed up as follows:

By the exercise of their rights of equal participation [the people] agree to a safeguard that prevents them, in the future exercise of their equal political rights, from later changing their minds and deviating from their agreement and commitment to a just constitution. . . . By granting to a non-legislative body that is not electorally accountable the power to review democratically enacted legislation, citizens provide themselves with a means for protecting their sovereignty and independence from the unreasonable exercise of their political rights in legislative processes. . . . By agreeing to judicial review, they in effect tie themselves into their unanimous agreement on the equal basic rights that specify their sovereignty. Judicial review is then one way to protect their status as equal citizens.[14]

As I said, the precommitment view is an attractive one. We are familiar with it in personal ethics: An individual may have reason to impose on himself certain constraints as far as his future decision-making is concerned. Ulysses decided that he should be bound to the mast in order to resist the charms of the Sirens, and he instructed his crew that "if I beg you to release me, you must tighten and add to my bonds."[15] A smoker trying to quit may hide his own cigarettes, a chronic oversleeper with a weakness for the "snooze" button may place his alarm clock out of reach on the other side of the bedroom, and a heavy drinker may give his car keys to a friend at the beginning of a party with strict instructions not to return them when they are requested at midnight.

These arrangements strike us not as derogations from individual freedom, but as the epitome of self-government. Freedom, after all, is not just moving hither and yon with the play of one's appetites. It is a matter of *taking control* of the basis on which one acts; it is a matter of the self being in charge of its desires and not vice versa.[16] The idea is sometimes explicated in terms of the related concept of *autonomy:* "Autonomy of the will is the property that the will has of being a law to itself."[17] Aware now of a way in which it might be determined by various forces in the future, the autonomous will seeks to limit such determination by responding to certain considerations of principle in advance.

So, similarly, it may be said, an electorate may decide collectively to bind itself in advance to resist the siren charms of rights violations. Aware, as much as the smoker or the drinker, of the temptations of wrong or irrational action, the people as a whole in a lucid moment may put themselves under certain constitutional disabilities – disabilities that serve the same function in relation to democratic values as are served by strategies like hiding the cigarettes or handing the car keys to a friend in relation to the smoker's or the drinker's autonomy. The smoker really desires to stop smoking; the drinker does not really want to drive under the influence. The mechanisms they adopt, therefore, enable them to secure the good that they really want and avoid the evil that, occasionally despite themselves, they really want to avoid. Similarly, the people really do not want to discriminate on grounds of race, to restrict free speech, or to allow the police to search people's homes without a warrant. They are aware, however, that on occasion they may be driven by panic into doing these things. And so they have taken precautions, instituting legal constraints as safeguards to prevent them from doing in a moment of panic what in their more thoughtful moments they are sure they do not want to do. As Stephen Holmes states the view (though this is not quite Holmes's *own* account of constitutional precommitment):[18]

A constitution is Peter sober while the electorate is Peter drunk. Citizens need a constitution, just as Ulysses needed to be bound to his mast. If voters were allowed to get what they wanted, they would inevitably shipwreck themselves. By binding themselves to rigid rules, they can better achieve their solid and long-term collective aims.[19]

Constitutional constraint, in other words, is a means by which the will of the people secures its own responsible exercise.

III. Causal Mechanisms versus External Judgment

In a seminal study of precommitment, Jon Elster has suggested that a decision at t_1 counts as a way of "binding oneself" vis-à-vis some decision at t_2 only if "[t]he effect of carrying out the decision at t_1 [is] to set up some *causal* process in the external world."[20] He means to exclude purely internal strategies like deciding to decide: "[O]ur intuitive notion of what it is to bind oneself seems to require that we temporarily deposit our will in some external structure."[21]

In the political case, we may want to ask: What counts as an *external* structure? Elster himself has doubts about the application of his analysis to constitutional constraints:

[T]he analogy between individual and political self-binding is severely limited. An individual can bind himself to certain actions, or at least make deviations from them more costly and hence less likely, by having recourse to a legal framework that is external to and independent of himself. *But nothing is external to society.* With the exception of a few special cases, like the abdication of powers to the International Monetary Fund, societies cannot deposit their will in structures outside their control; they can always undo their ties should they want to.[22]

His point is well taken as far as popular sovereignty is concerned: What the people can do, constitutionally, they can always *in some sense* undo.[23] Yet there is a sense nevertheless that constitutional provisions can be binding, a sense that has to do with the institutional articulation *within* the framework controlled overall by "the people" as popular sovereign. Even though the constraints are not external to that framework, they are in the relevant sense external to the particular agencies in which "the will of the people" is embodied for purposes of ordinary political decision. I shall return to these issues toward the end of the essay.[24]

A separate set of issues is raised by Elster's reference to causal mechanisms. A decision at t_1 counts, he said, as a precommitment only if its effect is "to set up some causal process in the external world."[25] Does this include or exclude strategies like the drinker giving his car keys to a friend? The friend's possession of the car keys is not really a *causal* mechanism ensuring or increasing the probability that the drinker will not drive home at midnight. Instead, it operates by virtue of the friend's undertaking at t_1 not to give him back the car keys at t_2, together of course with the friend's willingness at t_2 to actually honor that undertaking. My point is not that the friend may prove unreliable, for so may a causal mechanism. It is rather that the precommitment operates via the friend's judgment and decision, and to that extent its operation at t_2 is not entirely under the drinker's ex ante control at t_1.

An advantage of using a noncausal mechanism such as the judgment of a friend is that it enables the agent to bind himself to a principle that does not operate deontologically or rigidly. Most people who condemn drunk driving (in themselves and others) do so without considering that there may be circumstances in which driving with an elevated blood alcohol level is the right thing to do. Suppose I design a mechanism that prevents me from ever starting my car when my blood alcohol level exceeds 0.05 percent. Then I may be dismayed to find that I cannot drive my baby to the hospital if the child becomes desperately ill while I am hosting a cocktail party at my home (and no one else has a car, and no one else can drive, etc., etc.). I discover, in other words, the need for exceptions to the rule. Now if the exceptions are clear-cut, then perhaps a sophisticated mechanism can embody them as well: I install a device that also measures the body temperature of my baby and allows me to drive drunk whenever that temperature exceeds 102 degrees Fahrenheit. But if the exceptions are at all complicated or if delicate judgment is required in order to establish whether exceptional conditions obtain, then of course it will be better to abandon causal mechanisms altogether and instead entrust the car keys to a friend, hoping that the friend will make what is in the circumstances an ethically appropriate decision.

Clearly, if constitutional constraints are regarded as forms of democratic precommitment, then they operate more on the model of the friend's judgment than on the model of a causal mechanism. Except in rare cases (like "dual key" controls of nuclear weapons), constitutional constraints do not operate mechanically, but work instead by vesting a power of decision in some person or body of persons (a court) whose job it is to determine *as a matter of judgment* whether conduct that is contemplated (say, by the legislature) at t_2 violates a constraint written down at t_1.

As I said, the advantage of such forms of constraint is that they do not operate rigidly, but instead leave some room for judgment. The disadvantage is that they then become capable of operating in ways that do not represent the intentions of the agent who instituted them at t_1. Provided that one's intention is sufficiently simpleminded, a causal mechanism can embody it perfectly: The physical rigidity of the mechanism represents, as it were, the strength and single-mindedness of the agent's resolve. Though the machine is a mindless thing, its operation may for that very reason enhance rather than undermine the agent's autonomy, because it works to bind him to exactly the decision *he* intended. But if Agent A has vested a power of decision in someone else, B, with room for the exercise of judgment by B, then one may wonder whether this is really an instance of autonomous precommitment by A. Binding oneself to do at t_2 exactly what one intends at t_1 to do at t_2 is one thing; delivering one's power of decision as to what to do at t_2 over to the judgment of another person is something quite different. Person A may have good reason to do that of course (i.e., surrender his judgment to B) – and *in a sense* that would be a form of precommitment. That is, the *act* of precommitment may be autonomous, but its operation may be something less than a consummation of the agent's autonomy inasmuch as it is subject to the judgment of another. In other words, it would not be a form of precommitment that enabled one to rebut an objection based on the importance of A's hanging on to his autonomy or, in the case of constitutional constraints, an objection on democratic grounds. It would be more like the vote to vest power in a dictator that we discussed in Section I: When the people vote for dictatorship, maybe dictatorship is what they need, and maybe dictatorship is what they should have, but let us not kid ourselves that dictatorship is therefore a form of democracy.

I believe this point is *not* rebutted by showing that an independent power of judgment is indispensable to the sort of constraint that the agent (or the people) want to set up. In a recent book Ronald Dworkin has presented an attractive picture of the United States Constitution in which many of the provisions of the Bill of Rights are taken to embody abstract moral principles.[26] Dworkin argues that an accurate historical understanding of the equal protection clause, for example, precludes any interpretation that does not represent it as a moral principle framed at a very high level of generality.[27] Since it is obvious (and was obvious in 1868) that abstract moral principles cannot be interpreted and applied without the exercise of human judgment, Dworkin believes that the framers of the Fourteenth Amendment evidently intended members of the judiciary to employ their powers of moral judgment to determine how exactly the actions of state legislatures should be constrained in the name of equal protection. Since this is what the states voted for when the amendment was ratified, the arrangement amounts to a deliberate decision by various agents, not to constrain themselves by mechanical means as in Ulysses' case, but to have themselves constrained by others' judgment.

Furthermore, in cases like this, the necessity for judgment cannot be understood except on the assumption that it will sometimes be exercised – and exercised properly – in ways that were not foreseen by those who set up the constraint. After all, if its proper exercise could always be foreseen, then no exercise of judgment would ever really be required; constitutional jurisprudence would become, as we say, "mechanical." Dworkin is quite right to insist, therefore, that once one accepts the abstract-principle interpretation of the Bill of Rights[28] and the analytic connection between abstraction and judgment, it is a mistake to accuse modern judges of violating the framers' intentions simply because the framers did not contemplate or would have been surprised by some particular modern application of their principle.

But there is yet another point about the link between abstraction and judgment that *does* pose difficulties for the precommitment idea. Not only should we not expect particular applications of the principles embodied in the Bill of Rights to be ex ante foreseeable and unsurprising; we should also not expect them to be uncontroversial. The inference of particular applications from a complex principle is something on which people are likely to disagree, particularly if – as Dworkin rightly argues – the inference in every case should be from the whole array of abstract principles embodied in the constitution, not just the principle embodied in the particular provision appealed to.[29] Again, if we value judgment in relation to our constitutional commitments, we should not flinch at this conclusion. But it does eat away at any claim that precommitment is a form of self-government – that is, government not only of the people but *by* the people – or that it preserves the democratic or self-governing character of a regime. The argument to that effect goes as follows.

Early in our tradition, political theorists developed a taxonomy of various forms of constitution, of which the most familiar is the Aristotelian distinction between government by one man, government by a few men, and government by the many. The distinction was not necessarily a matter of whose *will* was to prevail in a society. According to Aristotle, the distinction was needed even in a society ruled by law, since the application of law required judgment and there was a question about who should apply the laws.[30] Judgment foreshadows disagreement, and in politics the question is always how disagreements among the citizens are to be resolved. It is, I think, important to remember that this includes disagreements about rights and justice, and thus disagreements about the things covered by the abstract moral principles to which the people have committed themselves in their constitution. Different forms of government amount to different answers to the question: Whose judgment is to prevail when citizens disagree in their judgments about matters as important as this?

Now there may be good reasons for the people to offer as their answer: "Not us, or our representatives, but the judiciary." If so, that amounts pro tanto to a refusal of self-government.[31] It amounts to the people's embrace of what Aristotle would call "aristocracy" – the rule of the few best.

Of course, it is not wholly aristocratic, for the few best are to exercise their judgment on the interpretation and application of principles that, initially at any rate and in their most general form, are chosen by the people. The fact that authority is accorded to the people's choice as to which abstract principles are to be adopted for interpretation by the judges makes this a mixed constitution.

But the aristocratic nature of the arrangement is not diminished by the mere fact that the aristocrats exercise judgment rather than will. For in our best understanding, politics is *always* a matter of judgment, even at the most abstract level: Even the framing of a provision like the Fourteenth Amendment is an act of judgment – by the people – as to what a good republic now requires (in light of its history, etc.). The democratic claim has always been that the people are entitled to govern themselves by their own judgments. So, to the extent that they invest the judiciary with an overriding power of judgment as to how something as basic as equal protection is to be understood, allowing that judgment to override the judgment of the people or their representatives on this very issue, it is undeniable that in terms of the Aristotelian taxonomy, they have set up what would traditionally be described as a nondemocratic arrangement.

Under these circumstances then – and there is no reason to believe that the problem will be any different with a British bill of rights – the constitutional arrangements we have been discussing cannot really be regarded as a form of precommitment by Agent A at time t_1 to a decision (for time t_2) that A himself has chosen. Instead, they involve a form of submission by A at t_1 to whatever judgment is made at t_2 by another agent, B, in the application of very general principles that A has instructed B to take into account.

One final observation to clarify the point I am making. It is sometimes said that what justifies judicial review is that it would be inappropriate for the representatives of the people (acting by majority decision) to be "judge in their own case," in determining whether a piece of legislation violates the rights of a minority.[32] But if a constitutional provision (protecting minority rights) is really a precommitment of the people or their representatives, then there is in principle nothing whatever inappropriate about asking them: Was this the precommitment you intended? If a dispute arises among the crew as to whether Ulysses wanted to be blindfolded as well as bound to the mast, there is nothing to do but *ask Ulysses*. To refrain from doing so on the ground that this would make him judge in his own case would be absurd – absurd, that is, if the name of the game really is precommitment. Precommitment cannot preserve the aura of autonomy (or democracy in the constitutional case) unless the person bound really is the judge of the point and extent of his being bound. Ulysses, of course, may not be able to give us a rational answer if we do not get around to asking him until he is already under the influence of the Sirens' song. Then there is nothing we can do but make our *own* decision about whether or not to blindfold him. At that stage we should stop justifying *our* decision by calling it a consummation of Ulysses' autonomy; the best we can now say on autonomy grounds is that we are acting, paternalistically, as Ulysses *would have acted* had he been lucid and in possession of full information, not that we are acting in the way he clearly wanted us to act in defense of his autonomy. So, similarly, if we follow the logic of precommitment in the political case, the people are presumably authorities – not judges in their own cause, but *authorities* – on what they have precommitted themselves to. If that authority is challenged – for example, because the people are now thought to be in the very state (of panic or anger, etc.) that they wanted their precommitment to counteract – then all we can say is that the notion of precommitment is now no longer useful in relation to the controversy. Once it becomes unclear or controversial what the people have committed themselves to, there is no longer any basis in the idea of precommitment for defending a particular interpretation against democratic objections.

IV. Disagreements or Weakness of Will?

We have concentrated for a while on the implementation of a precommitment: Is it a causal mechanism, or does it consist rather in entrusting a decision to somebody else's judgment? There are also things to be said about what motivates precommitment in the first place.

In cases of individual precommitment, the agent is imagined to be quite certain, in his lucid moments, about the actions he wants to avoid, the reasons for their undesirability, and the basis on which he might be tempted nevertheless to perform them. The smoker knows that smoking is damaging his health, and he can furnish an explanation in terms of the pathology of nicotine addiction of why he craves a cigarette notwithstanding his possession of that knowledge. The drinker knows the statistics about drunk driving and he knows too how intoxication works. He knows at the beginning of the evening that at midnight both his ability to drive safely and his judgment about his ability to drive safely will be seriously impaired.

These cases fall into recognized categories of decisional pathology, or *akrasia*.[33] Responsible individuals are aware of their own vulnerability to things like lust, laziness, impulse, anger, panic, passion, and intoxication. They are aware that these conditions can lead them to behave in ways they themselves believe to be undesirable. Though that belief may actually accompany the behavior in question, it is often referred to in the literature as a belief held and acted upon "in a calm moment" – a moment when the agent foresees the conditions of akrasia but is not actually afflicted by them, and so is able to make arrangements that lessen the probability that he will behave akratically in the future.

Much of this may be thought to apply in the political realm also. Constitutional constraints may be seen as prophylactics against political akrasia – that is, against the pathology of anger, panic, or greed that is often thought to be endemic in democratic politics. The history of political thought in the West is largely the history of warnings about the hasty, greedy, and intemperate courses on which the masses are likely to embark if they ever get power in their hands. "Men are not apt to change their character by agglomeration," wrote de Tocqueville. "Nor does their patience in the presence of obstacles increase with the consciousness of their strength."[34] If anything, James Madison said, "[b]odies of men are . . . *less* controlled by the dread of reproach and the other motives felt by individuals."[35] The point here is not merely that members of the majority are liable to act unjustly, but rather that they are likely to act in ways they will later regret. They have reason therefore to put themselves on guard against these temptations.

If we are worried about a majority falling upon the property of the rich or the rights of a minority in a moment of greed, panic, or anger, then constitutional precommitment seems an attractive idea. (We should note, however, that such precommitments have been singularly ineffective in the United States, at least as far as moments of national panic are concerned.)[36] But it is questionable whether we should take akrasia as our model for the circumstances in which bills of rights and the judicial review of legislation actually operate.

In most cases in which judicial review is contemplated by the defenders of constitutional constraints – certainly in most of the high-profile cases in the United States – the situation looks something like this:

1. The people commit themselves in their constitution (by a supermajority) to some fairly abstract formula about rights. Some of them (the minority) have misgivings about the principle – they think its adoption is wrong or unwise – while even among those who support its ratification, opinions differ as to what in detail it amounts to.
2. A legislature passes a measure that arguably violates the constitutional provision. The measure is supported by a majority of representatives,

some because they do not believe it falls under the constitutional principle, others because they oppose the constitutional principle and always did.

3. A court, deciding by a simple majority, holds that the legislature's enactment is unconstitutional. Four out of the nine justices argue, however, in dissent, that the legislation should not be struck down. They maintain that the interpretation of the bill of rights that would be required to sustain a finding of unconstitutionality is implausible, mainly on the ground that such interpretation would make the relevant constitutional provision quite unattractive from a moral point of view. Needless to say, their colleagues on the bench do not agree with this.

The disagreement among the justices, then, is in part about what makes a constitutional provision morally unattractive. That, of course, is exactly what the members of the legislature were disagreeing about when they voted on the bill. And it was also one of the focuses of disagreement among the people when the constitutional provision was originally adopted. It is the same disagreement all the way through, though the weight of opinion has shifted back and forth: a supermajority of the people on one side in Decision 1; a simple majority of their legislative representatives on the other side in Decision 2; and a simple majority of justices back in the other direction again in Decision 3. And this is what we should expect when a complex and highly charged moral issue is put in slightly different forms to different constituencies for decision at different times.

My theme in all this is reasonable disagreement, but I cannot restrain myself from saying that anyone who thinks a narrative like this is appropriately modeled by the story of Ulysses and the Sirens is an idiot. Ulysses is sure that he wants to listen but not respond to the Sirens' song; the people in our example are torn. If Ulysses were somehow to untie himself and get ready to dive over the side of the boat and swim to the Sirens, it would be clear to his crew that this was exactly the action he commanded them to restrain; but in most constitutional cases, opinions differ among the citizens as to whether the legislation in question is the sort of thing they wanted (or would or should have wanted) in a founding moment to preempt. What's more, all the judges and all the legislators know in our example that the issue they are facing is one on which reasonable people disagree, whereas in the *Odyssey* the crew members can be assured that Ulysses' straining at or breaking his bonds is the product of a decisional pathology that is well understood by everyone involved, including Ulysses.

In other words, in the constitutional case we are almost always dealing with a society whose members disagree in principle and in detail, even in their "calm" or "lucid" moments, about what rights they have, how those rights are to be conceived of, and what weight they are to be given in relation to other

values. They need not appeal to aberrations in rationality to explain or characterize these disagreements; disagreements about rights are sufficiently explained by the difficulty of the subject matter and what John Rawls refers to
as "the burdens of judgment."[37] A constitutional "precommitment" in these
circumstances is therefore not the triumph of preemptive rationality that it appears to be in the cases of Ulysses and the smoker and the drinker. It is rather
the artificially sustained ascendancy of one view in the polity over other
views while the complex moral issues between them remain unresolved. To
impose the template of precommitment on this situation would smack more
of Procrustes than Ulysses.

A better individual analogy – better, that is, than the case of Ulysses or the
drinker or the smoker – might be the following. Imagine a person – call her
Bridget – who is torn between competing conceptions of religious belief. One
day she opts decisively for fundamentalist faith in a personal God. She commits herself utterly to that view and abjures forever the private library of theological books in her house that, in the past, had excited and sustained her uncertainty. Though she is no book burner, she locks the door of her library and
gives the keys to a friend, with strict instructions never to return them, not
even on demand.

But new issues and old doubts start to creep into Bridget's mind after a
while ("Maybe Tillich was right after all . . ."), and a few months later she
asks for the keys. Should the friend return them? Clearly, this case is quite
different from (say) withholding car keys from the drinker at midnight. Both
involve forms of precommitment. But in Bridget's case, for the friend to sustain the precommitment would be for the friend to take sides, as it were, in a
dispute between two or more conflicting selves or two or more conflicting aspects of the same self within Bridget, each with a claim to rational authority.
It would be to take sides in a way that is simply not determined by any recognizable criteria of pathology or other mental aberration. To uphold the precommitment would be to sustain the temporary ascendancy of one aspect of
the self at the time the library keys were given away and to neglect the fact
that the self that demands them back has an equal claim to respect for *its* way
of dealing with the vicissitudes of theological uncertainty.

Upholding another's precommitment may be regarded as a way of respecting that person's autonomy only if a clear line can be drawn between the aber-
rant mental phenomena the precommitment was supposed to override, on the
one hand, and genuine uncertainty, changes of mind, conversions, and so on,
on the other.[38] In Ulysses' case and in the case of the potential drunk driver,
we can draw such a line. In Bridget's case, we have much more difficulty, and
that is why respecting the precommitment seems more like taking sides in an
internal dispute between two factions warring on roughly equal terms.

As if that weren't bad enough, if we were really looking for an analogy to the judicial review example, we would imagine the theological case with this difference – that Bridget hands the keys of the library to a *group* of friends, who then decide by majority voting when it is appropriate to return them to her. They find they have to decide by majority voting, since they disagree about the issue along the very lines of the uncertainty that is torturing Bridget herself.

Clearly there are dangers in any simplistic analogy between the rational autonomy of individuals and the democratic governance of a community. The idea of a society binding itself against certain legislative acts in the future is problematic in cases where members disagree with one another about the need for such bonds or, if they agree abstractly about the need, disagree about their content or character. It is particularly problematic when such disagreements can be expected to persist and to develop and change in unpredictable ways. And it becomes ludicrously problematic in cases where the form of precommitment is to assign the decision procedurally to another body, whose members are just as torn and conflicted about the issues as the members of the first body were.

If, moreover, the best explanation of these persisting disagreements is that the issues the society is addressing are themselves very difficult, then we have no justification whatever for regarding the temporary ascendancy of one or other party to the disagreement as an instance of full and rational precommitment on the part of the entire society. In these circumstances the logic of precommitment must simply be put aside, and we must leave the members of the society to work out their differences and to change their minds in collective decision-making over time, the best way they can.

V. Ulysses, the People

It may be thought that the model of Ulysses or the potentially drunk driver cannot be extended *anyway* to constitutional issues because in constitutional cases we are dealing not with one individual binding himself, but with a complex collective agent – consisting of millions of people – binding itself by setting certain of its own agencies at odds with one another. Moreover, if we apply this to instances like American constitutional law, we have to contemplate "the people" not just as millions of disparate individuals but as an entity that is continuous over several centuries, so that our being bound today by formulas laid down by a group of slaveholding revolutionaries in 1791 is represented as a form of autonomous precommitment *by us*. It might be thought that this strains the credibility of the elements of self, agency, and autonomy involved in the precommitment idea.

What difference does it make, then, when we move from decisional strategies by individuals, intended to last for a few hours or a few days, to the constitutional commitments of a whole people intended to endure over centuries?

The main difference is the one we have just finished discussing. In almost every case, a decision at t_1 by a whole people (comprising millions of individuals) to preclude a certain decision, D, by them at t_2 will be a subject of disagreement. At t_1, opinions will differ as to whether D is undesirable and, even if it is, as to whether it is properly the subject of constitutional constraint. Nevertheless, a precommitment will not be entered into a t_1 unless many more people think D is undesirable than favor D. What's more, those who vote for a constraint will do so, presumably, because they fear that among the present opponents of D, there are some who may be driven at some future time t_2 by panic, greed, or anger to vote in its favor; that is, they fear an akratic shift in the balance of opinion. But suppose now that we have reached t_2 and that despite the constitutional constraint, D has somehow found itself on the political agenda and it turns out that a majority of the people are in favor of D. If the desirability of D was controversial at t_1, then the akratic explanation is not the only possible explanation of the shift in opinion. An alternative and more charitable (more respectful) explanation is that, as public debate has gone on, many people have become convinced by the arguments in favor of D that were put forward originally by the minority at t_1 or by new arguments that have been put forward since.

The plurality of a political community, the inevitable existence of diversity of opinion and reasonable disagreement among them on all matters of rights and justice, and the dynamics of both formal and informal deliberation over time – these three things mean that we are seldom in a position to say, with any assurance, that majority support for a given position at t_2 represents the weakness or panic that opponents of the position thought at t_1 they had reason to fear. It *may* represent the akrasia they feared. But equally it may represent nothing more insidious than the sort of shift in the balance of opinion that we associate naturally with ongoing deliberation, particularly as circumstances change and one generation succeeds another in the body politic.

We saw in Section IV that it is possible to construct an individual analog of this: Bridget was genuinely torn over theological issues, and she resolved one way at t_1 but changed her mind at t_2.[39] This sort of thing is perfectly familiar. But although changes of mind are as familiar as constancy in the case of individuals, we are not familiar with anything remotely approaching Ulysses-like steadfastness and unanimity in the case of large political communities. Unanimous agreement, as John Locke pointed out, "is next impossible ever to be had."[40] So there is something spectacularly inappropriate about using the unequivocal precommitment of an individual as a model for constitutional constraint. The plurality of politics, the reasonableness of disagreement, and the dynamics of debate mean that Bridget should be our model, not Ulysses. And as we have seen, it is not possible to construct in Bridget's case the sort of account of precommitment that would allow us, in the political case, to finesse the democratic objection.

I mentioned earlier that one of the circumstances contributing to the dynamics of public debate and the corresponding shifts in public opinion is that the membership of the political community is constantly changing. Stephen Holmes cites Thomas Jefferson's calculation that actuarially (at the end of the eighteenth century) "half of those of 21 years and upwards living at any one instant will be dead in 18 years 8 months."[41] Why, then, said Jefferson, should a subsequent generation be bound by constitutional commitments entered into not by them but by their ancestors?

If political precommitments are understood primarily as individual strategies, then this objection succeeds. Suppose Tom votes for a law requiring the use of seat belts in automobiles because he wants to overcome his lazy and akratic neglect of his own safety.[42] And suppose the law passes. What Tom has done then is band together with a sufficiently large number of others, each hoping to set up and make use of this collective mechanism in order to bind him- or herself. Though the law is a coercive one, it can be defended against autonomy-based critiques, inasmuch as each of the coerced individuals deliberately sought it as a mechanism of enhancing his or her responsible individual autonomy. But once Tom and his original band of fellow citizens pass away, it will not be possible to offer *this defense* of the seat-belt law to their children and grandchildren. Of course, Tom's descendants may renew the law or allow it to remain on the books unrepealed for the very same reasons that led Tom to vote in its favor. Then again, they may not. And if they don't, we cannot defend the law *to them* as a precommitment, for it was at best a precommitment by the individuals of Tom's generation, not theirs.

However, when the precommitment idea is deployed in a political context, it is usually deployed in terms of a precommitment by *the people* as a collective entity, rather than as a series of precommitments by individual voters taking advantage of collective mechanisms such as laws. In cases where the precommitment is conceived to be collective, the intergenerational objection is not by itself decisive. After all, if citizens may *ever* be bound by legislation that commands anything less than unanimous support – and opponents of constitutional constraint, of course, believe that they may – then it must be because they have constituted themselves as a political entity, a community that is not simply the aggregate of its individual members. Ronald Dworkin asks:

Why am I *free* – how could I be thought to be governing *myself* – when I must obey what other people decide even if I think it wrong or unwise or unfair to me or my family? What difference can it make how many people must think the decision right and

wise and fair if it is not necessary that *I* do? . . . The answer to these enormously difficult questions begins in the communal conception of collective action. If I am a genuine member of a political community, its act is in some pertinent sense my act, even
when I argued and voted against it. . . .[43]

Opinions differ, of course, as to what this communal conception requires.
But at the very least, citizens must share some sense that they are "all in this
together." That is, they must share the sense that there are certain common
problems that are worth their while solving together despite their divergent
views as to what the solution ought to be. And they must connect this shared
sense to their support for mechanisms of collective decision that allow them
to precipitate out of their disagreements a single course of action that they accept as binding on all.

Their sense of sharing these concerns and commitments with others will involve some view – probably tacit – as to who these "others" are. That view
will have a temporal as well as a geographic dimension. People will ask themselves, "Among how many people must a common view be taken on these issues?" and their answers will yield theories of borders, federalism, and the
territorial separation of national and state jurisdictions. And they will also ask
themselves, "How important is it for our shared solution to a common problem to extend, and remain in force, over time?" Just as their answers to the
first question will indicate why a person on one side of a border is conceived
to be bound by a certain law while someone a few miles away is not, so their
answer to the second question will yield a theory as to why individuals may
sometimes be bound, not only by laws they voted against, but also by laws
voted upon decades before they were born.

I am not saying what their answers ought to be, and I am certainly not
saying that there is no political community unless its laws are taken to bind
future generations in perpetuity. But it is more than likely that the requi-
site sense of membership and community will extend across generations, so
that in principle there is no difficulty about being bound by the decision of
one's ancestors. So, if our forefathers deemed certain precommitments necessary, the mere fact that those precommitments are supposed to extend over
time, and outlast those who enacted them, is not in itself a reason for not honoring them or for condemning them as incompatible with the idea of self-
government.

That said, however, the intergenerational dimension might bear on our discussion in the following way. It is natural, when these possibilities are being
considered prospectively (as they are, presently, in the United Kingdom), to
focus on the ex ante rationality and autonomy of precommitment. It seems
like a good idea *now* for us to commit ourselves preemptively against *future*
violations of rights. But it is important that those who embark upon constitu-

tional change have the capacity to look upon what they are presently doing with the eyes of years, even centuries, to come.[44] We have to have in mind that at some future date a large number of people, favoring a change in some law or in the understanding of some right, will experience the force of the constraint that we are setting up as a restriction on their autonomy.

They might want to reform laws regarding electoral campaign finance, for example, but find that their efforts are constrained by a free speech provision in their constitution. Opponents of campaign finance reform may seek to mollify the anger that this constraint generates among the majority by defending it as a precommitment entered into by a previous generation. Now it is possible that the majority will be deaf to this characterization, and deaf to it for the very reason that the precommitment was set up: The majority is in precisely the pathological state that the precommitment was designed to counteract. But it is also possible that the members of the majority will resist the precommitment characterization, not because they are overwhelmed by passion or anger, but because they disagree with the ideas about free speech that seemed plausible to their ancestors. Ex ante the precommitment seemed to be a good idea; ex post, it might seem silly given what we know about democracies, mass media, and electoral campaigns. And if the majority now knows that even at the time the precommitment was entered into, there were voices warning against attempting to bind future generations in matters as complex as this, it will be particularly inclined to regard the constraint as unreasonable. Now, of course, that is hindsight; that is a view of the precommitment ex post. But it is a view that, imaginatively, the framers of the precommitment ought to take very seriously ex ante. They should ask themselves: Is there a reason now to doubt that this provision will seem reasonable as a precommitment to those whom it constrains in the future? It seems to me that the existence of good-faith disagreement about the content of the precommitment at the time it is proposed is *always* a reason for answering that question in the affirmative. Disagreement ex ante portends unreasonableness ex post.

So although the intergenerational dimension is not necessarily conclusive against the precommitment characterization of constitutional constraints, it is likely to be conclusive in fact inasmuch as the future has an uncomfortable tendency to vindicate the wisdom of those whose views or apprehensions might have been in the minority at the time the constraint was originally imposed.

I guess it follows from this that a constitutional constraint is less unreasonable *qua* precommitment the greater the opportunity for altering it by processes of constitutional amendment.[45] We need to bear in mind, however, that such processes are usually made very difficult; indeed, their difficulty – the difference, for example, between the majority required for constitutional amendment and the majority required for routine legislative change – is precisely definitive of the constraint in question. So if there is an objection to a certain constitutional constraint, we cannot rebut that objection by pointing to a formal opportunity for amendment or change; the limited nature and extent of that opportunity are precisely what are being objected to. All we can say is that the objection would have been even stronger if the opportunity for amendment had not existed. Certainly, the opportunity for constitutional amendment adds nothing to the case for considering a constitutional constraint as a *precommitment*.[46] At best, all it does is alter our understanding of what it is that we are trying to defend by presenting it in this light.[47]

VI. Constitutive Rules

I noted earlier that Jon Elster had some doubts about whether constitutional constraints could really be described as precommitments, since they were not "external" to the people who set them up.[48] We said that the answer to this is that the constraints are external to some of the institutions set up by the people to act in their name, even though they are not external to the people themselves, considered as "popular sovereign." I now want to return to this point, for it raises interesting questions about the relation between constitutional constraints and the constitutive rules of political institutions.

A bunch of individuals must constitute themselves as a people – that is, as a political community – even in order to frame a constitution. But mostly what they do in their framing is to construct what they hope will be an enduring set of institutions that can embody decision procedures and mechanisms of collective action. In *Passions and Constraint,* Stephen Holmes has argued that constitutional constraints have important *constitutive* functions in this regard:

[C]onstitutions may be usefully compared to the rules of a game and even to the rules of grammar. While *regulative* rules (for instance, 'no smoking') govern preexistent activities, *constitutive* rules (for instance, 'bishops move diagonally') make a practice possible for the first time. . . . Constitutions do not merely limit power; they can create and organize power as well as give it direction. . . . When a constituent assembly establishes a decision procedure, rather than restricting a preexistent will, it actually creates a framework in which the nation can for the first time, have a will.[49]

The point is clearest in the case of political procedures. A deliberative assembly needs procedural rules in order to facilitate and focus its debates.[50] If these rules are themselves up for grabs in the very sessions they are supposed to structure, then it will be hard for a large group of diverse deliberators to proceed with any assurance that they are not talking at cross-purposes or going around in circles. Like the rules of grammar, procedural rules cannot be regarded simply as a way of handcuffing or restraining participants.[51] Instead, they make participation possible, by setting out a matrix of interaction in which particular contributions can take their place and be "registered," so to speak. Of course, the rules of grammar are not really something we *decide* upon in order to facilitate speech. They just emerge; we find ourselves with them as part and parcel of our ability to communicate.[52] But in the context of an enacted constitution, procedural rules are the product of decisions made in order to constitute public decision-making. As Holmes puts it: "Decisions are made on the basis of pre-decisions. Electoral choices are made on the basis of constitutional choices. When they enter the voting-booth, for instance, voters decide who shall be president, but not how many presidents there shall be."

All this is very important. It is equally important, however, to notice the differences between this form of procedural "pre-decision" and precommitment properly so called.

Ulysses ties himself to the mast so that when the question arises as to whether he should leave the ship in response to the Sirens' song, any decision he makes to leave will be ineffective. Similarly, the drinker hands his car keys to a friend, to make it that much less likely that he will decide in favor of driving when the question about getting home from the party arises at midnight. Those are examples of precommitment. To adapt a definition from Jon Elster,[53] an agent carries out a certain decision at time t_1 in order to decrease the probability that he will carry out another decision at time t_2.

But in Holmes's example, the procedural rule ("only one president") adopted at t_1 is not supposed to operate when (or if) the people are deciding at a later time how many presidents to have; it is not intended to constrain any decision on that occasion. Instead, it is designed to operate at a time when people are choosing who is to be the president. Unlike Ulysses' tying himself to the mast or the drinker's giving his car keys to a friend, setting up a procedural rule is not designed to increase the probability of any particular decision at t_2; the point of it is simply to frame and constitute a type of decision-making procedure.[54] Its importance in structuring that procedure does not allow us to infer anything about its precluding any later reconsideration of the number of chief executives to have. (Likewise the constitutive importance of the rules of baseball or the conventions of English spelling does not show that it is wrong or unwise to vary these rules; all it shows is that, however much we vary the rules, they have to be settled on any occasion in which someone wants to engage in the practice or play the game that the rules constitute.)

Sure, there may be *other* arguments for not constantly revising the constitutive rules of various activities. If we change the rules of baseball too often, the fans will be confused and the players unable to develop a consistent set of skills. Change the conventions of spelling, and the vice-president may be unable to keep up. There are well-known conservative arguments in politics as well, of which the best known are those of Edmund Burke:

By this unprincipled facility of changing the state as often, and as much, and as in many ways as there are floating fancies or fashions, the whole chain and continuity of the commonwealth would be broken. No one generation could link with another. Men would become little better than the flies of a summer.[55]

Now this Burkean argument may well motivate constitutional precommitments as a precaution against hasty alteration of the constitutive procedures of our politics. We entrench our present procedures at t_1 against change at t_2 because we fear that if we were to indulge our half-baked reformist impulses at t_2 we would become little more than the "flies of a summer." And if we do this, our precommitment will be liable to all the difficulties about pluralism and disagreement that we have already considered – for nothing is surer than that Burke's arguments about the dangers of constitutional change are matters on which reasonable people disagree.

My present point, however, is that it would be a mistake to confuse those Burkean precommitments with the constitutive procedures themselves. Accordingly, it is misleading to suggest – as Stephen Holmes suggests – that constitutional constraints have the facilitating and enabling character of constitutive rules of procedure.

VII. Precommitment and Assurance

So far, we have established that constitutive procedures should not be assimilated to precommitments. But precommitments of other sorts may be practically or politically necessary in the constitution of a people.

In a purely formal sense, a political community may be constituted by a rule about voting, but such procedural rules constitute a meaningful political reality only in relation to the legal and social context that conditions the character of public debate. Government by popular majority is one thing if votes are taken after lengthy periods of argument back and forth among the citizens and their representatives; it is quite another thing if votes are taken without any deliberative interaction at all or if the political culture is such that most people are afraid to voice their opposition as soon as any hint of majority consensus begins to emerge. Indeed, these conditions concerning deliberation are arguably so important that majority decision may amount, in effect, to something quite different – to a different form of government, to the constitution of a quite different sort of "we, the people" – depending on the conditions. Holmes argues that, of all the different forms of government that may result, only some are entitled to be called "democracy":

Democracy is government by rational and free public discussion among legally equal citizens, not simply the enforcement of the will of the majority. . . . Not any 'will,' but only a will formed in vigorous and wide-open debate should be given sovereign authority. The legally guaranteed right of opposition is therefore a fundamental norm of democratic government; it provides an essential precondition for the formation of democratic public opinion.[56]

The idea is that in setting up democratic institutions, in constituting the very possibility of "the will of the people," the members of a society intend to commit themselves not just to any old form of majoritarianism but to a particular form of majority decision, namely the sovereignty of a popular "will formed in vigorous and wide-open debate." This they cannot do without, at the same time doing their best to create an open and tolerant climate for the effective expression of political opposition and dissent. And that in turn requires them to establish certain guarantees that minority opposition and dissent will not evoke any backlash from either temporary or permanent majorities. Such guarantees – the argument goes – are not credible unless the people have put in place constitutional mechanisms to restrain their own natural repressive response to the irritation of minority criticism. A precommitment of this kind may look negative, and members of the majority may feel that its immediate effect is to prevent them from doing things they want to do. But in the medium and long term, constitutional guarantees of free speech and loyal opposition are indispensable for meaningful political debate. Thus, they are necessary conditions for the very thing the members of the majority want from their constitution: the emergence, through majoritarian procedures, of an informed and effective basis for popular decision. That – as I understand it – is Holmes's argument.

It is an attractive argument. And I believe it would amount to a compelling case for the enactment of constitutional constraints immune to subsequent legislative revision if either of two conditions were met. It would be compelling if the people were constant and unanimous in their conception of majority decision and of the conditions necessary for its effective realization. Or – even if they did not agree about those issues – it would be a compelling argument for constitutional constraints if minorities had reason to fear that any legislative consideration of the rules about free speech and loyal opposition would be a way of crushing or silencing dissent.

In fact, neither condition is satisfied. Though almost every defender of majority decision is committed to *some* form of deliberative democracy, opinions vary widely as to what deliberation should amount to and as to the legal, political, and social conditions that should surround it. I should not need to labor the point, but here are a few of the issues about which reasonable democrats disagree: proportional representation, referendums, the frequency of elections, term limits, the basis of electoral districting, state-funded access to television airtime for candidates, and campaign finance generally. People disagree about the publication of opinion polls, about free speech in shopping malls, about the influence of special interest groups and political action committees, and about the public's interest in the internal workings of political parties. They disagree too about such fraught topics as heckling, hate speech, ethnic representation, criminal defamation, and the concepts of sedition, insurrection, and subversion.

We are blessed with a rich and thoughtful literature on all of this, from the *Federalist* papers to such modern tomes as Charles Beitz's *Political Equality*, Lani Guinier's *The Tyranny of the Majority*, and Cass Sunstein's *The Partial Constitution*.[57] The various opposing accounts put forward by these and other thinkers amount to diverse attempts to work out in detail the nature of the political system to which we have committed ourselves – or (more correctly) to which we are, in our ongoing political and constitutional practices, in the process of committing ourselves.

The persistence of these disagreements is characteristic of all modern democracies, and in most societies there is a natural connection between this sort of discussion among intellectuals, constitutionalists, and political scientists and the more formal processes by which the people and their representatives debate and vote on proposals for constitutional reform. Voters in New Zealand recently adopted and made use of a system of proportional representation; voters in the United Kingdom will soon have the opportunity to decide among various proposals for reform of the second chamber of their legislature; and electoral campaign finance is on the legislative agenda almost everywhere. Each country studies the constitutional experience of the others; in every one of these debates, citizens weigh complex arrays of pros and cons; and though people and their professors may plead passionately for one option or another, debates about constitutional structure are by and large conducted in a spirit of mutual respect and in common acknowledgement that this is not an area of life where the truth is well known and self-evident.

In some countries, effective decisions on constitutional structure may be made by parliaments, and of course the parliamentarians disagree among themselves as to what is desirable. In other countries, they are made by popular voting in referendums, and it turns out, predictably, that the people disagree as well. Even in countries like the United States where the political culture entrusts these issues largely to the courts, the justices' decisions are seldom unanimous. It turns out that the judges disagree as much as anyone else – and disagree reasonably and in good faith – about the nature of their constitutional stewardship and the commitments of principle that stewardship is supposed to embody.

All this is surely healthy; it is exactly what we should expect, and we can describe it – for the purposes of legal and political philosophy – in any number of ways. But one thing, it seems to me, we cannot say: We cannot describe this process in terms of a set of unequivocal popular precommitments to a particular form of political decision-making. How are collective decisions to be made in politics? All we can say is that this is something we are continuing to work on.

I said that the argument we have been considering in this section would amount to a compelling case for constitutional constraints immune to legislative revision if either of two conditions were satisfied – that is, either if the people's commitments in this respect were settled, constant, and unequivocal or if revisiting such issues threatened grave danger to dissidents or minorities. We have just seen that the first of these conditions is not satisfied. The second is not satisfied either.

Dissidents do need an assurance that their opposition will not elicit a repressive or murderous response. In some countries (including some that call themselves democracies) that assurance is tenuous or nonexistent. This is a matter of great concern, but it is not what interests us here; in those countries constitutional structures have failed altogether. There may, however, be one or two countries where the assurance that dissidents need actually does exist by virtue of constitutional structure, but where it is so fragile that any attempt by the people or their representatives to revisit and vote upon issues of political structure would reasonably be seen by minorities as a way of attacking and undermining their guarantee of freedom and loyal opposition. Perhaps some of the new democracies of Eastern Europe and the former Soviet Union fall into this category. Arguably, however, these are the countries that can least afford the constitutional rigidity that the precommitment idea involves;[58] their people need to be able to experiment with a variety of detailed procedural forms as, slowly, over the *decades,* they attempt to elaborate their own constitutional traditions. At any rate, the specifications I have given – opposition freedoms guaranteed in fact by constitutional constraints but in a way that is so fragile that they would be threatened by any legislative attempt to revisit or restructure those constraints – do not apply to the United States and they do not apply to the United Kingdom. In both countries there are robust and established traditions of political liberty (which have flourished often despite the best efforts of the judiciary), and in both countries there are vigorous debates about political structure that seem likely to proceed without threatening minority freedoms.

For that reason, then, and because these background issues of political structure, political procedure, and political culture remain the subject of ongoing, healthy, and benign disagreement, the panic-stricken model of Odyssean precommitment seems singularly inappropriate as a basis or template for constitutional theory.

Notes

This is a slightly modified version of chapter 12 of Jeremy Waldron, *Law and Disagreement* (Oxford University Press, forthcoming).
1 What this will involve is probably the incorporation into British law of the European Convention on Human Rights, conferring on British courts the powers of interpretation and enforcement presently vested in the European Court of Human Rights at Strasbourg.

2 It is remarkable how rarely books and articles on American constitutional law refer to constitutional arrangements in other countries. It is as though "Constitution" were a proper name rather than the name of a kind of thing whose nature could best be understood by examining and comparing a variety of instances. For a critique of American parochialism in this regard, see Mary Ann Glendon, *Rights Talk: The Impoverishment of Political Discourse* (New York: Free Press, 1991), 153–70.

3 See Alexander Bickel, *The Least Dangerous Branch: The Supreme Court at the Bar of Politics* (New Haven, Conn.: Yale University Press, 1962), 16.

4 Ronald Dworkin, *A Bill of Rights for Britain* (London: Chatto & Windus, 1990), 36–7.

5 Thomas Hobbes, *Leviathan,* ed. Richard Tuck (Cambridge University Press, 1991), 129–38; John Locke, *Two Treatises of Government,* ed. Peter Laslett (Cambridge University Press, 1988), II, para. 132, p. 354.

6 Thomas Hobbes, *De Cive: The English Version,* ed. Howard Warrender (Oxford: Clarendon Press, 1983), 129–40.

7 Locke, *Two Treatises,* II, para. 94, pp. 329–30 and para 149, pp. 366–7. I have discussed this view of Locke's at some length in "Locke's Legislature," in *The Dignity of Legislation* (the 1996 Seeley Lectures) (Cambridge University Press, forthcoming), ch. 5.

8 See Paul Brest, "Further Beyond the Republican Revival: Toward Radical Republicanism," *Yale Law Journal* 97 (1988): 1204–63.

9 See C. G. Tiedeman, *The Unwritten Constitution of the United States* (New York: Putnam's, 1890).

10 See Geoffrey Marshall, *Constitutional Conventions: The Rules and Forms of Political Accountability* (Oxford: Clarendon Press, 1984). There is also an accessible account of this aspect of the British constitution in Jeremy Waldron, *The Law* (London: Routledge, 1990), 56–87.

11 This example is adapted from Bruce Ackerman and David Golove, "Is NAFTA Constitutional?" *Harvard Law Review* 108 (1995): 799–929.

12 See Jeremy Waldron, "A Right-Based Critique of Constitutional Rights," *Oxford Journal of Legal Studies* 13 (1993): 18–51, at 27.

13 Samuel Freeman, "Constitutional Democracy and the Legitimacy of Judicial Review," *Law and Philosophy* 9 (1990): 353. See also Jeremy Waldron, "Freeman's Defense of Judicial Review," *Law and Philosophy* 13 (1994): 27–41.

14 Freeman, "Constitutional Democracy," 353–4.

15 Quoted in Jon Elster, *Ulysses and the Sirens: Studies in Rationality and Irrationality* (Cambridge University Press, 1984), 36.

16 See also the discussion of strong evaluation and second-order desires in Harry Frankfurt, "Freedom of the Will and the Concept of a Person" *Journal of Philosophy* 68 (1971): 55–81 and Charles Taylor, "What Is Human Agency?" in his collection *Human Agency and Language: Philosophical Papers* (Cambridge University Press, 1985), vol. 1.

17 Immanuel Kant, *Grounding for the Metaphysics of Morals,* trans. J. Ellington (Indianapolis: Hackett, 1981), 44 (p. 440 of vol. 4 of the Prussian Academy edition of Kant's Works).

18 We shall consider Holmes's somewhat more subtle view in Sections VI and VII.

19 Stephen Holmes, *Passions and Constraint: On the Theory of Liberal Democracy* (Chicago: University of Chicago Press, 1995), 135.

20 Elster, *Ulysses*, 42.

21 Ibid., 43 (my emphasis). In general, Elster says, decisions to decide have very little impact: "I decide that I shall decide that *p*" has the same ritual and redundant sound as "if someone were to buy several copies of the morning paper to assure himself that what it said was true." (Quoting Ludwig Wittgenstein, *Philosophical Investigations*, para. 265.)

22 Jon Elster, *Solomonic Judgments: Studies in the Limits of Rationality* (Cambridge University Press, 1989), 196 (emphasis in original).

23 See John Rawls, *Political Liberalism* (New York: Columbia University Press, 1993), 234–5.

24 See the discussion at the end of Section V.

25 Elster, *Ulysses*, 42.

26 Ronald Dworkin, *Freedom's Law* (Cambridge, Mass.: Harvard University Press, 1996), ch. 1. See also Ronald Dworkin, *A Matter of Principle* (Cambridge, Mass.: Harvard University Press, 1985), 69–71.

27 Dworkin, *Freedom's Law*, 8–10.

28 Not of all its provisions, of course. Dworkin argues that the Third Amendment, for example, does not on its face amount to a commitment of principle. Id. at 8–9.

29 Id. at 150. See also Ronald Dworkin, *Law's Empire* (Cambridge, Mass.: Harvard University Press, 1986), 250–4.

30 See Aristotle, *The Politics*, ed. Stephen Everson (Cambridge University Press, 1988), bk. III, ch. 15, p. 76 (1286a25–30).

31 This is Abraham Lincoln's position in the First Inaugural Address, in his *Speeches and Writings, 1859–1965* (New York: Library of America, n.d.), 215, at 220:

No foresight can anticipate, nor any document of reasonable length contain express provisions for all possible questions. Shall fugitives from labor be surrendered by national or by State authority? The Constitution does not expressly say. *May* Congress prohibit slavery in the territories? The Constitution does not expressly say. *Must* Congress protect slavery in the territories? The Constitution does not expressly say.

From questions of this class spring all our constitutional controversies, and we divide upon them into majorities and minorities. If the minority will not acquiesce, the majority must, or the government must cease. There is no other alterative; for continuing the government, is acquiescence on one side or the other. . . . Unanimity is impossible; the rule of a minority, as a permanent arrangement, is wholly inadmissible; so that rejecting the majority principle, anarchy, or despotism in some form, is all that is left.

And it was under *this* heading – "despotism in some form" – that Lincoln went on to discuss the prospect of the Supreme Court's having the final say, indicating his belief that if that were to happen, "the people will have ceased, to be their own rulers, having, to that extent, practically resigned their government, into the hands of that eminent tribunal" (id., 221).

32 See Dworkin, *Freedom's Law*, at 16.

33 This is Elster's description in *Ulysses*, 36–7. The classic discussion of weakness of the will is, of course, *The Nichomachean Ethics of Aristotle*, bk. VII. chs. 1–10.

34 Alexis de Tocqueville, *Democracy in America*, trans. Henry Reeve (New Rochelle, N.Y.: Arlington House, n.d.), 1: 249.

35 James Madison, Speech of August 7, 1787, excerpted in *The Mind of the Founder: Sources of the Political Thought of James Madison,* ed. Marvin Meyers (Hanover, N.H.: Banders University Press, 1973), 396. The passage continues: "Hence the liability of the rights of property, and of the impartiality of the laws affecting it, to be violated by Legislative majorities having an interest real or supposed in the injustice: Hence agrarian laws, and other leveling schemes: Hence the cancelling of debts, and other violations of contracts."

36 See, e.g., Debs v. United States 249 U.S. 211, 39 S.Ct. 252, 63 L.Ed. 566 (1919) and Korematsu v. United States 323 U.S. 214, 65 S.Ct. 193, 89 L.Ed. 194 (1944).

37 Rawls, *Political Liberalism,* 54–8.

38 For an excellent discussion, see Thomas C. Schelling, *Choice and Consequences: Perspectives of an Errant Economist* (Cambridge, Mass.: Harvard University Press, 1984), ch. 4. See also Thomas C. Schelling, "Ethics, Law and the Exercise of Self-Command," in Sterling McMurrin, ed., *Liberty, Equality and Law: Selected Tanner Lectures on Moral Philosophy* (Salt Lake City: University of Utah Press, 1987).

39 Schelling argues in "Ethics, Law, and the Exercise of Self-Command," that the political case can illuminate the individual case (as opposed to, or as well as, vice versa). He says that in all instances of individual precommitment, we are dealing in effect with the politics of two or more "selves" within a single person. This, of course, does not make the political cases any easier.

40 Locke, *Two Treatises,* II, para. 98, pp. 332–3.

41 Holmes, *Passions and Constraint,* 142, citing Thomas Jefferson, *Writings,* ed. Merrill Peterson (New York: Library of America, 1984), 961.

42 I am grateful to Amy Gutmann for this example and for this way of understanding precommitment.

43 Dworkin, *Freedom's Law,* 22.

44 See Hannah Arendt, *On Revolution* (Harmondsworth: Penguin Books, 1973), 198.

45 This point was made by Ronald Dworkin in discussion at the New York University Law School Program for the Study of Law, Philosophy and Social Theory, Fall 1996.

46 If we find Ulysses bound to the mast, the fact that the bonds are not as tight as they could be, and might have been loosened by him after a painful struggle, does not by itself show that the bonds represent a precommitment!

47 See also the discussion in the first few pages of Section III, above.

48 Elster, *Solomonic Judgments,* 196. See the beginning of Section III, above.

49 Holmes, *Passions and Constraint,* 163–4.

50 See Jeremy Waldron, "The Dignity of Legislation" (the 1994 Gerber Lecture), *Maryland Law Review* 54 (1995): 633–55 esp. 659–63.

51 See Holmes, *Passions and Constraint,* 163.

52 Cf. David Hume's observation about promises, conventions, and the emergence of language, in *A Treatise of Human Nature,* ed. L. A. Selby-Bigge (Oxford: Clarendon Press, 1888), bk. III, part II, sec. ii, pp. 490.

53 Elster, *Ulysses,* 39.

54 I think this is acknowledged in Holmes, *Passions and Constraints,* 174: "[T]he framers . . . did not have specific aims (to lose weight, to stop smoking) which

they wished to achieve despite the weakness of will which would foreseeably afflict their posterity."

55 Edmund Burke, *Reflections on the Revolution in France* (1789) (Harmondsworth: Penguin Books, 1969), 192–3.

56 Holmes, *Passions and Constraint,* 171.

57 Charles Beitz, *Political Equality* (Princeton, N.J.: Princeton University Press, 1989); Lani Guinier, *The Tyranny of the Majority* (New York: Free Press, 1995); Cass Sunstein, *The Partial Constitution* (Cambridge, Mass.: Harvard University Press, 1993).

58 See Stephen Holmes and Cass Sunstein, "The Politics of Constitutional Revision in Eastern Europe," in Sanford Levinson, ed., *Responding to Imperfection: The Theory and Practice of Constitutional Amendment* (Princeton, N.J.: Princeton University Press, 1995), pp. 275–306. The observations with which Holmes and Sunstein conclude their discussion are worth quoting at length: "The basic issues with which contemporary politicians in Eastern Europe must grapple concern territorial boundaries, the question of political membership, the assignment of first property rights and the sudden redistribution of private wealth (including *nomenklatura* privatization), settling scores or closing books on the past. These problems, faced by no Western democracy today, cannot be easily resolved by invoking liberal principles. And they cannot be addressed judicially, by a nonaccountable body of knowledgeable men and women. They will also not be imposed by a conquering army and accepted by a defeated and morally chastened people. They can be resolved only politically. Crucial decisions must be made with all the messiness of parliamentary bargaining and ad hoc compromise, carried out to some extent under the public eye. . . . It is futile and even illegitimate to attempt at the outset to entrench certain answers in a constitutional framework immunized against change. Attempts to depoliticize or juridify constitution making are unreasonable in societies where the future is so open and the choices so basic and so large" (305–6).

Index

abortion, 99, 118, 133
absolute entrenchment, 136n14
abstraction and judgment, 279–80
accountability, 85, 90–1
Ackerman, Bruce, 26, 76–7, 78, 80, 86,
  90, 97n64, 102, 135n11, 151n129,
  218–19
Act of Union (1707), 154
adjudicated Constitution, 240; gap
  between Constitution and, 241, 242;
  judicially unenforced constitutional
  rights at one with, 251; limited scope
  of, 243–4
adjudicated constitutional outcomes,
  265
adjudication: constitutional, 105, 111,
  213, 238–9; constitutional,
  interpretation central to, 177, 183;
  constitutional, pragmatist approach
  to, 146n78; non-rule-based, 48;
  pattern of, over time, 244
administrative regulation, authority of,
  210
affirmative action, 99, 133
African-Americans, 244
agency, authorship in default of, 85
akrasia, 2, 11, 13, 282, 286, 287
Alexander, Larry, 1–15
allegiance to Constitution, authorship
  and, 66–7
allocation of power, norms regarding,
  129

Amar, Akhil R., 228n11
amendment(s), 3, 8, 100, 101, 102–3,
  105, 153, 161, 185, 187, 219, 226–7,
  236; difficulty of, 137n15, 264–5;
  enforcing, 122; justification of, 174;
  opportunity for, 289–90; procedure
  for, 33–4, 195–6
amendment process, 135n11, 228n11
America, demo-graphy in, 211–26
American Civil Liberties Union, 140n41
American Legal Realism, 16
anarchy, 2, 3, 4
Andros, Sir Edmund, 40
Answer to the Nineteen Propositions, 18
antidiscrimination norm, 106–7, 112
architecture, constitutional, 237
argument, constitutional, 146n78
argument from consent, 162–4
argument from rule of recognition,
  160–2
aristocracy, 280
Aristotle, 279, 280
Arrow, Kenneth, 11, 13
Articles of Confederation, 255
associations, rights of, 21–2
assurance, precommitment and, 292–5
Austin, John, 207, 208
authoritative voice, 212
authority: consent as source of, 162; of
  constitutional law, 219, 222;
  constitutional-legal, 76; grounds of,
  210–11; legitimate, 194–7; of makers

countries: constitutional interpretation in, 157, 176–80, 185; constitutions in, 152, 159, 169; lacking constitutions, 154–5; legal traditions of, 156

courts, 10, 11, 12, 41–3, 49, 161; changing law by, 182; and constitutional meaning, 29; constitutional role of, 42; as courts of law, 207; doctrine of role of, 184–5; innovative interpretations by, 186; and interpretation, 177, 178, 179, 187, 189, 190; of last resort, 42, 43, 46; make the constitution, 191; moral considerations of, 184, 190–1; as norm-specifiers, 7, 113; other agencies of government complying with decisions of, 60n135; role of, 60n132; *see also* Supreme Court

Crown (the), 168

custom as social source of law, 171

customary law, 32, 154, 157, 158, 206; repealed, 161

Czech Republic, 168

Czechoslovakia, 168

decision making: mechanism of, 231n46; public, 291; *see also* democratic decision-making

decision-making authority, 52n25

decision procedures, 273

decisional pathology, 282, 283

decisional possibility (bindingness), 65–6, 85

Declaration of Independence, 17, 18, 19, 223

declarations of rights, 19, 21, 30

deference of Supreme Court in interpreting Constitution, 123–5

deliberation, 292, 293

democracy(ies), 4, 34, 74–82, 86–7, 153, 188; and constitutional justice, 247, 250–1; constitutional order and, 24–7; constitutionalism and, 218; defined, 292; deliberative, 293; as demo-graphy, 213, 214, 216, 218,

219, 226; disagreements in, 294; egalitarian logic of, 239; fundamental rights in, 212; ideal form of, 244; majority rule in, 231n46; and political justice, 249; and popular sovereignty, 271–4, 278; self-rule in individual sense/in group sense, 252; temporally extended, 214; theory of, 172

Democracy and Distrust (Ely), 127, 232n52, 244

democratarian theories of domain of constitutional justice, 244–7, 261, 265–6

democratic debate, 90, 91

democratic decision-making, 4–5, 6, 25–6; in conflict with constitutionalism, 10–13

democratic institutions, 293

democratic procedure, 88

democratic process, 91

democratic sovereignty, 74

democratic will, entrenched rules against, 13

demo-graphy: in America, 211–26; democracy as, 213, 214, 216, 218, 219, 226

Derrida, Jacques, 201, 229n23

Descartes, René, 229n23

determinacy, 114

Dickerson, Reed, 115

directives, constitutional, 100; bowing to old/issuing new, 101–4; fidelity to, 136n12

disagreement(s), 279–80, 293–4; good-faith, 289; about national laws, 120–4; precommitment and, 271–99; about rights, 282, 283–4, 286; or weakness of will, 281–5; *see also* reasonable disagreement

discourse, constitutional, 236

disestablishment of constitutional directives, 101–2, 103, 135n12

disobedience, 4

dissent/dissidents, 293, 295

distancing devices, 190, 191

sovereignty, 66; theory of, 74–82
Soviet Union, 295
specification, 6, 132, 143n56; of
    Constitution₂, 112–19, 125–33; of
    indeterminate norms, 150n113
speech, acts of, 231n45
speech-modeled self-government,
    211–13, 218
stability, 5, 25, 26, 34, 153, 155, 174–6,
    183, 185, 186, 187
standards, 7
state: constitutional obstacles to
    flexibility of, 25; courts as organs of,
    184–5; limiting power of, 18–19, 22,
    23; as means to accomplish corporate
    goals, 24; purpose of, 18, 20; as
    subject of constitutional restraint, 21;
    and subjects, 52n25
state agencies, mutual regulation of,
    41–2
state authority, specification of, 34
state constitutions, 19; declarations of
    rights in, 30
state governments, 105, 106, 112, 122,
    138n28, 264, 279
state law(s), 126–7
state power, 27, 33; in constitutionalism,
    34; to impose burdens "onerous and
    unexpected," 54n49; justification of,
    32; limits on, 29, 51n10; risks of, 17;
    scope of, 22
state ratification conventions, 26, 30–1,
    35
state regulation, danger of, 22
states, 21; politics of, 104
status quo neutrality, 269n16
statutes, 103, 161; authority of, 210;
    interpretation of, 206; old, 165;
    validity of, 157
Stevens, 141n41
Stevens, Wallace, 49
substantive legitimacy, 33–4, 35
Sunsten, Cass, 269n16, 294
supermajoritarian amendment process,
    226

Supreme Court, 5, 29, 42, 43, 48,
    49, 96n62, 108, 118, 213, 239,
    241–2, 243, 260; deference of, in
    interpreting Constitution, 123–33;
    and independence, 260–1; Lincoln
    on, 297n31; role of, in constitutional
    adjudication, 105, 111; striking down
    laws as unconstitutional, 104–7;
    supreme in interpreting Constitution,
    99, 119–33
Supreme Court justices, 43, 102, 109,
    112, 119, 120, 236
supreme law, Constitution as, 70, 153
supremacy of Supreme Court, 119–24
symbolic value in authority, 167, 168
symbols/symbolism, 2, 3, 6, 8

temporal orientation of self-government,
    211, 212
temporality, 213–14, 219; *see also* time
Tempting of America, The (Bork), 205
text (Constitution), 10, 58n108, 99, 112,
    134n6, 137n18, 219, 236, 240;
    interpreting, 118, 119; popular voice
    and, 211–13
text(s), 29–33, 67, 68, 218; "correct"
    interpretation of, 28; decoding, 237;
    democratically enacted, 196; giving
    lives, 214; historical inquiry into,
    110, 111; interpretation of, 114–16,
    200, 203–4; meaning of, 38; taking
    seriously, 219; true or correct
    meaning of, 201; unintelligibility of,
    108
Thayer, James Bradley, 117, 126, 128,
    129, 130, 227n3
theory of interpretation, 157, 179;
    general, 197–8; mistakes in, 182–3;
    unified, 203, 205, 210
Theory of Justice (Rawls), 232n55
theory of law, 159, 170, 207–8; unified,
    207
Thirteenth Amendment, 241, 242
Thomas, 225
Tiedeman, Christopher, 194

Printed in the United States
96827LV00004B/142-168/A

9 780521 799997